HUMAN
RELATIONS

HUMAN RELATIONS

Personal and Professional Development

SECOND EDITION

David A. DeCenzo

Beth Silhanek

Prentice
Hall

Upper Saddle River, N.J. 07458

Library of Congress Cataloging-in-Publication Data

DeCenzo, David A.
    Human relations: personal and professional development/David A. DeCenzo, Beth
Silhanek.--2nd ed.
        p. cm.
    Includes index.
    ISBN 0-13-014574-2
        1. Interpersonal relations. 2. Organizational behavior. 3. Success. I. Silhanek, Beth. II.
Title.

HM1106 .D43 2002
302--dc21

                                                            2001033914

Executive Acquisitions Editor: Elizabeth Sugg
Editorial Assistant: Anita Rhodes
Managing Editor: Mary Carnis
Production Management: WordCrafters Editorial Services, Inc.
Production Editor: Linda Zuk
Production Liaison: Brian Hyland
Director of Manufacturing and Production: Bruce Johnson
Manufacturing Manager: Ilene Sanford
Creative Director: Cheryl Asherman
Senior Design Coordinator: Miguel Ortiz
Formatting: Carlisle Communication, Ltd.
Printer/Binder: R.R. Donnelley & Sons, Willard
Copyeditor: Amy Schneider
Proofreader: Maria McColligan
Interior Design: Lee Goldstein
Cover Design: Lee Goldstein
Cover Printer: Phoenix Color Corp.

Pearson Education LTD
Pearson Education Australia PTY, Limited
Pearson Education Singapore, Pte. Ltd.
Pearson Education North Asia Ltd.
Pearson Education Canada, Ltd.
Pearson Educacíon de Mexico, S.A. de C.V.
Pearson Education—Japan
Pearson Education Malaysia, Pte. Ltd.

Prentice
Hall

10 9 8 7 6 5 4 3
ISBN 0-13-014574-2

BRIEF CONTENTS

CONTENTS

part two
HUMAN BEHAVIOR

3 THE HUMAN FACTOR   **49**

INTERPERSONAL COMMUNICATION

5 PERSONAL ISSUES

part three

ORGANIZATIONAL BEHAVIOR

 ORGANIZATIONAL STRUCTURES

ORGANIZATIONAL COMMUNICATIONS

8 POWER, POLITICS, AND STATUS

part four

HUMAN BEHAVIOR IN ORGANIZATIONS

9 BEING PART OF GROUPS AND TEAMS

EXCELLING ON THE JOB

11 INFLUENCING OTHERS

253

CHANGE, CONFLICT, AND CREATIVITY
278

part five
MAKING THE CONNECTIONS

CAREER SUCCESS: GETTING AND KEEPING JOBS 332

PREFACE

To The Instructor

*W*elcome to the second edition of *Human Relations: Personal and Professional Development.* This book, like its predecessor, represents a different paradigm in conveying information to students about human relations in organizations. The fact is, the world continues to change. Work conditions, technology, and the people with whom individuals work have a dynamism about them that is unprecedented in our history. People are more likely today to work with more diversified peers than at any other time. Furthermore, their interactions at work are changing as well. No longer are employees primarily a cog in a bureaucratic organization. Instead, they are more likely to be part of a work team, and they are expected to work together to be successful in accomplishing tasks. Employees may not have the strong supervisory influence that directed our work behavior in the past. Rather, they'll have to take on more of this responsibility themselves. As such, work behavior will have to adapt. Employees will no longer be looking at what organizations are doing to them, but how they may affect attainment of organizational objectives. It's issues like these that have led to the focus of this text—paying attention to the critical human relations at work—from the employee's perspective.

Writing this text was both exciting and frightening. The excitement came from being able to address topics that are important to our students as they apply to them at work. It gives each of us the opportunity to relate to students in a way that we think they can understand—and to prepare them for what lies ahead in their work interactions. The frightening part comes from doing something different. Books that are published often follow a similar structure. Sure, each of us puts our own spin on our material. We may give more weight to a topic that we have greater interest in or one that we feel is truly more critical to understand. Deviating from that norm is scary. But common sense dictates that when one attempts this, there has to be a well-grounded reason. For us, that reason came from the absolute belief that our students need to understand how to succeed at work today—no matter where or what type of work they do. Authors, however, don't simply go off on tangents without some basic premises. *Human Relations: Personal and Professional Development*, therefore, had to be rooted in an appropriate framework and assumptions. Let us explain what ours are.

The Assumptions

The first major assumption concerning this book and the revision is what students need to be exposed to—an order that makes sense. To address this issue, we've divided the book into five parts:

✪ **Part I: Starting the Journey** is written to provide students with sound foundational information about the field of human relations—past, present, and future challenges.

- ✪ **Part II: Human Behavior** begins the process of understanding why people do what they do. The chapters in this part focus on the fundamentals of individual behavior, how people develop interpersonal communications styles, and personal problems they may face. At the end of this part, students should have a better understanding of their own behavior. But recognizing that these behaviors are frequently exhibited at work, students need to understand the effect of their behaviors in a work setting.

- ✪ **Part III: Organizational Behavior** introduces students to the inner workings of organizations. Topics include why workers are grouped the way they are, how groups and teams affect individual behavior, the employment process, power, politics, status, and organizational communications. The nuances of each element and their behavioral implications are discussed.

- ✪ **Part IV: Human Behavior in Organizations** recognizes that individuals interact with others while at work and frequently deal with change and conflict. How each of these aspects of work life affects employees is highlighted.

- ✪ **Part V: Making the Connections** attempts to put all the pieces together. The focus is on one's career and what an individual can do to achieve personal goals.

A book on a topic like human relations must support a strong skills focus. These skills include interpreting data, processing information, making decisions, thinking critically, and developing personal qualities. Each of these skills was a driving force for the first edition of this book and continues to be strengthened in this edition.

Writing a book about human relations has an inherent benefit that other topic areas may not enjoy. That's because it's a book about people and how they behave. Although the material is often well rooted in organizational behavior and theoretical research, it does not have to be presented in a theoretical manner. Rather, we've taken a practical approach which we believe will assist in helping students understand the material in this book and meet their needs. To do this, we've written a text that is realistic to them, talks about issues they'll likely encounter at work, and discusses what they should do to be effective in their interactions with others in an organizational setting. We believe, too, that the book is written in an understandable manner with many examples drawn from students' everyday lives. We hope that writing style helps students learn about themselves and gives them an opportunity to explore their behavior and understand how to interact with others. Furthermore, a book for students should be interesting and user-friendly. The book should be performance-based, providing students an opportunity to develop a variety of competencies. We believe such characteristics make a text more interactive, and it's this performance-based approach that assists students in positioning themselves for success in tomorrow's jobs.

The Features

In deciding which features to include in this edition, several things came to mind. First, we wanted students to relate to this book. We wanted them to see themselves through the eyes of others who encounter situations that they may face in the future. Accordingly, we've used a rich base of relevant examples. Several features have been included in the book that can best be described as in-text learning aids:

- ✪ Learning Outcomes
- ✪ summaries linked to the learning outcomes

- ✪ review and discussion questions
- ✪ key terms and margin notes
- ✪ cases

But in order to make this text more interactive, we've taken another step. In each chapter, there are several learning stimuli designed to help students better understand themselves and the material and to build skills:

- ✪ **Unlocking Your Potential** vignettes ask students to respond to questions about themselves or how they perceive a particular event. Many of the Keys to Unlocking Your Potential also present the opportunity to go further—under a section called "extra effort." These extras may also be used as a graded writing assignment, thereby reinforcing another critical skill, effective communications.

- ✪ **Reviewing Your Understanding** features are designed to explain the important feature of some text-related material as it applies directly to the student. Students begin to formulate their personal profiles by completing the Unlocking Your Potential features and working through the Reviewing Your Understanding questions.

- ✪ **Value Judgment:** Today's students, as well as tomorrow's workers, are bound to face dilemmas not encountered by their parents. How students deal with the unexpected will often be a function of their value system. In response to this fact, each chapter contains a vignette called Value Judgment that links a situation to a particular facet in the chapter and asks the student his or her opinion on how they would deal with or resolve the dilemma.

Supplements

- ✪ **Companion Website on CD-ROM.** Packaged free with every copy of the book, the Companion Website on CD-ROM offers practice questions with immediate feedback and evaluation.

- ✪ **Companion Website** provides free access to the same questions as students will find on the CD-ROM, but set up for distance learning environments. Prentice Hall's Companion Websites offer automatic feedback, Internet communication support, and grading and gradebook features.

- ✪ **Student Study Guide** provides an additional set of questions and practice scenarios for students requiring more hands-on applications.

- ✪ **Self-Assessment Library on CD-ROM,** an option to the package provided with the text, provides students with greater insight into their own capabilities.

- ✪ **Instructor's Manual with CD-ROM and PowerPoint Files** provides a complete set of instructional tools, lecture guidance, classroom handouts, and test questions.

- ✪ **WIN PH Test Manager** is a computerized bank of test questions easily or randomly selected and printed with automatically generated answer keys.

- ✪ **JWA Video Offer:** Choose from a catalog of videos related to the topics in the book: one video for every adoption of 25 copies or two videos for every adoption of 50 copies or more.

Acknowledgments

No authors have ever had a book come off their word processor and magically appear. That simply cannot happen—although technology today is attempting to make it so. Publishing a book requires the concerted effort of a number of dedicated individuals. We've been fortunate to have been surrounded by a great team who continue to see the benefits of this book and have given of themselves to make our vision a reality.

Our first thank-you must go to Elizabeth Sugg, our Editor. Elizabeth took that first step years ago in making this book a reality and has continued to support us in this revision. Elizabeth, thanks for all you have done for us. Second, for a book to be useful, it must pass a major challenge—the reviewers. Our valued colleagues gave us useful feedback that helped shaped many of the ideas in the text. We'd like to recognize the following individuals for taking the time to become part of this text, and to say to them, we heard what you said: Therese Nemee, Fox Valley Technical College; Elton C. Evans, Los Angeles Trade and Technical College; Linda Mireh, J.D., West Valley College; Stuart C. Baker, Schoolcraft College; and Murlene Asadi, Scott Community College. This second edition is a significantly better product because of your involvement.

In addition to all the good feedback authors receive, there's a lot of work that has to be done to get the book in print, work done by production staff, copyeditors, designers, marketing representatives, and the like. We had the good fortune to have worked with many outstanding individuals on this project, and want to thank them for a job well done. Specifically, we'd like to recognize Anita Rhodes, Editorial Assistant; Cheryl Asherman, Creative Director; Miguel Ortiz, Senior Design Coordinator; Ilene Sanford, Manufacturing Manager; and Linda Zuk of WordCrafters for their careful and conscientious planning, checking, and follow-through.

Last, but certainly not least, we owe a debt of gratitude to our families, who have given us the precious time to meet our deadlines. Our spouses and children continue to be our lifelines. Time with them, and seeing them smile, is the inspiration that provides each of us with the willpower to work long hours writing this book

Reading a preface is like seeing an advertisement for a product. Sure, all authors make claims. But the proof is in the proverbial pudding. How these claims are supported, as well as how the features come to life, is truly your call. But as satisfied users have told us, they share our excitement in what we've set out to do.

chapter

1

INTRODUCTION TO HUMAN RELATIONS

Beginning the successful journey of understanding human relations requires us to develop a proper perspective of human relations, its history, and what affects it. Part one contains two chapters:

*L*earning Outcomes

After reading this chapter, you will be able to:

1. Describe what is meant by human relations.

2. Explain the importance of human relations.

3. List the critical factors affecting employee behavior.

4. Identify how the Industrial Revolution affected people at work.

5. Summarize the contributions of Frederick Taylor.

6. Explain how bureaucracies affect human relations.

7. Discuss the importance of the Hawthorne Studies.

8. Define the goal of the human relations movement.

9. Identify the approach of human relations advocates.

10. Define organizational behavior and identify its two goals.

Every day our lives are touched by people. How we interact with others depends largely on who and where we are and on what we want. For example, during class your professor interacts with students in a certain manner, but at a sporting event this same professor may act quite differently. Why? Because societal customs tell us that in one situation some type of behavior is appropriate, whereas the same behavior in another setting may be highly offensive. The behavior of a professor caught up in the excitement of a great game may not be viewed as acceptable by students or colleagues, if witnessed during class.

So how do we determine what is appropriate behavior, especially in the work environment? How do we properly interact with our co-workers and supervisors to meet our goals? Behavior that is appropriate in our everyday lives may or may not be appropriate behavior at work. The focus of this book on human relations, therefore, is on understanding our behavior and its effect—both personally and professionally—on others and on us.

What Is Human Relations?

➤ **human relations**
the composite of interactions that exist between people in all aspects of their personal and professional lives

*H*uman relations is the composite of interactions that exist between people in all aspects of their personal and professional lives. Studying human relations helps us understand ourselves and learn how to interact properly with others. Human relations can be either a formal interaction, such as a division meeting with workers and their supervisors, or an informal interaction, such as after-school sharing between a mother and her children. Furthermore, human relations occurs both when we are cooperating with others and when we are engaged in conflict with someone else.

Why Is Human Relations Important?

*W*e all have been learning about human relations throughout our lives. Through interactions with our families, friends, and teachers, we have absorbed information about ourselves. To a great extent, we know what motivates us, and we understand that what we do and say either helps us or hinders us in achieving our goals. We've learned what is acceptable behavior and what may get us into trouble. Often,

UNLOCKING YOUR POTENTIAL *1-1*

Understanding Your Relationships

*A*re you aware of the many different people who affect your life each day? It helps to stop for a moment and think about these relationships. Therefore, in the spaces provided, list the categories of people you interact with personally and professionally.

Personal Relationships   **Professional Relationships**

however, just knowing these lessons may not adequately prepare us for actually demonstrating effective human relations in the workplace. For instance, we all know that arriving late for a date or a friend's birthday party may be impolite. In these instances, we may be embarrassed and required to apologize for our behavior. But beyond that, there are usually no serious consequences for us. At work, however, arriving late is a problem. Continual lateness could result in serious repercussions. It's not that the organization is trying to punish you; it's that you're not doing what's expected of you. You are not present to start work on time. Furthermore, others may be waiting for you to arrive, especially if some of your work must be completed before they can start their work. As a result, your lateness affects not only you, but also your co-workers and their productivity. It is therefore very likely that you will be disciplined for regular lateness.

The field of human relations provides some rich information about work interactions. Because each of you will be involved with others in the workplace, it is important to understand how interactions with others affect you. All of us, to be successful in our jobs, must be able to work with others in the organization. Organizations, in order to meet their goals, depend on employees working together. The study of human relations provides an opportunity to learn about ourselves, as well as others, in an effort to work together effectively.

One hundred years ago, the interactions between individuals played a less significant role in an organization's success than they do today. Most employees were simply told what to do and how to do it. Then they were watched very closely as they performed their work. If problems arose, the supervisor saw that the problem was corrected immediately.

Over the last century, many organizations have come to the realization that employees are important to the organization. Sure, we live in a time when thousands of employees are being laid off and efforts for higher profits drive many organizational actions. Nonetheless, getting things done requires people—employees who perform a variety of tasks that help the organization succeed. After all, what would Toyota be without its employees? Many buildings, lots of equipment, and an impressive bank balance! Similarly, if you removed the employees from such varied organizations as the Department of Defense, Hewlett-Packard, Coors, or Los Angeles County Schools, what would you have? Very little. Consequently, it's the individuals—not buildings, equipment, financial balances, or brand names—that truly make a company.[1]

People help organizations become successful. Therefore, it is reasonable to infer that these individuals must be able to work together effectively. Specifically, in order to be able to effectively carry on day-to-day activities, employees need sound human relations skills—interpersonal skills such as being able to communicate effectively, deal with problems, interact as team members, and anticipate change. In fact, these skills are so critical that they often supersede job knowledge and technical skills. In many cases, individuals with exceptionally good technical skills have had their careers stymied because they lacked interpersonal skills. People who cannot deal effectively with others often create more problems than solutions.

The changes that organizations are experiencing are also pointing to the importance of human relations. For instance, organizations are increasingly focusing on structuring work groups as teams with shared responsibility for achieving work goals. Just like a family, teams come together to accomplish certain goals. Also like family members, teams experience conflicts. Knowledge of human relations helps employees understand their roles as part of a team, as well as how they can contribute to the team's goals.

---

[1]See Stephen P. Robbins and David A. DeCenzo, *Fundamentals of Management*, 3rd ed. (Upper Saddle River, NJ: Prentice-Hall, Inc., 2001), chapter 1.

1. Understanding human relations is important for a variety of reasons. Which of the following is not a primary focus in studying human relations?
   a. learning about acceptable work behaviors
   b. learning about work interactions
   c. learning about managing organizations
   d. learning about ourselves and others

2. Who is directly affected by human relations?
   a. the employee
   b. the co-workers
   c. the employee's family
   d. all of the above

Further, on these teams will be people from diverse backgrounds. The composition of the workforce today is drastically different from that of just a few decades ago. Accordingly, employees must appreciate the differences between them and find opportunities to reach their potential. For many, this means putting aside biases and preconceptions to work effectively with people who are different.

Organizations today are concerned with becoming more service-oriented, recognizing the needs of customers, and enhancing the quality of their products. To make this happen, employees must be actively involved in identifying problems and finding solutions. This means that employees must be able to provide substantial input on matters concerning improvement of the organization. They must also be competent in dealing directly with customers—whether that customer is the typical external customer who purchases goods or services or an internal customer, someone within the organization.

Another organizational change involves the location where employees do their jobs. Through the use of technology, today's workers are no longer confined to working on the employer's premises. Instead, they may be on the road or in the air most of the time, or they may work at home, interacting with colleagues and customers through telecommunications. Changes in the medium of communication and the absence of face-to-face interaction require some changes in the ways workers relate to others. Once again, understanding human relations can help create positive outcomes.

So what does all this add up to? Our work environment has changed. Moreover, it will continue to change rapidly and dynamically in the years to come. With these changes come new challenges and opportunities for employees and supervisors. The need for learning and applying positive human relations is more important today than ever before.

Critical Factors

*W*ork behavior is influenced by several critical factors—the personal characteristics we possess and the characteristics of the organization in which we work. Let's look at how each of these factors affects us. Exhibit 1-1 is a graphic representation of the discussion that follows. Study it now, and then review it again after you finish reading this section.

Personal Characteristics

If you were asked to describe yourself in ten words or less, what would you say? One way to face this challenge is to begin listing words that describe you. For example, you might say that you are outgoing, friendly, hardworking, intelligent, honest, and caring. When you describe yourself in this manner, what you are really doing is characterizing yourself in terms of your personality, attitudes, values, and communication style.

Personality.   Each individual brings to an organization a different *personality*—a unique combination of personal skills and abilities that contributes to successful job performance. Workers experience their work environments from their own particular perspectives. They bring their personal expectations to their jobs and presume that these jobs will provide them something they value. Employees do not all like to do the same things, nor do they all see the same things as being important. Along with personal characteristics of individual workers comes a set of corresponding behaviors. For instance, an entry-level accountant who views using spreadsheet applications as tedious and boring and wishes to do something else may lack commitment to that particular job. As a result, he or she may come to work late, frequently call in sick, or even quit. But another accountant who likes to work with spreadsheets and sees the job as a stepping stone to a business manager position may flourish. Research has shown that unless individuals are working in a job that gives them the opportunity to develop a positive self-concept and do the things they think are important, their success may be limited.[2]

---

[2]See K. Onstad, "No Jobs? No Problem!" *Canadian Business*, December 1995, p. 21; and J. Aley, "Wall Street's King Quant," *Fortune*, February 5, 1996, pp. 108–12.

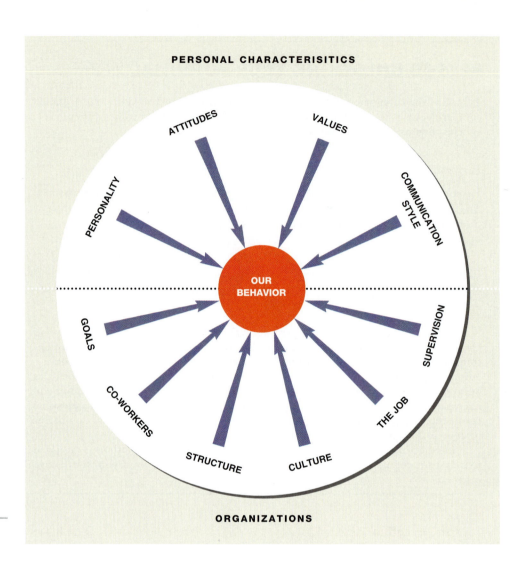

EXHIBIT 1-1
What Affects Work Behavior?

Attitudes. Individuals also demonstrate attitudes at work about their jobs and the organization. If you are unhappy about your level of pay, feel that the organization does not respect your talents, or believe that you are not treated fairly, you may do just enough work to get by. Your productivity is adequate for you to keep your job, but you perform at a level that is significantly below your ability. In essence, your attitude toward your job and the organization is to do only what you have to do. On the other hand, when an organization treats all its employees properly (giving them good pay, working conditions, and benefits, as well as the respect and dignity they deserve), productivity can soar. In this case, employees are more than willing to devote extra effort to their work.

Values. Values also play an important role in determining work behavior. If we see nothing wrong with padding our expense accounts or making personal long-distance calls from our offices, then we are going to act accordingly. If we dislike or are prejudiced against certain groups of people, then bias will also show up in our interactions with others. Our values are especially apparent in the ways we communicate.

VALUE JUDGMENT: Psychological Testing and the Honesty Test

Quickly, how would you respond to this question: Have you ever taken something that didn't belong to you? Yes. Sorry, we can't hire you because we don't hire thieves! No. Sorry again! Everyone has taken something that belonged to someone else. Therefore, you must be lying. We can't afford to hire someone who may not have the highest ethical standards.

Sound like a Catch-22? Welcome to the world of honesty tests. Although employers cannot use lie detector tests when hiring for the majority of jobs in the United States, they have found another means to get the information they want.

Much of the intent of honesty tests is to get applicants to provide information about themselves that otherwise would be hard to obtain. These integrity tests tend to focus on one's willingness to steal or to use illegal substances. Since applicants know that answers on these tests can be a factor in whether one is hired, they may try to answer questions vaguely, or they may lie. However, since inconsistency may indicate dishonesty, tests are frequently designed with multiple questions covering similar topics in order to detect inconsistent responses.

All of us know, however, that a simple paper-and-pencil test may not accurately characterize who we are. We may not take the test seriously, or we may simply get nervous when we are taking the exam. Should an organization make a decision about our employment on this one test? Should we be able to question an organization on its use of an honesty test—especially if that's the reason we didn't get the job? Do such tests further dehumanize the hiring process, making it almost mechanical? Or should we accept the fact that such tests are going to be used, and be better prepared to figure out how to respond to the items? What's your view of honesty tests being used in your hiring process?

Communication Style. Just as our personality is different from that of others, so too is the way we communicate with one another. If you are an introvert and not very expressive and are working with individuals who are more outgoing, they may view you as a dullard and a bore. That doesn't mean that they are correct. Instead, it points once again to the differences among us and the need to understand where everyone is coming from. The idea of "walking a mile in someone else's shoes" is quite relevant when dealing with interpersonal communications.

Organizational Characteristics

An **organization** is a planned grouping of people to accomplish a specific purpose. Your college is an organization. So are fraternities, sororities, government agencies, churches, the McDonald's Corporation, the American Medical Association, and your neighborhood gas station. Although organizations come in all varieties and sizes, each can be described using the same six categories of organizational characteristics.

➤ **organization**
a planned grouping of people to accomplish a specific purpose

Goals. Each organization has a specific purpose. This purpose is expressed in terms of a goal or a set of goals. Ford Motor Company's goal of "Quality is Job 1" sets the stage for what employees are expected to do—produce the highest-quality automobiles.

People. Organizations consist of people. These people do not just arrive, find a spot, and work in isolation. Rather, they are grouped together in a particular way.

Being part of a work group has a major effect on work behavior. Roughly one-third of your adult life will be spent at work. At work you'll be expected to interact with others, and these individuals will have a direct effect on you. How much you agree with the demands of the group will often dictate your level of success. The more cohesive your group is, or the more that you and your fellow employees cooperate with one another and share in the group's goals, the more effective each of you will be.[3]

Structure.   The behavior of organizational members is defined and limited by its structure. Structure might include creating rules and regulations, identifying some members as supervisors and giving them authority over other employees, and explicitly describing each member's job so that there is little confusion about what is expected. Organizations may create formal work teams. Why? Because work teams have been found to be more flexible in adapting to the changes that businesses face today. Teams are becoming more widespread because many managers view them as a means of enhancing worker morale, promoting faster and better decisions, and achieving better performance. Team members often expect and demand a lot from one another. They strive to cultivate and nourish a spirit of cooperation. Teams tend to encourage members to excel and, at the same time, create a work environment that increases job satisfaction. At Frito-Lay's plant in Lubbock, Texas, for example, team productivity has significantly reduced costs while making the plant one of the highest-quality-rated factories for the company. The employees have achieved this as a result of having more control over the day-to-day activities on their job, such as scheduling, making quality-control decisions, and interviewing potential co-workers. As one team member, Julia Garcia, has noted, being part of a team and having more say in how things operate has resulted in work now being "more fun."[4]

> **organizational culture**
the values, symbols, rituals, myths, and work practices that are shared by organizational members

Culture.   Just as we all have personalities, so do organizations. An organization's personality is called its organizational culture. **Organizational culture** reflects the values, symbols, rituals, myths, and work practices that are shared by organizational members.[5] These factors, in essence, dictate how each member will behave. Your organizational culture will typically provide very explicit signs on how hard to work, what level of output to have, when to look busy, when it's acceptable to goof off, how to dress, the expected level of demonstrated loyalty to the group and the organization, and so forth.

An organization's culture usually reflects the vision of the organization's leaders that has evolved over time. Organizational leaders establish the culture by communicating to employees and the outside world the ideals the organization values. For example, early leaders of IBM promoted research and development, product quality, proper employee attire, and excellent pay practices. This was nearly one hundred years ago, yet these same characteristics are still evident today.[6] Similarly, Lotus Development Corporation has established a culture that places great emphasis on "accepting" people. Lotus has been cited many times for its outstanding policies and employee benefit programs, which promote equal employment opportunities for its members regardless of their race, religion, or sexual orientation.[7]

[3]L. Berkowitz, "Group Standards, Cohesiveness, and Productivity," *Human Relations* (November 1954), pp. 509–519.

[4]Wendy Zellner, "Team Player: No More Same-Ol', Same-Ol'," *Business Week* (October 17, 1994), p. 95.

[5]J. H. Sheridan, "Culture-Change Lessons," *Industry Week*, February 17, 1997, p. 20.

[6]L. Hays, "Blue Period: Gerstner Is Struggling as He Tries to Change Ingrained IBM Culture," *Wall Street Journal*, May 13, 1994, p. A1.

[7]David Stipp, "Lotus Extends Company Benefits to Cover Domestic Partners of Homosexual Staff," *The Wall Street Journal* (September 9, 1991), p. B-6.

Job. Our job in an organization plays a very important part in influencing our behavior at work. Not every job is glamorous or provides the freedom to act completely as we would like. Some jobs are mundane and physically demanding and afford employees little opportunity to have a say in what they do. When you find yourself working in a difficult and undesirable job, problems may arise. For instance, your willingness to excel on the job may be significantly decreased if you consider your repetitive activities on an assembly line unrelated to your career goals. Similarly, if you hold a low-paying job in a fast-food restaurant, you may immediately quit that job when you find one that pays better. However, your current job may be the only job you can find for now. In the meanwhile, you will find that the features of the job itself play a key role in defining your work behavior and leading to your job satisfaction.

Supervision. Even though the trend today is toward more interdependent work groups and more satisfying jobs, we cannot overlook the fact that every organization still has management personnel. Traditionally, supervisors in organizations were those individuals who planned, organized, staffed, and controlled work activities. It was their job to set goals and dictate to employees what role they were to play. Although one-way directives from supervisor to employee are less prevalent than in previous centuries, your boss will still have a major effect on your behavior at work.

First of all, the supervisor is responsible for establishing the work environment. Positive work environments lead to improved performance and increased job satisfaction. Supervisors who afford you the opportunity to get involved in those things that affect you at work, allow you to have a part in setting work goals, give you opportunities for making decisions that affect your work, and involve you in most matters that require attention on the job ensure that the work environment is positive. Sure, there will always be some workers who do not view their being involved as positive. Yet research over the years has shown that supervisors who make involvement part of their supervisory practice do, in fact, have better-performing employees. Supervisors who involve employees and positively influence their performance truly function as leaders in the organization.

In contrast to leaders, many supervisors continue to view employees as things rather than assets, and they treat them accordingly. These supervisors are known as taskmasters. They focus much of their attention on gaining power for themselves even at the expense of workers, playing whatever politics are necessary to maintain their status in the organization, and getting the job done no matter what the cost to others. Power, politics, and status are part of every organization and, if properly used, can enhance your position in the organization. But taskmasters improperly use power, politics, and status to put employees down and to keep them there. Taskmasters operate on

✓ Checking Your Understanding *1-2*

3. Which one of the following would not be considered an organization?
   a. your family
   b. your church
   c. your college
   d. none of the above; all are types of organizations

4. Which of the following is not a true statement?
   a. Work behavior is influenced by both personal and organizational characteristics.
   b. Due to the success of work teams, the boss no longer plays an important role in work behavior.
   c. Every organization is made up of goals, structures, and people.
   d. Every organization has a personality.

one simple principle: as long as you do what they tell you, don't break any of their rules, and never question their authority, you will get along with them. True, these are traditional supervisory practices, but they may not be appropriate in today's world of work. Unfortunately, employees who experience this type of supervision and don't like it may have to grin and bear it for the time being. Working under such negative circumstances, however, will affect both the attitudes and behavior of employees toward their supervisors and organizations.

History of Human Relations in the Workplace

*H*uman behavior is complex. For many decades, researchers have been closely examining work behavior and human relations in the work environment. Let's take a look at the history of human relations in the workplace and examine how work behavior has evolved over time.

The McDonald's Corporation has fast-food restaurants all around the world. To achieve its claim that a hamburger in Berlin, Maryland, is the same as one in Berlin, Germany, McDonald's methodically trains its employees in how to do their jobs as efficiently as possible. Every McDonald's restaurant operates according to a 385-page manual. This manual describes in great detail how the restaurant will run. For instance, trainees at Hamburger University are taught that to maintain effectiveness and quality, every step of a job must be understood and performed exactly as directed. Cooking, salting, and bagging French fries, for example, consist of not three, but nineteen, separate steps. When to flip hamburgers on the grill is also not left to the cook's discretion. Flashing lights tell the cook precisely when to turn the hamburger over and when it is properly cooked.[8]

Does this rigid scheduling appear obsessive to you? Possibly. Do you think it guides employee behavior toward more productivity? Absolutely! In fact, McDonald's is one of the most efficiently managed companies in the world. It's also recognized as a profitable company. And from one restaurant to another, there's always consistency in any McDonald's product.

---

[8]Based on A. E. Serwer, "McDonald's Conquers the World," *Fortune* (October 17, 1994), pp. 103–105.

What's energizing these workers at Muni Financial Company? Their employer! Employees become more satisfied by working for an organization that treats them as assets and recognizes them for their hard work. They enjoy work more, are happier, and are more productive.

The case of McDonald's is similar to that of many other organizations that have learned from early research how to manage an organization efficiently and supervise its people effectively. Let's look at the historical development of the **human relations movement**—a twentieth-century organizational movement characterized by the belief that satisfied workers will be productive workers.

Forerunners of the Human Relations Movement

Prior to the formalization of work in organizations as we know it today, individuals typically performed their work at home. These individuals were farmers and craft workers. Farmers and craft workers produced their products from start to finish—whether food, clothing, cabinets, or shoes. Then, they would take their own goods to nearby markets to be sold. Although such an arrangement provided satisfaction for the workers—giving them total control of their jobs—productivity was significantly limited.

The answer to increasing productivity came with the Industrial Revolution. Begun in the eighteenth century in Great Britain, the Industrial Revolution crossed the Atlantic to America by the end of the Civil War. Machine power was rapidly replacing human power, and consequently it became more economical to manufacture goods in factories than in homes. The advent of machine power, the spread of mass production, the reduced transportation costs that resulted from the rapid expansion of railroads, and the almost total lack of governmental regulation fostered the development of big organizations. But these changes, however welcome at the time, came at the expense of the worker.

As members of a large organization, workers began to lose their identities. Rather than being proud workers who displayed and sold the fruits of their labor, employees became cogs in the wheels of production. They became one of hundreds, sometimes thousands, of employees brought under one roof working diligently to meet the goals of the boss. Unfortunately, many times the boss took advantage of the employees. Labor was plentiful and cheap. Coming to the cities hoping for prosperity, workers found that the jobs paid very little. Work was grueling, and workdays were long. In fact, it was common for workers to labor fourteen to sixteen hours per day, six or seven days a week. Workers faced terrible work conditions. There were no protective devices for workers, nor were there laws requiring employers to make the workplace an acceptable place to work. Instead, the environment was hot, dirty, unhealthy, and unsafe. As a result, many workers were exhausted, injured, or killed on the job. Those who couldn't work because of injury were simply cast aside. There was no such thing as unemployment or disability insurance. Many of the workers were seeking realization of the "American dream." Unfortunately, very few found a prosperous life through employment in the factories.

Frederick Taylor and Scientific Management. Frederick Taylor was a college professor who spent more than two decades researching work behavior, mostly at the Midvale and Bethlehem Steel companies in Pennsylvania. Taylor observed that since no work standards existed at the time, employees doing the same job used vastly different techniques. Workers were placed into jobs with little or no concern for matching their abilities and aptitudes with the tasks they were to do. There were no clear responsibilities between workers and the owners or their representatives, and consequently workers were prone to take it easy on the job. Furthermore, owners and employees perceived that they were in continual conflict with each other. Rather than working to reconcile their differences, they behaved as if any gains for one side would have to come at the expense of the other side. Taylor believed that worker output in these steel plants was only about one-third of what was possible.

➤ **scientific
management**
a set of principles that were
designed to make
employees more productive,
while providing greater
profits for the organization
that could be shared with
employees

Frederick Taylor set out to improve the inadequate work situations on the shop floors at Midvale and Bethlehem Steel. In 1911, Taylor formulated his philosophy of **scientific management** by proposing a set of principles that were designed to make employees more productive, while providing greater profits for the organization that could be shared with employees.

By defining clear guidelines for improving production efficiency, Taylor sought to create a mental revolution between the workers and the owners. He defined four principles of management that, if followed, would result in prosperity for both workers and supervisors. (See Exhibit 1-2.) With great passion, Taylor argued the benefits of applying scientific methods to each job and defining the one best way for each to be done. Workers would know exactly what they were supposed to do, and they would have job security. Owners, on the other hand, would receive more profits. This philosophy, in part, is what drives McDonald's.

Frederick Taylor's principles of scientific management were immediately popular with business owners and managers. However, the response was not as positive from the employees. Merely implementing changes in the work environment based on the principles of scientific management afforded no guarantee that workers would share in growing company profits. Moreover, after changes were implemented according to the principles, some workers found themselves being treated even more poorly than before. Scientific management required workers to learn new techniques so as to be able to perform a large variety of tasks. The opportunity to expand one's skills is usually considered a work-related benefit. However, as a result of scientific management, workers often were viewed as interchangeable parts that could be pulled from one location to another at any time without regard to employee preference or well-being. Too often, the organization's only focus was to keep productivity up at any cost. As a result, jobs in America became even more dehumanized for workers in the early 1900s.

The Gilbreths and Gantt.   Taylor's ideas inspired others to study and develop methods of scientific management. His most prominent disciples were Frank and Lillian Gilbreth and Henry Gantt.

A construction contractor by background, Frank Gilbreth gave up his contracting career in 1912 to study scientific management after hearing Taylor speak at a professional meeting. Along with his wife, Lillian, a psychologist, he studied work arrangements to eliminate wasteful hand-and-body motions. The Gilbreths also experimented in the design and use of the proper tools and equipment for optimizing work performance.[9] Frank Gilbreth is probably best known for his experiments in reducing the number of motions in bricklaying.

---

[9]See, for example, Frank B. Gilbreth, *Motion Study* (New York: Van Nostrand, 1911); and Frank B. Gilbreth & Lillian M. Gilbreth, *Fatigue Study* (New York: Sturgis & Walton, 1916).

Develop an exact method for performing each element of an employee's job.

Properly match individuals to the job. Then train, teach, and develop them to do the job the best way.

Cooperate with employees to ensure that all work is done properly according to the exact methods established for the job.

Divide work responsibility almost equally between owners and workers. The owners should do all the work they are better able to do rather than making the workers do everything.

EXHIBIT 1-2
**Frederick Taylor's
Principles of Management**

The Gilbreths were among the first to use motion-picture films to study hand-and-body motions. They devised a microchronometer that recorded time to 1/2000 second, placed it in the field of study being photographed, and thus determined how long a worker spent enacting each motion. Wasted motions missed by the naked eye could be identified and eliminated. The Gilbreths also devised a classification scheme to label seventeen basic hand motions—such as *search*, *select*, *grasp*, and *hold*—which they called *therbligs* (*Gilbreth* spelled backward with the *th* transposed). This allowed the Gilbreths a more precise way of analyzing the exact elements of any worker's hand movements.

Another notable associate of Taylor was a young engineer at Midvale and Bethlehem Steel named Henry L. Gantt. Like Taylor and the Gilbreths, Gantt sought to increase worker efficiency through scientific investigation. But Gantt extended some of Taylor's original ideas and added a few of his own. For instance, Gantt devised an incentive system that gave workers a bonus for completing their jobs in less time than the allowed standard. The supervisor also received a bonus for each worker who earned one. If all the workers under a supervisor completed their jobs in less time than the allowed standard, the supervisor received an extra bonus. Gantt's incentive system expanded the scope of scientific management to encompass the work of supervisors as well as that of employees.

Gantt is probably most noted for creating a graphic bar chart that could be used by managers as a scheduling device for planning and controlling work. The *Gantt chart*, a graphic bar chart used by managers as a scheduling device for planning and controlling work, shows the relationship between work planned and completed on one axis and time elapsed on the other. An example of a Gantt chart is shown in Exhibit 1-3.

The Rise of the Bureaucracy.   As organizations continued to grow larger, owners recognized that they couldn't control every aspect of the operation. Training all

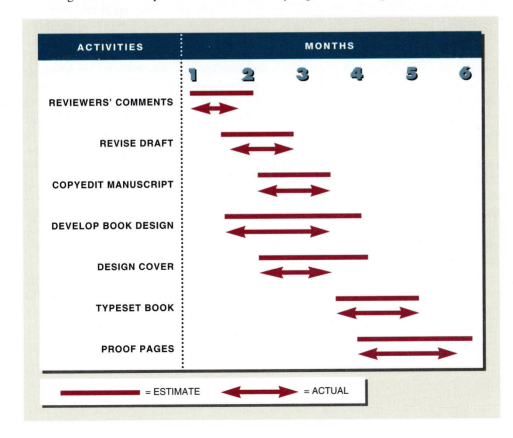

EXHIBIT 1-3
A Sample Gantt Chart for Publishing a Book

workers in the one best way to do everything was too cumbersome. Largeness bred ambiguity and inefficiency. Organizations were just too big to handle, even with scientific management principles. What was needed was a system of management for large organizations that included a professional manager who could plan, organize, direct, and control the work of large groups of workers. Two individuals—Henry Fayol and Max Weber (pronounced *VAY-ber*)—proposed the underlying principles for such a system.

Henry Fayol wrote during the same time as Taylor. However, whereas Taylor was concerned with directing activities at the shop level (or what we today would describe as the job of a supervisor) and used the scientific method, Fayol's attention was directed at the activities of all the managers, and he wrote from personal experience. Taylor was a scientist. Fayol, the managing director of a large French coal-mining firm, was a practitioner.

Fayol described the practice of management as distinct from accounting, finance, production, distribution, and other typical business functions. He argued that management was an activity common to all human undertakings in business, in government, and even in the home. He then proceeded to state fourteen principles—fundamental or universal truths—of management that could be taught in schools and universities. These principles are shown in Exhibit 1-4.

Max Weber was a German sociologist and a contemporary of Taylor and Fayol. Writing in the early 1900s, Weber developed a theory of authority structures and described organizational activity based on authority relations.[10] He described an ideal type of organization, a bureaucracy. A **bureaucracy** is an organizational structure that analyzes jobs according to simple, routine, well-defined tasks. Employees are hired and trained to perform specific tasks and only those tasks. Jobs are organized in an orderly way such that each worker at a lower job is controlled and supervised by a worker at a higher one. Furthermore, rules and regulations are put in place so that all workers at any given level are supposed to be treated the same—regulating the actions of both employees and supervisors.

Although bureaucracies may have served some purpose when they were first implemented, they created one significant problem for workers: bureaucracies are impersonal. Everything is decided by consistent rules and work controls. Managers in bureaucratic organizations avoid any involvement with the personalities or personal preferences of their employees. As a result, the organization's structure further dehumanizes the worker on the job.

It shouldn't come as any surprise, then, that some of the greatest conflicts between workers and managers occurred during the first third of the twentieth century. Workers were not regarded as an important part of the organization. Rather, they were viewed as a necessary cost of doing business—just like the buildings they worked in or the machines they ran. But this situation for workers could not continue. Workers were revolting. They began to organize themselves into groups called unions, and thus acquired a collective voice for confronting management, settling disputes, and making demands. Consequently, management was compelled to treat workers more fairly.

Unionization was one of the major initiatives of the twentieth century for improving employee work conditions, but it was not the only one. At the same time, other researchers recognized that the dehumanizing of corporate America was leading to serious problems. Owners and managers needed to begin to recognize and focus on the human side of their enterprises.

> **bureaucracy**
> an organizational structure that analyzes jobs according to simple, routine, well-defined tasks

---

[10]Max Weber, *The Theory of Social and Economic Organizations*, ed. Talcott Parsons, trans. A. M. Henderson and Talcott Parsons (New York: Free Press, 1947).

1. **Division of work.** This principle is the same as Adam Smith's "division of labor." Specialization increases output by making employees more efficient.

2. **Authority.** Managers must be able to give orders. Authority gives them this right. Along with authority, however, goes responsibility. Wherever authority is exercised, responsibility arises.

3. **Discipline.** Employees must obey and respect the rules that govern the organization. Good discipline is the result of effective leadership, a clear understanding between management and workers regarding the organization's rules, and the judicious use of penalties for infractions of the rules.

4. **Unity of command.** Every employee should receive orders from only one superior.

5. **Unity of direction.** Each group of organizational activities that have the same objective should be directed by one manager using one plan.

6. **Subordination of individual interests to the general interest.** The interests of any one employee or group of employees should not take precedence over the interests of the organization as a whole.

7. **Remuneration.** Workers must be paid a fair wage for their services.

8. **Centralization.** Centralization refers to the degree to which subordinates are involved in decision making. Whether decision making is centralized (to management) or decentralized (to subordinates) is a question of proper proportion. The task is to find the optimum degree of centralization for each situation.

9. **Scalar chain.** The line of authority from top management to the lowest ranks represents the scalar chain. Communications should follow this chain. However, if following the chain creates delays, cross-communications can be allowed if agreed to by all parties and superiors are kept informed.

10. **Order.** People and materials should be in the right place at the right time.

11. **Equity.** Managers should be kind and fair to their subordinates.

12. **Stability of tenure of personnel.** High employee turnover is inefficient. Management should provide orderly personnel planning and ensure that replacements are available to fill vacancies.

13. **Initiative.** Employees who are allowed to originate and carry out plans will exert high levels of effort.

14. **Esprit de corps.** Promoting team spirit will build harmony and unity within the organization.

Source: Management, 4/e by Robbins, © 1994. Adapted by permission of Prentice-Hall, Inc., Upper Saddle River, NJ.

EXHIBIT 1-4
Fayol's Principles

The Human Side of Organizations

Supervisors get things done by working with people. If people are upset with the way they are being treated, or if they work in harmful or dangerous environments, they simply will not be as productive as they could be. That's what experts like Hugo Munsterberg, Mary Parker Follet, and Chester Barnard believed.

Like Taylor, Hugo Munsterberg was interested in a scientific study of individuals at work that would maximize their productivity. But rather than focusing solely on job skills, Munsterberg looked at differences among individuals. Munsterberg suggested that results from psychological tests could be used to better match employees to jobs and to determine the most effective ways to motivate employees.

Mary Parker Follet focused her attention on both individual and group behavior. She believed that organizations should be based on a group ethic rather than on rigid bureaucratic principles. Follet asserted that individual potential would remain merely potential unless it was released through group association. The manager's job, according to Follet, was to coordinate group efforts. Follet is credited with introducing the foundations of the team concept, as we know it today, in organizations and the world of work.

Chester Barnard, like Follet, recognized the need to humanize organizations. Although Barnard understood the reasons for bureaucratic structures, he also knew that human cooperation is needed even in bureaucracies for them to function effectively. He believed that organizations were made up of people who interact with one another. According to Barnard, the major role of managers was to communicate with employees and to stimulate them to work at high effort levels. The managers would be effective only if their workers cooperated. Thus, organizational success depended on maintaining good relations with employees.

Munsterberg, Follet, Barnard, and many others were instrumental in raising awareness of the human side of organizations. Yet many other factors were not yet identified that affected work behavior.

Hawthorne Studies

> **Hawthorne Studies**
> an attempt to examine the effect of various work factors—such as lighting and ventilation levels, individual pay plans versus group wage plans, and length of workday and workweek—on worker productivity

Without question, the most important contribution toward understanding work behavior came out of the Hawthorne Studies, undertaken at Western Electric's Hawthorne Works in Cicero, Illinois. These studies began in the mid-1920s and lasted for about ten years. Initially originated by researchers employed by Western Electric, and later directed by Harvard University professor Elton Mayo, the **Hawthorne Studies** were an attempt to examine the effect of various work factors—such as lighting and ventilation levels, individual pay plans versus group wage plans, and length of workday and workweek—on worker productivity.[11] The researchers ran numerous experiments. In one study, two groups were picked to determine what effect lighting changes would have on productivity. Group One was presented with variations in lighting, whereas Group Two worked in constant light. These researchers anticipated that productivity would be directly related to light intensity. However, they found that as the light level was increased for Group One, productivity for both groups rose. Even when the lights were dimmed, productivity continued to increase for both groups. It was not until Group One was faced with light intensity equivalent to moonlight did productivity decline. Repeating this study in other parts of the plant, and with different groups of employees, brought similar results. The researchers concluded that environmental factors were not related to group productivity. More important, however, they could not initially explain what they saw happening.

In another experiment, a study was designed to evaluate the effect of an incentive plan. Researchers expected that workers would maximize their output, which would result in their receiving more pay. In this case, much to their surprise, employees did not increase productivity. Instead, the group controlled output at a level that they determined was appropriate for a day's work. Why? Because workers in this study didn't trust management and felt that if they increased productivity, the incentive rate might be cut at some point in time, or some workers might be laid off. So the group established its own output level—neither too much nor too little. And they made it look as though everyone contributed equally.

What did the Hawthorne Studies teach supervisors? First, productivity in the lighting experiments was directly related to involving employees. Workers in both groups felt special that they had been chosen to be part of the experiment. That recog-

---

[11]Elton Mayo, *The Human Problems of an Industrial Civilization* (New York: Macmillan, 1933); and Fritz J. Roethlisberger & William J. Dickson, *Management and the Worker* (Cambridge, Mass.: Harvard University Press, 1939).

5. Which statement about the Hawthorne Studies is most correct?
   a. Group norms play an important role in determining group productivity.
   b. Environmental factors such as lighting and ventilation have a major effect on employee productivity.
   c. Employee involvement and recognition are less important than employee pay.
   d. Supervisory orders dominate employee behavior.

6. Which of the following is not a conclusion of the Hawthorne Studies?
   a. A strong informal organization controls employee behavior.
   b. Employees are different from machines.
   c. Taylor found that lighting had little effect on an employee's productivity.
   d. Involving employees and recognizing their work creates more satisfied employees.

nition, as well as the challenge to do the best they could, made them exert more effort. Furthermore, workers were being given more freedom to do their jobs during the experiment and faced less interference from their supervisors. They were also given a lot of feedback on their performance—something that had been lacking in the past. In the incentive pay experiment, the studies showed that there was a strong informal organization that controlled employees' behaviors. The work group managed itself, even when what they were doing was not what the supervisor wanted. These social norms or group standards, therefore, became key elements of individual work behavior.

The conclusions of the Hawthorne Studies, though leading to a new emphasis on the human factor in organizations, have not been without critics. Attacks have been made on the researchers' procedures, analysis, and conclusions.[12] However, it is not as important to us now whether the studies were academically sound or their conclusions justified as it is that the Hawthorne Studies went a long way in changing how employers view their employees. At the time, employers believed that people were no different from machines: You put them on the shop floor, crank in the inputs, and they produce a known quantity of outputs. But employees are more, much more than machines. The Hawthorne Studies have shown that employees have needs and that these needs must be met for them to be satisfied and productive.

The Human Relations Movement

Other individuals notable for their unflinching commitment to making work practices more humane are the early members of the human relations movement. The common thread that united the human relations supporters was an unshakable optimism about people's capabilities. These people uniformly believed in the importance of employee satisfaction—a satisfied worker is a productive worker. They believed strongly in their cause and were inflexible in their beliefs—even when faced with evidence that contradicted them. Names associated with the human relations movement include Dale Carnegie, Abraham Maslow, and Douglas McGregor—individuals whose views were shaped more by their personal philosophies than by substantial research evidence.

Dale Carnegie's ideas and teachings have had an enormous influence on human relations. His book *How to Win Friends and Influence People*[13] has been read by millions

---

[12]Stephen R. G. Jones, "Worker Interdependence and Output: The Hawthorne Studies Reevaluated," *American Sociological Review* (April 1990), pp. 176–190.

[13]Dale Carnegie, *How to Win Friends and Influence People* (New York: Simon & Schuster, 1936).

UNLOCKING YOUR POTENTIAL *1-2*

Job-Related Needs

What are you looking for in a job? List ten factors that, if present, will create a more satisfactory work experience for you.

1.
2.
3.
4.
5.
6.
7.
8.
9.
10.

since its publication. Carnegie's main theme is simple: Your success is achievable only through winning the cooperation of others.[14] Thus, according to Carnegie, if you mistreat others and cannot work well with them, your career goals will be blocked.

Abraham Maslow proposed a theoretical hierarchy of five needs as they relate to one's motivation: physiological, safety, social, esteem, and self-actualization.[15] In terms of motivation, Maslow argued that each step in the hierarchy must be considerably satisfied before the next can be activated. Then, once a need is substantially satisfied, it no longer motivates employee behavior. Therefore, supervisors need to have an understanding of where employees are in the hierarchy and provide those things that will help them fulfill that need.

Douglas McGregor is best known for his formulation of two sets of assumptions—Theory X and Theory Y—about human nature.[16] Briefly, Theory X presents an essentially negative view of people. It assumes that they have little ambition, dislike work, and need to be closely supervised. On the other hand, Theory Y offers a positive view. It assumes that people can exercise self-control and accept responsibility. McGregor believed that Theory Y assumptions best captured the true nature of workers and should guide how they are to be supervised. Both Maslow and McGregor gave us much insight into our willingness to work.

Organizational Behavior

There are many ways of looking at how organizations operate. Organizations can be viewed by how workers are grouped, how goods and services are produced, how information and technology are handled in the operation, or how new ways are found to increase quality. But if we want to look specifically at human behavior in organizations, we must turn our attention to the field of organizational behavior. **Organizational behavior (OB)** is a field of study concerned specifically with the actions of people at work. Based on the tenets of members of the early human relations movement and

➤ **organizational behavior (OB)**
a field of study concerned specifically with the actions of people at work

---

[14]Daniel A. Wren, *The Evolution of Management Thought*, 3rd ed. (New York: Wiley, 1987), p. 422.
[15]Abraham Maslow, *Motivation and Personality* (New York: Harper & Row, 1954).
[16]Douglas McGregor, *The Human Side of Enterprise* (New York: McGraw-Hill, 1960).

drawing from such diverse fields as psychology and sociology, OB looks at formalizing and supporting those beliefs that support the human relations movement. OB investigators are not content to rely on personal philosophies and experiences; rather, they seek understanding through objective research.

One of the challenges for organizational behavior investigators is that many of the roots of human behavior are not obvious. Like an iceberg, much of employee behavior is not visible to the naked eye. (See Exhibit 1-5.) Organizational behavior provides us insight into both the visible and hidden aspects of human behavior in the workplace.

The goals of organizational behavior are to explain and to predict human behavior in the workplace. In doing so, OB focuses primarily on two major areas. First, OB looks at individual behavior. Based predominantly on contributions from psychologists, this area includes such topics as worker attitudes, personality, perception, learning, and motivation. Second, OB is concerned with formal and informal group behavior, using the work of sociologists and social psychologists in the areas of norms, roles, team building, and conflict. OB researchers know that the behavior of a group of employees cannot be understood by merely adding up the actions of each individual, because individuals in a group behave differently from individuals acting alone. This is evident when disgruntled employees in a group slow down their work efforts or purposely create quality problems with the products they produce. The employees, acting

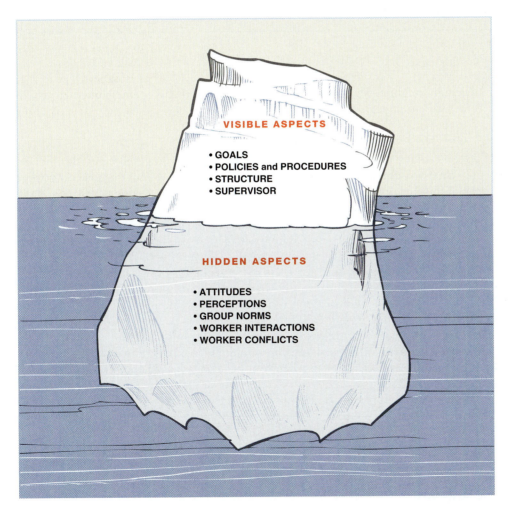

EXHIBIT 1-5

The Organization as an Iceberg

KEYS TO UNLOCKING YOUR POTENTIAL *1-2*

Although each of us will have unique needs and wants from our jobs, there are a number of needs and wants that most employees desire. They have been listed here (though not in any priority order). Compare your list in Unlocking Your Potential 1-2 with the list given here. What are the similarities? What are the differences? Compare your list with those of other students. What might this tell you about your needs, as well as the needs of others?

1. Challenging work
2. Fair pay
3. Decent supervisors
4. Making own decisions
5. Opportunity to advance
6. Trustworthy co-workers
7. Good employee benefits
8. Working in teams
9. Job security
10. Recognition for good performance

individually, might never engage in such behavior. Put them together, and they act differently. OB attempts to find out why.

Human Relations and You

The study of human relations is designed to help you get along with others at work. Unless you are a hermit and independently wealthy, you are not going to go through this life alone. Instead, you will have to interact with others at work and depend on them for your success. But before you can venture out into the world of work, you need to understand yourself. Who are you, and what makes you do the things you do? Are you aware of your needs and how you plan to fulfill them? Do you know what you want from work and from your career? Studying human relations begins the process of helping you formulate answers to these questions. It gives you the opportunity to take a close look at the person you call *you*.

The study of human relations also provides you the opportunity to understand others. Each of us must recognize that those around us have needs, too. We must understand that in order to work effectively, we need to communicate effectively with co-workers and build a working relationship with them based on mutual respect and trust. Human relations skills can help us shape our behavior toward others, both co-workers and supervisors.

But remember, changes in attitudes and behavior take time and effort. You must be open to learning new things—about yourself and others. You must be flexible in your views and open to information that may be different from what you had thought before. You must be willing to experiment and to make the effort necessary to develop yourself. Fortunately, topics and exercises in human relations give you this opportunity in a setting that is painless and that supports your efforts. Studying human relations can be the first step in unlocking your potential and your keys to success.

SUMMARY

This summary corresponds to the Learning Outcomes found on page 1.

1. Human relations is the composite of interactions that exist between people in all aspects of their personal and professional lives. Human relations can be either a formal or an informal interaction and occurs both when we are cooperating with others and when we are engaged in conflict with someone else.

2. Human relations is important in today's organizations for several reasons. Success in achieving organizational goals requires employees to interact together effectively. Furthermore, organizational changes such as work teams, the composition of the workforce, customer service, and technology are all placing more emphasis on effective human relations skills for employees.

3. Critical personal factors affecting employee behavior are personality, attitudes, values, and communication style. Additionally, critical organizational factors affecting employee behavior are goals, people, structure, culture, the job, and supervision.

4. The Industrial Revolution made it possible for owners to manufacture goods more economically in factories than in homes. As a result, workers began to lose their identity. Rather than proudly displaying his or her crafts, each employee became one of hundreds of workers brought under one roof working to meet the goals of the boss. Furthermore, working conditions were terrible. Many workers faced exhaustion, injury, and loss of life as a result of their jobs in the factories.

5. Frederick Taylor's contributions to human relations focused on his principles of scientific management. Taylor believed that workers should be highly trained to improve production. As a result, both the workers and owners could prosper. However, owners using Taylor's principles began to view employees as interchangeable parts—resulting in jobs becoming even more dehumanized.

6. A bureaucracy is an organizational structure that analyzes jobs according to simple, routine, well-defined tasks. Workers are guided by consistent work rules and controls. Bureaucracies became impersonal structures and contributed to further dehumanization of jobs.

7. The conclusions of the Hawthorne Studies placed a new emphasis on people in organizations. The studies began a change in how workers were viewed. Rather than seeing employees as machines, the Hawthorne Studies concluded that employees have needs and that these needs must be met for them to be satisfied and productive.

8. The goal of the human relations movement was to demonstrate that satisfied employees would be productive employees.

9. Early advocates of the human relations movement held strong convictions about people at work. They believed in the abilities of employees and promoted supervisory practices that would increase employee satisfaction.

10. Organizational behavior (OB) is a field of study concerned specifically with the actions of people at work. The goals of OB are to explain and to predict human behavior in the workplace.

REVIEWING YOUR UNDERSTANDING

1. In what ways can studying human relations help you at work?

2. Why are people an important component in an organization?

3. "Employees work better with the co-workers they like best." Do you agree or disagree with this statement? Explain.

4. How did the Industrial Revolution dehumanize jobs for workers in the United States?

5. What were Frederick Taylor's four principles of management, and how were they supposed to help workers? Did Taylor's principles achieve that goal? Explain.

6. "Bureaucratic organizations are built on formality and fairness. In a bureaucracy, no one is given special treatment, and career growth is based purely on job performance." Do you agree or disagree with this statement? Support your position with examples.

7. What contributions to the human relations movement did Hugo Munsterberg, Mary Parker Follet, and Chester Barnard make?

8. What organizational activities exist today that can be attributed to the conclusions of the Hawthorne Studies?

9. Describe the human relations implications of employees working in a location other than the employer's premises. Discuss this situation from both Theory X and Theory Y assumptions about human nature as proposed by McGregor.

10. Given the goals of organizational behavior, specify two or three types of activity in your classroom that could be investigated by an OB researcher. Discuss how the results of the OB study could be used to improve the work behavior of the instructor and students.

ANSWERS TO CHECKING YOUR UNDERSTANDING

1. c **2.** d **3.** d **4.** b **5.** a **6.** c

LEARNING TOGETHER

A. Discuss with classmates how to foster good human relations (1) at school, (2) in sports, (3) at home, and (4) on the job. Draw some conclusions about the human relations similarities and differences that you identified in each setting.

B. Make a list of characteristics that you believe are vital to good work behavior. Then, with a classmate, interview a human relations or personnel manager of a local business to determine how many of the factors are important to him or her. Ask the individual to rank each item from 1 (lowest) to 5 (highest). Add any factors that this person mentions that were not on your initial list. Share the results and your conclusions with the class.

C. Research the life of one of the pioneers of the human relations movement. Give an oral report to your class or write a paper on his or her contributions. Identify, if you can, what it was that made the person's contribution so important to (1) the movement and (2) human relations today. Then, identify at least one present-day person who exemplifies the person or contribution you selected. Describe how the person's influence or contribution can be applied to other present-day situations.

D. Role play with classmates the pros and cons of honesty testing. Draw some conclusions about the exercise.

E. In teams of four to six people, identify the elements that are vital to teamwork. Together, describe and write down a plan for improving the human relations within your school. Present the plan to your class. Implement your plan. (The key to this exercise is implementation. It is much easier to develop plans for others to implement than for your own team. Be realistic.)

The Human Relations Movement

Rodney McCullock and Ana Quintirez work as checkout clerks at Anderson's Food Mart. They are two of nineteen checkout clerks who work for Marge Rider, Anderson's store manager. Ms. Rider has been with the Food Mart for about two years—eight months as store manager. Ms. Rider is a conscientious person who puts her customers' needs first. She is straightforward with her employees but finds ways to help each one maximize his or her strengths and potential. She is good at building teamwork among her employees. She practices good human relations and expects her employees to do the same.

Rodney has a very outgoing personality, likes to joke, and enjoys life to its fullest. He likes to be with his friends and they with him. Usually one or two friends stop by during the day to buy something or come by when he gets off work. Rodney is always upbeat, is dependable, and is liked by customers and his co-workers. He has been working at Anderson's for about three months. He is happy to have a steady job to help him with his car payments.

Ana has a more reserved personality and approaches life in a very conservative way. She is very observant and is pleasant with customers and co-workers. She works the same shift as Rodney and he can always depend on her to know the sale items and assist him with price checks. Frequently other co-workers also rely on Ana to assist them. Ana is creative and constantly strives to improve her productivity and efficiency. Ana's goal is to work her way up to become a store manager, just as Marge has done.

Questions

1. Identify the human relations skills of Marge, Rodney, and Ana. What are the strengths of each person? What are the potential weaknesses?

2. Explain how the statement, "People are the most important element," is exemplified in this case.

3. The critical factors of work behavior are personal characteristics and organizational characteristics. Describe how each of these factors is important at Anderson's Food Mart and why it is important for Marge, Rodney, and Ana to understand the components of these two factors.

4. What are some of the things Marge might do to practice good human relations and build teamwork?

21st-CENTURY CHALLENGES

*L*earning Outcomes

After reading this chapter, you will be able to:

1. Identify significant changes that have occurred in the composition of the workforce.

2. Describe human relations implications of the changing composition of the workforce.

3. Explain how globalization affects human relations.

4. Explain what is meant by parochialism as it relates to the global village.

5. Describe what is meant by corporate downsizing and discuss its effect on human relations.

6. Describe what is meant by total quality management (TQM) and identify its goals.

7. Explain the reengineering phenomenon of the early 1990s and its effect on human relations.

8. Explain why jobs are disappearing in the United States and the human relations implications of this.

9. Identify the components of a socially responsible organization.

10. Define *ethics*.

11. Explain what companies can do to prevent workplace violence.

It's been stated that the only thing that remains constant is change. And it's true. People must always be prepared for changing events that may have some significant effect on their lives. Human relations is no different in this regard. Changing events have always helped shape the interactions that exist between people and will always continue to do so. Some of the more recent changes include workforce diversity, globalization, corporate downsizing, total quality management, reengineering, the shifting of jobs in the United States, the increase in contingent workers, and issues of social responsibility and ethics. Let's look at how these changes are affecting human relations in organizations.

Working in a Diverse Society

Nearly six decades ago, our workforce was strikingly homogeneous. In the 1950s, for example, the U.S. workforce consisted primarily of white males employed in manufacturing who had wives who stayed at home, tending to the family's two-plus children.

Until very recently, organizations took a "melting-pot" approach to differences in organizations. It was assumed that people who were different would somehow automatically want to integrate. But reality tells us that employees do not set aside their cultural values and lifestyle preferences when they come to work. The challenge for organizations today, therefore, is to become more accommodating to diverse groups of people by addressing different lifestyles, family needs, and work styles. The melting-pot assumption is being replaced by the recognition and celebration of differences.[1]

Workforce Diversity

Much of the change that has occurred in the workforce can be attributed to the passage of federal legislation in the 1960s prohibiting employment discrimination. Based on such laws, avenues began to open up for minority and female applicants. These two groups have since become the fastest growing segment in the workforce, and accommodating their needs has become a vital responsibility for human resources managers. Furthermore, during this time, birthrates in the United States began to decline. The baby boomer generation had already reached its peak in terms of employment opportunities. And as globalization became more pronounced, Hispanic, Asian, and other immigrants came to the United States and sought employment.

Projecting into the future is often an educated guess at best. Trying to predict the exact composition of our **workforce diversity** is no exception, even though we do know it will be made up of "males, females, white, blacks, Hispanics, Asians, Native Americans, the disabled, homosexuals, straights, and the elderly."[2] Nonetheless, some excellent predictors are available to us, the results of which give us a good indication of what is to come. The landmark investigation into workforce composition was conducted by the Hudson Institute and the Department of Labor.[3] Their findings, originally published in 1987, illuminated the changes we could expect over the next several decades (see Exhibit 2-1). Although there is some debate over the original findings of the Hudson Report, including the Hudson Institute's own sequel to the study, and how rapidly the workforce composition change will occur, three groups in particular are projected to supply significant increases of workers to U.S. firms: minorities, women, and immigrants.

> **workforce diversity**
the differences that diverse groups bring to the workplace, such as gender, nationality, age, and race

[1] I. Taylor, "Winning at Diversify," *Working Woman*, March 1999, p. 36; L. Urresta and J. Hickman, "The Diversity Elite," *Fortune*, August 3, 1998.

[2] Sharon Nelton, "Winning with Diversity," *Nation's Business* (September 12, 1992), p. 18.

[3] The Hudson Institute, *Workforce 2000: Work and Workers for the 21st Century* (Indianapolis, Ind.: The Hudson Institute, 1987).

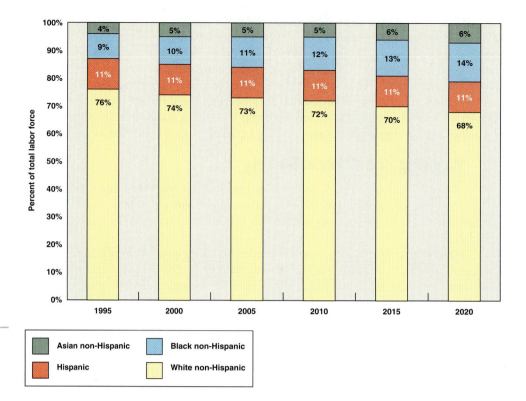

EXHIBIT 2-1
Workforce Diversity
Source: Bureau of Labor
Statistics projections to
2005; Hudson Institute
projections 2010–2020

Legend:
- Asian non-Hispanic
- Black non-Hispanic
- Hispanic
- White non-Hispanic

How Diversity Affects You

Diversity in the workforce will require each of us to recognize the differences that diverse groups bring to the workplace. We must be flexible enough in our views to be accepting of others who are different in what they want and need from work. This may mean significantly reducing our biases for or against any one particular group. Our challenge, therefore, is to embrace diverse groups of people by accepting and respecting different lifestyles, family needs, and work styles.

Globalization

Back in 1973, with the first oil embargo, U.S. businesses began to realize the importance that international market forces had on their profit and loss statements. The world was changing rapidly, with other countries making significant inroads into traditional U.S. markets. Unfortunately, U.S. businesses did not adapt to this changing environment as quickly or adeptly as they should have. The result was that U.S. businesses lost out in world markets and have had to fight much harder to get back in. Only by the late 1980s did U.S. businesses begin to get the message. But when they did, they aggressively began to expand into what is now commonly called the global village.

In a **global village,** the world and organizations in it are no longer constrained by national borders. For example, Burger King is owned by a British firm, and McDonald's sells hamburgers in China. Exxon, considered an American company, receives almost 75 percent of its revenues from sales outside the United States. Honda makes cars in Ohio, General Motors makes cars in Brazil, and Toyota and General Motors jointly own a plant that makes cars in California. Parts for Ford Motor Company's Crown Victoria come from all over the world: Mexico (seats, windshields, and fuel

➤ **global village**
a term indicating that the world and organizations in it are no longer constrained by national borders

Debra Richards recognizes the importance of valuing diversity. As a communications manager for Aetna Life and Casualty, she has seen how corporate emphasis on diversity can create opportunities for minorities. Although diversity programs can always be improved, Richards delights in diversity programs, such as the one at Aetna, that are showing steady progress.

tanks), Japan (shock absorbers), Spain (electronic engine controls), Germany (antilock brake systems), and England (key axle parts). These examples illustrate that the world has become a global village and that to be effective in business, people must adapt to cultures, systems, and techniques that are different from their own.

The Globalization of Business

In the 1960s, Canada's prime minister described his country's proximity to the United States as analogous to sleeping with an elephant: "You feel every twitch the animal makes." By the 1990s, this analogy could be generalized to the entire world. A rise in interest rates in Germany instantly affected organizations throughout the globe. The fall of communism in Eastern Europe and the collapse of the Soviet Union created unlimited opportunities for business firms throughout the free world.

Globalization has long been with us. For instance, companies such as Siemens, Remington, and Singer were selling their products in many countries in the early 1900s. By the 1920s, companies such as Fiat, Ford, Unilever, and Royal Dutch/Shell had gone multinational. However, it wasn't until the mid-1960s that **multinational corporations (MNCs)** became commonplace. These corporations—which maintain significant operations in two or more countries simultaneously but are based in one home country—initiated the rapid growth of international trade. Most of the companies in Exhibit 2-2 are MNCs, with subsidiaries and manufacturing facilities in countries throughout the world.

In the 1990s globalization extended the reach and goals of MNCs to create an even more generic global organization—the **transnational corporation (TNC).** This type of organization doesn't seek to repeat its domestic successes by managing foreign operations from home. Rather, decision making in TNCs takes place at the local level. Individuals in the host countries, called *nationals,* typically are hired to run operations in each country. Further, the products and marketing strategies for each country are uniquely tailored to that country's culture. Nestlé, for example, is a transnational corporation. With operations

> **multinational corporations (MNCs)** corporations that maintain significant operations in two or more countries simultaneously but are based in one home country

> **transnational corporations (TNCs)** corporations in which decision making takes place at the local level and products and marketing strategies are uniquely tailored to each country's culture

ExxonMobil	115,464
IBM	50,337
Ford Motor	50,138
General Motors	46,485
General Electric	35,350
Texaco	32,700
Citigroup	28,749
Hewlett-Packard	23,398
Wal-Mart Stores	22,728
Compaq Computer	21,174

Source: Forbes.com, "Forbes 100 US Multinationals," *Forbes* (July 2000), p. 1.

EXHIBIT 2-2

Top 10 U.S. International Corporations and Their Foreign Revenues ($mil)

in almost every country on earth, it is the world's largest food company. Yet Nestlé matches its products to its customers and sells products in areas of Europe, for instance, that aren't available in the United States or Latin America.

Though organizations have become increasingly global in their perspectives and accept the reality that national borders no longer define corporations, the general public has been slower to accept this fact. For example, controversies over fair trade with Japan often lead to backlash against Japanese products being sold in the United States. Many people feel that the sale of Japanese products takes jobs from Americans. The national cry often is "Buy American." The irony is that many of the supposedly Japanese products that critics cited were actually made in the United States. For example, most Sony televisions sold in the United States are made in California. Zenith televisions, on the other hand, are made in Mexico. The message should be obvious: A company's national origin is no longer a very good gauge of where it does business or the national origin of its employees. Companies such as Sony and Samsung employ thousands of people in the United States. At the same time, firms such as Coca-Cola, Exxon, and Citicorp employ thousands of workers in India, Hong Kong, and the United Kingdom. So phrases like "Buy American" represent old stereotypes that fail to reflect the changing global village.

How Does Globalization Affect Human Relations?

A world without boundaries introduces new challenges for us. We need to assess our views of people from foreign countries and develop a deeper understanding of their cultures. One specific challenge is to recognize the cultural differences that might exist among individuals, while at the same time finding ways to make our interactions with them more effective. One of the first issues we must deal with, then, is our perception of foreigners.

Americans, in general, have held a rather parochial view of the world. **Parochialism** means that we often see things solely through our own eyes and within our own perspectives. We believe that what *we* do is best. We simply do not recognize that other people have different ways of doing things and live differently than Americans. In essence, our parochialism leads to our **ethnocentric view.** That is, we view ourselves as superior to people from other cultures and our ways as being better than those in other cultures. Obviously, we know this cannot be the case—nor is it the dominant view. But changing this perception requires us to understand different cultures and their environments.

➤ **parochialism**
situations in which individuals see things solely through their own eyes and within their own perspectives

➤ **ethnocentric view**
a view that one is superior to people from other cultures and one's ways are better than those in other cultures

All countries have different values, morals, customs, and laws. Although cultural diversity is much more involved than this and goes beyond the scope of this book, we should try to understand the cultural issues others bring to our organizations. For example, in the United States, laws guard against employers using the services of someone "less qualified" when that decision was based on a personal characteristic. Similar laws do not exist in all other countries. Understanding cultural environments, then, is critical to the success of interacting with others in the global village. This becomes especially relevant if we find that our jobs take us abroad. For example, there's an adage that states, "When in Rome, do as the Romans do." That is, if you go to another country, you must understand that country's legal, political, economic, and cultural systems. Failure to do so may result in your not succeeding in the assignment or, at the very least, experiencing **cultural shock**—the confusion and the frustration that occurs when we are first exposed to a different culture. Although cultural shock is normal, some of it is preventable if you know ahead of time what you may experience.

> **cultural shock**
confusion and frustration that occurs when one is first exposed to a different culture

One of the better-known studies about cultural environments was done by researcher Geert Hofstede,[4] who analyzed various aspects of a country's culture. He found that a country's culture had a major effect on employees' work-related values and attitudes. By analyzing the various dimensions, Hofstede developed a framework for understanding what one might find when going abroad or working with someone from another culture. These findings, and countries that share similar cultures, are represented in Exhibit 2-3. Hofstede's findings allow us to group countries according to such cultural variables as status differences, societal uncertainty, and assertiveness. These variables indicate a country's means of dealing with its people and how the people see themselves. For example, in an individualistic society, people are primarily concerned with their own family. On the contrary, in a collective society (the opposite of individualistic), people care for all individuals that are part of their group. Thus, a strongly individualistic U.S. employee may not work well if sent to a Pacific Rim country where collectivism dominates, unless he or she adapts to that country's culture. Thus, flexibility and adaptability are key components for employees going abroad.

When working with individuals from different cultures, individuals informally learn the differences that exist between them and their respective cultures. An organization such as Mars (the candy producer), for example, builds on this informal development by providing formalized training to employees that focuses on the "major differences which may lead to problems."[5] Workers learn that they must be flexible in their dealings with one another. Initially, fellow employees may not understand you either. People must learn, therefore, to recognize differences in others—their backgrounds, customs, and work schedules—and appreciate, even celebrate, those differences.[6] Organizations such as Honeywell and Xerox have found that extensive training in recognizing these differences and changing "the way employees think about people different from themselves"[7] has positive outcomes.

---

[4]Geert Hofstede, *Culture's Consequences: International Differences in Work-Related Values* (Beverly Hills, Calif.: Sage Publications, 1980).

[5]See, for example, L. B. Pincus, and James A. Belohlav, "Legal Issues in Multinational Business Strategy: To Play the Game You Have to Know the Rules," *Academy of Management Executive*, November 1996, pp. 52–60.

[6]Ibid.

[7]"Riding the Tide of Change," *The Wyatt Communicator* (Winter 1991), p. 11.

Variable	Similarities
Individualism	Refers to a social framework in which people look after their own interests and those of their immediate family. Its opposite is collectivism, in which people expect others in groups of which they are a part to look after them and protect them when they are in trouble. The U.S. culture is more individualistic.
Power distance	Refers to how society accepts that power in institutions and organizations is distributed unequally. In a high-power-distance society, employees show a great deal of respect for those in authority. In contrast, a lower power distance society plays down inequalities as much as possible. The U.S. culture is low on this variable.
Uncertainty avoidance	Characterized by an increased level of anxiety among its people. People feel threatened by uncertainty and ambiguity in these societies. The United States is low on uncertainty avoidance.
Quantity versus quality of life	Some cultures emphasize the quantity of life and value things like assertiveness and the acquisition of money and material goods. Other cultures emphasize the quality of life and the importance of relationships, and show sensitivity and concern for the welfare of others. Culturally, the United States focuses on the quantity dimension.

EXHIBIT 2-3

Hofstede's Cultural Variables and Country Similarities

Changing How We Do Business

*T*he American workplace today is changing dramatically in many ways. Big corporations dominated the American scene during the last half of the twentieth century, but that's not necessarily the case today. Many small and medium-sized companies are growing significantly, primarily because they tend to be more customer-responsive than big businesses. However, the big businesses are not throwing in the towel. In order to maintain their share of the profits, they have been making some major changes

UNLOCKING YOUR POTENTIAL *2-1*

Working in the Global Village

*I*n today's global business setting, you are very likely to come into contact with individuals from other countries. Interacting with people from different cultures is not as easy as it would be if they originally came from next door. It helps to recognize the differences they bring to the work setting and to find commonalities among us. List as many ways as you can that describe how people from around the globe are different from you and how they are similar.

Differences   *Similarities*

in their organizations. The most obvious of these organizational changes are downsizing, total quality management, and reengineering. Let's look at these three changes and discuss how they will affect you on the job.

Doing More with Less

American companies have been working to become lean and mean organizations. As a result of deregulation in certain industries, foreign competition, mergers, and takeovers, organizations have cut employees from their payrolls. In fact, by the mid-1990s, almost all Fortune 500 companies—including Sears, Kodak, IBM, and Toyota—had cut staff and reshaped their operations. In business terms, the action of reshaping or restructuring an organization by reducing the number of workers employed is called **downsizing.**

Organizations downsize to accomplish two primary goals: to create greater efficiency and to reduce costs. In many cases, corporate downsizing necessitates the reduction of large numbers of workers, including managers and supervisors, from the organization's employment list. Organizations don't lay off employees lightly—they are forced to do so because business-world changes demand that payrolls be trimmed to only the most essential employees.

➤ **downsizing**
reshaping or restructuring an organization by reducing the number of workers employed

1. What statement best represents what is meant by an ethnocentric view?
   a. When in Rome, do as the Romans do.
   b. Use your own practices and techniques no matter where in the global village you operate.
   c. Seek consensus to blend your practices with those of the foreign culture.

   d. Adapt to the political, social, and economic systems in the global village.
2. Which of the following was not identified by Hofstede as a cultural variable?
   a. status difference
   b. assertiveness
   c. consensus building
   d. individualism

In order to deal effectively with increased global competition in a rapidly changing world, corporations had to become more flexible about how work got done. Formal work rules that dominated bureaucracies wouldn't permit changes to occur fast enough. There were just too many people involved in making decisions—either in how they were made or in their implementation. Workers in the organizations may not have had the necessary skills to perform the newly emerging jobs. In some cases, the organization didn't plan far enough ahead. In other cases, the organization was unwilling to spend the money to ensure that employee skills would remain current. As a result, people outside the organization had to be contracted to do the work. Some corporations realized that it would be cheaper to let contracted workers continue to do the work than it would be to train and pay for full-time employees. Downsizing, therefore, furnished organizations both flexibility in how the work was done and significant savings in who did the work.

Although downsizing seemed to make sound business sense, a few ethical questions are associated with it. Many employees in organizations suffered by being laid off, and others worked in constant fear that their jobs might be eliminated at any time. Yet some corporations were paying executives exorbitant salaries. Furthermore, company profits in some of these organizations were at all-time highs. As a result, many employees entered the new millennium frustrated; employee morale in many companies was at an all-time low; and trust between employees and their managers in the organization had all but disappeared. As large organizations continue downsizing efforts in this century, their chief executives must carefully consider the ethical implications of their actions.

Implementing Total Quality Management

> **total quality management (TQM)**
> a quality revolution, inspired by a small group of quality experts, taking place in both business and the public sector

A quality revolution is taking place in both business and the public sector.[8] The term that has evolved to describe this revolution is **total quality management (TQM).** TQM was inspired by a small group of quality experts, the most prominent of them being the late W. Edwards Deming.

An American, Deming found few managers in the United States interested in his ideas. Consequently, in 1950 he went to Japan and began advising many top Japanese managers on how to improve their production effectiveness. Central to his management methods was the use of statistics to analyze variability in production processes. A well-managed organization, according to Deming, was one in which statistical control re-

---

[8]Marshall Saskin and Kenneth J. Kiser, *Total Quality Management* (Seabrook, Md.: Ducochon Press, 1991).

duced variability and resulted in uniform quality and predictable quantity of output. That meant, from Deming's perspective, that the 64,233rd light bulb produced should have the same quality and properties that the first one had. Deming developed a fourteen-point program for transforming organizations. Today, Deming's original program has expanded into TQM—a philosophy of management that is driven by customer needs and expectations. (See Exhibit 2-4.) In today's business world, the term *customer* in TQM has also expanded beyond the traditional definition to include everyone who interacts with the organization's product or service either internally or externally. So TQM encompasses employees, suppliers, and the people who buy the organization's products or services. The primary objective of TQM is to create an organization committed to continuous improvement.

TQM represents a counterpoint to earlier management theorists who believed that low costs were the only way to increased productivity. The American automobile industry, in fact, represents a classic case of what can go wrong when attention is focused solely on trying to keep costs down. Throughout the 1970s and 1980s, companies such as GM, Ford, and Chrysler ended up manufacturing products that a large part of the auto-buying public rejected. When the costs of rejects, repairs of shoddy work, recalls, and expensive controls to identify problems in quality were factored in, American auto manufacturers were actually less productive than many foreign competitors. The Japanese demonstrated that it was possible for the highest-quality manufacturers to also be among the lowest-cost producers. Their implementation of many of the basic components of TQM—quality-control groups, process improvement, teamwork, improved supplier relations, and listening to the needs and wants of customers—accounted for their global success in manufacturing quality products at a low cost. Only recently have American auto manufacturers realized the importance of total quality management and implemented it in their companies. They have learned that TQM, or at least the commitment to continuous improvement in quality, is necessary for an organization to be globally competitive in any business endeavor.

Reengineering Our Work Efforts

TQM, focusing on continuous improvement or ongoing incremental change, is definitely a positive initiative in many U.S. organizations. Such action—the constant and permanent search to make things better—is intuitively appealing. Many U.S. companies,

1. **Focus on the customer.** The customer includes not only outsiders who buy the organization's products or services, but also internal customers (such as shipping or accounts payable personnel) who interact with and serve others in the organization.

2. **Continuous improvement.** TQM is a commitment to never being satisfied. "Very good" is not enough. Quality can always be improved.

3. **Improve the quality of everything the organization does.** TQM uses a very broad definition of quality. It relates not only to the final product but also to how the organization handles deliveries, how rapidly it responds to complaints, how politely the phones are answered, and the like.

4. **Measure accurately.** TQM uses statistical techniques to measure every critical variable in the organization's operations. These are compared to standards or benchmarks to identify problems, trace them to their roots, and eliminate their causes.

5. **Involve employees.** TQM involves the people on the line in the improvement process. Teams are widely used in TQM programs for finding and solving problems.

EXHIBIT 2-4
The Foundations of TQM

however, live in a time of incredibly rapid and dynamic change. As the elements around them change ever so quickly, a continuous-improvement process may still leave them behind the times.

The problem with continuous improvement is that it provides a false sense of security if not also accompanied by meaningful change. Continuous-improvement activities allow managers to feel that they're actively doing something positive. But this may be a twenty-first-century version of rearranging the deck chairs on the *Titanic*. Why? Unfortunately, ongoing incremental change avoids facing up to the possibility that what the organization may really need is radical or quantum change, commonly referred to as reengineering.[9] **Reengineering** is the evaluation and alteration of most of the work done in an organization. It requires organizational members to rethink what work should be done, how it is to be done, and how to best implement these decisions. Reengineering efforts in companies such as Federal Express, Bell Atlantic, and Vortex Industries are designed to lead to improvements in production quality, speed, and customer service.[10]

> **reengineering**
> evaluation and alteration of most of the work done in an organization

If you read the previous section closely, you may now be wondering if this doesn't contradict what was written a few paragraphs ago about TQM. Not so. The distinction is that while TQM is an important philosophy for organizations and can lead to improvements in most of them, TQM may not always be the right strategy initially. If an organization is producing an outdated product, an improved version of the outdated product may not be helpful to the company. Rather, in a number of instances, major change is required. Only after major change has occurred, can continually improving the product (TQM) have its rightful place. Let's see how this may be so.

Assume you are the individual responsible for implementing some type of change in your roller skate manufacturing process. If you took the continuous-improvement approach, your frame of reference would be a high-toe leather shoe on top of a steel carriage, with four wooden wheels. Your continuous-improvement program might lead you to focus on things such as using a different grade of cowhide for the shoe, adding speed laces to the uppers, or using a different type of ball bearing in the wheels. Of course, your new skate may be better than the one you previously made, but is that good enough? Compare your action to that of a competitor who reengineers the process.

To begin, your competitor poses the following question: How can I design a skate that provides mobility and is safe, fun, and fast? Starting from scratch, and not being constrained by the current manufacturing process, a product is designed that looks much like today's popular in-line skates. Your improved leather-and-metal skates are now competing against molded boots. Your competitor's molded skate is better than one made from leather, and it has no laces to tie. Additionally, it uses four to six high-durability plastic wheels, which are placed in-line for greater speed and mobility than traditional skates.

In this contrived example, both companies made progress. But which competitor do you believe made more progress, given today's dynamic environment? This example clearly reinforces the reasons why companies such as Union Carbide, GTE, and Mutual Benefit Life opted for reengineering as opposed to incremental change.[11] It is imperative in today's business environment for all managers to consider the challenge of reengineering their organizational processes. Why? Because reengineering can lead

---

[9]Michael Hammer and James Champy, *Reengineering the Corporation* (New York: HarperCollins, 1993).

[10]John Byrne, "Reengineering: What Happened?" *Business Week* (January 30, 1995), p. 16.

[11]Thomas A. Stewart, "Reengineering: The Hot New Managing Tool," *Fortune* (August 23, 1993), pp. 41–43.

to "major gains in cost, service, or time."[12] These kinds of gains will keep companies profitable and expanding throughout the twenty-first century.

Human Relations Implications

Although downsizing, total quality management, and reengineering are activities pertaining to the operations of organizations, they do affect employees. Therefore, employees must be prepared to deal with the ramifications of these organizational changes. Let's take a look at some of these issues.

Downsizing and Human Relations. When an organization downsizes, the most obvious effect may be that people lose jobs. Therefore, from a human relations viewpoint, we can expect some significant changes in employee behavior. Employees get angry. They conclude that the organization no longer cares about them as individuals, but is concerned only about profits. This leads to deep resentment against the organization and its policymakers. Furthermore, knowing that an organization can downsize at any time, employees no longer freely give their loyalty to the employers. Instead, the employer must now earn employee loyalty. Furthermore, this loyalty is very fragile and can be lost at any time if the employer makes an unwise decision or takes an action unfavorable for employees.

Downsizing may also cause increased competition among employees. If decisions are made to eliminate jobs based on a performance criterion, employees may understandably be less likely to help one another. Every employee looking out for himself or herself defeats any chance of fostering genuine teamwork.

Finally, downsizing may cause serious problems for the workers who are fortunate enough to keep their jobs. Unless the work process has been revamped substantially, many of the major tasks of jobs that were cut may still be necessary. Thus, workloads are often substantially increased for the remaining employees. This can lead to longer workdays for them, which may create conflicts between their work and family life.

TQM and You. Each one of us must understand what quality means in our work and what effort we need to exert to achieve the required quality in our jobs. We must recognize that failing to provide quality products and services leads to unsatisfied customers, who take their purchasing power to competitors who do provide them. Without quality, our very jobs might be in jeopardy. Knowing the close relationship between TQM and job security may even create feelings of work-related anxiety or cause fear of losing our jobs.

The premise of TQM or continuous improvement, however, can generate a positive outcome for us. The foundations of TQM are built on our participation—the people closest to the work. TQM allows us to make suggestions for the best way to do our work. As a result, we'll have more direct involvement in those things that affect us and our performance. As such, TQM can eliminate many of the obstacles that have hampered our efforts in the past and allow us to focus more on quality. We consequently will find far more satisfaction in our jobs than ever before.

Reengineering and Human Relations. If we accept the premise that reengineering will change how we do business, it stands to reason that we, too, will be directly affected. First of all, reengineering may have left us confused and angry. Although a preferred method of change would have been to involve us throughout the process, we need to recognize that reengineering may have left some of us frustrated

---

[12]Ibid., p. 42.

and unsure of what to expect.[13] Longtime work relationships may now be severed. Emotionally, we may be devastated. (See Exhibit 2-5.)

Reengineering definitely has its skeptics and its opponents. Yet, it can generate some benefits for us. We may now be working with the latest technology, be working in teams, or have more decision-making authority. Reengineering may provide us opportunities to learn new skills. These are the same skills that will keep us marketable and help us move to another organization should that time ever come. Additionally, we will more than likely have more control over our own work efforts and be subject to less supervision. Finally, as these changes sweep across corporate America, we may see changes in how we are paid. Under a reengineered work arrangement, we may be in a better position to be compensated for the work we do and receive bonuses and incentives when we excel.

---

[13]Julie Connelly, "Have We Become Mad Dogs in the Office?" *Fortune* (November 28, 1994), p. 197.

3. How do total quality management and reengineering differ?
   a. TQM looks at major changes in the organization. Reengineering looks at fine-tuning the organization's processes.
   b. Reengineering is people-based change. TQM focuses on organization-based change.
   c. TQM looks at incremental change. Reengineering focuses on continuous process improvements.
   d. Reengineering looks at making major changes in the organization. TQM focuses on continuous improvements.

4. Which one of the following is not a human relations implication of downsizing?
   a. Increasing employee involvement in the change process.
   b. Keeping skills up to date in preparation for finding employment elsewhere.
   c. Understanding severance pay and health insurance issues.
   d. Doing the job previously done by two or more people.

Understanding the New Workforce

*Y*ears ago, the job market was relatively predictable. In good times, when work was plentiful, organizations hired a large number of employees. Then as the economy went into a recession and consumers purchased fewer goods, companies simply laid off workers they didn't need. When the economic picture improved, a new cycle started. But downsizing, restructuring, and reengineering have all changed these practices.

In a number of organizations, this dynamic situation has led to employment of two very different types of workers: core employees and contingent workers. **Core employees** ordinarily provide some essential job tasks—such as *marketing manager* or *treasurer*—that require commitment and permanence in the organization. They may work in either part-time or full-time positions. Core employees usually are considered permanent workers and receive all the benefits that traditionally go to regular employees—such as health insurance, sick leave, paid vacation, and job seniority. **Contingent workers** are not employees of the organization, but rather sell their services to an organization on an individual contracted basis. They perform specific tasks that often require special job skills and are especially needed when an organization is experiencing significant deviations in its workflow. Like core employees, they may work in either part-time or full-time positions. Contingent workers have no seniority rights in the organization, nor do they receive any of the employee benefits that are provided to core employees. Contingent workers are typically hired for temporary periods. When there is no longer a need for their special skills or when their specific task is completed, they are let go. However, the layoffs of contingent workers have none of the characteristics of the traditional employee terminations. When their projects are completed, so is their affiliation with the organization. By 2000, about one-third percent of the workforce consisted of contingent workers, and that number, given the trends in restructuring and reengineering, is expected to climb significantly during the twenty-first century.

> **core employees**
> workers who are employees of an organization, provide some essential job tasks that require commitment and permanence in the organization, and receive all the benefits that traditionally go to regular employees

> **contingent workers**
> workers who are not employees of an organization, perform specific tasks that often require special job skills and are especially needed when an organization is experiencing significant deviations in its workflow, and do not receive the benefits that traditionally go to regular employees

We Don't All Have Full-Time Jobs

So who makes up the contingent workforce? Contingent workers are temporaries, consultants, contract workers, or adjunct professors. They work as secretaries, accountants, nurses, assembly-line workers, lawyers, dentists, computer programmers, engineers, and marketing representatives.

Are we freely becoming contingent workers out of our desire to fulfill personal work, family, lifestyle, or financial needs? Or have we been forced into this employment limbo as a result of organizational activities? The answer to both is unequivocally affirmative. Many individuals prefer the contingent work relationship. It offers them flexibility in work scheduling, which is something that they want. With the increasing diversity of the workforce, contingent work arrangements permit one to blend family and career goals. Using this logic, contingent positions are, in fact, beneficial to many employees. Furthermore, hiring contingent workers protects core employees' jobs.[14] For example, Blue Cross and Blue Shield of Rhode Island was able to trim its workforce by more than 40 percent over a five-year period without having to lay off one full-timer.

But we cannot overlook the other side of this issue. Many organizations are using contingent workforce concepts merely to save money. An organization can save about 40 percent in labor costs by employing contingent workers without providing them employee benefits. Therefore, many employers opt to fill a position with one or more contingent workers rather than with one full-time core employee. Consequently, some people are being forced into contingent worker roles if they want to work. And although some of these individuals will be working less than forty-hour workweeks, many will be working forty or more hours each week since they will be working for several different organizations at one time. However, they won't have the benefits associated with working full-time for the same organization.

The Contingent Workforce and You

When an organization makes a long-term decision to employ you, it is likely that you will be considered a core employee. But even though you have full-time status, working with contingent workers may create some conflict between you and them. For example, you may become upset over what contingent workers are getting paid. If you look strictly at paychecks (and don't consider the value of your benefits), contingent workers could be making more money. For instance, contracting with a freelance computer programmer and paying her $30,000 over a twelve-month period for developing a computer program for the organization's accounting department might create some ill feelings when you realize that as a core employee you are paid only $25,000. Although these feelings are natural, your organization should anticipate such events and provide incentives so that you won't leave. And you need to take a good look at the benefits, both monetary and nonmonetary, that you receive by being a core employee.

Core employees generally have more career stability than contingent workers. So how do you keep yourself employable if you're one of the many who make up the contingent workforce? Although specific answers are impossible, some suggestions can be offered. And they are revealed in the acronym DATA.[15] Let's look at each letter.

The *D* stands for *desire*. In the past, experience was once perceived as the best preparation for the future. Today, that may not be so. The past may promote the status quo, which is ill-fitted to a dynamic environment. Instead, your desire will be a key factor in your career. Those of you who strive to be the best and to excel will have an advantage over those who don't.

The first *A* denotes the *ability* to do the work required in today's organizations. This means that you can never sit back and bask in your glory. Instead, you must continually upgrade your skills so that you can offer something to the organization.

---

[14]Keith H. Hammonds, Kevin Kelly, and Karen Thurston, "The New World of Work," *Business Week* (October 17, 1994), p. 85.

[15]Based on William Bridges, "The End of the Job," *Fortune* (September 19, 1994), p. 72.

You must also have the *T*, an appropriate *temperament*. Yesterday's job security is gone. You will be on your own in many circumstances. For instance, when the job is done, so might be your association with the organization. Consequently, you must have a disposition that easily adjusts to an ever-changing work situation.

Finally, you must possess the second *A*, many *assets*. This means that whatever the job requires, you must be able to do. You must have the skills and knowledge to meet the needs that contribute to the success of the organization—and ultimately to your success. These assets may be in the form of your own expertise, but also may include equipment, good contacts, and even sufficient time.

Being a contingent worker, especially if not by choice, need not be a hopeless cause. If you recognize that proper preparation and a positive attitude will be keys to

VALUE JUDGMENT: The Contingent Workforce

Hiring contingent workers can be a blessing for both organizations and individuals. Contingent workers provide employers with a rich set of diverse skills on an as-needed basis. Furthermore, hiring precisely when the specific work is to begin is very cost-effective. Likewise, individuals who desire to work less than full-time or for intermittent intervals also have the opportunity to keep their skills sharp. Contingent workers can also balance personal matters and their careers.

Many of the blessings for individuals, however, revolve around a central theme; that is, being a contingent worker is something that an individual voluntarily chooses. Unfortunately, that is not always the case. Many employees are put into the contingent workforce involuntarily. Jobs in America have shifted (disappeared or changed to a service orientation), and that trend is expected to continue. Consequently, the involuntary contingent workforce is expected to grow in the years ahead.

Being part of the contingent workforce—even if not by choice—might not be as bad if these workers received the benefits typically offered to full-time employees of an organization. Although hourly rates are sometimes higher for contingent workers than for core employees, these individuals do not receive the benefits that organizations typically provide for core employees. For instance, contingent workers are required to pay their entire social security premium. Core employees, usually share this tax with the employer. As a result, some of that extra hourly rate for contingent workers must be reserved for extra tax withholdings. In addition, contingent workers must pay for their own health, life, and disability insurance. Buying insurance through an organization, which often receives group rates, is generally cheaper than having to buy the insurance yourself. So insurance coverage is another major expense the contingent workers must subtract from their income. As for time-off-with-pay benefits, forget about it. Vacation, holidays, sick leave? It's simple. Take all you want. But remember, when you don't work, you don't get paid.

So are contingent workers benefiting organizations greatly and encouraging them to continue this trend? Are individuals who are forced into the contingent workforce being exploited by this organizational activity? Should organizations be forced to provide some basic level of benefits—such as health insurance, vacation pay, sick leave, and retirement—to contingent workers? What's your view of this dilemma?

success, then you can succeed in whatever any organization expects of you. Remember, being prepared and positive is solely up to you.

Can Organizations Be Good and Still Be Profitable?

*E*very organization has one simple goal: to survive. Survival, though, may take on different forms. For many, it means being profitable; for others, it means continuing the organization's work for the good of society. The former often raises questions. Can an organization do the right thing and still make money? Although the answer is yes, newspapers are filled with stories about organizations that may not operate in a manner that we feel is appropriate. For instance, if Dow Corning knew that its breast implants could have serious side effects for women if they leaked, should they have withdrawn the product before the courts made them do so? Should tobacco companies such as RJ Reynolds and Philip Morris continue to sell billions of cigarettes when there is documented evidence that cigarette smoking may lead to serious medical problems or even death? But we cannot condemn such organizations. They are, after all, obeying the law. And that's all that's required of them. We assume that businesses obey the law and do what is rightfully necessary to ensure survival. Moreover, many organizations today are implementing policies and practices that focus on socially responsible behavior. Let's look at this phenomenon.

Socially Responsible Organizations

> **social responsibility**
> an organization's voluntary commitment to improve society

Social responsibility is an organization's voluntary commitment to improve society. It means that an organization considers more than legal boundaries and profit making; it pursues long-term goals that are good for society. *Society*, in this context, refers to such groups as an organization's employees, customers, and the environment in which it operates.

> **social obligation**
> an organization's economic and legal responsibilities to society

> **social responsiveness**
> an organization's moral responsibility to do those things that make society better and not to do those that could make it worse

We can understand social responsibility better if we contrast it with two similar concepts: social obligation and social responsiveness.[16] **Social obligation** is the foundation of a business's social involvement. A business has fulfilled its social obligation when it meets its economic and legal responsibilities to society. It does the minimum that the law requires. In contrast to social obligation, both social responsibility and social responsiveness go beyond merely meeting basic economic and legal standards. **Social responsiveness** adds a moral responsibility to do those things that make society better and not to do those that could make it worse. It is the capacity of the organization and its people to adapt to changing societal conditions. Social responsiveness, then, requires business to seek fundamental truths and determine what is right or wrong. Societal norms guide this process. Social responsiveness is primarily reactive to societal norms. In contrast, social obligation requires organizations to react to law rather than societal norms. Social responsibility, on the other hand, is clearly a proactive process voluntarily undertaken by a company. Let's look at an example to make this more clear.

When a company meets pollution control standards established by the federal government, or doesn't discriminate against employees on the basis of their race in a promotion decision, the organization is fulfilling its social obligation—and nothing more. Various laws say that employers may not pollute, or be biased against certain groups, and this company is abiding by those laws. However, when another company

---

[16]S. Prakash Sethi, "A Conceptual Framework for Environmental Analysis of Social Issues and Evaluation of Business Response Patterns," *Academy of Management Review* (January 1979), pp. 68–74; and Donna J. Wood, "Corporate Social Performance Revisited," *Academy of Management Review* (October 1991), pp. 703–708.

packages its products in recycled paper, or provides health insurance for an employee's significant other, this firm is being socially responsive. How so? Although pressure may be coming from a number of societal groups, such businesses are providing something society desires—without having to be told to do so by law. They are doing the right thing because society norms indicate that it is the right and moral thing to do. A third company wants to do more than merely provide a good service; it wants to leave a lasting legacy behind and to help society advance. In addition to maintaining a reputation as a leading financial institution, it sponsors international programs and scholarships for underprivileged youth. This company is not only socially responsive, it is also socially responsible because of its voluntary commitment to better society.

It's often easy for us to sit back and talk about a company being socially responsible. But what about when "they" become us? Socially responsible behavior for individuals can be viewed from a perspective that we call *ethics*.

The Ethical Individual

Are we currently suffering a moral crisis in the United States? Behaviors that were once thought reprehensible—lying, cheating, misrepresenting, covering up mistakes—have become, in many people's views, acceptable or necessary practices. Stock traders have profited greatly from illegal use of insider information. A few congressmen have allegedly mistreated and abused their female staff. Even college students seem to have become caught up in this wave. A Rutgers University study of more than six-thousand students found that, among those anticipating careers in business, 76 percent admitted to having cheated on at least one test, and 19 percent acknowledged having cheated on four or more tests.[17] Do these examples—and many others just like them—affirm that we have little moral character? That answer lies in the concept of ethics.

Ethics commonly refers to the rules or principles that define right and wrong conduct. People who lack a strong moral character are much less likely to do the wrong things if they are constrained by rules, policies, job descriptions, or strong cultural norms that frown on such behaviors. Conversely, very moral people can be corrupted by an organizational culture that permits or encourages unethical practices. For example, suppose you are in a class where a copy of the final exam is being sold for $50. Department members have heard the rumors, but nothing is done. Do you buy a copy because without it you'll be disadvantaged, or do you do without and try your best? If your professor suspects a copy is floating and does nothing, and then gives no curve on the exam because the grades are so high (mainly because of those who had a copy of the exam), the professor is doing little to dissuade cheating. In that case, you may rationalize getting a copy for yourself.

> **ethics**
> the rules or principles that define right and wrong conduct

This example illustrates how ambiguity about what is ethical can be a problem for employees. Codes of ethics are an increasingly popular response for reducing that ambiguity.[18] A **code of ethics** is a formal document that states an organization's primary values and the ethical rules it expects employees to follow. It has been suggested that codes be specific enough to guide employees in what they're supposed to do. Unfortunately, you may not have such a policy to fall back on. In that case, you must respond in such a way that you feel is appropriate—and deal with the consequences. Let's look at this more closely.

> **code of ethics**
> a formal document that states an organization's primary values and the ethical rules it expects employees to follow

Suppose you are asked by your boss to fix prices with competitors and at the same time steal technology from the same groups you are colluding with. Your boss knows that

---

[17]Rick Tetzeli, "Business Students Cheat Most," *Fortune* (July 1, 1991), p. 14.
[18]M. Cash Matthews, "Codes of Ethics: Organizational Behavior and Misbehavior," in William C. Frederick & Lee E. Preston, eds., *Business Ethics: Research Issues and Empirical Studies* (Greenwich, Conn.: JAI Press, 1990), pp. 99–122.

in doing so, your organization can create an unbeatable market for its products and possibly run your competitors out of business. Further, if you do these things, you'll be rewarded handsomely—in fact, you may be put in charge of the entire organization.[19] What are your options? First of all, you can do what the boss has asked. After all, he's the boss, and he can make your life great or miserable. But recognize that if you go to such extremes as price fixing or stealing trade secrets, you might be criminally liable. You, not the boss, may face the charges. Even though you did it for the good of your organization, realize that the boss may not protect you if you get caught. In essence, your career may be tarnished.

---

[19]This example is adapted from Mark Whitcare, "My Life as a Corporate Mole for the FBI," *Fortune* (September 4, 1995), pp. 52–62.

SKILLS CHECKLIST

Acting Ethically

1. **Obtain the organization's policy on ethics.** Company policies on ethics, if they exist, describe what the organization perceives as ethical behavior and what it expects you to do. This policy will help you clarify what is permissible for you to do—and becomes your code of ethics to follow.

2. **Understand the ethics policy.** Just having the policy in your hand does not guarantee that it will achieve what it's intended to do. You need to fully understand it. Ethical behavior is rarely a cut-and-dried process. But the guidance of the policy will provide a basis from which you will do things in the organization. Even if a policy doesn't exist, there are still several steps you can take before you deal with the difficult situation.

3. **Think before you act.** Ask yourself why you are doing what you're about to do. Is it for the right reasons? Or are there ulterior motives? It's your behavior that will be seen. You need to make sure that you are not doing something that will jeopardize your reputation.

4. **Ask yourself, "What if?"** If you thought ahead about why you're doing something, you should also be asking yourself some what-if questions: What if I make the wrong decision? What will happen to me? To my job? What if I get caught? What if I refuse to do something? How will others view what I did?

5. **Seek opinions from others.** If it is something major that you must do, whenever possible, ask for others' advice. Maybe another person has been in a similar situation and can give you the benefit of his or her experience. Or maybe others can just listen and act as a sounding board for you.

6. **Do what you truly believe is right.** Each of us has a conscience, and we all must be responsible for our own behavior. Whatever you do, if you truly believe it was the right thing, then what others say is immaterial. Can you live with yourself for what you're going to do or not do?

Another option may be to talk to your boss and register your displeasure with being asked to do this deed. It's doubtful your boss will change his mind, but at least you can state your position. You may even refuse to do what you've been ordered to do. But this refusal could create problems for you. You may find an organization member in a position of higher authority that could help you. But you cannot count on that happening. You might also give the impression that you'll do what the boss asked, but never give the information requested. You might make up excuses that prices couldn't be fixed because other companies wouldn't agree to the request. In such an instance, you're hoping that the boss will accept your excuse or simply forget to follow up on his request. Again, it's a risk you'll have to take.

Assuming that the boss continues to press you to do what he asked, you'll have another choice available to you. This, however, is the most extreme. That is, if the request goes clearly against your beliefs and you cannot get any help from others in the organization, you may have to think about quitting. You may even go outside the organization to report what is happening. Sure, there are disadvantages to doing so, but at least you'll know that you've done the right thing.[20]

In situations involving ethical decisions, you'll never know what you'll face. The most you can do is prepare yourself for making good ethical decisions and try to anticipate what you'd do when faced with one. The more you do prepare, the easier it will be when and if that day arrives and you're asked to do something that tests your personal and professional ethics.

Workplace Violence

*I*nasmuch as there is growing concern for the safety of our workers, a much greater emphasis today is being placed on the increasing violence that has erupted on the job. No organization is immune from such happenstance, and the problem appears to be getting worse.[21] Shootings at a local post office by a recently disciplined employee, an upset purchasing manager who stabs his boss because they disagreed over how some paperwork was to be completed, a disgruntled significant other who enters the workplace and shoots his mate, an employee upset over having his wages garnished—incidents like these have become all too prevalent. Consider the following statistics. More than 1,000 employees are murdered, and more than 1.5 million employees are assaulted on the job each year. Homicide has become the number-two cause of work-related death in the United States.[22]

Many individuals note that in U.S. cities, violent behaviors are spilling over into the workplace. Two factors have contributed greatly to this trend: domestic violence and disgruntled employees.[23] The issue for companies, then, is how to prevent the violence from occurring on the job. Because the circumstances of each incident are different, a specific plan of action for companies to follow is difficult to detail. However, in many cases in which violent individuals caused mayhem in an office setting and didn't commit suicide, one common factor was apparent: these employees were not treated

---

[20]Ronald Henkoff, "So Who Is Mark Whitcare and Why Is He Saying These Things about ADM?" *Fortune* (September 4, 1995), p. 68.

[21]Daniel Costello, "Stressed Out: Can Workplace Stress Get Worse?—Incidents of 'Desk Rage' Disrupt America's Offices—Long Hours, Cramped Quarters Produce Some Short Fuses; Flinging Phones at the Wall," *Wall Street Journal* (January 16, 2001), p. B-1.

[22]U.S. Department of Labor, Occupational Safety and Health Administration, Workplace Violence (Washington, D.C.: Government Printing Office, 2000), p. 1; and Lynn Miller, Karen Caldwell, and Laura C. Lawson, "When Work Equals Life: The Next State of Workplace Violence," *HR Magazine* (December 2000), pp. 178–180.

[23]Michael Lynch, "Go Ask Alice," *Security Management* (December 2000), pp. 68–73.

with respect or dignity. They were laid off without warning, or they perceived they were being treated too harshly in the discipline process. Effective company practices can help to ensure that respect and dignity are accorded employees, even in the most difficult of situations, such as terminations.

Organizations must also train their supervisory personnel to identify troubled employees before the problem results in violence.[24] Furthermore, if supervisors are better able to spot the types of demonstrated behaviors that may lead to violence, then those who cannot be helped by company programs can be removed from the organization before others are harmed. Organizations may also need to implement stronger security mechanisms. For example, many women who are killed at work following a domestic dispute die at the hands of someone who should not have been on company premises. These individuals, as well as violence paraphernalia—guns, knives, and so forth—must be kept from entering the facilities altogether.

Sadly, no matter how careful the organization is and how conscientiously it attempts to prevent workplace violence, such violence may occur. In those cases, the organization must be prepared to deal with the situation and to offer whatever assistance it can to its employees.

---

[24]See, for example, Kate Walter, "Are Your Employees on the Brink?" *HRMagazine* (June 1997), pp. 57–63.

SUMMARY

This summary corresponds to the learning outcomes on page 24.

1. Compared to years ago when the workforce consisted primarily of white males, the workforce of today has become more diverse. Passage of federal legislation that prohibits employment discrimination, changing population demographics, and globalization of businesses have contributed to this change.

2. The changing workforce means that individuals will be interacting with people who are different from them in terms of gender, race, ethnicity, physical ability, sexual orientation, and age—all of whom have different lifestyles, family needs, and work styles.

3. Globalization affects human relations in many ways. For example, we need to recognize differences that exist between people from various cultures and to understand that language differences may block effective communications.

4. Parochialism in the global village refers to a situation in which individuals see things solely through their own eyes and within their own perspectives. It means that these individuals believe that what they do is best. Parochialism leads to an ethnocentric view, in which individuals believe that they are superior to people from other cultures and their ways are better than those in other cultures.

5. Corporate downsizing involves reshaping or restructuring an organization by reducing the number of workers employed in an effort to create greater efficiency and to reduce costs. The human relations effect is twofold. First, individuals must keep their skills up to date to keep from having their job eliminated, or they must look for work elsewhere. Second, if their job remains, they will more than likely be doing the work of two or three people, which can create anger, frustration, anxiety, stress, and so on.

6. Total quality management (TQM) is a quality revolution, inspired by a small group of quality experts, taking place in both business and the public sector. TQM focuses on the customer (both internal and external), seeks continual improvement, strives to improve the quality of work, seeks accurate measurement, and involves employees.

7. Reengineering is the evaluation and alteration of most of the work done in an organization. It involves what work should be done, how it is to be

done, and how best to implement these decisions. For human relations, reengineering may lead to severing long-term work relationships. It may leave employees confused, angry, and frustrated. But it may also give them opportunities to learn new skills, more control over their daily work activities, and better compensation.

8. Downsizing, restructuring, and reengineering have all led to the decline of jobs in the United States. As a result, two groups of employees have emerged: (1) core employees, who are employees of an organization, provide some essential job tasks that require commitment and permanence in the organization, and receive all the benefits that traditionally go to regular employees; and (2) contingent workers, who are not employees of an organization, perform specific tasks that often require special job skills and are especially needed when an organization is experiencing significant deviations in its workflow, and do not receive the benefits that traditionally go to regular employees. The new workforce requires all employees to keep their skills up to date, as well as to learn to deal with any conflict that may arise between core employees and contingent workers.

9. Social responsibility is an organization's voluntary commitment to improve society. It means that an organization considers more than legal boundaries and profit making; it pursues long-term goals that are good for society in a proactive and voluntary manner.

10. Ethics refers to rules or principles that define right or wrong conduct. In an organization, those rules or principles may be defined in a code of ethics, a formal document that states an organization's primary values and the ethical rules it expects employees to follow.

11. A company can help prevent workplace violence by ensuring that its policies are not adversely affecting employees, by developing a plan to deal with the issue, and by training its managers in identifying troubled employees.

REVIEWING YOUR UNDERSTANDING

1. What is workforce diversity, and what direct effect do you believe it will have on you?

2. Describe how globalization has changed the way American companies are doing business. Do you believe this change has made American organizations better for their customers? Explain.

3. How can an ethnocentric view be damaging to an organization that operates in a global village?

4. What advice would you give to a friend who doesn't understand downsizing and knows her company is going to be restructuring in about six months?

5. "Total quality management is not new. Organizations have been concerned with quality for years and don't need some catchy title and a bandwagon to jump on to continue what they've been doing already." Do you agree or disagree with this statement? Discuss.

6. Explain how reengineering can ultimately lead to greater worker satisfaction.

7. Do you believe the disappearance of jobs in America is taking us back some one-hundred years when people didn't work in organizations, but rather worked for themselves? Explain your response.

8. "Contingent workers are getting the best of both worlds. They can pick and choose when they want to work, and when they do, they get paid a higher wage." Do you agree or disagree with this statement? Discuss.

9. Can organizations be socially responsible and still be profitable? If you think so, cite some examples of companies you believe fit this profile, and describe what they are doing.

10. Is it ethical to cheat on an exam knowing that it would not affect another student's grade and knowing that you wouldn't get caught? Why or why not?

ANSWERS TO CHECKING YOUR UNDERSTANDING

1. b **2.** c **3.** d **4.** a

LEARNING TOGETHER

A. In teams of three or four students, create a display depicting global aspects that might affect today's businesses. Discuss the similarities and differences among the displays. How do the displays demonstrate that all the world is a global village? What can be learned from the displays about conducting business in this global village?

B. Debate with your classmates how total quality management differs from reengineering. Identify some companies that have been successful at one or both concepts. Why have they been successful?

C. Form teams of two to four students. Under the headings of desire, ability, temperament, and assets, identify the attributes associated with each term that are needed in today's businesses. Are these attributes different from those needed twenty-five or more years ago? Why or why not? Share your opinions with the other groups in the class.

The Changing Work World

Loren Waggoner's father works in the customer service division at TransAtlantic Airways (TAA). Mr. Waggoner has worked at TAA for more than fifteen years and plans to retire in about four years. Recently, however, rumors have been circulating around TAA that the company is considering some restructuring. The buzzwords are *reengineering* and *downsizing*. Mr. Waggoner finds the rumors somewhat unbelievable because of the investment the company has just made toward implementing some total quality management programs.

At dinner one night, Mr. Waggoner shared with his family the restructuring rumors at TAA. Loren was quite interested in what his father had to say because his instructor in his human relations class was discussing reengineering, downsizing, rightsizing, and many of the other challenges that face today's businesses. Loren told his father and family about some of the ways companies were responding to the changing global economy.

Each evening the Waggoner family continued their dinner discussions about the new developments at TAA. Then one night, Mr. Waggoner said he had heard pink slips were going to be handed out at the end of the month. Rumor had it that nearly 30 percent of TAA employees were going to be laid off. Issues of concern to TAA seemed to be workplace diversity, globalization, and contingent workers. Loren told his dad that he would see many positive employees become negative about their work and the company. Probably complaints and accidents would increase.

Sure enough, over the weeks, Mr. Waggoner heard more and more complaints about nearly everything. Although a few people left the company to find employment elsewhere, there were those who complained about how devoted they were to the company and how unfair, unethical, and heartless the company was becoming. Being fired was going to be their reward for their dedication and many years of service to the company. To some, the company owed them and they were going to make sure the company would pay. Loren was amazed at how accurate his instructor had been in describing the human relations changes that can occur over such a short period of time when a company's proposed actions threaten employee job security. Loren was also noticing his dad becoming more serious and despondent.

Questions

1. Why is change considered a constant in today's society? Even though 70 percent of TAA employees would not lose their jobs, why do you believe the morale of most employees went down?

2. Does TAA have any social responsibilities or obligations to its employees? If contingent workers are brought in to replace terminated employees, what changes in human relations skills seem inevitable?

3. What human relations skills may be needed by TAA as a transnational corporation versus a multinational company? What factors of the new workforce make human relations different than in previous work environments?

Now that you have a basic understanding of human relations, it's time to begin focusing your attention on the most critical component of human relations—you. Why you act the way you do, how you communicate with others, and how you deal with life's problems are the subjects of this section. Part two contains three chapters:

chapter 3

THE HUMAN FACTOR

*L*earning Outcomes
After reading this chapter, you will be able to:

1. Identify several recognized methods for classifying personalities by traits.

2. Describe Holland's personality-job fit theory.

3. Define *perception* and describe the factors that can shape or distort perceptions.

4. Describe the factors that influence value systems.

5. Identify and describe three components of attitudes.

6. Show how consistency plays a role in attitude.

7. Describe what is meant by the term *positive attitude*.

8. Explain why companies use organizational surveys.

9. Define *learning*.

10. Explain what is meant by the term *operant conditioning* and describe four ways in which behavior can be shaped.

What do your family, your instructor, your special friend, and your employer have in common? That's an easy one. The answer is you. Whenever you interact with others, you show them a side of you that is unique to who you are. You are different from every other individual. You behave and react in ways that no one can accurately predict. You do things that at times are viewed as odd—but only to those who do not understand you. As individuals, we each try to live the way we want—within the conditions set by society's cultural norms. Our behaviors in our personal lives and in the workplace are determined by many human factors that shape who we are.

To understand human behavior, it's important to understand the basic makeup of individuals—or at least begin to recognize why we do the things we do. To achieve that goal, you need to understand who you are—what makes you unique.

Character

➤ **character**
the way one defines oneself and shows this to others through behavior

Character is a term that has many meanings. It can mean the role an actor portrays in a play. It can refer to the funny and witty way you act when your mom says, "He's a character." **Character** is also the way you personally define yourself and the way you show this to others through your behavior. Character is something you

UNLOCKING YOUR POTENTIAL 3-1

Understanding Who You Are

Understanding who you are means recognizing your positive and negative personality traits and thinking through what advantages and disadvantages they create for you. To begin this process, describe yourself using ten adjectives that honestly reflect who you are.

_____   _____

_____   _____

_____   _____

_____   _____

_____   _____

Now answer the following questions by circling Agree or Disagree. Respond according to how you feel most of the time. Certainly you'll find exceptions to even your general rules, but try to give your typical response.

1. Much of anyone's success is due to fate and a lot of good luck.   Agree   Disagree

2. I believe in the golden rule. That is, the one with the gold, rules.   Agree   Disagree

3. Getting an A in this class is important to me. I'll do whatever it takes to get that grade—even if it means doing something I'm not proud of.   Agree   Disagree

4. I often find faults in things I do.   Agree   Disagree

5. Given the choice between $10 in cash and a chance to choose—while wearing a blindfold—one bill out of a hat in which there are nine blank pieces of paper and one $100 bill, I'll take the chance for the big payoff.   Agree   Disagree

develop. It's a way of life, a way of dealing with others, and the way others react to you. It's your pride, your integrity, and the basic moral fiber of your life. Your character goes to your very being, and it directs the action you take in life.

Character, then, plays a major role in human relations. Your interactions with others will be a function of the character you have developed. How consistent you are in dealing with others, how sensitive you are toward the people you interact with, and how confident you are in your abilities are derived from the individual characteristics you possess.

In the current advertising slogan for the U.S. Marines—"The Few, the Proud, the Marines"—the message is that this branch of the military prides itself on developing high levels of character. But what, exactly, goes into developing character? Specifically, character is made up of personality traits and learning experiences over a lifetime. Each of us was born with certain traits that developed throughout childhood and adolescence as a result of interaction with the environment. Your experiences have helped shape who you are, and each new experience continues your character evolution.

Personality

*P*ersonality is an individual's pattern of thinking, feeling, and acting over time. Of the many different views of personality, we have selected three major perspectives that seek to define and explain personality: the trait perspective, the humanistic perspective, and the social-cognitive perspective.

> ▶ **personality**
> an individual's pattern of thinking, feeling, and acting over time

The Trait Perspective

Personality Traits. Some people are loud and aggressive, whereas others are quiet and passive. Such terms as *quiet, passive, loud, aggressive, ambitious, extroverted, introverted, loyal, tense,* or *sociable* describe people in terms of personality traits. There are dozens of personality traits. An individual's personality is the combination of the various psychological traits we use to classify that person.

Classifying Personalities. Through the years, researchers attempted to focus specifically on traits that would lead to identifying sources of one's personality. Several of these efforts to classify or type personalities have been widely recognized. One effort by Cattell was the formation of sixteen primary personality dimensions.[1] (See Exhibit 3-1.) The varying degrees of these sixteen factors combine to form each person's personality combination. Identifying each, however, is nearly impossible. Because each trait is rated on a scale from 1 to 10, there are 10^{16} (ten *quadrillion*) different personality combinations.

A more widely used method of identifying and classifying personalities, especially in business and career counseling, is the **Myers-Briggs Type Indicator (MBTI).** Based on the work of Carl Jung, the MBTI uses four dimensions of personality to identify sixteen different personality types derived from responses to a 126-item questionnaire. (These sixteen personality types are different from those noted in Exhibit 3-1.) The four MBTI dimensions are extroversion versus introversion (EI), sensing versus intuitive (SI), thinking versus feeling (TF), and judging versus perceiving (JP). The EI dimension measures an individual's orientation toward the inner world of ideas (I) or the external world of the environment (E). The SI dimension indicates an individual's reliance on information gathered from the external world (S) or from the world of ideas (I). The TF dimension reflects one's preference for evaluating information in an analytical manner

> ▶ **Myers-Briggs Type Indicator (MBTI)**
> a method that uses four dimensions of personality to identify sixteen different personality types

---

[1]Raymond B. Cattell, "Personality Pinned Down," *Psychology Today* (July 1973), pp. 40–46.

Reserved	vs.	Outgoing
Less intelligent	vs.	More intelligent
Affected by feelings	vs.	Emotionally stable
Submissive	vs.	Dominant
Serious	vs.	Happy-go-lucky
Expedient	vs.	Conscientious
Apprehensive	vs.	Venturesome
Tough-minded	vs.	Sensitive
Trusting	vs.	Suspicious
Practical	vs.	Imaginative
Forthright	vs.	Shrewd
Self-assured	vs.	Apprehensive
Conservative	vs.	Experimenting
Group-dependent	vs.	Self-sufficient
Uncontrolled	vs.	Controlled
Relaxed	vs.	Tense

EXHIBIT 3-1
Primary Personality Factors

Source: Raymond B. Cattell, *The Secret Analysis of Personality* (Chicago: Aldine Publishing, 1966).

(T) or based on values and beliefs (F). Lastly, the JP dimension reflects one's attitude toward the external world, which is either task-completion-oriented (J) or information-seeking (P). Using this information, then, let's describe someone who is identified as an INFP (introvert-intuitive-feeling-perceptive). According to Myers-Briggs, the INFP individual would be someone who is quiet and reserved and generally in deep thought, sees the big picture, is flexible and adaptable, likes a challenge, looks for complete information before making a decision, and cares for others.[2]

> **risk propensity**
willingness to take chances

The trait of **risk propensity,** or willingness to take chances, has also been used to classify personalities. A preference to assume or to avoid risk has been shown to have an impact on how long it takes a person to make a decision and how much information is required before making a choice. High-risk-taking individuals make more rapid decisions and use less information in making their choices than do low-risk-taking individuals. Research over the years has shown that the decision accuracy for both groups is about the same.

Risk propensity, like many of the other traits, must be aligned with specific job demands. For instance, a high risk propensity may lead to more effective performance for a stock trader in a brokerage firm. This type of job demands rapid decision making. On the other hand, this personality characteristic might prove a major obstacle to computer programmers designing new software packages. This latter job might be better filled by someone with low-risk propensity.

> **authoritarianism**
a belief that there should be formal differences among people in organizations, based on authority

Individuals have also been classified as high or low authoritarian. **Authoritarianism** refers to a belief that there should be formal differences among people in organizations, based on authority. People who have a high authoritarian personality trait

[2]Adapted from Isabel Briggs-Myers, *Introduction to Type* (Palo Alto, Calif.: Consulting Psychologists Press, 1980), pp. 7–8.

are likely to be intellectually rigid, judgmental of others, respectful primarily to those above them in the organization, somewhat distrustful of others, and resistant to change. What does this mean in the workplace? Specific conclusions are difficult to generate because it depends on the situation. It seems reasonable to conclude that having a strong authoritarian personality would lead to poor performance on a job that demands sensitivity to the feelings of others, diplomacy, or adapting to rapidly changing situations. On the other hand, in a job that is highly structured and in which success depends on close conformity to rules and regulations (a bureaucratic organization), the highly authoritarian individual should perform quite well.

Closely related to authoritarianism is the characteristic of **Machiavellianism** (Mach), named after Niccolo Machiavelli, who wrote in the sixteenth century on how to gain control over and manipulate others. An individual who is high in the Machiavellianism trait—in contrast to someone who is low—is practical, maintains emotional distance from others, and believes that ends can justify means.[3] "If it works, use it" is consistent with those who have a high Mach. If you are high in the Mach trait, will you make a good employee? Again, the answer depends on the type of job you have. In jobs that require negotiating skills (such as a lawyer or a labor negotiator) or that have substantial rewards for winning (such as a commissioned salesperson), you would be very productive. In jobs in which the ends do not justify the means or that lack precise standards of performance, it is difficult to predict the performance of a high Machiavellian personality.

> **Machiavellianism**
> a belief that it is desirable to gain control over and to manipulate others

---

[3]R. G. Vleeming, "Machiavellianism: A Preliminary Review," *Psychological Reports* (February 1979), pp. 295–310.

Anne Beiler always wanted to run her own business. She had that special drive and the willingness to take risks in opening up Auntie Anne's Pretzel Shop. Through her efforts, she's built a pretzel empire that now boasts nearly 300 shops and millions in annual revenues.

Personality and Job Choices.   One application of the trait perspective is matching an individual employee's personality with the personality of the job. Psychologist John Holland's theory of **vocational preferences** and work choices consists of two primary components.[4] First, Holland found that people have varied occupational preferences based on their personality. Second, Holland demonstrates that if people are properly matched to their jobs, they'll place more importance on their jobs and be more productive. For instance, assume Alice hates her job. She thinks it's boring and a waste of time packing and unpacking crates and stocking shelves in her job at Radio Shack. Bob, on the other hand, enjoys the routine of the work. He likes the daily rhythm of loading and unloading equipment and doesn't want to be bothered by others. Will Alice and Bob get the same satisfaction from their jobs? There's a good chance they won't. Why not? Their occupational interests are not the same. Alice's personality doesn't appear to be well matched to this job.

Holland has identified six vocational types: realistic, investigative, social, conventional, enterprising, and artistic. Exhibit 3-2 describes each of the six types, the personality characteristics, and examples of compatible occupations. An individual's occupational personality is expressed as some combination of high and low scores on these six themes. High scores indicate that the individual enjoys those kinds of activities expressed in a vocational type. Although it is possible to score high or low on all six vocational types, most people are identified by three dominant scales. The six themes, then, are arranged in a hexagon, as shown in Exhibit 3-3. This hexagon represents the fact that some of the themes are opposing, whereas others have mutually reinforcing

---

[4]John L. Holland, *Making Vocational Choices: A Theory of Vocational Personalities and Work Environments*, 2nd ed. (Upper Saddle River, N.J.: Prentice-Hall, 1985).

EXHIBIT 3-2

Holland's Six Vocational Themes

Type	Personality Characteristics	Sample Occupations
Realistic—Prefers physical activities that require skill, strength, and coordination	Shy, genuine, persistent, stable, conforming, practical	Mechanic, drill press operator, assembly-line worker, farmer
Investigative—Prefers activities involving thinking, organizing, and understanding	Analytical, original, curious, independent	Biologist, economist, mathematician, news reporter
Social—Prefers activities that involve helping and developing others	Sociable, friendly, cooperative, understanding	Social worker, teacher, counselor, clinical psychologist
Conventional—Prefers rule-regulated, orderly, and unambiguous activities	Conforming, efficient, practical, unimaginative, inflexible	Accountant, corporate manager, bank teller, file clerk
Enterprising—Prefers verbal activities where there are opportunities to influence others and attain power	Self-confident, ambitious, energetic, domineering	Lawyer, real estate agent, public relations specialist, small business manager
Artistic—Prefers ambiguous and unsystematic activities that allow creative expression	Imaginative, disorderly, idealistic, emotional, impractical	Painter, musician, writer, interior decorator

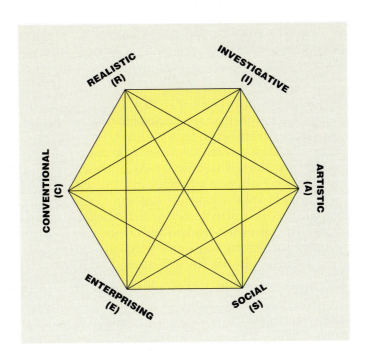

EXHIBIT 3-3
Relationship among Occupational Personality Types
Source: Reproduced by special permission of the Publisher, Psychological Assessment Resources, Inc., *Making Vocational Choices,* copyright 1973, 1985 by Psychological Assessment Resources, Inc. All rights reserved.

characteristics. For instance, realistic and social are opposite each other in the diagram. A person with a realistic preference wants to work with things, not people. A person with a social preference wants to work with people, no matter what else he or she does. Therefore, they have opposing preferences about working alone or with others.

An example of mutually reinforcing themes is the social-enterprising-conventional (SEC) vocational preferences. Debbie, for example, likes working with people, being successful, and following routines. That combination is perfect for someone willing to climb the organizational ladder in a bureaucracy. But what about Kevin? He's realistic-investigative-artistic. How would Kevin fit into a large, rule-oriented, organization? Probably not very well. He might even be viewed as a troublemaker. Where would Kevin fit better? Probably somewhere like a research lab. Both the preference of the scientist and the environment of the research lab are characterized by a lack of interruptions and a concentration on factual data.

What does all this mean? The theory argues that satisfaction is highest and turnover lowest where personality and occupation are in agreement. Social individuals, for example, should be in social jobs, conventional people in conventional jobs, and so forth. A realistic person in a realistic job is in a more compatible situation than is a realistic person in an investigative job. A realistic person in a social job is in the most dissimilar situation possible. The key points of this model are that (1) there do appear to be natural differences in personality types among individuals, (2) there are different types of jobs, and (3) people in job environments compatible with their personality types should be more satisfied and less likely to resign voluntarily than should people in incongruent jobs.

Understanding your personality is one of the first steps to making a good job choice. The closer the match between your personality and what the job requires, the greater the chance for achieving your career goals.

The Humanistic Perspective

Although early personality trait theories helped describe behavior and classify individuals in terms of personality types, they did little to explain why people did what they did. Researchers continued to look for links between personality and behavior in organizations. Building on the findings of prominent humanistic psychologists of the early 1900s, researchers turned to whole-person theories for explanations of human behavior. Two areas receiving attention in this search were self-esteem and self-serving bias.

self-esteem
the degree to which one likes or dislikes oneself

Self-Esteem.   The degree to which you like or dislike yourself is called **self-esteem.** The research on self-esteem offers some interesting insights into human behavior. For example, self-esteem is directly related to your expectations for success. If you have high self-esteem, you believe you possess more of the needed abilities to succeed at work. You will take more risks in job selection and are more likely to choose unconventional jobs than are others with low self-esteem. In contrast, those who have low self-esteem are more likely to seek approval from others and are more likely to feel compelled to conform to the beliefs and behaviors expected by those they respect. Not surprisingly, self-esteem has also been found to be related to job satisfaction. A number of studies confirm that people with high self-esteem are more satisfied with their jobs than are people with low self-esteem.

self-serving bias
a person's tendency to take credit for successes while putting blame for failures on others

Self-Serving Bias.   More recent studies, however, provide evidence that individuals may have inflated confidence in the accuracy of their beliefs and judgments. A **self-serving bias** is a person's tendency to take credit for his or her successes while blaming his or her failures on others. Most individuals suffer from a self-serving bias, accepting more responsibility for good deeds than bad and for successes than failures. Many see themselves as better than average.

The Social-Cognitive Perspective

Social-cognitive psychologists look at how personality is derived from interactions with our environment. Do we control our environment, or are we controlled by it? One important aspect of personality is **locus of control,** our sense of the center of control or authority in our lives. Human behavior is affected by whether people perceive the control of their lives as external (at the mercy of the outside world) or as internal (in themselves).

locus of control
the center of control or authority

Who has control over your behavior? Do you see yourself as a pawn of fate, believing that what happens to you is due to luck or chance? Or do you believe that you control your own fate? The locus of control in the first case is external, meaning that you believe that your life is controlled by outside forces. In the second case, the locus of control is internal, meaning that you believe that you control your destiny. The evidence indicates that individuals with an external locus of control are less satisfied with their jobs, more alienated from the work setting, and less involved in their jobs than those with an internal locus of control.[5] We might also expect to find that employees

---

[5] Dennis W. Organ & Charles N. Greene, "Role Ambiguity, Locus of Control, and Work Satisfaction," *Journal of Applied Psychology* (February 1974), pp. 101–102.

✓ Checking Your Understanding *3-1*

1. Which one of the following is not a trait used to classify personality?
   a. authoritarianism
   b. risk propensity
   c. social need
   d. extroversion

2. Which type of job would least interest a person with an investigative vocational preference?
   a. nuclear engineer
   b. computer programmer
   c. professional chess player
   d. aerobics instructor

with an external locus of control blame work problems on their boss's prejudice, their co-workers' incompetence, or other events outside their control. Employees with an internal locus of control explain the same problems in terms of their own actions.

Personality and National Cultures

Undeniably, there are no common personality types for a given country. You can, for instance, find high-risk takers and low-risk takers in almost any culture. Yet a country's culture does influence the dominant personality characteristics of its population. We can see this by looking at two personality characteristics: authoritarianism and locus of control.

KEYS TO UNLOCKING YOUR POTENTIAL *3-1*

*T*he words you used to describe yourself in Unlocking Your Potential 3-1 can be any that you truly believe portray who you are. You may have used words such as *sincere, quiet, outgoing, friendly, thinker, problem solver,* and *athletic*. Did you include any negative ones?

The second part of Unlocking Your Potential 3-1 asked you to respond to five questions. Each question focused on a particular personality trait. Although your responses are not cast in concrete, nor are they 100 percent scientifically accurate, the responses would indicate the following:

	Agree	*Disagree*
1. Much of anyone's success is due to fate and a lot of good luck.	External locus of control	Internal locus of control
2. I believe in the golden rule. That is, the one with the gold, rules.	Strong authoritarian	Weak authoritarian
3. Getting an A in this class is important to me. I'll do whatever it takes to get that grade—even if it means doing something I'm not proud of.	High Mach	Low Mach
4. I often find faults in things I do.	High self-esteem	Low self-esteem
5. Given the choice between $10 in cash and a chance to choose—while wearing a blindfold—one bill out of a hat in which there are nine blank pieces of paper and one $100 bill, I'll take the chance for the big payoff.	High-risk taker	Low-risk taker

Extra Effort

Just describing yourself, or quickly seeing how you rate on five personality traits, isn't enough to fully appreciate or understand who you are. You need to begin asking yourself many questions. Is there a pattern to what you see? Do the words you used to describe yourself tell you—and maybe others—something about your personality? If so, what? Do you see some consistency in how you see yourself? Do you believe that others, if asked to describe you, would come up with a similar list? Would that list be different if a family member wrote it, in contrast to a close friend?

Authoritarianism is closely related to the concept of power distance. In high power-distance societies, such as Mexico or Venezuela, there should be a large proportion of individuals with authoritarian personalities, especially among the ruling class. In contrast, because the United States rates below average on this dimension, one should expect authoritarian personalities to be less prevalent here than in the high power-distance countries.

National cultures also differ in terms of the degree to which people believe they control their environment. Many North Americans, for example, believe that they can dominate their environment, whereas other societies, such as Middle Eastern countries, believe that life is essentially predetermined. Notice the close parallel to internal and external loci of control. Therefore, there's more likely a larger proportion of people with an internal locus of control among U.S. and Canadian workers than among workers of Saudi Arabia or Iran.

Perception

> **perception**
a process by which an individual organizes and interprets sensory impressions to give meaning to his or her environment

Perception is a process by which you organize and interpret sensory impressions to give meaning to your environment. Your perceptions are the basis for developing your very personal and unique system of beliefs. Research on perception consistently demonstrates that an individual may look at something and perceive it very differently from someone else. One of your family members, for instance, may interpret the fact that you regularly take several days to make important decisions as evidence that you are slow, disorganized, and afraid to make decisions. Another family member, however, might interpret the same action as evidence that you are thoughtful, thorough, and deliberate. As a result, the first family member would probably perceive your actions negatively, whereas the second would probably perceive them in a positive light. The point is that no one actually sees reality. People interpret what they see and call these perceptions reality. Moreover, they act according to their personal perceptions of reality, not reality itself.

What Influences Perception?

How do you explain the fact that people can perceive the same thing differently? A number of factors shape and sometimes distort perception: how you see something, the object being observed, the context of the situation in which the perception is made.

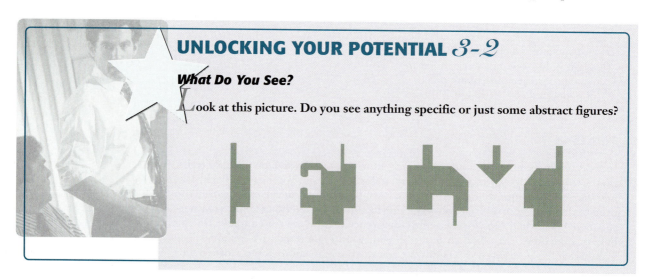

UNLOCKING YOUR POTENTIAL 3-2

What Do You See?

Look at this picture. Do you see anything specific or just some abstract figures?

When you look at something and attempt to interpret what you see, personal characteristics will heavily influence your interpretation. These personal characteristics include your personality, attitudes, motives, interests, experiences, and expectations. The characteristics of what you're observing, the target, can also affect what you perceive. Loud people are more likely than quiet people to be noticed in a group, as are extremely attractive or unattractive people. Because targets are not looked at in isolation, the relationship of a target to its background also influences perception, as does your tendency to group together close things and similar things. The context in which you see objects or events is also important. The time at which you see an object or event can influence attention, as can location, light, heat, and any number of other situational factors.

Using Perceptions to Judge Others

We typically use a number of shortcuts when we judge others, often relying on our perceptions. Perceiving and interpreting what others do is burdensome. As a result, we tend to develop techniques for making the task more manageable. These techniques are frequently valuable—they allow us to make accurate perceptions rapidly and provide valid data for making predictions. However, shortcut techniques relying solely on perceptions are not foolproof; they can and do get us into trouble. Understanding these shortcut techniques can be helpful in recognizing when they might result in significant distortions. (See Exhibit 3-4.)

We cannot absorb all we see, so we engage in a shortcut technique called selective perception. **Selective perception** involves taking in only bits and pieces of information from infinite sensory data. These bits and pieces are not chosen randomly; rather, they are selectively chosen depending on a person's interests, background, experience, and attitudes. For example, if you perceive that you are a well-prepared student because you graduated from Sensational High School, then you would view others who graduated from the same school in the same way. Graduates from a competing

▶ **selective perception**
interpretation of objects and events based on personal interests, background, experience, and attitudes

Shortcut	*What It Is*	*Distortion*
Selective perception	People assimilate certain bits and pieces of what they observe depending on their interests, backgrounds, experiences, and attitudes	May draw an inaccurate picture of others by speed-reading them
Assumed similarity	People assume others are like them	May fail to take into account individual differences, resulting in incorrect similarities
Stereotyping	People judge others based on their perception of a group to which others belong	May result in distorted judgments because many stereotypes have no factual foundation
Halo effect	People form an impression of others based on a single trait	May form inaccurate assumptions because of failure to take into account the total picture of a person

EXHIBIT 3-4

Distortions in Shortcuts in Judging Others

high school that you felt didn't adequately prepare its students for college would selectively be viewed by you as educationally inferior. Selective perception allows you to speed-read others, but not without the risk of drawing an inaccurate picture.

It is easy to judge others if you assume that they are similar to you using another shortcut technique. In **assumed similarity**, or the *like-me effect*, your perception of others is influenced more by your own characteristics than by those of the person observed. For example, if you want challenge and responsibility in your job, you will assume that others want the same. Assuming that others are like you can, of course, be right; but, most of the time, that's an incorrect assumption.

When you judge someone on the basis of your perception of a group to which he or she belongs, you are using the shortcut called **stereotyping.** "Married people are more stable employees than singles" and "Union people expect something for nothing" are examples of stereotyping. To the degree that a stereotype is based on the truth, it may produce accurate judgments. However, many stereotypes have no foundation in reality. In such cases, stereotypes distort judgments. The distinction here is one between facts and inferences. A **fact** is anything that is actual or true. For example, you are currently reading Chapter 3 of this text. That is a fact. On the other hand, for us to say that you are thoroughly enjoying this book because you are still reading it would be an inference. An **inference** is a conclusion drawn without fact, but based on probabilities. Because you are still reading the book (fact), we might presume that you like it (inference). Otherwise, you'd not be reading it at all (unless you're forced to).

When you form a general impression about an individual based on a single characteristic such as intelligence, sociability, or appearance, you are being influenced by the **halo effect,** yet another shortcut. This effect may occur when you evaluate your classroom instructors. You may isolate a single trait—such as enthusiasm—and allow your entire evaluation to be tainted by your perception of this one trait. Your instructor, however, might be quiet, assured, knowledgeable, and highly qualified. But if your instructor's style lacks intensity, you may rate him or her lower on a number of other characteristics.

Creating Positive Perceptions about Yourself

Each of us has been evaluated since birth. Moments after you were born, you were assessed on something called an Apgar score.[6] The closer your score was to ten, the healthier you were said to be. During your early years, your height and weight were monitored and evaluated against some preset standards. Elementary and secondary schools, and even college, evaluate how you are progressing. The more you meet the objectives as set by the teacher, the better grades you will earn. Work is no different. You are constantly evaluated. But evaluation (a form of judging) is also subject to the evaluator's perceptions. Therefore, you need to understand how those perceptions may affect you.

Your evaluators will generally judge your behavior not only on the action itself but also according to what they perceive as the cause of the behavior.[7] Basically, when your behavior is observed, an evaluator attempts to determine whether what was seen was internally or externally caused. That is, was your behavior something you controlled (internal), or was it a reaction to something out of your control (external)? For example, if you failed to complete a project that you had six months to complete, your

[6]An Apgar score reflects an assessment of respiration, color, heart rate, and muscle tone.
[7]Sandy J. Wayne & K. Michele Kacmar, "The Effects of Impression Management on the Performance Appraisal Process," *Organizational Behavior and Human Decision Processes* (February 1991), pp. 70–88.

assumed similarity
a perception of others influenced more by an individual's own characteristics than by those of the persons observed

stereotyping
judging a person on the basis of one's perception of the group to which he or she belongs

fact
anything that is actual or true

inference
a conclusion drawn without fact, but based on probabilities

halo effect
a general impression about an individual based on a single characteristic

supervisor may view this negatively if she believes the delay is attributed to how you handled the project or budgeted your time (internal control). On the other hand, if the project is delayed because she requested that you work on something with a higher priority (external control), she may see the incomplete project in more positive terms. In essence, in the former situation, you are perceived totally responsible; in the latter, your behavior was forced by situations outside your control. Situations like this one, however, are not always crystal clear. Perceptions of you are often a function of whether others see the behavior as unusual, unique to you, or happening frequently. Let's explore these through an example.

Suppose you come in late today for work. Are you likely to get nailed? The answer will depend on how you're perceived. If in addition to being late, your supervisor has received complaints about your being a goof-off, then he may see your lateness as another indication of your character. Accordingly, he could hold you responsible, and you may face the appropriate discipline one gets for coming in late for work. But your supervisor is also going to look at what happened to others this morning. If others who came to work traveling the same route you did were also late, then extenuating circumstances (external control) may have been the reason. So even though he still has complaints about your being a goof-off, the fact that others were also late may excuse your particular behavior. Finally, your supervisor will look for consistency in your actions. Are you regularly late? Do you behave in ways that are inappropriate for the organization? If so, you are held responsible.

So how do you guard against negative perceptions? Generally speaking, to avoid problems associated with negative perceptions by your evaluators, you need to do the right thing. That means developing and maintaining the impression that you are a good employee, one who cares about work and work relationships. It means presenting an image that is consistent with the values the organization holds. In most places, that means getting to work on time, working diligently on the tasks you're responsible for, and relating well with others. Realize, too, that you need to be accountable for your own behavior. We all make mistakes—take ownership of them. Even the most patient individual gets tired of someone's self-serving bias. Accepting blame when it is appropriate demonstrates your maturity and goes a long way toward creating a positive perception of you. For instance, maybe the low grade you earned last semester wasn't your instructor's fault because of tricky questions. Maybe, just maybe, you needed to devote more time to studying that material. Although you shouldn't let anyone walk over you and you shouldn't

KEYS TO UNLOCKING YOUR POTENTIAL *3-2*

*T*hese abstract shapes show how perceptions can differ. If you look closely at the picture, you should notice the word *FLY*. If you're having trouble seeing *FLY*, use the background color. Now do you see the word? If you now can, it's because changing the background changes your perception.

Extra Effort

How can something look so clear to you and still not be what everyone else sees? Do you make mistakes in your life by not being open to new experiences or by seeing things only one way? What do you think?

take responsibility for things that are not your fault, your basic response to problems should be to look at where your responsibility lies. When you are not at fault (and even when you are), people around you are more likely to excuse you because you don't frequently cry wolf. That's a powerful perception to leave with others.

Values

*P*erceptions lead to beliefs and beliefs lead to values. **Values** are strongly held beliefs that guide your behavior. Values define what's important to you and your life, and they determine how you view your behavior. They dominate how you see things, and they often determine how you act. They can drive your very existence. They include such things as your integrity, honesty, trust, and loyalty. Values also define what society views as acceptable behavior. Furthermore, they help you decide between right and wrong, determining your ethics. Values are learned. As you learn them and form your ethical opinions, you develop your **value system,** beliefs formed over time by taking in and processing thousands of pieces of information from varied sources.

Many factors influence your value system. To understand how your values are formed, think of your value system as a sponge, taking in and processing thousands of pieces of information in your formative years. As you absorb all these facts, you begin to make sense of them and define what you like. These information sources come from all aspects of your life. Sources can be your parents, brothers and sisters, extended family members, significant others, friends, teachers, public figures, significant events occurring in your life, movie stars, professional athletes, coaches, supervisors, the media, your religion, and the like. (See Exhibit 3-5.)

Although your life is touched by many people, the foundation of your value system begins with the family. You were taught right from wrong at an early age and were often reinforced for good behavior. Maybe that meant getting an extra dessert or the privilege of staying up late to watch a special TV show. Instinctively, you knew that your family meant well. But sometimes there were inconsistencies. You heard family members say things, but act differently. For instance, you were told to always be honest. Yet when family members got too much change at the grocery store, they didn't return it. Even though they told you not to get involved in drugs, you watched them drink a bottle of wine at dinner and blow cigarette smoke around you. And the list could go on. This is not to indict your family. Most of you have good ones that you

values
strongly held beliefs that guide behavior

value system
beliefs formed over time by taking in and processing thousands of pieces of information from varied sources

UNLOCKING YOUR POTENTIAL *3-3*

Who Shaped Your Values?

*O*ur values were not born with us. They have been formed over the years. Values reflect what we see as being right—however we define *right*. List the ten most influential people in your life who have helped you form your value system.

_____   _____

_____   _____

_____   _____

_____   _____

_____   _____

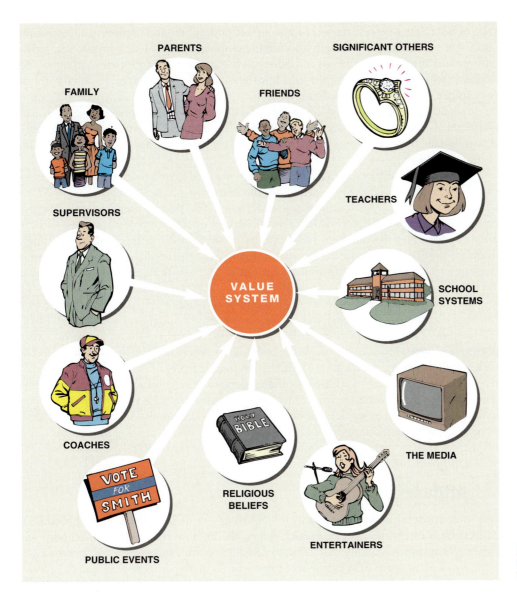

FAMILY

PARENTS

FRIENDS

SIGNIFICANT OTHERS

SUPERVISORS

TEACHERS

VALUE SYSTEM

SCHOOL SYSTEMS

COACHES

THE MEDIA

VOTE FOR SMITH

HOLY BIBLE

RELIGIOUS BELIEFS

ENTERTAINERS

PUBLIC EVENTS

EXHIBIT 3-5
Some Factors Influencing Your Value System

love very much. But it demonstrates that you learned from their behaviors just as from what they told you. And both their words and their behaviors shaped your values.

As the world has changed over the past decades, so too have home environments, which include single parents, high divorce rates, dual-career couples, career responsibilities, latchkey kids, and so on. Children's values are affected. Family members, the primary teachers of values, aren't as available to today's generation of children as they were decades ago. The result is more pressure on young people to form values more by what they observe in society than by what they experience in the home. It's a difficult world, a world that presents a challenge to developing a sound value system. For many, teaching values has become the responsibility of their educators—individuals who may be uncomfortable with accepting that duty.[8]

[8]Sonia L. Nazario, "Schoolteachers Say It's Wrongheaded to Try to Teach Students What's Right," *The Wall Street Journal* (April 6, 1990), p. B-1.

The media you're exposed to also affect you. The entertainment industry has come under attack lately over its dominant emphasis on violence in movies, video games, and song lyrics. The issue is that such entertainment glorifies violence and makes it appear that maiming or killing others is not only acceptable behavior, but fun. Impressionable individuals may be swayed into believing that this type of behavior is acceptable in society. They may make heroes of villains or mimic antisocial elements. They may try to do what these idols are doing or saying. That's why there was so much flack over two of "gangsta" rapper Ice-T's songs, "Cop Killers" and "Home Invasion."[9]

But not all media are negative. There are positive media that extol the goodness that does exist in society. There are children's television shows—such as *Sesame Street* and *Barney*—or family-oriented movies and music like that of the Disney Company or the musical group 4PM (For Positive Music) that promote positive values. Others are designed to teach you about family values or working hard for the things you get. Today, however, there are fewer positive influences in the media than there are negative ones. Once again, forming appropriate values is challenging, given what is thrown at you.

Regardless of how you formed your values, one important aspect is worth mentioning. You shouldn't impose your values on others. Although some values held by a fellow student may be unpopular with you, you don't have the right to dictate how that person is supposed to act—nor he you. And this is particularly true in a workforce that is rich with diversity. You should recognize that people from different cultures have different values. You need to appreciate and understand those values; otherwise, serious conflict can occur. Some organizations offer help dealing with these potential problems. At DuPont, for example, that help is part of the company's "A Matter of Respect" program,[10] which is designed to assist all employees in understanding one another and respecting one another's rights. Similar programs exist at Federal Express, General Mills, and Levi-Strauss.[11]

Attitudes

> **attitudes**
> statements that reflect values—either favorable or unfavorable—concerning objects, people, or events

*A*ttitudes are statements that reflect values—either favorable or unfavorable—concerning objects, people, or events. They reflect how you feel about something. When, for instance, you say, "I like my college," you are expressing an attitude.

Look at an attitude as being made up of three main components. The first component is the beliefs, opinions, knowledge, or information you hold. For example, if you believe that not associating with others because of their sexual orientation is wrong, this illustrates an attitude based on a belief. The second component is the emotional or feeling segment of an attitude. This component would be reflected in the statement, "I don't like Eric because he belittles people who are different from him." Finally, the behavioral component of an attitude refers to an intention to behave in a certain way toward someone or something. To continue the example, you might choose to avoid Eric because of your feelings about him. Looking at attitudes as being made up of three components helps show their complexity.

---

[9]Bernie Ward, "Rap Street on Gangstas," *San Francisco Examiner* (July 11, 1995), p. 17.
[10]Commerce Clearing House, *Human Resources Management: Ideas and Trends* (March 5, 1992), p. 39.
[11]Anne B. Fisher, "Sexual Harassment: What to Do," *Fortune* (August 23, 1993), p. 88.

The Need for Consistency

Consistency in attitudes is considered important in human behavior; we are continually making adjustments to maintain consistency between our attitudes and our behavior. Did you ever notice how people change what they say so that it doesn't contradict what they do? Perhaps a friend of yours has consistently argued that American cars had been poorly built and that he'd never own anything but a foreign import. But his dad gives him a late-model American-made car, and suddenly American cars are not so bad. Or, when going through sorority rush, a freshman believes that sororities are good and that pledging a sorority is important. If she fails to make a sorority, however, she may say, "I recognized that sorority life isn't all it's cracked up to be, anyway!"

Research has generally concluded that we seek consistency among our attitudes and between our attitudes and behavior. This means we try to adjust differing attitudes and align our attitudes and behavior so that they appear rational and consistent. When there is an inconsistency, we take steps to correct it. This can be done by altering either our attitudes or behavior or by developing an excuse for the difference.

For example, a recruiter for Bank of America visits college campuses, identifies qualified job candidates and sells them on the advantages of the bank as a place to work. This individual will be in conflict if he personally believes the bank has poor working conditions and few opportunities for new college graduates. However, over time, his attitudes toward the organization may become more positive. By continually explaining the merits of working for Bank of America, he may convince himself that Bank of America is a good place to work. Another alternative is for the recruiter to become overtly negative about the bank, expressing his concerns about the opportunities within the firm for prospective candidates. In this scenario, the original enthusiasm the recruiter may have shown would dwindle and be replaced by open cynicism toward the company. Obviously, taking this route may lead to his dismissal. Finally, the recruiter might acknowledge to family and friends that the bank is an undesirable place to work, but as a professional recruiter his obligation is to present the positive side of working for the company. He might further rationalize that no workplace is perfect. Therefore, his job is not to present both sides of the issue, but rather to present a rosy picture of the company.

Can You Change Your Attitude?

You can change your attitudes. Throughout your life, you are going to be confronted with significant changes. Some of these changes may be positive (such as

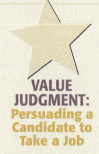

VALUE JUDGMENT: Persuading a Candidate to Take a Job

You work for a large international organization that manufactures and sells computer components. In your position as a recruiter, you have been given primary responsibility to hire individuals to fill open entry-level positions in your company. Your organization has found that hiring recent college graduates for these entry-level manufacturing and marketing positions works well for the company. It can hire individuals who have the latest knowledge in their fields at a cheaper price than experienced workers.

Your job requires you to travel extensively. In fact, over the past several years, you have averaged visiting thirty-five colleges during a semester. Your performance rests on one factor—how many people you hire. Your goal is to fill the vacancies that exist in the organization.

Over the past several months, you've noticed a surge in open positions. These aren't new positions, but replacements for employees who have quit. A little investigating on your part indicates that after about five years with the organization, employees hired into entry-level positions quit. It appears that there is no upward mobility for them and that they have been burned out by being asked to work as many as twelve hours a day, six days a week. Furthermore, you know that employee benefits—such as vacation pay and sick leave—for entry-level employees are nearly nonexistent. There is little doubt why they quit.

On the other hand, almost everyone who has quit has gone on to bigger and better jobs—jobs with more responsibility and greater pay. To get the most productivity out of these employees, your company invested heavily in their training. Almost everyone in these positions receives more than forty hours of specialized training each year. These employees came to the job well skilled and, after a time, they developed themselves into top-quality workers.

Nevertheless, your organization, although spending a lot of money on these people, isn't interested in advancing them in the organization. It just prefers to start the cycle over again. Although philosophically you don't totally agree with the treatment of employees in the organization, you recognize that the company is giving many of these individuals a great start in their career.

But what about the people you've hired over the past two years, or the ones you'll be hiring in the future? Do you tell them what you know: that the jobs you're hiring them for are dead-end jobs in the organization; they'll have no future in the company; they'll probably work sixty- to eighty-hour weeks; their pay and benefits will be below that of competing organizations; but, if they endure all this for about five years, they can go to any organization in the world and find a job? Or, do you say very little, if anything, and keep hiring to meet your quota? After all, your job is to hire them. If you don't, you will likely be replaced. And if they quit sooner than five years, well, that's just more job security for you. So what do you do?

promotions or technology that make your job easier), whereas others may be negative (such as the same technology leading to the elimination of your job). Attitudes go a long way toward defining who you are. If you are always negative and continually blaming others for all of your ills, people are going to avoid you. You know people who see the downside of everything. You hear their remarks: They don't like their classes. The latest movies all stink. They've got too much work. Life just doesn't treat them fairly. They don't like this, they don't like that. In fact, they often don't like themselves. And it's more than just a bad hair day! It's a way of life and how they live it.

The greatest advantage you can give yourself in any situation—personal life, relationships, work—is a **positive attitude,** a frame of mind that reflects seeing good things in yourself, in others, and in what you do. (See the Skills Checklist.) See the good in things, in yourself, in others, and in what you do. Have a sense of humor. Learn to recognize that there's hope, not only despair, in the world. And know that you can make a difference. No one questions that your life is trying at times, but getting through the tough times is often a function of how you approach the problem. For example, disagreeing with your professor's grading of a term paper and verbally attacking him or her in front of the whole class is unlikely to get you anywhere. On the other hand, meeting with the professor after class or during office hours in order to seek clarification and learn where you may have erred just might gain an advantage. Even if the grade on the paper stands—because it was the correct assessment of your work—you now know how to do better in the future.

Developing a positive attitude, however, is not always easy. Even if you want to give it a chance, others may try to drag you down. Your attitude is often a reflection of those with whom you associate. If your social group bad-mouths most things surrounding them, then you may lose your positive attitude. Therefore, you may have to make a choice. And often that choice may mean hanging out with others who share the attitudes you like. At work, it's no different. If your work group finds most things wrong with the organization (pay's poor, supervisor's unfair, work's no fun), you're going to have problems. You'll be guilty by association.

I (Dave) remember one of the greatest pieces of advice I got when I first entered the workforce: If you're ever asked how things are, smile and say everything is great! Every time some person from management asked me that question—no matter the situation or the place—they got the same response. Soon I developed a good reputation of being a positive and enthusiastic individual—and that meant greater autonomy and more frequent pay raises. Sure, I had problems like everyone else. But I didn't voice them every chance I got. My co-workers who did weren't getting better assignments. As a result, many of them gave up and quit or were asked to leave. And not one supervisor shed a tear. When I left to teach college, many from upper management—even the president of the company—made a special trip to attend my going-away party. I have no doubt it was because I kept a positive attitude.

Closely aligned with a positive attitude is common courtesy. Many in our society have lost one of the basic fundamental issues of human relations—respecting others. Courtesy means saying "please" and "thank you." It means respecting and caring for the rights of others around you. As kids, you were taught that "you can get more flies with honey than with vinegar." Yet somewhere along the way, you may have lost that understanding. If you treat people poorly, no matter who they are, you're going to regret it one day. That one time you need help out of a difficult situation, those to whom you have been discourteous will watch you fall, and they will probably enjoy it. Treating others as you want to be treated is part of the Golden Rule for a reason. It's an attitude and a way to act to be successful— in your personal life and your work life.

Assessing Attitudinal Changes

When you change your attitude, the attitudes of others may also change. If you and most of the members in your class like the way the professor teaches and find the material interesting, you'll probably continue coming to class each meeting. You will be excited about the material and the learning that is taking place. Why? You feel this

> **positive attitude**
a frame of mind that reflects seeing good in things, in oneself, in others, and in what one does

faculty member has created an enjoyable way to learn. But if the opposite is true, attendance may drop off quickly (unless, of course, you are penalized for not showing up). You may tell your friends to avoid this class in the future. Either way, how you and your classmates feel may determine whether you reach your goals for this class.

SKILLS CHECKLIST

Developing a Positive Attitude

1. **Build a more positive attitude in one environment, and you will be more successful in another.** You don't change your attitude like you change your clothes. Your attitude generally sticks with you, and you continually wear it. It's reasonable to assume, then, that if you become more positive in one environment—such as with friends—you will begin to take that attitude with you wherever you go. Start to be more positive where you feel most comfortable. Sooner or later, it will become habit-forming for you.

2. **Talk about positive things.** No one likes a complainer. Stop griping about the things that bother you. We joke about it when someone says, "How's it going?" and we respond, "If I told you, you wouldn't care." We may be right; he or she may not care. There's a time and place to talk about what bothers you—but that's usually with a special person. Telling everyone your troubles won't build healthy or exciting relationships.

3. **Look for good things in people you interact with.** Not one of us is perfect. We all have faults. But all of us do some things well. Focus on your good qualities. Celebrate them if need be. Let people know you see the glass as half full, not half empty. You'll notice that they react to you differently, too.

4. **Look for good things in your organization.** Just like people, organizations have good attributes, too. Look for the things you like, and try to change the things you don't like. A positive person making a constructive and thoughtful suggestion on improving the workplace goes further than a negative person who's always complaining.

5. **Don't let others who have a negative attitude trap you in their way of thinking.** You probably won't be able to change their attitude, so don't let them change yours. Remember, misery loves company. If the company is miserable, go elsewhere.

6. **Remember, life's short.** Each of us has only a limited time on this earth. We can spend life enjoying it—even with life's ups and downs—or we can trudge through the agony. It's really up to each of us in how we see it. How do you want to go through life?

Source: Your Attitude Is Showing: A Primer on Human Relations, 6/e by Chapman, © 1991. Adapted by permission of Prentice-Hall, Inc., Upper Saddle River, N.J.

3. Which of the following statements is the best example of an inference?
   a. The Houston Rockets is the best professional basketball team in the United States.
   b. Christmas Day falls on December 25.
   c. Robots displace human workers.
   d. Leap year occurs every four years.
4. Which of the following statements about attitudes is false?
   a. Attitudes are statements that reflect values.
   b. Attitudes are formed at birth.
   c. Attitudes consist of beliefs, feelings, and opinions.
   d. Attitudes and behaviors are generally consistent.
5. Why is a positive attitude important?
   a. It fools everybody into thinking you are great.
   b. It eliminates the need for having to do the required work.
   c. It gives you a sense of being in control when facing problem situations.
   d. Positive attitudes are not important for success in organizations.

Attitudes of employees in organizations may change also, and these changes in employee attitudes can affect productivity. To keep apprised of employee attitudes, an increasing number of organizations are regularly surveying employees. Typically, organizational surveys present a set of statements or questions. Ideally, the items will be tailor-made to solicit specific information about how employees see their job, co-workers, supervisor, and the like.[12]

Learning

*T*he last behavior concept to be introduced in this chapter is learning. We include it for the obvious reason that almost all complex behavior is learned. If you want to understand why you do certain things, you need to understand how you learn. What is learning? **Learning** is the process of bringing about relatively permanent change in thinking, feeling, and behaving through experiences. This can be done through direct experience—by doing—or indirectly through observation. Regardless of the means by which learning takes place, you cannot measure learning per se; you can measure only the changes in your attitudes and behavior that occur as a result of learning. Therefore, we will emphasize *how* we learn rather than *what* we learn.

Two concepts have dominated learning research over the years: operant conditioning and social learning theory. Let's look at these two processes.

Learning through Consequences

Operant conditioning describes learning as a behavioral change brought about by its consequences. You learn to act in a specific manner to achieve something you want or to avoid something you don't want. The tendency for you to repeat such behavior, then, is influenced by the reinforcement (or lack thereof) stemming from the consequences of the behavior. Reinforcement, therefore, strengthens your behavior and increases the likelihood that it will be repeated.

> **learning**
> the process of bringing about a relatively permanent change in thinking, feeling, and behaving through experiences

> **operant conditioning**
> a model describing learning as a behavior change brought about by its consequences

---

[12]See, for example, P. Hise, "The Motivational Employee Satisfaction Questionnaire," *Inc.* (February 1994), pp. 73–75.

Operant conditioning (or behavior modification) focuses on learning from external sources.[13] Relying on extensive research, B. F. Skinner and his followers argued that by creating consequences to follow certain behaviors, the frequency of that behavior will be altered. That is, you will most likely engage in appropriate behaviors if you are reinforced for doing so. For example, suppose you're unsure about spending the time to take the Self-Assessments in the Learner's Manual for each chapter of this text. Your professor does not require you to complete these but has offered the class the opportunity to turn them in for review. You complete a couple of Self-Assessments, answering the questions to ponder, and turn them in. When you get them back, you notice that you received several extra-credit points. Operant conditioning, then, indicates that you'll continue completing the Self-Assessments (modified behavior) because there was a positive reward (extra-credit points) for doing so. This same analogy applies to your work. If your organization increases your pay each time you learn another skill the organization values, this reward will foster your continued learning.

In operant conditioning, there are four ways in which behavior can be shaped: positive reinforcement, negative reinforcement, Type I punishment, and Type II punishment. Positive reinforcement encourages a specific behavior by providing a pleasant consequence for your actions. A raise, a promotion, or even praise for a job well done would encourage you to continue your behavior. Negative reinforcement encourages a specific behavior by withdrawing or stopping something unpleasant. Not having your pay docked by your supervisor now that you're coming to work on time would be an example of negative reinforcement. Punishment penalizes you for specific undesirable behaviors. Being fired for coming to work under the influence of a substance would be an example of a Type I punishment, presenting you with an unpleasant consequence for your behavior. Finally, a Type II punishment might discourage you from an undesirable behavior by withdrawing a pleasant consequence, such as losing your staff lounge because of employee damage to the furniture in the room.

As an individual, you may face any or all of the four types of consequences. Although all four affect how you learn, positive reinforcement appears to have the greatest influence on fostering a permanent behavioral change.[14] Human nature, and common sense, indicate that individuals respond better to such positive support.

Learning from Experiences

Another perspective views learning as an ongoing interaction between you and your environment. This is called **social learning theory**—learning from our experiences.[15] Social learning theory acknowledges that you can learn by observing what happens to others, by being told about something, or through direct experience. That is, much of what you learn comes from watching others—family members, teachers, co-workers, the media, and so on. Since much of the learning for college students is observational, this theory has considerable application to you.

Social learning theory can be seen as an expansion of behavioral modification because it, too, recognizes the importance of consequences on behavior. But social learning theory also focuses on what you observe and the importance of perceptions on your learning. That is, you respond to situations with respect to how you perceive the consequences that will affect you—not necessarily the consequences themselves. For example,

> **social learning theory**
> a view of learning as an ongoing interaction between an individual and his or her environment

---

[13]B. F. Skinner, *Contingencies of Reinforcement* (East Norwalk, Conn.: Appleton-Century-Crofts, 1971).

[14]Stephen P. Robbins, *Organizational Behavior: Concepts, Controversy, and Applications*, 9th ed. (Upper Saddle River, N.J.: Prentice-Hall, 2001), pp. 115–116.

[15]Albert Bandura, *Social Learning Theory* (Upper Saddle River, N.J.: Prentice-Hall, 1977).

6. In Skinner's operant conditioning theory, the type of consequence that occurs when we are penalized for a specific undesirable factor is:
   a. extinction
   b. positive reinforcement
   c. negative reinforcement
   d. punishment

7. In Skinner's operant conditioning theory, the type of consequence that occurs when one is given a bonus for a job well done is:
   a. extinction
   b. positive reinforcement
   c. negative reinforcement
   d. punishment

using the Self-Assessment example, if you know that your professor will give extra-credit points for completing the Self-Assessments, but you perceive that your final grade will be an A even without the extra points, then you may decide not to complete them.

A Final Word

You have been reading about character, personalities, perceptions, values, attitudes, and learning processes. Understanding these can greatly benefit you and improve your interactions with others. In what way? Having read this material, you should be coming to the conclusion that everyone is different. Accepting these differences can go a long way in reducing problems you may have with others. For instance, understanding that someone's values may be different from yours may help you see his or her point of view—and him or her to see yours. That's not to say that you'll change your views. It simply helps you understand where the other person is coming from and open up positive interpersonal interactions. It can also help you learn more about yourself and others around you.

As you continue to learn throughout your life, you need to know how you best comprehend new things. You know by now that the dynamic world in which you live will continually require you to make changes—changes that will require you to possess more and finer skills to succeed. Others around you are available to help. For instance, your instructor has a good grasp on the best way to help you learn. But that, too, is an assumption. Tailoring teaching to a method that helps you best is something your instructor cannot do without your input. As such, if you know what works best for you, you need to let your teachers know—be they in college or in organizations. Everyone will be better off because of it. But giving that information requires good communication skills. And that's the topic of the next chapter.

SUMMARY

This summary corresponds to the Learning Outcome, found on page 49.

1. Two methods for classifying personalities by traits are Cattell's sixteen primary personality dimensions and the Myers-Briggs Type Indicator (MBTI). Other methods include degree of risk propensity, authoritarianism, and Machiavellianism.

2. Holland identified six basic personality types and six sets of compatible occupations. He found that when properly matched with occupations that were compatible with their personality types, employees experienced higher job satisfaction and improved productivity.

3. Perception is the process of organizing and interpreting what you sense and giving meaning to it. Several factors operate to shape, and sometimes distort, your perceptions. These include how you see something, the object being observed, and the context of the situation in which the perception is made. Selective perception, assumed similarity, stereotyping, and the halo effect may also distort perceptions.

4. Your value system is formed over time by taking in and processing thousands of pieces of information from such varied sources as parents, brothers and sisters, extended family members, significant others, friends, teachers, public figures, significant events occurring in your life, movie stars, professional athletes, coaches, supervisors, the media, and your religion.

5. Your attitudes are made up of three components: your beliefs, opinions, knowledge, and information; your emotions or feelings; and your intention to behave in a certain manner toward someone or something.

6. You seek consistency among your attitudes and between your attitudes and behavior. You seek to harmonize different attitudes and to align your attitudes and behavior so that they appear rational and consistent.

7. A positive attitude is a frame of mind that reflects seeing good things in yourself, in others, and in what you do.

8. Companies use organizational surveys to elicit responses from employees through questionnaires about how they feel about their jobs, co-workers, supervisors, and the organization.

9. Learning is the process of bringing about relatively permanent changes in your life. Learning can take place through direct experiences or through observation.

10. Operant conditioning describes learning as a behavior change brought about by its consequences. The four types of consequences in operant conditioning are positive reinforcement (encouraging a desired behavior by providing a pleasant consequence), negative reinforcement (encouraging a desired behavior by withdrawing an unpleasant consequence), Type I punishment (discouraging an undesired behavior by providing an unpleasant consequence), and Type II punishment (discouraging an undesired behavior by withdrawing a pleasant consequence).

REVIEWING YOUR UNDERSTANDING

1. What is a personality, and how is it formed?
2. "We can change our personality to fit any job." Do you agree or disagree? Explain.
3. What is a self-serving bias?
4. "A perception is more than one's view, it's reality. As such, perceptions become facts." Do you agree or disagree? Explain.
5. Name four different shortcuts used in judging others. What effect does each of these have on perception?
6. Distinguish between a fact and an inference. Can an inference ever be a fact? Discuss.
7. "Religion and family influence our value systems most. Everything else is just secondary to how we see things. Accordingly, all the scare tactics some politicians use to force the cleaning up of the entertainment industry are a waste of time." Do you agree or disagree? Explain.
8. How are attitudes formed?
9. How do we adjust inconsistencies between attitudes and behaviors?
10. Why do organizations want to know our attitudes, and how do they get that information?
11. Describe four situations in which each of the four consequences of operant conditioning might work best.

ANSWERS TO CHECKING YOUR UNDERSTANDING

1. c **2.** d **3.** a **4.** b **5.** c **6.** d **7.** b

LEARNING TOGETHER

A. In teams of three, identify four different types of workers (bank manager, construction worker, TV personality, carpet layer, and so on). Make a list of the personality traits you feel are needed by each worker. Draw some conclusions about your listings.

B. In teams of four or five, develop a bulletin board on the components that make up personality traits (or on another main concept of this chapter such as attitudes or values). Then, critique and discuss the meaning of the bulletin boards of the other teams. Exchange your perceptions with the entire class. Did your classmates perceive your team's bulletin board as it was intended? Why or why not?

C. In teams of three, make a list of attitudes and values. Rate the other two team members and yourself on each of the items. Discuss. Are there differences between how you see yourself and how others see you? Why or why not?

D. Draw a vertical line down the middle of a sheet of paper. At the top of one column write "Negative People I Have Known." At the top of the other column write "Positive People I Have Known." Then list names of people in each column, followed by the reasons you labeled each person as negative or positive. Form groups of five to six individuals. In your group, discuss the impact these individuals had or have in your life. Who inspired you the most? The least? What conclusions did you draw from this discussion?

Understanding the Individual

Tiffany was very popular when she was in high school and participated in all the school's social activities. She especially enjoyed the drama club and acted in several of the school's theatrical productions. Tiffany has always been able to make friends and get along with people of all ages and personalities. She has a positive attitude about everything and is happiest when she is with people and engaged in conversation—she especially likes to discuss politics and Hollywood movie personalities. She is an avid moviegoer and reads lots of magazines that focus on TV and movie personalities. She likes to predict the winners of movie awards, and usually she is very good at it.

This is Tiffany's second year in college. Her uncle is an attorney and she has always thought she would like to be a lawyer. She has found history, law, debate, and communications classes fun and interesting. She knows she is definitely interested in a "people" career, but is having a difficult time deciding what career choice would be best for her. Her grades, so far, are probably good enough to get into law school, but a new program in hotel and restaurant management sounds attractive. A career in hotel and restaurant management could possibly offer her opportunities to work in various parts of the world. Undoubtedly in the hotel business, she would meet lots of people from all walks of life—maybe even some celebrities. As a hotel manager she could arrange all sorts of social events, still participate in community theater acting, and maybe even do some creative writing associated with some of her experiences.

Questions

1. List and describe Tiffany's personality traits. Which of her traits match well with a career in hotel and restaurant management? Which ones do not? Is it important to match personality and job requirements? Why or why not?

2. Do you think Tiffany has high or low self-esteem? Support your response. What can you expect from Tiffany as she interacts with other people?

3. List as many statements as you can from this case under the headings "Facts," "Stereotyping," "Inferences," and "Halo Effect." Draw some conclusions from your statements.

4. List pros and cons of the statement, "Tiffany's greatest asset is her positive attitude."

5. What have you learned from this case that you can apply to yourself?

chapter 4

INTERPERSONAL COMMUNICATION

*L*earning Outcomes

After reading this chapter, you will be able to:

1. Define *communication* and explain why it is important to everyone.

2. Explain the communication process.

3. Identify the ways individuals communicate with one another.

4. Describe the barriers blocking effective communication.

5. List techniques for overcoming communication barriers.

6. Define *interpersonal style*.

7. Differentiate between a strength and a weakness in interpersonal styles.

8. Identify three types of interpersonal styles and their characteristics.

9. Explain how the Johari Window can be used to tap into your hidden potential.

10. List the guidelines for giving feedback.

The importance of effective communication for each of us can't be overemphasized. *Everything* you do involves some form of communication. Your clock tells you the time for getting up in the morning. Calling a friend for a ride to class helps you arrive at your destination. Logging on to your computer, you read written words and follow prompts. In order to go out with that special person, you have to ask! You cannot make a decision without information. That information has to be communicated. And once a decision is made, communication must again take place, or no one will know that you've made a decision. Your best ideas, your most creative suggestions, and even the greatest plan you've developed cannot take form without communication.

Just look at the syllabus your instructor has given you for this course. He or she has more than likely given you all the information you need to successfully complete the class. Assignments, readings to be completed before a class period, test dates, and how grades will be determined are all spelled out. Having this information helps you plan your schedule and properly prepare for the class.

You need effective communication skills to interact well with others. Of course, good communication skills alone will not make human relations effective. However, ineffective communication skills can lead to a continuous stream of problems for you and those with whom you interact.

In this chapter, we'll look at communications from two perspectives. First, we'll explore the concept called communication—defining the process, the barriers, and the ways one can become a more effective communicator. We'll then take a closer look at interpersonal styles, the various ways in which individuals interact and communicate with others. The attention in this chapter will be on **interpersonal communications,** interactions that exist between two or more people in which the parties are treated as individuals rather than objects. Organizational communications will be covered in Chapter 7.

> **interpersonal communications**
interactions that exist between two or more people in which the parties are treated as individuals rather than objects

> **communication**
the transfer and understanding of meaning

What Is Communication?

*I*n its purest form, **communication** involves the transfer and understanding of meaning. If no information or ideas have been conveyed, communication has not taken place. The speaker who is not heard or the writer who is not read does not communicate. The philosophical question, "If a tree falls in a forest and no one hears it, does it make any noise?" must, in a communicative context, be answered negatively.

For communication to be successful, the meaning must be not only imparted but also understood. If you do not understand Japanese, a letter written in that language is not communication until it is translated. Perfect communication, if such a thing were possible, would exist when a transmitted thought was received and perceived by someone else exactly as it was intended by the person sending the message.

Good communication is often mistakenly defined by agreement instead of clarity of understanding. If you disagree with me, I may assume that you just didn't fully understand my position. In other words, I may be defining good communications as having you accept my views. But you may understand very clearly what I mean and not agree with what I say. I might erroneously conclude that a lack of communication must exist because our disagreement has continued for a long time. However, a closer examination might reveal that there is, in fact, plenty of effective communication going on. Each of us fully understands the other's position. We just don't buy the other's position. The problem, therefore, is one of equating effective communication with agreement.

The Communication Process

Although communication occurs in many different ways, explaining how messages get from one individual to another is rather easy. All communications follow a general process.

Before communication can take place, a purpose expressed as a message to be conveyed must exist. The message is converted by the sender to symbolic form (**encoding**) and passed by way of some medium (**channel**) to the receiver, who translates the sender's message (**decoding**). The result is the transfer of meaning from one person to another.[1]

Exhibit 4-1 depicts the **communication process**. This model is made up of seven components: the sender, the message, encoding, the channel, decoding, the receiver, and feedback. In addition, the entire process is susceptible to **noise**—that is, disturbances that interfere with the transmission of the message (depicted in Exhibit 4-1 as lightning bolts). Typical examples of noise include illegible print, telephone static, inattention by the receiver, and the background sounds of shuffling papers. Anything that interferes with understanding—whether internal (such as the low speaking voice of the speaker/sender) or external (such as the loud voices of fellow students talking at adjoining desks)—represents noise. Noise can create distortion at any point in the communication process. The impact of external noise on communication effectiveness is self-evident. Potential internal sources of distortion in the communication process are complex and require some exploration.

Working through the Process

An individual, the sender, initiates a message by encoding a thought. Four conditions affect the encoded message: skills, attitudes, knowledge, and culture.

Without the necessary communication skills—speaking, writing, graphic representation, listening, reading, and visual interpretation—success in communicating is limited. Attitudes, the preformed ideas we hold on numerous topics, influence our behavior and affect the content of our communications. Furthermore, we are restricted in our communication activity by the extent of our knowledge of a particular topic. We cannot communicate what we do not know, and extensive knowledge can lead to trying to communicate more information than the receiver can understand. Finally, just as our attitudes influence our behavior, so does the culture in which we live. For

> **encoding**
> converting a message to symbolic form

> **channel**
> a medium through which a message travels

> **decoding**
> translating a sender's message

> **communication process**
> components of communication that include the sender, the message, encoding, the channel, decoding, the receiver, and feedback

> **noise**
> disturbances that interfere with the transmission of a message

---

[1]David K. Berlo, *The Process of Communications* (New York: Holt, Rinehart, & Winston, 1960), pp. 30–32.

EXHIBIT 4-1

The Communication Process

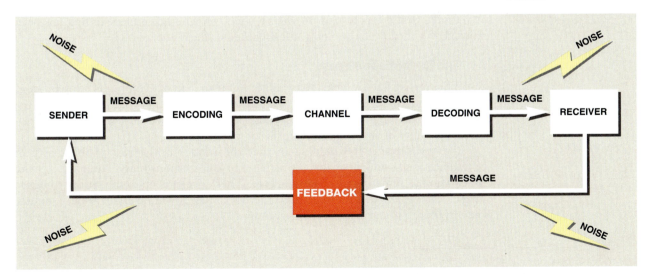

example, a word used in different parts of the country (or with different groups of people) can be interpreted differently. Take the word *arrest*.

It has an entirely different meaning to cardiac surgeons (a heart attack) than to police officers (incarceration). Accordingly, our beliefs and values (all part of our culture) act to influence us as senders.

The message itself can cause distortion in the communication process regardless of the supporting apparatus used to convey it. Our message is the actual product we encode. "When we speak, the speech is the message. When we write, the words are the message. When we paint, the picture is the message. When we gesture, the movements of our arms, the expressions on our face are the messages."[2] Our message is affected by the code or group of symbols we use to transfer meaning, the content of the message itself, and the decisions that the sender makes in selecting and arranging both code and content. Each of these three segments can act to distort the message.

The channel is the medium through which a message travels. It is selected by the sender. The most common channel is a face-to-face conversation, using spoken words and gestures to transmit a message. But there are numerous choices. A message—an invitation to a party, for example—can be communicated orally or in writing. In an organization, certain channels are more appropriate for certain messages. Obviously, if the building is on fire, a memo to convey the fact is inappropriate. If something is important, such as when tests will be given in this class, an instructor might want to use multiple channels—for instance, highlighted dates on the syllabus, followed by recurring verbal reminders in class as the dates draw near. By using multiple channels for the same message, the instructor decreases the potential for misunderstandings about when the tests will be given.

The receiver is the individual to whom the message was sent. But before the message can be received, the symbols in it must be translated into a form that can be understood by the receiver. When the receiver does this, it is called decoding the message. Just as encoding reflects the sender's skills, attitudes, knowledge, and culture, decoding reflects the receiver's skills, attitudes, knowledge, and culture. In an organization, people from all walks of life and very diverse backgrounds must communicate with one another. The closer the sender and the receiver are in age, background, language, and so on, the easier it is to communicate successfully. When there is significant diversity between sender and receiver, problems may arise in the communication process.

The final link in the communication process is a feedback loop. Feedback returns the message to the sender and provides a check on whether understanding has been achieved. We'll take a closer look at feedback later in this chapter.

The Responsible Party

Thus far, we have referred to two different people in our communication process, the sender and the receiver. We have said that both have some work to perform in order for understanding to occur. The question that arises, however, is who has the greatest responsibility in enabling this transfer of meaning?

On the surface, it would seem that the sender is the responsible party in communications—and in many cases, has the sole responsibility. After all, it's the sender who has something to communicate. Therefore, it is up to the sender to figure out the best way for that message to get across so that it will be understood. Unquestionably, there's sound logic in that reasoning.

---

[2]Ibid., p. 54.

Another argument could be made for placing the responsibility for successful communication on the receiver. The argument goes something like this. I know I've got a good message to send to you. I've done my best to get it to you in a way that it can be understood. But if you don't listen to what I say, then how can the message get through? For example, your instructor has studied hard to receive the credentials necessary to teach. She also does her homework in preparing for the class. She knows the topics to teach, how to run the class, and how to get you involved. But if you don't come to class, or if you daydream through most of her lecture, should she be responsible if you don't understand the material? Of course not. She's put the message out there. It's your responsibility to get it. Period.

Therefore, a good case can be built for holding either the sender or the receiver responsible for communication. However, in the majority of situations, both receiver and sender must take responsibility for achieving successful communication. Placing the responsibility—or the blame—on one individual when communication doesn't reach its goal usually does not accurately reflect the way communication works. It is more productive to view the communication process as a responsibility shared between the sender and the receiver. The sender must do his or her job in sending the message appropriately. This means that the message must be conveyed in such a format that it can be easily understood. The receiver, on the other hand, has the responsibility to stay alert, to attend to the message, and to meet the sender halfway. With give and take, successful communication can be achieved. Or will it?

Inasmuch as a dual responsibility seems to make sense, we must be realistic. Senders cannot always count on receivers to do their part. Receivers may be preoccupied with millions of other things going on in their lives. They may even indicate they understand, but how will we really know if they do? Therefore, we conclude that the sender, and no one else, is the primary responsible party in communication. When communication is not successful, the sender needs to reflect on the message, the medium, and the receiver to understand why the message did not get across. If the message was vague, how could it be made more precise? For instance, it's eleven A.M. Thursday when you ask a classmate for a copy of his notes for a class you missed. You say you'd like to get the notes as soon as possible because there's a test coming up Tuesday. You know exactly what you mean—you'd like the notes now. But the other person is working on something critical at the moment and can't stop. He'll get you what you want as soon as he possibly can. Two days later, no notes. You're upset and frustrated. How could he not understand? The point is, he did understand. As soon as possible is what you said. Three days later is when it's possible for him. If you had asked for the notes by two o'clock Thursday afternoon, it would be a different story. Knowing that getting the notes to you that day was impossible given what he was working on, your classmate at least could have said so. You would have had time to make other arrangements. In addition, your

Checking Your Understanding *4-1*

1. Which one of the following statements is most reflective of the term *communication?*
   a. sender–receiver interaction
   b. agreement between two or more people
   c. transfer of meaning
   d. encoding–decoding process

2. Telephone static, illegible print, and inattention by the receiver are all examples of _____ in the communication process.
   a. feedback
   b. noise
   c. encoding
   d. channels

Effective communications in both our personal and work lives are built on the expectation that appropriate and accurate information is being given. In most communication encounters, people should be afforded the respect and dignity of being given complete and factual information. Under what circumstances is it appropriate to withhold information from someone? Discretion in conveying information is required when the issue of confidentiality is involved. The decision to withhold confidential information is sometimes a must—especially at work. Assume, for example, that a co-worker has just been diagnosed with a treatable form of cancer. Being a close friend of yours, he's confided in you about the status of his health. He's also asked you not to say a word to anyone because he considers his health to be a personal matter.

Over the next few months, your friend is absent frequently, especially during his radiation treatments. His supervisor knows about his condition, so his absences are not a major problem. Some of your friend's duties involve direct computer work, which he can do at home and forward electronically to the appropriate people. The supervisor has discreetly divided the rest of his work among you and your co-workers. However, your fellow employees are wondering what is wrong. Many have come to you to find out. You simply and politely decline to discuss your friend with other co-workers. However, a number of them think that your friend is getting special treatment, and they are ready to go to the supervisor to complain. You know that if they only knew what was going on, they'd understand. But you can't reveal the reason for his absence. On the other hand, if some individuals begin to make trouble for your friend, this could create even more problems for him. That's something he doesn't need right now in his life. You're stumped. Should you tell the other people the whole story? What would you do?

classmate and you could have come to a clear understanding of what you were asking and what the response would be. The misunderstanding and disappointment could have been eliminated by simply being specific about when you needed to get the notes. You incorrectly assumed that saying that the test was on Tuesday made your "as soon as possible" time frame clear. When you accept responsibility for your communication, you don't assume that the receiver will figure out what you mean. Taking time to think clearly and state things clearly and precisely will save you from many frustrating experiences.

How We Communicate with Others

So far, we've viewed communication as a generic process and from the perspective of the sender's responsibility. Let's now turn to the most common ways we communicate with one another: oral, written, and nonverbal communication.

Oral Communication. We communicate with each other most often by oral communication. Forms of oral communication include conversations, speeches, formal and informal group discussions, and the rumor mill or grapevine.

The advantages of using oral communication are quick transmission and quick feedback. An oral message can be conveyed and a response can be received in a minimum amount of time. If the receiver is unsure of the message, rapid feedback allows the uncertainty to be corrected immediately. The major disadvantage of oral communication surfaces whenever a message has to be passed through a number of people. The more people who are involved, the greater the potential for distortion. Each person interprets the message in his or her own way and repeats it accordingly. The message's content, when it reaches its destination, is often very different from the original content.

Written Communication. Written communication includes memos, letters, reports, bulletin boards, or any other medium (such as e-mail) that transmits written words or symbols. The advantage of using written communication is that the message is permanent, tangible, and verifiable. Both the sender and the receiver have a record of the communication that can be stored for an indefinite time. If there are questions about the content of the message, it is physically available for later reference. This is particularly important for complex or lengthy communications such as reports and planning documents. For instance, a marketing plan contains a number of tasks spread out over several months. A team of workers involved in writing and implementing the plan can readily refer to it over the life of the project. A final benefit of written communication comes from the process itself. Except in rare instances, such as when presenting a formal speech, more care is taken with the written word than with the spoken word. Having to put something in writing forces us to think more carefully about what we want to convey. Therefore, written communication is more likely to be well thought out, logical, and clear than oral communication.

Of course, written messages also have their drawbacks. Although writing may be more precise, it consumes a great deal more time. You could convey far more information to your college instructor in a one-hour oral exam than in a one-hour written exam. In fact, you could probably say in ten to fifteen minutes what it takes you an hour to write. The other major disadvantage is feedback or the lack of it. In oral communication, receivers can respond rapidly to what they think they heard you say. However, written communication does not have a built-in feedback mechanism. There is no assurance that a recipient will interpret a letter or memo as the sender meant or that feedback will be given. Therefore, it is incumbent on the writer to specifically state what kind of response is expected and when the response is needed. If the receiver does not respond as expected, the writer may need to follow up with subsequent written or oral communication.

Nonverbal Communication. Some of the most meaningful communications are neither spoken nor written. These are **nonverbal communications.**[3] A loud siren or a red light at an intersection tells you something without words. When a college instructor is teaching a large lecture class, she doesn't need words to tell her that her students are bored. Heavy eyelids, nodding heads, or students reading the school newspaper clearly send the message. Similarly, when papers start to rustle and notebooks begin to close, the message is also clear. It's almost time for the class to end. The size of a person's office and the quality of her desk and chair often indicate her importance to the organization. The clothes an executive wears also convey messages of status to others. There is no limit to the examples of nonverbal messages that most of us readily recognize.

Two categories of nonverbal communication that are essential for us to understand are body language and verbal intonation. **Body language** refers to gestures, facial configurations, and other movements of the body. A snarled face, for example, says something different than a smile. Hand motions, facial expressions, and other gestures

► **nonverbal communication**
communication that is neither spoken or written, such as body language or verbal intonation

► **body language**
gestures, facial configurations, and other movements of the body

---

[3]Mark Henricks, "More Than Words," *Entrepreneur* (August 1995), pp. 54–57.

What do Catherine Sellman, Lee Taylor, and Anne Brown have in common? Each left the hustle and bustle of big-city life for a calmer, more sedate environment in Telluride, Colorado. But thanks to technology such as laptops, modems, and fax machines, these offsite workers didn't have to leave behind their jobs (environmental engineer, computer software developer, and marketing researcher). They can continue to do their work and electronically communicate with their employers and co-workers from anywhere in the world.

➤ **verbal intonation**
emphasis given to words or phrases

can communicate emotions such as aggression, fear, shyness, arrogance, joy, and anger. **Verbal intonation** refers to the emphasis we give to words or phrases. To illustrate how intonations can change the meaning of a message, consider the student who asks the instructor a question. The instructor replies, "What do you mean by that?" The student's reaction will vary depending on the tone of the instructor's response. A soft, smooth tone creates a different meaning than one that is abrasive with a strong emphasis on the last word. Most of us would view the first intonation as coming from someone who sincerely sought clarification, whereas the second suggests that the person is aggressive or defensive.

The fact that every oral communication also has a nonverbal message cannot be overemphasized. Why? Because the nonverbal component is likely to carry the greatest impact. One researcher found that 55 percent of an oral message is derived from facial expression and physical posture, 38 percent from verbal intonation, and only 7 percent from the actual words used.[4] Most of us know that animals respond to how we say something rather than what we say. Apparently, people respond likewise.

Barriers to Effective Communication

*I*n our discussion of the communication process, we noted several factors that create the consistent potential for distortion. What causes such distortions? In addition to the possible distortions identified in the communication process, such as inconsistent nonverbal cues, there are other barriers to effective communication. These are presented next, and summarized in Exhibit 4-2.

➤ **filtering**
the deliberate manipulation of information to make it appear more favorable to the receiver

Filtering is the deliberate manipulation of information to make it appear more favorable to the receiver. For example, when we tell someone what he or she wants to hear, we are filtering information. In the work environment, the extent of filtering tends to be related to the formality of the organization and its culture. The more layers that exist in an organization, the more opportunities there are for filtering. Like-

---

[4]Albert Mehrabian, "Communications without Words," *Psychology Today* (September 1968), pp. 53–55.

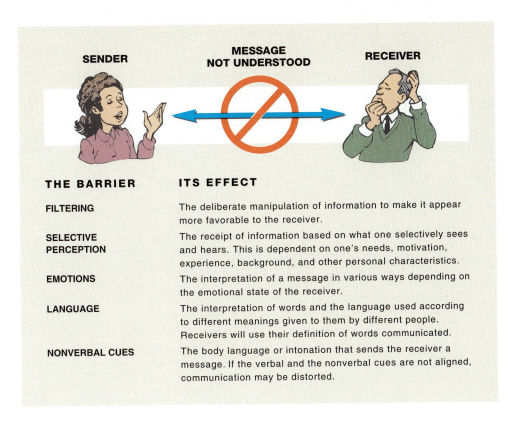

SENDER	MESSAGE NOT UNDERSTOOD	RECEIVER

THE BARRIER   **ITS EFFECT**

FILTERING	The deliberate manipulation of information to make it appear more favorable to the receiver.
SELECTIVE PERCEPTION	The receipt of information based on what one selectively sees and hears. This is dependent on one's needs, motivation, experience, background, and other personal characteristics.
EMOTIONS	The interpretation of a message in various ways depending on the emotional state of the receiver.
LANGUAGE	The interpretation of words and the language used according to different meanings given to them by different people. Receivers will use their definition of words communicated.
NONVERBAL CUES	The body language or intonation that sends the receiver a message. If the verbal and the nonverbal cues are not aligned, communication may be distorted.

EXHIBIT 4-2
Barriers to Effective Communication

wise, the organizational culture encourages or discourages filtering by the type of behavior it emphasizes through rewards. The more rewards emphasizing style and appearance, the more we are motivated to alter communications.

The second barrier can be identified as selective perception. This was mentioned in the last chapter in regard to factors that distort perception. Receivers in the communication process selectively see and hear information depending on their interests, backgrounds, experiences, and attitudes. Receivers also project their interests and expectations onto communications when decoding them. The employment interviewer who expects a female applicant to put family before career is likely to see that characteristic in all female candidates regardless of what the candidates actually say or do. As a rule, we don't see reality; instead, we interpret what we see and call it reality.

Another obstruction in communications comes from emotions. How someone feels when a message is received influences how he or she interprets it. Extreme emotions such as ecstasy or depression are most likely to hinder effective communication. In such instances, we often disregard our rational and objective thinking processes and substitute emotional judgments.

Words, too, mean different things to different people. Age, education, and cultural background are three of the more obvious variables that influence the language a person uses and the definitions he or she gives to words. The language of the legal profession is clearly different from everyday conversational language. Most of us who are not trained in law undoubtedly have trouble understanding much of the legal vocabulary.

In many work settings, employees come from diverse backgrounds. This diversity may mean that words and language are used differently by different people. A knowledge of how each of us modifies the language would minimize communication difficulties. However, members of an organization usually don't know how others with whom they interact have modified the language. Senders tend to assume that their words and terms will be appropriately interpreted by the receivers. This, of course, is often incorrect and creates communication difficulties.

Enhancing Our Communication Effectiveness

Now that you have examined the difficulties in achieving effective communication, you must be wondering, "Can it work the way it should?" If so, what can you do to reach that goal? By and large, you can become more effective communicators by following some simple rules. These are using feedback, simplifying and targeting language, listening actively, restraining emotions, and aligning verbal and nonverbal cues. Let's look at each of these.

Using Feedback

Many communication problems can be directly attributed to misunderstandings and inaccuracies. These problems are less likely to occur if you use the feedback loop in the communication process. This feedback can be verbal or nonverbal.

If you ask the receiver to restate your message in his or her own words, the response you get represents feedback. If you hear the intended message, you can be assured of understanding and accuracy.

Of course, feedback does not have to be conveyed in words. Actions can speak louder than words. When you give a speech to a group of people, watch their eyes and look for other nonverbal clues to tell you whether they are getting your message. If they are nodding and appear attentive, you're getting feedback that the audience is listening.

Simplifying and Targeting Language

Because language can be a barrier, it is important to choose words and structure messages in ways that will make them clear and understandable to the receiver. Simplify your language. Consider the audience to whom your message is directed and tailor your language to the audience. Remember, effective communication is achieved when a message is both received and understood. This means, for example, that an information systems manager should try to communicate in clear, easily understood terms when explaining a new computer system to employees and should purposely use language different from that used with other computer technicians. Jargon can facilitate understanding when it is used within a group who knows what it means, but it can cause innumerable problems when used outside that group.

Listening Actively

When someone talks, we hear, but too often we don't listen. Listening is an active search for meaning, whereas hearing is passive.

Many of us are poor listeners. Why? Because listening, in fact, is often more tiring than talking, and it is usually more satisfying to have others listen to us. **Active listening** demands intellectual effort. Unlike hearing, active listening demands total concentration. The mind works faster than the mouth. The average speaker talks at a rate of about 150 words per minute, whereas the average listener has the capacity to listen at a rate of nearly 1,000 words per minute.[5] This leaves a lot of time for the mind to wander. We must work hard to focus on what is being said, while tuning out miscellaneous thoughts that come to mind to fill the spaces between words. An active listener

> **active listening**
> placing oneself in the sender's position, reserving judgment on the message's content, and carefully listening to what is being said

---

[5]T. D. Lewis and G. H. Graham, "Six Ways to Improve Your Communication Skills," *Internal Auditor* (May 1988), p. 25.

fills the void by mentally summarizing what has been said and putting each new piece of information into its proper context.

Active listening is enhanced by developing empathy with the sender—that is, by placing yourself in the sender's position. Because senders differ in attitudes, interests, needs, and expectations, empathy makes it easier to understand the actual content of a message. An active listener reserves judgment on the message's content and carefully listens to what is being said. The goal is to receive the full meaning of a communication without having it distorted by premature judgments or interpretations.

SKILLS CHECKLIST

Active Listening Techniques

1. **Make eye contact.** Most people interpret a lack of eye contact as aloofness or disinterest. Making eye contact with the speaker focuses your attention, reduces the likelihood that you will become distracted, and sends a nonverbal cue to the speaker that you're interested in what is being said.

2. **Provide affirmative nods and appropriate facial expressions.** As an effective listener, you show interest in what is being said through your body language. Affirmative nods and appropriate facial expressions, coupled with good eye contact, tell the speaker you're listening.

3. **Avoid distracting actions that suggest boredom.** If affirmative nods and appropriate facial expressions can indicate you're listening, other nonverbal cues indicate the opposite. Looking at your watch, shuffling papers, playing with your pen, and the like tell the speaker that you're bored, disinterested, and not fully attentive.

4. **Ask questions.** As an active listener, you analyze what has been said and ask clarifying questions. This action helps you fully understand what was said and assures the speaker that you're listening.

5. **Paraphrase using your own words.** Using phrases such as "What I hear you saying is . . ." or "Do you mean. . . ?" is an excellent device to check whether you're listening carefully. Such a technique also helps verify that what you've heard is accurate.

6. **Don't interrupt the speaker.** Human nature being what it is, most of us would rather speak our own mind than listen to what someone else says. Talking might be more fun and silence might be uncomfortable, but you can't talk and listen at the same time. Let the speaker speak. Don't try to respond before he or she is finished. Don't second-guess where the speaker's thoughts are going. Listen carefully. When the speaker is done, it's your turn to talk.

7. **Make a smooth transition between the roles of speaker and listener.** As an effective listener, you'll need to make smooth transitions from listener to speaker and back to listener. From a listening point of view, this means concentrating on what the speaker has to say and not thinking about what you're going to say as soon as you get your chance.

Restraining Emotions

It would be naive to assume that people always communicate in a fully rational manner. Emotions can severely cloud and distort the transfer of meaning. Someone who is emotionally upset over an issue is more likely to misconstrue incoming messages and fail to express outgoing messages clearly and accurately. What can you do when this happens to you? The best alternative is to end the communication until you have regained composure. After calming down, you will probably be able to see the issue in a different light or at least feel open enough to accept another point of view.

Aligning Verbal and Nonverbal Cues

Communication problems often arise because people say one thing and do another. Actions usually do speak louder than words. Therefore, it is important to make sure that your actions align with and reinforce the words that go along with them. This is true of nonverbal messages that are communicated while you are speaking, as well as actions you may take subsequent to a communication. Failure to follow through, or doing the opposite of what you said, is a sure way to lose credibility as a communicator.

Developing Your Interpersonal Style

No matter who you are, you have a particular way of doing things. You act in a certain manner that is consistent with the way you see the world. You know from Chapter 3 that much of your behavior is attributed to your personality, perceptions, and attitudes. How do you prefer to deal with others, and how do others want you to react to them? Much of that answer lies in your **interpersonal style.** Because the way you interact and communicate with others is one of the fundamental demonstrations of your behavior, it's important to gain an understanding of your interpersonal style.

➤ **interpersonal style**
the way in which an individual interacts and communicates with others

The Assumptions of an Interpersonal Style

Exhibit 4-3 lists some common elements of interpersonal style. Everyone has an interpersonal style. Interpersonal style gives individuals the unique flair in their speech, determines the amount of empathy heard in their words of consolation, and rules their desire to examine what is said. It influences their preferred way of using language, the degree to which they listen, and the way they respond to others.

People often ask whether there is one interpersonal style that works best in fostering effective communications. The answer is that no style is best for all situations. There are times when a particular style will work well and times when it will not. For instance, suppose you've been patiently waiting for service in a restaurant, but you are getting no response. Your preferred style of communicating is to be assertive. You find it easy to

---

- Everyone has an interpersonal style.
- Each individual possesses some of every style.
- Each style has strengths associated with it.
- Each style has potential weaknesses.
- A weakness is a strength carried to an extreme.
- When faced with difficult times, our style may change—possibly to the weakness side of another style.

EXHIBIT 4-3

Elements of Interpersonal Style

Source: Adapted from Elias H. Porter and Sara E. Maloney, *Personal Values Inventory* (Anaheim, Calif.: Personal Strengths Publishing, Inc., Rev. 1983).

draw attention to the fact that you haven't been served, while others who have waited less time are being helped. In this situation, your assertiveness is a strength for you. Each interpersonal style has its strengths. But styles, too, have weaknesses. Using your preferred style in every situation may lead to communication problems. For example, suppose a friend has volunteered to help you study for a test. After waiting a half hour for him to arrive, you call and demand to know why he hasn't shown up. In this situation, assertiveness may cost you a friend's help. Your preferred style just became a weakness. A **weakness** is a strength carried to an extreme. It's something you do too much of or do inappropriately. For instance, being assertive while waiting in a restaurant shows a strength in that you don't let people walk all over you. But being assertive with a friend whose help you need might be perceived as aggressiveness used inappropriately.

➤ **weakness**
a strength carried to an extreme

Understanding your preferred interpersonal style not only helps you make your strengths work for you but also helps you recognize when a strength carried to an extreme might create a communication barrier. Remember, effective communication relies on your message reaching your targeted audience. Communication is more effective if you can recognize and understand the preferred styles—and strengths—of others. If another person's interpersonal style is similar to yours, communication between the two of you may be effective. But if your styles differ, there may be communication problems. Have you ever been in a situation where you ask friends what they want to do tonight? And their response is something like, "Oh, it doesn't matter, surprise us!" And when you did surprise them, your idea was something they didn't want to do? Sound vaguely familiar? Probably. This situation highlights one of the problems at the heart of communications—conflicting interpersonal styles.

Understanding interpersonal styles not only helps you assess your own strengths and weaknesses in communicating, but also provides you insight into effectively reaching and responding to others, even when conflicting interpersonal styles are involved. Successful communication may require that you adapt your style so that others can better understand the message you are sending.

Identifying Interpersonal Styles

Over the years, there has been much research into identifying the various personality attributes of individuals—such as their dominance and sociability—and translating these findings into communication patterns.[6] The theoretical aspects of that discussion, and their corresponding styles, go far beyond the scope of this book. However, to provide you with some basic insight into three primary interpersonal styles—dominant, analytical, and caring—we have found it useful to liken them to three animals—lions, foxes, and Saint Bernards.[7] Let's look at each of these three types.

Lions. Lions are individuals who like to control things. They are good at managing and getting things done through others. They like to compete, and more important, they like to win. Lions are strong people who possess strong characteristics—they are assertive, controlling, dominant, and forceful. They view themselves as leaders—people who can direct the actions of others. The lions' strengths are sometimes viewed rather negatively by others. An assertive person can be seen as being too

---

[6]For example, see David W. Johnson, *Reaching Out: Interpersonal Effectiveness and Self-Actualization* (Upper Saddle River, N.J.: Prentice-Hall, 1981); Stuart Atkins, *The Name of Your Game* (Beverly Hills, Calif.: Ellis & Stewart, 1981); Gerald L. Manning & Barry L. Reece, *Selling Today: An Extension of the Marketing Concept*, 5th ed. (New York: Allyn & Bacon, 1992); and John Gottman, "What Makes a Marriage Work," *Psychology Today* (March–April 1994), pp. 38–45.

[7]These three primary interpersonal styles address attributes of individuals of the dominant culture of U.S. society. They may not be applicable to people from other cultures.

aggressive. Lions may be regarded as too controlling and authoritarian. Individuals like Dennis Rodman, G. Gordon Liddy, Rosie O'Donnell, Hillary Clinton, George Steinbrenner, Madonna, and Ted Turner are representative of the lion group.

How do lions behave in the classroom? What are they like? Classic lions will often ask tough questions, challenging instructors to prove they know what they're teaching. They'll raise exceptions or cite how they've experienced things. And, you guessed it, they'll always have a response. They like for everyone to know that they know.

Foxes. Foxes are truly analytical people. They study everything. They value logic, processes, planning, and truth. Foxes like to investigate things and render decisions. They are time-oriented, cautious, calculating, investigative, and methodical. Others may view the cautious behavior of foxes as calculating. They may regard foxes as being nitpicky, cunning, and insensitive. Fox-type interpersonal styles are found in such diverse individuals as Abraham Lincoln, Bill Gates, Davey Johnson, Connie Chung, Colin Powell, and Judge Judy.

What behaviors characterize foxes in class? Foxes come to class carrying everything they may need. "Be prepared" is their motto. Foxes take copious notes, usually transcribing them later in a manner that they find more beneficial to their studying. They compare their notes with information in the text, which is often highlighted and coded in some manner. They bring calculators, recorders, or laptops to class, hoping not to miss one shred of information in the lecture. If the professor has given a breakdown by class periods, or even weeks, foxes have checked off exactly where the professor is. At any time, foxes can cite exactly the state of the semester.

Saint Bernards. Saint Bernards are people who truly value pleasing others. They're caring and supportive. They often put the feelings and well-being of others ahead of their own. Saint Bernards are also optimistic, adaptable, and helpful. However, when Saint Bernards carry these characteristics to an extreme, they may be viewed by others as unrealistic, spineless, and able to be manipulated. Individuals with strong

UNLOCKING YOUR POTENTIAL *4-1*

Interpersonal Styles

Imagine yourself in a room where there's a lion in one corner, a fox in another, and a Saint Bernard in a third. You're standing in the center of the room and are asked to go over to the animal that best represents you. You must pick only one. (Don't worry, these are trained animals.) Why did you pick the animal you did? Why didn't you select one of the others? Jot down the characteristics of the animal you chose in the left column. Then, in the right column, list characteristics of the two animals you didn't choose, focusing on why you didn't select them.

Most Like Me	*Least Like Me*
_____	_____
_____	_____
_____	_____
_____	_____
_____	_____

Saint Bernard characteristics include Martin Luther King, Drew Carey, Herb Kelleher, Oprah Winfrey, and Mother Teresa.

What can we expect from Saint Bernards in class? They are the ones that show up early. They want to get the best seat possible. And you never know, the instructor may need some help—such as arranging seats or readying a VCR. Saint Bernards thoroughly enjoy participating in group activities because it gives them a chance to be with people. They freely share their notes—being open to letting their lion friends copy them. As for the tough questions the lion poses to the instructor, Saint Bernards will try to intervene so as to help the instructor. And after class, they are the ones who will usually tell the instructor how much they enjoyed a particular class activity.

Speaking Their Language

Lions, because of their domineering interpersonal style, typically communicate in short sentences. They get to the point quickly and don't often see the value in small talk. They view that as mush—something that wastes their valuable time. So how do you speak to lions? As far as we can tell, you need to be direct. You need to demonstrate confidence. If you have a request, you need to make it and be specific about what you want. That means you'll need to think through exactly the outcomes you will achieve and the help you desire from the lion. Then you need to get out of the lion's way and let him or her work. Lingering or getting emotional usually won't be received well by lions. A report to a lion should be concise—probably no more than a couple of pages. The acronym *KISS*, "keep it simple, stupid" (or "keep it short and simple"), probably best reflects how to interact with lions. In personal relationships, lions also need to be told what you want. They simply frown on indecisiveness.

To get messages to foxes, you need to communicate in a way that is organized and rational. You need to show the logic of your message. Yes, foxes prefer some of the pleasantries but not too much. Instead, they want you to get down to business. But this time, you don't present what outcomes you want. Rather, you leave that for the fox to determine. Because foxes have a great need for an orderly approach, they'll need to come to the conclusion themselves. They'll need to make sure what you're asking is correct. Because foxes like analysis, they want data. Reams of data if you have it. Whereas the lion wants a two-page report, the fox wants everything associated with your request. Computer printouts with statistical analyses are especially useful when speaking the fox's language. In personal relationships with foxes, you need to remember that order, schedules, and values dominate their lives. Telling them what to do will only create a problem. They want to have input and to help orchestrate what goes on.

Saint Bernards generally like all the warm fuzzies they can get. If you, as a lion or a fox, tell Saint Bernards what to do in a harsh or matter-of-fact manner, you've committed a big error in communication. It's not that Saint Bernards won't do what you'd like; it's just that they'll spend most of their time asking themselves what they did to upset you. Remember, Saint Bernards often place your happiness above theirs. They want to be helpful and to do whatever it takes to please you. When you do not reciprocate, you're telling them that you don't care. That's a feeling they can't accept. They just want to be viewed as having some importance in your life.

As we leave this discussion, let's make a few points clear. Interpersonal styles have no bearing on one's position or level in an organization. Don't make that false assumption. There are as many lion supervisors and managers as there are foxes and Saint Bernards. Realize, also, that there's a little of all three styles in you. It's just that you usually have one dominant style that you prefer. When you send information, you need to draw on the attributes of the other styles in order to speak the receiver's language. It would be nice if people came with signs on their foreheads announcing their preferred interpersonal styles. But that's ridiculous. Or is it? Paying attention to the

KEYS TO UNLOCKING YOUR POTENTIAL *4-1*

Which animal did you select in Unlocking Your Potential 4-1? The specific animal you chose is less relevant than the characteristics you used to describe yourself—and the animals. For example, in the "Most Like Me" column, you probably listed many of the characteristics that were presented in the previous sections describing lions, foxes, and Saint Bernards. These are characteristics that you see working for you—they are your strengths.

How did you describe the other two animals in the "Least Like Me" column? More than likely, you described them from your perceived "weakness" of the animal. For instance, if you are a lion, you may see foxes as sly or sneaky, and you may see Saint Bernards as lazy and weak. Foxes and Saint Bernards, on the other hand, may view you, the lion, as all talk and no action and too aggressive. This is counter to your view of yourself as assertive and in control of things. That's the point of this exercise. Individuals tend to see themselves from a position of strength and to view others from a position of perceived weaknesses. For example, accusing foxes of being manipulative when, in fact, they are just analyzing the situation (and that's using their strengths) is not recognizing and understanding individual differences. How then, if we don't understand others, will we ever learn to communicate successfully?

The adage that we don't know a person until we walk a mile in his or her shoes is very appropriate for communication. Unless we take the time to get to know those with whom we interact and determine what their communication needs are, we'll have a difficult time relating to them. Being a lion, fox, or Saint Bernard—or whatever we want to label individual interpersonal styles—is not the critical point. Rather, it's becoming more attuned to how others behave, attempting to learn more about their interpersonal styles, and then speaking to them in a way that they can understand. Doing so will not only enhance your communications with others, but also go a long way toward ensuring that your personal interactions will be positive.

behavior and demeanor of individuals can help you make educated guesses about their interpersonal styles. As you get to know people better, you will develop a deeper understanding of them and learn to adapt automatically. If you're having trouble recognizing someone's interpersonal style, there is always the old-fashioned way: ask. Although they may not be open initially to giving you the information you want, there is something you can do to open up these lines of communication: a communications model called the Johari Window.

Checking Your Understanding *4-2*

3. The emphasis one gives to words or phrases in communication is most reflective of:
   a. verbal intonation
   b. body language
   c. nonverbal communication
   d. excited speech

4. Which one of the following is not a potential barrier to effective communication?
   a. filtering
   b. emotions
   c. selective perception
   d. feedback

The Johari Window

*Y*ears ago, two individuals—Joseph Luft and Harry Ingram—developed a feedback model called the **Johari Window.**[8] This model was designed to explain communication relationships and interactions with others. It is based on the premise that whenever two individuals interact, certain factors must be taken into account. You have information about yourself that others do not know. Conversely, others may be aware of things about you that you aren't. The Johari Window attempts to show how you both can gain an understanding of what we know about each other. The goal of the model is to increase your self-awareness, build greater trust between you and those with whom you interact, and develop more accurate communications.

The premise behind this model is simple. Through the use of feedback, both parties can improve. **Feedback** is receiving information about yourself from others. When people tell you something about yourself, they are giving you feedback. But what about when you say something about yourself. Is that feedback? Yes. However, in the Johari Window, this kind of feedback is called self-disclosure. **Self-disclosure** is the process of sharing information about yourself with others. When you tell someone what you like, what you want, or how you feel about something, you disclose information about yourself. Disclosure is revealing your innermost thoughts and sharing those things that others couldn't possibly know about you—until you tell them. For instance, suppose you're attracted to another individual. Maybe you've been dating that person for some time and you've fallen in love. Does that person love you? You won't know until you ask. But in tender moments like this, you don't blatantly ask, "Do you love me?" Rather, you disclose to him or her, "I love you!" And then, if you're lucky, and the love is real, you get some feedback—"I love you, too!" A great moment because you took the risk to share something about yourself. Well, that's precisely what the Johari Window is about. Let's see how this model works.

The Model

In any interaction, there are at least two people. In the Johari Window, we'll represent these people as you and me (Dave). Now each of us has some information that may be crucial to both of us. There are things I know about myself and things I don't know. Likewise, there are things about me that you know and things that you don't. Accordingly, if we take just this information and construct a matrix diagram, we'll get something that looks like Exhibit 4-4. Let's work though each cell.

There are things I know about myself that you, too, know. This is called common knowledge. **Common knowledge** is information about yourself that both of us know and understand. For example, it's common knowledge that I co-authored this book about human relations. In fact, as presented in "Memo to Students" in the front matter, you even have access to me for answering questions about the book. That's the purpose of common knowledge. It's something we both understand and can talk about from a common perspective. In other words, the more commonalties we have, the more we speak each other's language.

Our second cell is one where I know something about myself, but you don't—my secrets. A **secret** is privately held, and it will remain a secret until I tell someone. So for me, a secret could be that this is the tenth book I've written. Sure, that's unimportant to you, but a sentence or two ago, you didn't know that about me. Now it's common knowledge. Maybe it's trivial, but for someone interested in writing a book, it could open up the communication lines between us to have some of his or her questions answered. Another example was something we did a few pages back when we

> ➤ **Johari Window**
> a model designed to explain communication relationships and interactions with others

> ➤ **feedback**
> receiving information about yourself from others

> ➤ **self-disclosure**
> sharing information about yourself with others

> ➤ **common knowledge**
> information about yourself that is known by you and others

> ➤ **secrets**
> information about yourself that is known by you but is not known by others

[8]Joseph Luft, *Group Processes: An Introduction to Group Dynamics* (Mountain View, Calif.: Mayfield, 1984).

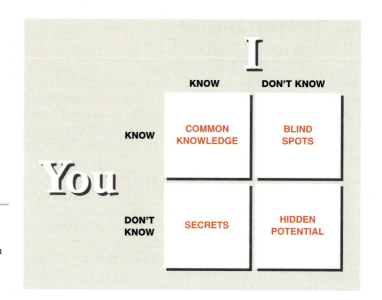

EXHIBIT 4-4
The Johari Window
Source: Joseph Luft, *Group Processes: An Introduction to Group Dynamics* (Mountain View, Calif.: Mayfield Publishing, 1984). Used with permission.

talked about interpersonal styles. If I tell you that I'm a Saint Bernard, it could open up our dialogue to where I find out you're a lion. Then, it becomes common knowledge. Even more obscure, I often tell my students that I'm a pizza freak and disclose another of my secrets—where I think the best pizza in town is sold. Most laugh, but I've had hours of conversation with students about where their favorite pizza parlor is. In fact, one time, the entire offensive line of Towson's football team visited my favorite spot. Eleven large pizzas later, they agreed with my assessment.

Now let's be realistic about secrets. Even in our personal lives, there are some things we'll never tell. It's nobody's business. Although it has been fashionable on television talk shows to reveal one's innermost secrets to strangers, some privacy is in order. The Johari Window recognizes that. Total self-disclosure is not expected. Instead, we share those things that are appropriate and necessary for increasing our self-awareness and building trust. Obviously, you'd be more open to a spouse than to co-workers. But even then, some things may remain a secret.

Thus far in the model, we've covered me. But what about you and what you know? The third cell of the Johari Window involves those things you know about me but I don't know about myself. These are called my **blind spots.** I'm unaware of them. I don't know they exist—unless, that is, you tell me about them. For example, suppose you've found a typographical error in this book. Obviously, if I knew it existed, I would have corrected it before it went to final print. Maybe I missed it in proofreading the final pages. Whatever the reason, it got past me (and several other pairs of eyes, too). Therefore, if you see one, consider it a blind spot of mine and please let me know.

Finally, there's an area in this model where I don't know something about myself, and you don't know it either. Such an occurrence is called my hidden potential. **Hidden potential** can be anything that I may be capable of but that I haven't yet discovered and that remains unrecognized by others. Maybe I could become a professional golfer. That's a sport I've never played, but maybe I'd have a natural swing and could excel at the game. It's doubtful that it could happen, especially considering I'd be starting to play at age forty-five. But it could happen. It could just be my hidden potential. But I'll never know unless I disclose my desire to play to some golf pro, sign up for lessons, and get some critical feedback. Therein lies the potential for the Johari Window.

▶ blind spots
information about yourself that is not known by you but is known by others

▶ hidden potential
anything you may be capable of but that is yet unknown by you and others

Tapping into Hidden Potential

Thinking of the Johari Window as simply a communication model is not allowing it to work to its fullest. The Johari Window relies on human interaction, and it can help us grow as a person by developing areas that are unrealized. How? Let's answer that by working through the four cells of the model with a work-related example.

Your company wishes to relocate one of its offices three hundred miles away within six months and your supervisor selects you to manage the project. When your supervisor meets with you and explains the details of the relocation, you gladly agree to manage the project (your positive attitude is showing). Your supervisor wants you to use project management tools in laying out your plan, estimating the costs of the move, and developing a timeline for the events that will take place. You understand that you have six months to get the job done (common knowledge). But you don't have a clue about what your supervisor wants in terms of project management tools. You've never been trained in this, nor have you had any exposure to using such techniques. More important, your supervisor doesn't know this (your secret). Do you flounder for the next six months and run the risk of not succeeding, or do you disclose that project management is new to you? Let's hope you choose the latter and tell your supervisor that you aren't up to date on project management skills (self-disclosure). "No problem," he states. "The company is offering a training program in the basics of project management next week" (blind spot). He picks up the phone and enrolls you in the seminar. You attend the sessions and learn what is expected of you and what you'll have to do to manage a project. As a result of the training seminar, you were able to meet your boss's requirements and successfully relocate the office. The learning that took place means you tapped into your hidden potential. (See Exhibit 4-5.) You've added to your skill repertoire and are now a more productive employee in your supervisor's eyes. All because you gave up a secret.

Developing Feedback Skills

You can also use the Johari Window to assist others by helping them see what they can't—their blind spots. Often we do that by providing constructive feedback. Giving feedback to others, however, may not be easy. Even giving or receiving positive feedback sometimes makes us uncomfortable. We need to learn how to give feedback

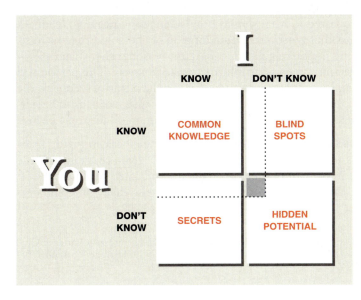

EXHIBIT 4-5

Tapping into Your Hidden Potential

Source: Joseph Luft, *Group Processes: An Introduction to Group Dynamics* (Mountain View, Calif.: Mayfield Publishing, 1984). Used with permission.

5. In the Johari Window, things that others know about you that you don't know about yourself are called:
   a. personality quirks
   b. blind spots
   c. the unknown
   d. hidden potential

6. What is the difference between feedback and self-disclosure in the Johari Window?
   a. Feedback refers to information you give others about yourself. Self-disclosure is information given to others by you.

   b. Feedback involves receiving information from others about yourself. Self-disclosure involves talking to yourself.

   c. Feedback refers to information you receive from others about yourself. Self-disclosure is information you give to others about yourself.

   d. Feedback is associated with the secrets cell of the Johari Window. Self-disclosure is associated with the hidden potential cell of the Johari Window.

EXHIBIT 4-6
Guidelines for Giving Feedback

1. Give feedback to be helpful.
2. Assess the readiness of the receiver.
3. Make it recent.
4. Describe behaviors rather than evaluate them.
5. Don't demand change.
6. Focus on those things a person controls.
7. Be empathetic.
8. Confirm understanding.

---

properly so that it is beneficial to others. Are there any easy techniques for giving feedback to others? Although there are no foolproof methods, we can follow some guidelines to help us in this process.[9] (See Exhibit 4-6.)

Give Feedback to Be Helpful.   Ask yourself, why am I giving this person feedback? Even if he or she requested it, what should I say? Generally speaking, feedback should be given to help the other person see something he or she doesn't see or to fix a problem he or she is having. If you're giving feedback for reasons other than these—for instance, to hurt the person—keep your information to yourself. The person will be better off and so will you. Remember, even though it may be negative feedback, the person's attitude and perception toward you are at stake. If you give feedback to be self-serving—or primarily to help yourself gain an advantage—your credibility may be lost.

Assess the Readiness of the Receiver.   A primary element in giving feedback is the person's willingness to hear what you have to say. If you're lucky, and the person has asked for some information, then he or she has indicated readiness. But it often doesn't happen like that. Instead, you need to set the stage so that your comments

---

[9]Adapted from Cyril R. Mill, "Feedback: The Art of Giving and Receiving Help," in Larry Porter & Cyril R. Mill, eds., *The Reading Book for Human Relations Training* (Bethel, Maine: NTL Institute for Applied Behavioral Sciences, 1976), pp. 18–19.

UNLOCKING YOUR POTENTIAL *4-2*

Giving Feedback

*F*or each question, choose a response that describes how you actually react, or would react, in a particular situation. (Do not respond in the way you think you should react.)

	Usually	Sometimes	Seldom
1. When giving someone feedback, I focus my attention on behaviors I see.	3	2	1
2. I evaluate the behavior rather than describe it.	1	2	3
3. I prefer to collect a lot of information about someone, and then I give detailed feedback all at once.	1	2	3
4. I verify that the receiver understands what I have said by asking that person to tell me what he or she heard.	3	2	1
5. I offer my help to the other person when I am giving constructive feedback.	3	2	1
6. When I give someone feedback about something I don't like, I expect that person to change his or her behavior immediately.	1	2	3
7. When I have something to say to someone, I simply say it.	1	2	3
8. I give feedback to others to benefit me, too.	1	2	3

A maximum of 24 points and a minimum of 8 points are possible. If you scored 20 or more points, you have a good understanding of how to give feedback to someone. This indicates that you are using the guidelines for giving feedback when you interact with others. A score of 15 to 19 indicates that you are on the right track, but you could do better. Look to see where you strayed from the guidelines and work to fine-tune how you give feedback. A score below 15 indicates you have much room for improvement. Review Exhibit 4-6 and compare it to your responses. See if you can pinpoint where some of your deficiencies lie.

Extra Effort

Why not put the Johari Window into practice? Meet with several people to whom you have given feedback. Ask these individuals to give you some information on how effective you were in giving them feedback. Use the eight statements as a basis for your discussion. You might ask the individuals to rate you on each of the eight items. Ask how you could have done a better job in providing feedback and what you can do to improve your feedback skills.

Source: The idea for this exercise came from Stephen P. Robbins, *Training in InterPersonal Skills: TIPS for Managing People at Work* (Upper Saddle River, N.J.: Prentice-Hall, 1989), pp. 64–65.

can get through. That may mean telling someone you'd like to meet with him or her by a specific time. For instance, it's ten A.M. and you tell the other person you'd like to meet to talk about a particular topic before four P.M. that day. Remember, don't be vague here. Saying you'd like to talk with the individual as soon as possible could lead to that person never showing up.

Make It Recent.   Have you ever been in a situation with someone close to you and said something that proved to be the straw that broke the camel's back? Then, for the next ten minutes, you were read the riot act, and everything you've ever done that upset him or her came out? It happens all too frequently. We store upsetting information and tolerate it until we can no longer deal with it. That's not healthy. Instead, following a general twenty-four-hour rule in giving feedback appears to work best. That is, if someone has done something you don't like, address it within the next twenty-four hours or forget it. You'll both be better served by doing so.

Describe Behaviors Rather Than Evaluate Them.   One of the pitfalls of giving feedback is that you can be led astray. Rather than focusing on a behavior, you become subjective in your judgment. For example, if your instructor returned a report to you and said it "stunk," you got little information. That's the instructor's subjective evaluation. There's a difference between writing "This paper stunk" and "There were twenty-five typos and three incomplete sentences in the first paragraph alone." The latter you can see and correct. The resulting grade might be the same, but the instructor's saying your paper stunk doesn't help you fix the problem. Remember, attack the behavior, not the person. Doing so will also help keep communication lines open and emotions out of the process.

Don't Demand Change.   Often, when people place demands on others, the initial reaction is rebellion. If you demand that someone do something—even if it is the right thing to do—the change may not take place. There are ways of bringing about a change in behavior without being demanding. For instance, describing the consequences if the current behavior continues lets the individual know that he or she must do something different to avoid negative consequences. You've achieved the same goal, but you did so without demanding a change.

Focus on the Things a Person Controls.   Providing feedback—especially constructive feedback—and making recommendations will do little if the person has little or no control over the conditions you are discussing. Your instructor may be upset because you aren't reading the text and reprimands you for not being prepared for class. However, this feedback will have little positive effect if the reason you're not reading the text is that the bookstore didn't order enough copies of it, and no other copies are readily accessible to you. Therefore, before you ask someone to do something or criticize what he or she has done, make sure it's within the person's control.

Be Empathetic.   Realize that receiving constructive feedback is often difficult for most people. Let the person know that you understand and care. Share your feelings with the individual. More important, tell him or her what you'll do to help improve the situation.

Confirm Understanding.   Was your message received and understood? Check to see whether that's the case. If not, for whatever reason, you'll likely be witnessing the same behaviors continue in spite of your feedback.

KEYS TO UNLOCKING YOUR POTENTIAL *4-2*

*T*he purpose of Unlocking Your Potential 4-2 was to give you some feedback on how well you give feedback to others. To calculate your score, circle the point value that matches with your response to the question. You'll notice that Questions 1, 4, and 5 are scored alike, as are Questions 2, 3, 6, 7, and 8. Then total your score by adding up what you've circled.

	Usually	Sometimes	Seldom
1. When giving someone feedback, I focus my attention on behaviors I see.	3	2	1
2. I evaluate the behavior rather than describe it.	1	2	3
3. I prefer to collect a lot of information about someone, and then I give detailed feedback all at once.	1	2	3
4. I verify that the receiver understands what I have said by asking that person to tell me what he or she heard.	3	2	1
5. I offer my help to the other person when I am giving constructive feedback.	3	2	1
6. When I give someone feedback about something I don't like, I expect that person to change his or her behavior immediately.	1	2	3
7. When I have something to say to someone, I simply say it.	1	2	3
8. I give feedback to others to benefit me, too.	1	2	3

SUMMARY

This summary corresponds to the Learning Outcomes found on page 75.

1. Communication is the transfer and understanding of meaning. It is important because everything you do—such as making a decision, planning activities, or influencing others—requires that information be communicated.

2. The communication process begins with a sender who has a message to convey. The message is converted to symbolic form (encoding) and passed by way of a channel to the receiver, who decodes the message. To ensure accuracy, the receiver should provide the sender with feedback as a check on whether understanding has been achieved.

3. The ways we communicate with one another are oral communications, written communications, and nonverbal communications.

4. Several barriers to communication exist. They can take many forms. Among them are filtering, selective perception, emotions, language, and nonverbal cues.

5. Some techniques for overcoming communication barriers include using feedback, simplifying and targeting language, listening actively, restraining emotions, and aligning verbal and nonverbal cues.

6. An interpersonal style is the way in which an individual interacts and communicates with others. It's one's preferred way of doing things.

7. A communication strength is something that works best for an individual. It's a personal characteristic that gives an individual the ability to handle what he or she faces. On the other hand, a weakness is a strength carried to an extreme. It's the overuse of something that has worked well in most situations.

8. There are three types of interpersonal styles: dominant, analytical, and caring. A dominant interpersonal style reflects assertive, controlling, dominant, and forceful characteristics. Characteristics of the analytical interpersonal style include cautious, calculating, investigative, and methodical behaviors. A caring interpersonal style reflects optimistic, adaptable, and helpful characteristics.

9. The Johari Window can help individuals tap into their hidden potential through self-disclosure and feedback. When individuals disclose secrets, they invite feedback that may reduce their blind spots. This feedback can help individuals gain new knowledge and skills.

10. Recommendations for giving feedback include the following: give feedback to be helpful; assess the readiness of the receiver; make it recent; describe behaviors rather than evaluate them; don't demand change; focus on the things a person controls; be empathetic; and confirm understanding.

REVIEWING YOUR UNDERSTANDING

1. Describe how effective communication differs from agreement.

2. Where in the communication process is distortion likely to occur? Explain.

3. "Ineffective communication is the fault of the sender." Do you agree or disagree with this statement? Support your position.

4. What are some methods used to maximize communication?

5. Explain why effective communication skills are necessary for success in human relations?

6. Why do interpersonal styles differ?

7. Describe how a strength carried to an extreme can be considered a weakness.

8. What similarities exist between one's interpersonal style and Holland's vocational preferences?

9. Using the Johari Window, describe a situation in a class setting where you could tap into your hidden potential.

10. "If a person is not ready to receive feedback, the sender shouldn't provide it." Do you agree or disagree with this statement? Explain your position.

ANSWERS TO CHECKING YOUR UNDERSTANDING

1. c   2. b   3. a   4. d   5. b   6. c

LEARNING TOGETHER

A. Send an e-mail message to two friends asking for a definition of *communication*. Analyze the responses as to their similarities and differences. Exchange the definitions with your friends and try to find agreement on one definition. Share with your class what you learned from your friends' responses and interaction.

B. Debate with your class the statement, "More than 50 percent of communication is body language and less than 10 percent is words."

C. In groups of two to four students, identify three people who can be characterized by the statement, "Actions speak louder than words." Explain your choices. Then compare and contrast the personality and interpersonal style of each of the three individuals. Share your conclusions with your class.

D. Discuss with classmates why people usually see other people's styles from a weakness standpoint. Share some examples. Identify and discuss several steps that can be taken to change the way you see each other's styles. How will changing your view of others help you communicate better?

CASE 4

Communicating Effectively

Your English instructor just told you there will be a retake exam next week for anyone who did poorly on the first test. When you ask your instructor what *poorly* means, she replied, "I will leave that up to you to interpret." You do not know the range of scores on the exam, but decide that your score of 79 does not qualify as poorly. When you asked a couple of your classmates if they were going to take the second exam, they said, "Probably not." You decide you have other, more important things to do, so you dismiss the idea of taking the exam again.

Two weeks later your instructor announces that about one-fourth of the class completed the retake exam. Because of their conscientiousness, she is going to add a 5 percent bonus to the higher score of either the first or second exam. You and several others react with glances to each other, which your instructor totally ignores. One student said, "If I had known extra credit was going to be given, I would have taken the retake exam." Your instructor replied, "Yes, hindsight is better than foresight."

Personally you don't think foresight had anything to do with the situation. It was just plain miscommunication (or was it intentional withholding of information?) by your instructor. You feel upset, uncomfortable, and betrayed. After class, you found out that three of your classmates made scores of at least 87 on the first test. Because they completed the retake exam, they now have A's! You're angry with these classmates for not telling you their scores or that they were going to take the exam. You are really angry with your instructor. In fact, each time you go to class you are having more and more trouble concentrating on the topic. Your instructor's lectures really don't seem to add much to what you have already read in the book.

Questions

1. Describe the communication barriers (and their sources) that exist in this case.

2. How could communication be improved by (a) the instructor, (b) by you, and (c) by your classmates?

3. What actions could be taken at this point by (a) the instructor, (b) by you, and (c) by your classmates to improve communication for the rest of the term?

4. Assume that the instructor can change her interpersonal style. Determine which style would be most effective for her in improving communication for the rest of the term.

5. What have you learned from this case that you can apply to yourself?

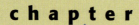

chapter 5

PERSONAL ISSUES

*L*earning Outcomes

After reading this chapter, you will be able to:

1. Define *stress* and *burnout*.

2. Describe the characteristics of Type A and Type B personalities.

3. Explain the differences between role overload, role conflict, and role ambiguity.

4. List several stress reduction strategies.

5. Explain how time management strategies can reduce stress.

6. List six steps for better time management.

7. Describe the effect of alcoholism on behavior.

8. Describe the purpose of employee assistance programs.

9. Explain why companies offer wellness programs to their employees.

10. Explain what is meant by the term *sexual harassment*.

The vast majority of us meet life head on, accepting whatever happens in a day-to-day fashion. We experience the happy times and celebrate. When there are sad times, we mourn. We anticipate these events, realizing that everything can't be a joyous occasion, nor (thankfully) is everything a tragedy. Although we think we are prepared to deal with anything, sometimes things do happen that are more than we can handle. Consider what happened to Charles Dorsey on the morning of July 20, 1995.[1]

As on any other morning, Charles, his wife, Kim, and their children, Keisha and Channel, awoke early. After scurrying around the house together getting ready for the busy day ahead, the family headed off in separate directions. As usual, Charles drove off to his job while Kim and the children met up with Kim's sister and her two children, intending to all ride the bus to downtown Baltimore together. Kim and her sister planned to leave the children in a downtown daycare near their workplace. This morning appeared no different than any other workday—until, that is, about 6:50 A.M. While the Dorseys were standing at the bus stop, an out-of-control car jumped the curb, striking several waiting bus riders. Kim, Keisha, and Channel Dorsey, as well as two other children, were killed instantly. In that instant, the life of Charles Dorsey changed forever. For Charles Dorsey and anyone who has ever suffered a similar tragedy, the memory of loved ones will always remain. But so will the pain. The lives of these people will be drastically different. Yet despite their sorrow, most people eventually find the inner strength to go on.

Fortunately, most of us have never faced such a personal tragedy. But that's not to say we are free of problems. Instead, we face many different types of dilemmas from one day to the next. As we face our day-to-day ventures, our lives and our behavior may change as well.

Stress

The need to seek relief from the difficulties in your daily life can lead you to do things you normally wouldn't. You may deal with anxieties by engaging in a variety of new behaviors, such as changing eating and sleeping habits or turning to a chemical substance for relief. Collectively, these anxieties are called *stress*. Let's look at stress and how it affects you.[2]

What Is Stress?

Stress is something you feel when you face opportunities, constraints, or demands that you perceive as both uncertain and important.[3] Stress is complex, showing itself in both positive and negative ways. Stress is said to be positive when the situation offers you an opportunity to gain something. For example, intense studying prior to an exam may produce positive stress. Conversely, when constraints or demands are placed on you, stress can become negative. Constraints are barriers that keep you from doing what you desire. Attending college may be your desire, but if you cannot afford the tuition, you are constrained from enrolling in college classes. Accordingly, constraints restrict you by taking control of a situation away from you. If you cannot afford college now, you may not be able to immediately meet your educational goals. Demands, on the other hand, may cause you to give up something you want. If you wish to attend a

> **stress**
> something an individual feels when faced with opportunities, constraints, or demands that are perceived as both uncertain and important

---

[1] John Rivera and Elaine Tassy, "Tragedy Strikes Woodlawn," *The Baltimore Sun* (July 21, 1995), p. A-1.

[2] This discussion of stress was drawn heavily from David A. De Cenzo & Stephen P. Robbins, *Human Resource Management*, 5th ed. (New York: Wiley, 1996), chapter 15.

[3] Adapted from Randall S. Schuler, "Definition and Conceptualization of Stress in Organizations," *Organizational Behavior and Human Performance* (April 1980), p. 189.

Having a bad day? It's more than that for Gordy Bennett. This 27-year-old systems analyst is having serious problems—all associated with personal issues in his life. As a result, he's losing the battle with stress. But with help, Gordy can learn and practice stress reduction strategies.

party on campus Thursday night but have a major examination Friday morning, the examination may take precedence. Thus, demands preoccupy your time and force you to shift priorities.

Constraints and demands can lead to potential negative stress. When they are coupled with uncertainty of the outcome and importance of the outcome, potential stress becomes actual stress. However, if you remove the uncertainty or the importance of the outcome, you remove stress. For instance, you may have been constrained from attending college because of tuition costs. But if you find out you've just been awarded a merit scholarship that will pay your tuition and living fees, the uncertainty element is significantly reduced. Your stress is likewise reduced. Accordingly, if you are auditing a class for no grade, the importance of the major examination is reduced. Consequently, stress is reduced also. However, when constraints or demands actually do have an impact on an important event and the outcome is unknown, pressure is added—pressure resulting in stress.

Causes of Stress

> **stressors**
> personal and on-the-job factors that cause stress

Stress can be caused by a number of factors called **stressors.** Factors that create stressors can be grouped into two major categories: personal and on-the-job. (See Exhibit 5-1.) Both of these categories directly affect us and, ultimately, our jobs. Because personal factors affect and are affected by on-the-job factors, we will address them first.

Almost anything of a personal nature can cause us stress. The three broad categories most cited are personality types, family matters, and financial problems.

Personality Types. Do you have a friend who always appears consumed with time? Does he or she always seem to take on too much work and hurriedly attempt to get everything done? If you know this type of individual, you've already been introduced to a particular personality type. For years, psychologists have been writing about two extreme types of personalities, described as Type A and Type B people.[4]

---

[4]See, for example, Meyer Friedman and Ray H. Rosenman, *Type A Behavior and Your Heart* (New York: Knopf, 1974).

EXHIBIT 5-1
Causes of Stress

Type A personalities are time-driven, aggressive, and competitive and have a strong desire for achievement. They often are extremely ambitious. Type A people tend to work on tasks rapidly and often work on many projects simultaneously. They are also impatient and irritated with others who do not share their love of demanding schedules and precise, detailed plans. Type A people also prefer to work exceptionally long hours—rarely taking time off for leisure activities. When they do have time for relaxation, they often feel guilty about it. Type A people easily earn themselves the label of "workaholic."

Many Type A people are highly successful. Their work habits and willingness to focus for long periods on multiple projects make them extremely productive. But at what cost do they achieve success? Over extended time periods, their drive causes problems for Type A people. They become shut-ins focusing solely on their work. They have little or no time for family or friends. They can't relax, for they are constantly thinking about the next thing that needs to be done. Eventually, the constant pressure Type A individuals bring on themselves overpowers them—often resulting in poorer health.[5]

The opposite of the Type A personality is the **Type B personality.** Type B people are more relaxed, easygoing, even-tempered, flexible, and friendly. They take time to reenergize themselves by doing things for fun. Everything does not have to be work-related for Type B people. They don't feel guilty for taking time off. Nor do they feel

➤ **Type A personality**
an individual who is time-driven, aggressive, and competitive and has a strong desire for achievement

➤ **Type B personality**
an individual who is relaxed, easygoing, even-tempered, flexible, and friendly

[5]Ibid.

that their every movement has to lead to some successful goal attainment. Type B individuals tend to be more creative individuals, allowing their minds to wander in search of new and different solutions. They are less conscious of time, accept change easily, and aren't likely to experience many of the anxiety-related ailments that their Type A counterparts do.

What can you learn from looking at these personality types? As with the interpersonal styles, it's unlikely that you are purely Type A or Type B. Those two points represent endpoints on a continuum, and you will fall somewhere in between the two extremes. Yet most individuals are more dominant in one type than the other. What you need to do is learn from the strengths of both personality types. Career success can be supported by some of the Type A characteristics, such as the drive for success.[6] Focus and ambition can help you achieve personal goals. But you need to place limits on your desire for achievement. Life doesn't always go as planned. You encounter obstacles in almost everything you do. You need to be resilient to change—to anticipate, expect, and accept change. Learn to go with the flow. Type B individuals have shown that these latter attributes help reduce the anxiety-related problems you may bring on yourself.[7]

Family and Finances.   No matter who you are, or how far you advance in your career, one thing is certain: Family is important. When you are faced with a family crisis—divorce, a problem child, illness, and the like—your behavior is going to change. So, too, will your behavior change during a financial crisis. You may attribute much of the stress in any relationship to lack of money. There's no doubt that finances play an important part. But there are as many people earning more than $100,000 a year who are experiencing severe stress as there are people earning less than $25,000. The key to minimizing your stress level is learning to manage your money and live within a budget.

An important fact to remember is that positive stressors can cause as much stress as negative stressors. Certainly, the death of a family member, a divorce, or being fired from work can cause major stress, but so can the birth of a child, a wedding, or getting a new job. For example, remember the time you finally got that date with the person of your dreams? Was it a happy time? Hopefully. But what did you go through to get ready? You debated over what clothes to wear, what to talk about, how you looked, and so on. Moreover, you were nervous when you finally found yourself alone with your date. All in all, you may have had a good time on the date, but this good time caused you a lot of stress.

From the Job.   No matter what personal factors are causing you stress, one thing is certain: sooner or later you will bring it to work. Also, organizational factors such as the changing workforce, downsizing, reengineering, and technological advancements that are occurring in U.S. companies are changing how you do your job and determining whether you even have a job. It's little wonder, then, that stress is so rampant among workers in today's organizations. Just how rampant? Various surveys indicate that up to three-fourths of workers experienced high job stress.[8] And stress on the job knows no boundary. In Japan, worker stress has been identified in 70 percent of the workers by a Fukoku Life Insurance Company study.[9] In fact, in Japan there is

---

[6]John W. Newstrom & Keith Davis, *Organizational Behavior: Human Behavior at Work*, 9th ed. (New York: McGraw-Hill, 1993), p. 466.

[7]Lynn Beresford, "Workaholics Anonymous," *Entrepreneur* (August 1995), p. 13.

[8]Robert McGarvey, "On the Edge," *Entrepreneur* (August 1995), p. 76.

[9]This information is adapted from a news wire report by Mari Yamaguchi as cited in "Stress in Japanese Business," *Audio Human Resource Report*, vol. 2, no. 2 (March 1991), pp. 6–7.

Type	Symptoms
Physiological	Physiological symptoms of stress are the most difficult to detect with the naked eye. They relate to internal medical changes that can occur, including increased heart and breathing rates, higher blood pressure, headaches, backaches, and stomachaches. At the extreme, they can lead to heart attacks and strokes.
Psychological	Psychological symptoms of stress can be seen as tension, anxiety, irritability, boredom, and procrastination. When these are present, we begin to lose interest in things around us and begin to feel overwhelmed.
Behavioral	Behavioral symptoms of stress are the most visible. They include decreased productivity, increased absenteeism and turnover, and increased smoking and alcohol consumption.

EXHIBIT 5-2
Symptoms of Stress

a concept called *karoshi*, which refers to sudden heart attacks caused by overworking. *Karoshi*, experts cite, affects more than 10,000 Japanese workers each year.[10]

Worker stress is costing U.S. industry billions of dollars. One estimate revealed that almost $150 billion is lost each year because of stress and its related implications.[11] (See Exhibit 5-2.) Things such as the demands of job roles, work relationships, the organization's structure, and supervisors can all contribute to stress. For example, most recognize that the forty-hour work week is a thing of the past. Most workers today work sixty hours a week or more, experiencing **role overload.** They just have more work than time in which to complete it. Role overload for you may lead to **role conflict,** being torn between two or more major responsibilities, such as your work and your family. You may lose your ability to deal effectively with others and feel inadequate in handling various situations. Co-workers, too, may make unreasonable demands on you. After all, they're stressed out, too. The problems you face, then, may have a spiraling effect. At a time when you need others most, you may alienate them because of the stress you're under. Organizations have become leaner and meaner. More work may now be expected from you. Although technological advancements are supposed to help out, they just

> **role overload**
> having more work than time in which to complete it

> **role conflict**
> being torn between two or more major responsibilities

---

[10]Robert McGarvey, "On the Edge," *Entrepreneur* (August 1995), p. 76; and K. L. Miller, "Now Japan Is Admitting It: Work Kills Executives," *Business Week* (August 3, 1992), p. 17.
[11]K. Lynch, "Humor Can Beat Stress," *Industry Week*, May 4, 1998, p. 55.

✓ Checking Your Understanding *5-1*

1. Which one of the following characteristics is not associated with Type A personality?
   a. workaholic
   b. aggressive
   c. easygoing demeanor
   d. success-driven

2. When one is torn between the responsibilities of work and family, the stress associated with this situation is best reflective of
   a. role conflict
   b. role overload
   c. role controversy
   d. role ambiguity

can't buy you all the time you need. Your job may also be ill defined, creating **role ambiguity:** you simply may not know what you are supposed to do. Your job may not allow you to make the decisions that affect you at work. That, coupled with a lack of proper tools, can compound the situation. Furthermore, your supervisor may be part of the problem rather than the solution. If his or her attitude is "Get the job done at all costs or else" (because he or she is being pressured by a boss), fear and anxiety are likely to dominate the work setting. In the end, serious stress becomes constant. When that occurs, you may experience **burnout**—chronic emotional distress. Burnout is the physical and emotional exhaustion that you encounter.[12] Burnout is a serious physical and emotional disorder that affects many workers; long-term boredom that we frequently refer to as burnout is not the same thing. In order to escape burnout, stress sufferers must learn ways to reduce their stress. Let's look at some suggestions.

Stress Reduction Strategies

Recognizing that stress is a fact of life and must be channeled properly, both you and your organization must find ways to reduce stress levels before they result in burnout. Although no clear-cut remedies are available for every case, there are some guidelines that you can follow.

Take a Good Look at Yourself. Have you stopped for a moment and assessed who you are? Are you more susceptible to Type A characteristics? Do you know what causes stress for you? One of the first things to do in managing your stress is finding out how you bring stress on yourself and what in your life creates stress for you. Only then can you begin to think about making some worthwhile changes in your behavior. Self-awareness is the initial key. Without it, reducing stress is difficult, at best.

Be Flexible. Tolerate life's curve balls. Realize that most things happen no matter what you may do to prevent them. Accept that fact. Many of life's experiences will be painful, but time heals pain—if we let it. No one is perfect, and we can neither expect nor demand perfection of ourselves. Excellence is always a worthy goal, but if you don't achieve excellence in everything you attempt, don't beat yourself up. There's a saying that goes something like this: "The way to a stress-free life is not to sweat the small stuff. Ninety-nine percent of life is small stuff." Save your anxiety for that 1 percent that really matters.

Be Positive. Here comes that positive attitude sermon once again. But it's true. How you see things determines your stress level. There's no sense becoming irritated about an unexpected traffic jam caused by road construction two miles ahead—even if you're going to be late for work. After all, you're still alive. Use the time wisely. Listen to a tape, jot down ideas that you haven't yet put on paper, or work on your plan for tomorrow.

Don't Let People Get to You. No one can make you angry, sad, or frustrated. People cannot upset you. They can do things that may annoy you, but only you can allow yourself to get upset. Let things bounce off you. Giving others control over your thoughts too often leads to letting them influence your body. Your blood pressure rises and your heart rate increases. The more frequently you respond with unrestrained emotion, the more harmful it is to you physically. Likewise, there's no reason to allow other individuals to bring you emotionally down with them. If they choose to be negative or depressed, let it be their choice. But you don't have to join them. Just walk away if need be.

---

[12]Baron Perlman & E. Alan Hartman, "Burnout: Summary and Future Research," *Human Relations*, vol. 35, no. 4 (1982), p. 284.

Get Some Exercise.　The medical community has shown that one of the greatest stress reducers is exercise. Do something other than sitting. Go for a walk, jog, or swim; go for a bike ride; wash the car; clean the house. Exert yourself at something you enjoy—other than watching television or playing video games. Be physical.

Seek Help from Someone Else.　No one is an island. Each of us needs someone else. We all need special people—friends, family members, counselors, or clergy members—in whom we can confide. Find someone who will actively listen to you and let you vent your frustrations. Share with him or her what's on your mind. Sometimes getting whatever it is off your chest is the best medicine. You and your special confidant may not be able to solve every difficult matter, but at least you can relieve some of the stress you are facing. Keeping things to yourself and allowing them to fester inside you may only make matters worse. Unresolved problems and worries not discussed with others may even contribute to substance abuse.

Plan Your Activities.　Too many times, you may leave things to chance. You may not set schedules, or you may fail to follow the schedules you set. You may put things off until later. And when later comes, you become overwhelmed. Planning activities helps you focus your attention on what needs to be done and when it needs to be done. But don't be so rigid in your schedule that, if something unforeseen happens, you flounder. Type A people plan very well, but often their clinging rigidly to the plan becomes a stressor. Remember, a plan is a plan; it is not cast in concrete. You work the plan; don't let the plan work you. Manage your plan well.

A Special Stress Reduction Strategy: Manage Your Time

*W*hat is time? It's something that can be your best friend in that it gives you an opportunity to experience life's many wonders. Time can also be your biggest enemy. You, like everyone else, have a limited time on this earth. No matter how you view time, it's one of those things that is exceptionally difficult to define. Dictionaries generally agree that time is an indefinite, unlimited duration in which things are considered as happening in the past, present or future—every moment there ever has been or ever will be. But what does that definition mean to us? Alan Lakein, one of the leading authorities on the subject of time, has probably said it best: "Time is Life, and if you want to reduce your stress and enjoy life, you have to take control of your time."[13] Lakein's quotation is precisely at the root of the subject of time management.

Effective time management strategies help individuals schedule their personal and professional lives, take control of their own life activities, and balance the requirements of both work and play. Think for a moment about the activities in which you're involved—whether they're school, work, or personal projects. How many hours a day do you need to get everything done? Well, guess what? Time is limited. Like everyone else, you have only twenty-four hours a day. It's what you do in those twenty-four hours that makes the difference between your being successful (and less stressed) or not. You probably have some friends who always seem to have time to do whatever they want. Maybe you do not understand why. Perhaps they manage their time very effectively.

Learning to manage your time better will improve your ability to plan. A time management program provides the structure and self-discipline to keep your attention focused on those things you need to do. Every day you face a number of time wasters—people and events that rob you of time to complete priority activities at work and at home. You need to recognize these time wasters and look for ways to overcome them.

---

[13] Alan Lakein, *How to Get Control of Your Time and Your Life* (New York: New American Library, 1974).

The Time Wasters

What wastes your time? Is it the annoying interruptions you get throughout the day? The telephone ringing constantly? Too much work that has to get done in too little time? Your mind wandering? Any and all of these things may waste your time. It may be somewhat easy to identify common time wasters in our life, but it's more difficult to acknowledge who's really responsible for wasted time. Clearly, you are. You do and say things that give people the chance to interrupt you and, therefore, create your time management problems yourself. Following are some examples of typical time wasters:

✪ A classmate walks into your dorm room and asks if you've got a minute. Thirty minutes later, you're still talking.

✪ You're spending some quiet time with someone special, and the phone rings. You answer it.

✪ You attend a meeting not knowing why you're going or what is going to happen. An hour later, you still don't have a clue.

✪ You work on easy tasks before tackling the harder ones. You like the feeling of accomplishment and continue working on the easy tasks, leaving the harder ones for later.

✪ You thrive on chaos. The urgency of having to get something done at the last minute gives you a rush.

✪ You shuffle paper after paper, moving the stack from one place to another, and then move it again.

And the list could go on. Although identifying what wastes your time is a critical first step, you need to pay more attention to what you can do to better manage the situation. There's a saying in time management seminars that goes something like this: "Be kind to others, but ruthless with your time." Remember, you have only twenty-four hours each day. If you let others take control of your time, you are the one wasting your time. For example, why answer that telephone call? Technology today gives us the opportunity to screen calls before we answer the phone. Why disrupt a special moment with a friend or your scheduled quiet time because of your habitual urgency to answer the telephone? Let it ring or screen your calls. Yes, the call could be an emergency, but that's highly unlikely. Even if you do answer, look for ways to minimize lost time. For instance, some companies intentionally schedule calls to people's homes around dinner time. If you answer the phone and hear a computer message, hang up. If a live person is calling and you're not interested in what is being sold, thank the person and hang up. Be assertive. It is your time.

➤ **procrastination**
putting off for tomorrow things that should be done today

Another substantial time waster for many individuals is **procrastination,** putting off for tomorrow things that should be done today. One form of procrastination is consistently spending time on easier tasks before tackling harder ones. Finishing easy tasks gives you a pleasant sense of completion, but is it completion that leads to your success? More than likely, no. You may actually tend to do the easier and unimportant things first because you really don't want to tackle the hard problems at all. You may even justify your choice by saying "that's all time would allow me to do." However, if you really wish to improve the way you manage your time, you will need to change your mindset and habits regarding the order of selecting tasks. Why? Your success may depend on it. You'd be better off spending just a few minutes on an important item—even if it's just planning how to do it—than ignoring it totally. Important tasks not done eventually become urgent as well as important, and then getting them done can cause you great stress. For example, not once when we were students did either of us ever see a term paper assigned the weekend before it was due. But we both remember waiting until Sunday

UNLOCKING YOUR POTENTIAL *5-1*

Identifying Time Wasters

Listed here are many of the typical reasons people cite as time wasters. Check all those that apply to you in both Column A and Column B.

A   *B*

_____ Interruptions   _____ Procrastination
_____ Attending meetings   _____ Too much work to do
_____ Drop-in visitors   _____ Complete easy tasks first
_____ Telephone   _____ Messy desk
_____ Red tape   _____ Unnecessary mail
_____ Unclear expectations   _____ Can't say no
_____ Lack of clear goals   _____ Failure to listen
_____ Lack of help   _____ Waiting for others
_____ Unrealistic time estimates   _____ Lack of self-discipline
_____ Too many bosses   _____ Visual distractions
_____ Lack of motivation   _____ Misplaced items

After you've checked those that apply, study your answers. What patterns or common characteristics do you notice? Place your response here.

_____
_____
_____
_____
_____

night to start writing a term paper due Monday afternoon. Furthermore, as instructors neither of us has ever assigned a term paper the weekend before it was due. However, we both have suspicions that more than a few of our students have likewise started writing term papers on the Sunday night just before the Monday deadline. Perhaps these students, like we did, erroneously claim that assignments completed under pressure are better-quality, when, in reality, far better term papers could have resulted if more time had been spent planning and revising the composition. In the work setting, giving yourself enough time for important projects becomes even more crucial. A late term paper may cause a lower grade, but at work a late project may cost a job. The excuse of a weekend illness preventing the completion of a major project doesn't carry a lot of weight when the employee had six months to complete the assignment.

Techniques for Managing Your Time

There are no hard and fast rules for managing your time. Nonetheless, you need to look at a variety of techniques and tailor them to meet your needs. Doing so will make you a better time manager. Let's look at suggestions drawn from time management experts and others who manage their time well.

Identify Your Time Wasters.   The first step in better managing time is to find out what wastes your time. You need to identify who and what steals time from you. The best way of uncovering this mystery is to track and record your daily events. Time logs, such as the one presented in Exhibit 5-3, should be kept for about two weeks—using a new sheet every day. Experts suggest logging items every fifteen minutes. That means from the time you wake up to the time you go to sleep, you should keep a diary of what happens in your life. Record everything—people's names, what took place, what you did, how long it took, and so on—even if it appears boring to you. After a couple of weeks, study these sheets. Look for patterns. For example, did someone call you most mornings at nine A.M. and did the calls last thirty minutes or so? Were you interrupted by the same people over the two-week period? If so, where did the interruptions take place? Take a hard look at these sheets; they may give you answers that will help you better control your time by significantly reducing your time wasters.

Make a List of Things to Do.   Planning is really the key here. If you don't plan what you need to do, chances of getting done what you want are slim. Most people claim that they plan. But how many write it down? To manage your time effectively, put that plan on paper—on what is most appropriately called a To Do list. You should

EXHIBIT 5-3
A Sample Time Log

Date:_____

Time	What I Did	Interrupted By	Time	What I Did	Interrupted By
Pre-7:00 A.M.	_____	_____	2:45 P.M.	_____	_____
7:00 A.M.	_____	_____	3:00 P.M.	_____	_____
7:15 A.M.	_____	_____	3:15 P.M.	_____	_____
7:30 A.M.	_____	_____	3:30 P.M.	_____	_____
7:45 A.M.	_____	_____	3:45 P.M.	_____	_____
8:00 A.M.	_____	_____	4:00 P.M.	_____	_____
8:15 A.M.	_____	_____	4:15 P.M.	_____	_____
8:30 A.M.	_____	_____	4:30 P.M.	_____	_____
8:45 A.M.	_____	_____	4:45 P.M.	_____	_____
9:00 A.M.	_____	_____	5:00 P.M.	_____	_____
9:15 A.M.	_____	_____	5:15 P.M.	_____	_____
9:30 A.M.	_____	_____	5:30 P.M.	_____	_____
9:45 A.M.	_____	_____	5:45 P.M.	_____	_____
10:00 A.M.	_____	_____	6:00 P.M.	_____	_____
10:15 A.M.	_____	_____	6:15 P.M.	_____	_____
10:30 A.M.	_____	_____	6:30 P.M.	_____	_____
10:45 A.M.	_____	_____	6:45 P.M.	_____	_____
11:00 A.M.	_____	_____	7:00 P.M.	_____	_____
11:15 A.M.	_____	_____	7:15 P.M.	_____	_____
11:30 A.M.	_____	_____	7:30 P.M.	_____	_____
11:45 A.M.	_____	_____	7:45 P.M.	_____	_____
12:00 noon	_____	_____	8:00 P.M.	_____	_____
12:15 P.M.	_____	_____	8:15 P.M.	_____	_____
12:30 P.M.	_____	_____	8:30 P.M.	_____	_____
12:45 P.M.	_____	_____	8:45 P.M.	_____	_____
1:00 P.M.	_____	_____	9:00 P.M.	_____	_____
1:15 P.M.	_____	_____	9:15 P.M.	_____	_____
1:30 P.M.	_____	_____	9:30 P.M.	_____	_____
1:45 P.M.	_____	_____	9:45 P.M.	_____	_____
2:00 P.M.	_____	_____	10:00 P.M.	_____	_____
2:15 P.M.	_____	_____	Post-10:00 P.M.	_____	_____
2:30 P.M.	_____	_____			

KEYS TO UNLOCKING YOUR POTENTIAL *5-1*

*L*et's look again at the time wasters presented in Unlocking Your Potential 5-1.

A

_____ Interruptions
_____ Attending meetings
_____ Drop-in visitors
_____ Telephone
_____ Red tape
_____ Unclear expectations
_____ Lack of clear goals
_____ Lack of help
_____ Unrealistic time estimates
_____ Too many bosses
_____ Lack of motivation

B

_____ Procrastination
_____ Too much work to do
_____ Complete easy tasks first
_____ Messy desk
_____ Unnecessary mail
_____ Can't say no
_____ Failure to listen
_____ Waiting for others
_____ Lack of self-discipline
_____ Visual distractions
_____ Misplaced items

Irrespective of the time wasters you checked, did you see any similarities among the items in the columns? Look closely and you will see that Column A lists those things that waste your time but seem beyond your direct control. Column B, on the other hand, lists time wasters we obviously bring on ourselves. Unfortunately, time management isn't that simple. Contrary to what most of us believe, every item in both columns is actually within our control. Even though we may think it's impossible for us to eliminate many of the time wasters in Column A, it's actually quite possible to do so. That's the primary reason for learning about and using good time management strategies.

Extra Effort

Develop a plan of action for identifying and eliminating your time wasters. Refer to the suggestions and strategies in the text and incorporate these into your plan. Once you have implemented your action plan, how will you recognize and measure success with it?

plan out and schedule your activities. Your To Do list should cover, at a minimum, the things that need to be done over the next few days. Review the list throughout the day and update it when necessary. Cross out completed items. You've probably listed many items on your To Do list, but not every activity is equally important nor is every activity urgent. Therefore, you must begin to figure out what are the most important and most urgent activities.

Prioritize Your To Do List. If I told you that I could show you a way in which you could do roughly half your job yet be 99 percent effective, would you try it? Well, I can. Let's look at a theory called **Pareto's Law of Optimality.** Pareto showed that in most things an individual does, 20 percent of the items account for 80 percent of the results. For example, 20 percent of all items in a warehouse take up 80 percent of its space, 20 percent of the items an organization sells account for 80 percent of its income, and

▶ **Pareto's Law of Optimality**
a theory asserting that in most things an individual does, 20 percent of the items account for 80 percent of the results

20 percent of your items or activities take up 80 percent of your time. (See Exhibit 5-4.) The issue is, how do you identify those critical activities? A number of people have developed a lettering or numbering scheme that can help, focusing on items that are important or urgent. For example, Lakein suggests going through your To Do list and classifying each item as A, B, or C. Items marked A are most important, those marked B are moderately important, and those marked C are least important. Then, within each letter, the activity can be classified further by numbers. For example, items marked 1 must be done now; items marked 2 should be done soon; items marked 3 can be done later; and for items marked 4, time is not an issue. Thus, A1's get your immediate attention, followed by A2's, and so on. Note that a C activity usually does not have a level 1 urgency associated with it. If it does, it might have been misclassified in importance. But that's not to say a classification of C1 can't happen, especially when the activity is a necessity for completing an A1 that will occur in a day or so.

Schedule Your Day. After prioritizing your activities, develop a daily plan. Each morning (or the night before), identify what you want to accomplish during the day. If you used your ABC's and 123's properly, your schedule should be nearly set. Obviously, you'll work on the A1's first, followed by the A2's, and so on. But be realistic in your schedule. Given the nature of your activities, you may be unable to complete everything. In fact, if your scheduled list of activities gets too big—some contend that too big is more than a dozen items—you'll have difficulty completing everything, and you may become frustrated. Be reasonable in deciding what you can accomplish. If you prioritize your time well, there should be no more than one A1 item (although exceptions do occur—such as two major final exams on the same day). The key is to concentrate on the A's, making sure they get done; completing B's and C's demonstrates your progress in managing your time.

Prepare Yourself for Work. Any craftsperson can attest that without proper tools, good work is nearly impossible. The car mechanic without wrenches, the cook without a stove, or the word processor without a computer will not be effective. Likewise, you cannot be an effective time manager without appropriate tools. Make sure you have what you need to begin working on your A1 items. If you need a book for a

---

Well, here's the challenge. Can you do half your job and still be 99 percent effective? Using Pareto's Law, you can. Assume that on your job you have twenty-five tasks to perform. From that, we can show the following:

Activities		Percent Effectiveness	
25		100%	
(applying Pareto's Law in each of three rounds)			
20% of 25 = 5	20 activities left	80% of 100% = 80%	20% left
20% of 20 = 4	16 activities left	80% of 20% = 16%	4% left
20% of 16 = 3	13 activities left	80% of 4% = 3%	1% left
Totals 12		99%	

Thus, performing just twelve of your twenty-five activities has led to you achieving 99 percent effectiveness. So what's the key? You've got to identify the top 12 activities. This involves setting priorities. (It also assumes that you won't get fired or fail a class for not performing the remaining thirteen activities.)

EXHIBIT 5-4
Applying Pareto's Law of Optimality

report, make sure you obtain it ahead of time. Getting the book may have been a C item for you several days ago, and you didn't get around to going to the library for the book. Now the day to start your A1 item has arrived, and you can't proceed without the book. That one C item of several days ago has become a time waster for you today—getting the book right now is an A1. Anticipate situations like this one and you'll manage your time much better.

The Four D Strategies.   There's an adage that says a cluttered desk is the sign of a cluttered mind. Of what is an empty desk a sign? Not what we might think. An empty desk, or at least an organized one, is certainly a sign of a worker who has eliminated many time wasters. Most time management experts agree that any type of paper should be handled only once. Reading it, putting it down, and then coming back to it later wastes your time. Dealing with paper in more efficient ways, such as with the four D strategies, makes better use of your time.

The first D strategy is *dump it*. Don't waste your time reading word-for-word unimportant pieces of paper, junk mail, or memos that don't concern you. Throw them away. I know there's someone wondering, what if you're wrong about the importance of a written communication? What if it's a memo from your boss, for example? What if you misjudge the importance of something and throw it away, and now you need it? No problem—if it's really that important, someone around you probably kept a copy of the memo, or you can ask your boss for it again. Eventually, you'll catch on to what you need to keep and what can be tossed. When in doubt, however, dump it.

For magazines and similar publications, I recommend the second D strategy: *defer it*. Put them in a pile. Then, when you have some free time (waiting for someone, before you go to bed, or between classes), read them. Scan the table of contents and go to the articles that interest you. As with a newspaper, we don't need to read every word in every article. Scan for the things that appear important or interesting to you, focus your attention on them, and bypass the rest.

The third D strategy is *delegate it*. See if others can do some things for you. Something that is low in priority for you just might be high for someone else. Maybe you can approach that person as a resource. For instance, suppose you get a notice saying that a book you need tomorrow has just arrived in the library. But your time is really pressed right now since you are studying for tomorrow's exam. However, your roommate mentions that he is going out for a walk to get some fresh air and then plans to study for a while in the library. Ask your friend if he wouldn't mind getting the book for you. Delegating can be useful. Remember, there'll also come a time when you can help that person out in exchange for the assistance now.

You've dumped much of your paper, deferred reading some of the rest, and delegated what was possible. But still something is nagging at you. Remember the C1 we discussed earlier that rarely exists? Maybe it's unimportant to you, but to another— such as your supervisor—it's an A1. In that case, rather than fret over it, get stressed out over it, or send your blood pressure skyrocketing, just *do it*—the fourth D strategy. You'll probably find it takes less time to do than the time you might waste getting upset over the thing because it seems so unimportant to you and takes time away from your A1 priorities. Don't sweat the small stuff.

Abusing Substances

*W*hen you face difficult times (such as the loss of a loved one or the loss of a job), you generally work through them. You find an inner strength that gives you the fortitude to deal with trying times, and then you move on with your life. But for about 25 percent of the U.S. workforce, that fortitude frequently comes in the form of alcohol or other drugs.[14] Turning to alcohol or other drugs creates even greater problems; though pain may be temporarily eased or hidden, the fact remains that one problem has been substituted for another.

---

[14]Janet Gemignani, "Substance Abusers: Terminate or Treat?" *Business and Health* (June 1999), pp. 32–38.

UNLOCKING YOUR POTENTIAL 5-2

Do You Drink Too Much?

Most of us know the dangers associated with alcohol abuse. We also know that, if asked, we often say we can handle our booze. But is our drinking affecting our behavior? As you answer each of the following twenty questions, don't answer the way you think you're supposed to. Rather, answer each question as honestly as you can.

	Yes	No
1. I have missed class because I drank too much the night before.	___	___
2. I drink because it helps me interact with other people.	___	___
3. Drinking makes me feel self-confident.	___	___
4. I sometimes drink alone.	___	___
5. People talk about my drinking.	___	___
6. Drinking takes me away from school or work worries.	___	___
7. I get upset after I have been drinking.	___	___
8. It bothers me when someone says I'm drinking too much.	___	___
9. I have to take a drink before I go out on a date.	___	___
10. I perform better (at work, play, or school) after I have a drink.	___	___
11. I sometimes spend too much money on alcohol.	___	___
12. I feel a sense of power when I drink.	___	___
13. I hang out with people who like to drink alcohol.	___	___
14. I have lost a friend since I started drinking.	___	___
15. My friends drink less than I do.	___	___
16. I drink until I've finished what I bought.	___	___
17. I sometimes can't remember what I did when I was drinking.	___	___
18. I sometimes drink and drive.	___	___
19. I think lecturers about drinking are a waste of my time.	___	___
20. I think I have a problem with alcohol.	___	___

Source: Applied Human Relations: An Organizational Approach, 5/e by Benton, © 1995. Adapted by permission of Prentice-Hall, Inc., Upper Saddle River, N.J.

Alcohol Abuse

It's not unusual for adults to have a drink now and then. In fact, there is growing evidence that drinking in moderation, such as having a glass of red wine each day, can help reduce heart disease.[15] However, when alcohol becomes a crutch for you, or when the overindulgence of alcohol reduces your ability to function effectively, you have become an **alcoholic.**

Alcoholism is an illness and should be treated as one. Alcoholism causes great pain to afflicted individuals and their families, friends, and employers. For instance, organizations lose billions of dollars each year because of employees with alcohol-related problems. These losses include reduction in employee productivity, increased absenteeism, more on-the-job accidents, and higher health care costs. Companies, therefore, are paying more attention to how their employees act on the job in an effort to identify those who might have serious drinking problems. But identifying someone with a drinking problem is not always easy. Individuals who abuse alcohol are usually very good at covering up their addictions, especially in the early stages. They make reasonable excuses, and supervisors generally accept these. But excuses work for only so long. At some point, the behavior changes significantly as frequent alcohol abuse becomes a way of life. Individuals who chronically abuse alcohol begin to call in sick more often. They may take longer lunch breaks than usual or simply not return after lunch. Their behavior becomes erratic as they become moody, forgetful, and argumentative. All in all, their job becomes less important to them. Consequently, their performance begins to fall off drastically. Although companies today are offering to help the alcoholic employee, some individuals just can't or won't accept the help. Once workers with serious alcohol addiction think they have gone too far, the least of their worries is that they may lose their jobs.

Other Substance Abuse

People who abuse alcohol and other substances are often seen as creating similar problems. Workers with both these problems have increased absences and accident

> **alcoholic**
> an individual for whom alcohol has become a crutch or for whom overindulgence reduces that person's ability to function effectively

---

[15]Eric B. Rimm, "Moderate Alcohol Intake and Lower Risk of Coronary Heart Disease: Meta-analysis of Effects on Lipids and Haemostatic Factors, *British Medical Journal* (December 11, 1999), p. 1–4.

KEYS TO UNLOCKING YOUR POTENTIAL *5-2*

*A*nswering yes to any one of the twenty questions in Unlocking Your Potential 5-2 by itself doesn't indicate you have an alcohol problem. It should only provide an awareness of your specific alcohol-related behavior. However, answering yes to several questions may mean you have a potential drinking problem. If, for example, you answered yes to five or more questions, don't discount what this is saying. Look closely and honestly at your behavior. Is it dominated by alcohol? Is drinking becoming the centerpiece of your life? Is drinking affecting how you do things or how others see you? Without labeling or condemning yourself, take a good look at yourself. If you don't like what you see or what drinking may be doing to you, seek help from others. There are many people around you—family members, friends, co-workers, counselors—who are available to help. Take advantage of their assistance. Your life and the lives of those around you will be better if you do.

rates. They have caused 40 percent of all on-the-job injuries and about half of all work-related deaths.[16] Yet although there are similarities between alcohol abuse and abuse of other substances, there are differences that are worth noting. Alcohol, for the most part, can be legally obtained, whereas, most other abused substances are illegal. (See Exhibit 5-5.) Even though the behavior may be very similar, people who abuse substances are apt to more boldly deny they have a problem than are those who abuse alcohol. They are also more likely to steal at home and at work to support their habit. Society has been more tolerant of alcohol abuse (unless it leads to driving under the influence) than other substance abuse, although alcohol is the most abused substance in the United States. But that has been changing in the last decade. Laws have been passed, and company practices have been implemented that focus primarily on eliminating illegal substances and those who use them from the workplace. For example, Toys "R" Us and Motorola require drug tests of all current employees as well as job applicants.[17] For example, appli-

---

[16]"An Alternative to Drug Testing?" *Inc.* (April 1995), p. 112.

[17]"Fewer Employers Are Currently Conducting Psych and Drug Tests," *HR Focus* (October 2000), p. 78. It is important to note that drug testing may be constrained by collective bargaining agreements or state laws. See Erica Gordon Sorohan, "Making Decisions About Drug Testing," *Training and Development* (May 1994), pp. 111–117.

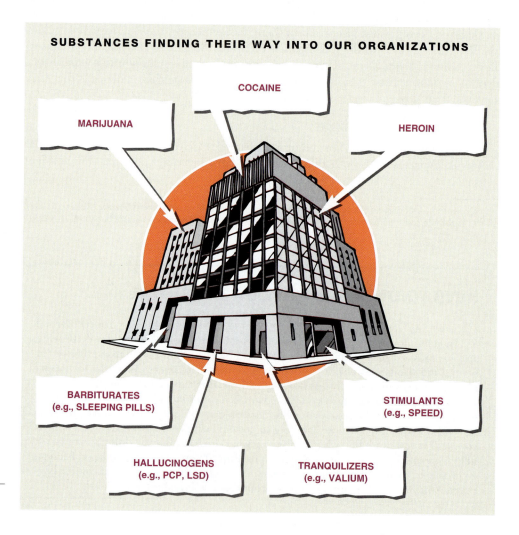

SUBSTANCES FINDING THEIR WAY INTO OUR ORGANIZATIONS

COCAINE

MARIJUANA

HEROIN

BARBITURATES
(e.g., SLEEPING PILLS)

STIMULANTS
(e.g., SPEED)

HALLUCINOGENS
(e.g., PCP, LSD)

TRANQUILIZERS
(e.g., VALIUM)

EXHIBIT 5-5

Most Common Drugs Found in the Workplace

cants who successfully complete the hiring process are given a conditional job offer. If their drug test is negative, they may start work. If their test is positive, however, the job offer is withdrawn. In fact, walk into any Toys "R" Us store, and you'll see prominently displayed at the entrance a sign that says something to the effect that "The employees of this store are drug-free. Applicants who cannot pass a drug screening test should not apply." The intent of drug testing is to identify substance abusers and either help them overcome their problem or not hire them in the first place.

How an organization deals with a substance-abusing employee is a matter of preference. Some may simply fire the employee immediately, whereas others may provide counseling programs. And although many questions have been raised regarding an employee's right to privacy with respect to drug testing, the courts have generally given organizations a lot of leeway. The use of illegal drugs, including alcohol, is so rampant and its effects so severe that some tough measures are permitted. We as a society must learn to better recognize the early signs of substance abuse in the workplace and find better ways to prevent workers from turning to drugs in self-defeating attempts to cope with life. Our future may depend on it.

Seeking Help from the Organization

Keeping with the theme that all of us will face difficulties in our lives—either personal or work-related—we may need to turn to others for help. Earlier we looked at what we could do for ourselves. But we don't have to do these things alone. Given

VALUE JUDGMENT: Should Employees be Required to Take Drug Tests?

Apply for most any type of job today, and you'll likely experience something new in the hiring process. Before you can officially start work, you'll have to take a drug test. If the test comes back negative, the job is yours—that is, as long as you remain substance-free. Many organizations today also have a policy requiring employees to submit to random drug tests. At any time, but especially after an accident has occurred, employers may direct all employees to take a drug test. Most of us understand why organizations are doing this. Drug testing helps an organization reduce dangerous effects of substance abuse during job-related activities and avoid serious problems such as lower productivity, higher absenteeism, and job-related accidents.

There's no argument against employers wanting to achieve these goals. But the rights of employees must be protected.* How can employees be assured that the tests are administered properly and their dignity is respected? Should people be subjected to the humility of having to fill a cup while being monitored to ensure that what's in the cup is actually theirs? Can employers guarantee that the test is valid? What about the many instances when drug tests have given false readings or the specimens were improperly handled? In many cases, tests produced negative results because the employees took legitimate medication or ate certain foods.

Should employees be drug tested? What should employers do if employees fail the test? Should the organization provide help, or should employees be fired for substance abuse? What is your view of the employer's right to drug test? How would you ensure respect for employee rights pertaining to drug testing?

*For an overview of employee rights in drug testing, see David A. De Cenzo and Stephen P. Robbins, *Human Resource Management*, 6th ed. (New York: Wiley, 1999), pp. 391–394.

that some of our stress—and its related behaviors—is brought on by work factors, organizations have taken a more active role in providing us some help. What are organizations doing? The answers to that question lie in a discussion of employee assistance and wellness programs.

Employee Assistance Programs

► **employee assistance program (EAP)**
a program designed to help employees overcome their personal problems and to return them to the job as soon as possible

Employee assistance programs (EAPs) as they exist today are extensions of programs that began in companies in the 1940s. Companies such as DuPont, Standard Oil, and Kodak recognized that a number of their employees were experiencing problems with alcohol.[18] To help their employees, companies implemented special programs to educate these workers on the dangers of alcohol and to help them overcome their addiction. The purpose of these programs is to get productive employees back on the job as swiftly as possible. For example, consider Sally. She has been with an organization for a number of years and has always been a solid performer. But lately something has happened. The quality of Sally's work is tapering off, and she has been late three times the past two weeks; what's more, she's having marital problems. The organization would have every right to fire Sally. But that would not solve anyone's problem. The organization would lose a once-productive employee, and Sally's problems would be exacerbated. Instead, Sally is referred to the company's EAP. Knowledgeable EAP professionals first work with Sally to determine the causes of her problems and then help her overcome them.

From their early focus on employees with alcohol-related problems, EAPs have expanded into new areas. EAPs are now used to help control rising health care costs, especially in the areas of mental health and substance abuse services.[19] For example, at Campbell's Soup Company, the company's EAP is the first stop for individuals seeking psychiatric or substance abuse help. By providing an EAP for employees, Campbell's was able to cut its health care insurance premiums by 28 percent.[20] Similar findings have occurred elsewhere. Studies suggest that organizations that have EAPs save from $5 to $16 for every EAP dollar spent.[21] That's a significant return on investment.

But no matter how beneficial EAPs may be to an organization, there is always the question of whether the employee will participate. The employee will participate as long as he or she perceives the EAP as worthwhile—that is, as long as it is designed to help deal with such problems as "alcohol and chemical dependency, emotional problems, stress, preretirement planning, marital problems, careers, finances, legal matters, or termination."[22] And most important, the organization must guarantee that an employee's participation is confidential.

Although EAPs are a good resource when you have problems, more and more companies are giving thought to implementing programs that attempt to eliminate some factors that may lead to your having problems in the first place. In doing so, organizations have promoted wellness programs.

[18]Valla Howell, "The Groggy Beginnings of EAPs," *JEMS* (November 1988), p. 43.

[19]Wayne Pancratz, "Employee Assistance Program a Valuable Benefit," *FDM* (December 2000), pp. 56–58; and "EAPs Adopt Broad Brush Approach to Helping Employees," *Employee Benefit Plan Review* (October 1999), pp. 44–46.

[20]Edward Stetzer, "Bringing Sanity to Mental Health Costs," *Business and Health* (February 1992), p. 72.

[21]William Atkinson, "Wellness, Employee Assistance Programs: Investments, Not Costs," *Bobbin* (May 2000), pp. 42–48.

[22]John S. McClenahen, "Working with AIDS," *Industry Week* (November 17, 1997), pp. 51–52.

Wellness Programs

A **wellness program** is any organizationally sponsored event designed to keep employees healthy and to prevent problems. These programs are varied and may focus on such things as smoking cessation, weight control, stress management, physical fitness, nutrition education, and high blood pressure control.[23] In return, these programs are designed to help cut employer health costs and lower absenteeism and turnover by preventing health-related problems.[24] For instance, it is estimated that over a ten-year period, the Adolph Coors Company saved several million dollars in decreased medical premium payments, reduced sick leave, and increased productivity.

As with EAPs, wellness programs don't work unless employees view them as valuable. Unfortunately, the number of people participating in wellness programs across the United States has not been substantial. It is estimated that only about 20 percent of employees who have access to these programs actually use them.[25] Reasons cited for this low turnout include the absence of top management support and use of the programs, the limitation that entire families are not permitted to use them, and most important, a lack of employee input in determining what they want and would use. Simply put, an organization offering something we don't want will be money ill-spent.

But let's not throw wellness programs out the door. These programs are there to help you maintain your health, and you should take advantage of them whenever possible. And if your organization isn't providing what you want, you need to suggest programs that would better serve your needs. EAPs and wellness programs aren't meant to create conflict between employers and employees. Rather, they should be viewed as a win-win opportunity for both. EAPs and wellness programs are beneficial for employees in that they provide opportunities to maintain good health, and they are beneficial for organizations in that they keep productive employees on the job.

> **wellness programs** organizationally sponsored events designed to keep employees healthy and to prevent problems

Sexual Harassment

Sexual harassment is a serious issue for both you and your organization. Thousands of complaints are filed by employees each year. Not only have settlements in these cases cost companies substantial amounts of money in terms of litigation; it is estimated that sexual harassment is the single biggest financial risk facing companies today—and can result in upwards of a 30 percent decrease in a company's stock price.[26] At Mitsubishi, for example, the company paid out more than $34 million to 300 women for the rampant sexual harassment they were exposed to.[27] But the problem encompasses more than simply jury awards. Sexual harassment results in millions of dollars lost to absenteeism, low productivity, and turnover."[28] Sexual harassment, further-

[23]Stephanie L. Hyland, "Health Care Benefits Show Cost-Containment Strategies," *Monthly Labor Review* (February 1992), p. 42; and Therese R. Welter, "Wellness Programs: Not a Cure-All," *Industry Week* (February 15, 1988), p. 42.

[24]Leah Ingram, "Many Healthy Returns," *Entrepreneur* (September 1994), p. 84; and Harry Harrington, "Retiree Wellness Plan Cuts Health Costs," *Personnel Journal* (August 1990), p. 60.

[25]James W. Busbin & David P. Campbell, "Employee Wellness Programs: A Strategy for Increasing Participation," *Journal of Health Care Marketing*, vol. 10, no. 4 (December 1990), p. 22.

[26]Norman F. Foy, "Sexual Harassment Can Threaten Your Bottom Line," *Strategic Finance* (August 2000), pp. 56–57.

[27]"Federal Monitors Find Illinois Mitsubishi Unit Eradicating Harassment," *Wall Street Journal* (September 7, 2000), p. A-8.

[28]Liberty J. Munson, Charles Hulin, and Fritz Drasgow, "Longitudinal Analysis of Dispositional Influences and Sexual Harassment: Effects on Job and Psychological Outcomes," *Personnel Psychology* (Spring 2000), p. 21; and "Cost of Sexual Harassment in the U.S.," *Manpower Argus* (January 1997), p. 5.

more, is not only a U.S. phenomenon. It's a global issue. For instance, sexual harassment charges have been filed against employers in such countries as Japan, Australia, Netherlands, Belgium, New Zealand, Sweden, Ireland, and Mexico.[29] While discussions of sexual harassment cases often focus on the large awards granted by a court, there are other concerns for employers. Sexual harassment creates an unpleasant work environment for organization members and undermines their ability to perform their job. But just what is sexual harassment?

> **sexual harassment**
any unwanted activity of a sexual nature that affects an individual

Sexual harassment is any unwanted activity of a sexual nature that affects you. Sexual harassers can be either male or female and can harass individuals of the same or the opposite sex.[30] Sexual harassment exists under two conditions: (1) when such an activity results in your getting something for giving something (called *quid pro quo*) or (2) when the activity creates a hostile environment for you.[31]

> **quid pro quo**
getting something for giving something

Most would agree that *quid pro quo* instances are clear-cut cases of sexual harassment. If you fail to submit to unwelcome advances, your job, a passing grade, a promotion, or the like may be jeopardized. No person in power, such as a supervisor or instructor, should ever force another person into making such a decision. It is obviously illegal to do so. Understanding sexual harassment in the form of a hostile environment, however, is more problematic for many organizations.

> **hostile environment**
an environment in which the unwelcome actions of another create an abusive work setting for an individual

Just what is a hostile environment? (See Exhibit 5-6.) A **hostile environment** occurs when the unwelcome actions of another create an abusive work setting for a person. Unlike *quid pro quo* cases, you do not have to be threatened with the loss of a job, a poor grade, the withholding of a promotion, or the like for this type of sexual harassment to occur. Rather, if you are placed in an uncomfortable position as a result of unwanted sexual attention, you may be experiencing sexual harassment. For example,

---

[29]See, for instance, Gerald L. Maatman, Jr., "A Global View of Sexual Harassment," *HR Magazine* (July 2000), pp. 151–158; Glenda Strachan and Suzanne Jamieson, "Equal Opportunity in Australia in the 1990s," *New Zealand Journal of Industrial Relations* (October 1999), p. 319; "Mexico: Sexual Harassment in the Workplace," *Manpower Argus* (March 1997), p. 8; Susan Webb, *The Webb Report: A Newsletter on Sexual Harassment* (Seattle, Wash.: Premier, January 1994), pp. 4–7, and (April 1994), pp. 2–5.

[30]Although female-male, male-male, and female-female sexual harassment cases have been reported in the courts, the majority of sexual harassment cases still involve a male harassing a female.

[31]See, for example, Jacqueline F. Strayer & Sandra E. Rapoport, "Sexual Harassment: Limiting Corporate Liability," *Personnel* (April 1986), pp. 30–31.

Listed here are several events that occur in the world of work. Do you believe they fall under the definition of sexual harassment? If so, why? If not, why not?

1. A male supervisor makes comments regularly to his secretary about how she's dressed for the day.

2. A female supervisor asks her male employee to join her for dinner so that they have some quiet time away from work to go over his performance evaluation.

3. A student offers sexual favors to an instructor in return for a passing grade. The instructor agrees, and the student gets a passing grade.

4. A customer in a restaurant grabs the rear end of a waitress. She complains about the customer to the owner, who says, "Oh, ignore it, you'll probably get a bigger tip."

5. You willingly dated a co-worker for the past three years. Now you've met someone else and do not want to continue the relationship with your co-worker. Your co-worker does not want to end your relationship and is posting derogatory notices about you and your new friend around the workplace.

EXHIBIT 5-6
You Be the Judge

3. The main distinction between employee assistance programs and wellness programs is:
   a. Employee assistance programs focus on helping employees prevent problems. Wellness programs focus on helping employees overcome problems.
   b. Employee assistance programs focus their efforts on alcoholic employees. Wellness programs focus their efforts on other substance abusers.
   c. Employee assistance programs return $5 for every $1 invested in them. Wellness programs return only $3 for every $1 invested in them.
   d. Employee assistance programs focus on helping employees overcome their problems. Wellness programs focus on helping employees prevent problems.

4. Which one of the following situations would not be considered sexual harassment?
   a. being given a passing grade in return for sexual favors
   b. being repeatedly teased and called names because you're overweight
   c. being exposed to pinup calendars in your work setting
   d. being given a raise in exchange for wearing seductive clothing

consider what happened to an employee of Baker and McKenzie, one of the world's largest law firms, located in San Francisco.[32]

Rena Weeks was hired as a secretary by the firm. Listed among her duties was responsibility for a variety of secretarial tasks, including word processing, copying, and answering the phone. What Rena wasn't hired for, however, was to be a playmate for one of the firm's leading trademark attorneys. Yet for twenty-five days, Rena was subjected to some of the most humiliating behavior any person could imagine. For example, it was alleged that this attorney "grabbed her breast while pouring M&Ms down the front of her shirt pocket, lunged at her in the office with his arms outstretched, and grabbed her hips and pressed himself against her."[33] Needless to say, the attorney created a work environment for Rena in which she could not function productively.

Of course, what Rena Weeks experienced was unacceptable behavior for the workplace. But when Rena reported it, her complaint apparently fell on deaf ears. The members of the firm did little to help her; they neither investigated her allegations nor stopped this attorney from harassing her. Eventually, Weeks felt she had no other recourse than to quit her job. Consequently, Rena lost her source of income, and the firm lost a potentially productive employee. But Rena wasn't willing to put this experience behind her, chalking it up to good-old-boys behavior. She would not simply forget about her ordeal. Instead, Rena realized that she was not at fault for these incidents—it was her harasser and her employer that were wrong. And the courts agreed. A jury awarded Rena Weeks more than $7 million, $250,000 of which was to be paid personally by the harasser. The Weeks case and countless others have serious implications for organizations. However, for us there are two primary issues: (1) How do we protect ourselves from being sexually harassed by another, and (2) how do we determine whether something we do is offensive to another?

---

[32]Jolie Solomon & Susan Miller, "Hero or Harasser?" *Newsweek* (September 12, 1994), pp. 48–50; Seema Nayyar and Susan Miller, "Making It Easier to Strike Back," *Newsweek* (September 12, 1994), p. 50; "Jury Finds Firm Knew of Lawyer's Harassment," *The Baltimore Sun* (August 28, 1994), p. 21A; and Commerce Clearing House, "$7 Million Award Says Take Prevention Seriously," *Human Resources Management: Ideas and Trends* (September 14, 1994), p. 149.

[33]"Jury Finds Firm Knew of Lawyer's Harassment," p. 21A.

Protecting Yourself from Sexual Harassment

1. **Know the organization's policy on sexual harassment.** Almost all organizations, large and small, public and private, have some sort of sexual harassment policy. Get a copy of that policy—it's often printed in your employee or student handbook. Learn what your organization considers inappropriate behavior.

2. **Let the offending individual know specifically which behaviors you consider harassment.** Sometimes things are said or done inadvertently or in jest. If that happens to you, let the person know you're offended by his or her behavior and that it constitutes sexual harassment. Also let the person know exactly what you will do if he or she harasses you again.

3. **Document offensive behavior.** Even things said or done in jest should be documented. Record the day, date, and time of the offensive behavior. List the names of people who may have witnessed the incident. Keep this information in a safe place. If the behavior stops, you won't need this data. But if the behavior continues, you'll have documentation to support your case.

4. **If the harassment is repeated, file a complaint.** You need to seek help. In your handbook is the name of the designated contact person. This person may be someone in human resources in a business or corporation or the dean of students at a university. Go immediately to the contact person with your documentation. In many places, if you fail to file a complaint within a specific time period, you lose your right to do so. After receiving your written complaint, the contact person should begin an immediate investigation.

5. **Keep documentation of your work record, such as tests, performance appraisals, and any other official personnel actions affecting you.** If after an incident when you refused to submit to unwelcome sexual advances, you begin to get more unfavorable evaluations or lower test grades, you then have solid and indisputable evidence of *quid pro quo* sexual harassment.

6. **Seek help from an attorney if you're not satisfied with what the organization has done in response to your complaint**. Remember, sexual harassment is a legal matter. You may need legal help. Don't overlook the fact that it may come down to your word against that of the harasser and the organization. Don't expect the organization to play anything but hardball. For your own protection, seek legal advice.

7. **Keep your spirits high.** You're entering one of the more difficult times you'll ever face in an organization, especially if the harasser is the boss or owner. You'll feel emotional, stressed, and badgered at times. Be aware that almost everyone in the organization will know what is happening—even though the charge and the investigation are both supposed to be confidential. Don't expect the harasser to accept responsibility for his or her behavior. You're in a battle that could last for months or even years if it goes to the court. Therefore, be sure to seek help from others—family, friends, support groups, professionals, and so on. Remember, it's not your fault!

Sources: Adapted from Clifford M. Keon, Jr., "Sexual Harassment Claims Stem from a Hostile Work Environment," *Personnel Journal* (August 1990), pp. 97–98; Martha E. Eller, "Sexual Harassment: Prevention, Not Protection," *The Cornell H.R.A. Quarterly* (February 1990), p. 87; Maureen P. Woods and Walter J. Flynn, "Heading Off Sexual Harassment," *Personnel* (November 1989), p. 48; and Jacqueline F. Strayer and Sandra E. Rapoport, "Sexual Harassment: Limiting Corporate Liability," *Personnel* (April 1986), pp. 32–33.

Sexual harassment is often likened to a power game. It is not sex, but one's desire to exert his or her power to control you.[34] Most of us, as students or employees beginning our careers, are vulnerable to those who make decisions about us. If they use sex as a means of exploiting us, it's a difficult thing for us to handle. But we don't have to submit to their demands. Rather, we can fight back and stand up for our rights. It's often not easy and, in many cases, it's your word against theirs. If you read Michael Crichton's book *Disclosure* (or saw the movie), you'll recognize that alleging sexual harassment against a supervisor is, at best, an uphill battle. But it's not an impossible task. There are many things you can do to protect yourself from sexual harassment. (See the Skills Checklist.)

When unwanted sexual advances or innuendoes exist, the course of action is clear. But what about the less obvious situation, the hostile environment? For instance, does the use of sexually explicit language in the classroom or the office create a hostile environment? How about telling off-color jokes at work or school or displaying nude pictures of people in the dorm or office? It depends on whether anyone is offended. We all must be attuned to what makes others—classmates or fellow employees—uncomfortable. If you don't know what that may be, then ask. And if you are asked to stop some behavior that offends someone (a blind spot revealed), comply immediately. Success in today's organization will, in part, reflect how sensitive you are toward others—your ability to apply effective human relations skills.

[34]Brian S. Moskal, "Sexual Harassment: An Update," *Industry Week* (November 18, 1991), p. 18.

SUMMARY

This summary corresponds to the Learning Outcomes found on page 100.

1. Stress is something individuals feel when they are faced with opportunities, constraints, or demands that they perceive to be both uncertain and important. Chronic, long-term stress can lead to burnout.

2. Type A personalities are time driven, aggressive, and competitive and have a strong desire for achievement. Type B people are relaxed, easygoing, even-tempered, flexible, and friendly.

3. Role overload exists when one has more work than time in which to complete it. Role conflict exists when an individual is torn between two or more major responsibilities, such as work and family. Role ambiguity exists when individuals are unclear about and don't understand what is expected of them.

4. Several recommended stress reduction strategies include assessing yourself, being flexible, being positive, not letting people get to you, getting some exercise, seeking help from someone else, and planning your activities.

5. Time management strategies can reduce stress by empowering individuals to face tasks that they perceive to be both uncertain and important. Effective time management strategies help individuals schedule their personal and professional lives, take control of their own life activities, and balance the requirements of both work and play.

6. Six steps for better time management are identifying your time wasters, making a list of things to do, prioritizing your To Do list, scheduling your day, preparing yourself for work, and following the four D strategies.

7. When overindulgence in alcohol reduces one's ability to function effectively, that person is an alcoholic. As alcoholism progresses, the person's behavior becomes more erratic. Alcoholics are moody, forgetful, and often argumentative.

8. Employee assistance programs (EAPs) are designed to help employees overcome their personal problems. By having employees work out their problems with knowledgeable people in the EAP, the employer can get these once-productive employees back on the job as soon as possible.

9. Wellness programs are organization-sponsored events that are designed to keep employees healthy and prevent problems from occurring. They include programs on such topics as smoking cessation, weight control, blood pressure control, stress management, and physical fitness.

10. Sexual harassment is any unwanted sexual activity that affects an individual. Sexual harassment can exist when this unwanted activity is required for getting something (*quid pro quo*) or when it creates a hostile environment for the individual.

REVIEWING YOUR UNDERSTANDING

1. Identify three causes of stress in your life and describe what you are doing to reduce it.

2. "Type A individuals are better suited for the work world. They are driven and like to succeed, just as a business needs to be." Do you agree or disagree with this statement? Explain your position.

3. Do you believe people can actually work themselves to death? Support your position.

4. Explain how you might experience role conflict, role ambiguity, and role overload as a college student. Give examples.

5. How can you manage your time better?

6. Which is more problematic for an organization, an employee who abuses alcohol or one who abuses an illegal substance? Why?

7. Give three reasons why an organization might start an employee assistance program for its employees.

8. How is a wellness program different from an employee assistance program?

9. Under what conditions can sexual harassment exist? What would you do if you were sexually harassed?

10. In your opinion, what creates a hostile environment?

ANSWERS TO CHECKING YOUR UNDERSTANDING

1. c **2.** a **3.** d **4.** b

LEARNING TOGETHER

A. Form three teams in the class. Have each team identify and discuss the characteristics associated with one of the main types of stress symptoms—physiological, psychological, and behavioral—and prepare a debate strategy that the group's symptom is "worse" than the other two. After each team presents its case, conduct a debate of the issue.

B. With two or three classmates, design what you believe would be a good employee assistance program for a local business or for your school. Collect facts from library sources, local businesses, school records, and so on to help you identify the measures that will be effective and that can be implemented with reasonable resources. Be sure you can support your recommendations.

Dealing with Difficulties

Mike Jasmine and Richard Alderman have been best friends since before grade school. In high school they did nearly everything together—both were on the basketball team, debate team, and school newspaper staff. Mike and Richard liked similar music and both played in the school marching band. It was almost ironic that both even made similar grades and were senior class officers. Now that they are in college, Mike and Richard share an apartment and both have part-time jobs.

But that is where similarities between Mike and Richard end. Mike has decided he wants to be an accountant. He likes math and enjoys working out solutions to find a better way to do things. He enjoys working crossword puzzles and sometimes can't put them down until he has them completely solved. He likes to cook, but he has two rules for others to follow when he is in charge in the kitchen: (1) cleanup must be done as you go along and (2) no one can sit down to eat until the kitchen is tidy. Mike likes to keep the apartment in an orderly fashion too. Mike seems to be having more difficulty studying and finding time to just stay up with things.

Richard is extremely creative and likes to daydream. He thinks he will pursue a career in commercial art. He frequently will get an idea that he will sketch out on any piece of paper he can find—the back of an envelope, a scrap piece of paper, the margin of a book, or a napkin. One can find Richard's bits of creative thought nearly anywhere in the apartment, especially in his room. He has things scattered on his desk, table, chair, and the floor. Things are pinned to walls, curtains, and doors. He even has a haystack of papers and books piled in his closet. Richard also likes to cook and is very creative in his cuisine, but he drives Mike crazy in the kitchen. Mike is sure that Richard uses every dish in the kitchen when he cooks. Richard is pretty good at cleanup, but sometimes it doesn't get done until the next day.

Questions

1. Why are Mike and Richard having some difficulty coexisting in an apartment even though they have known each other and have been friends for nearly their entire lives?

2. What Type A and B personality characteristics may be creating some tension between Mike and Richard? What can they do about them?

3. What are some of the symptoms of stress for (a) Mike and (b) Richard? What types of physiological, psychological, or behavioral stress symptoms may be present with each of them?

4. Identify some ways Mike and Richard could reduce their stress.

5. Could Mike and Richard benefit from some good time management advice? What advice would you give to each of them?

part three

ORGANIZATIONAL BEHAVIOR

chapter

6

ORGANIZATIONAL STRUCTURES

Most of us will spend a portion, if not all, of our careers working for others. We will perform our jobs in organizations that have some unique and some common characteristics. Part II looked at human behavior by viewing the individual as an entity, exploring personal communications and addressing some areas related to dealing with personal issues. In Part III, in order to better understand organizational behavior, we will view the organization as an entity, explore organizational communications, and address some areas related to dealing with organizational issues. Part three contains three chapters:

chapter **6**

ORGANIZATIONAL STRUCTURES

chapter **7**

ORGANIZATIONAL COMMUNICATIONS

chapter **8**

POWER, POLITICS, AND STATUS

*L*earning Outcomes

After reading this chapter, you will be able to:

1. Identify the components of organizational structure.

2. Define *adhocracy*.

3. Identify four classical principles that guide how employees are grouped.

4. Describe the advantages and disadvantages of standardized jobs.

5. Compare authority and responsibility.

6. Identify the strengths and weaknesses of grouping employees by the products they produce.

7. Explain what the term *matrix* means.

8. Define a simple structure and identify its strengths.

9. Explain what is meant by the term *horizontal organization*.

10. Describe how flatter structures benefit employees at work.

In the 1920s and 1930s, as organizations got bigger and more formal, managers felt a need to provide more coordination of activities and tighter control over operations. Early management theorists argued that formal bureaucracies would best serve the company. That was true sixty or more years ago; these bureaucratic structures flourished. But by the 1980s, our world was changing. The global marketplace, rapid technological advancements, diversity in the workforce, and socioeconomic conditions were making a formal bureaucratic structure inefficient and inappropriate for many businesses. As a result, since the late 1980s, most organizations have restructured to be more customer- and market-oriented and to increase productivity.

It's critical today for an organization to have the right structure. Although setting up the organization's structure is typically done by top management in an organization (or the owner in a small business), it's important for us to understand how these structures work. Why? Because each of us works in some type of structure, and we need to know why we are arranged as we are. For example, will we be grouped with people who perform essentially the same jobs as we do? Will we work together to produce a specific product? Will we be grouped according to the customer we serve or where we are geographically? Or will we see some combination of these factors? In this chapter, then, we'll look at the traditional components that go into developing a structure, discuss the various ways that we may be grouped, address the value systems of organizations, and look at how organizational structures change over time.

Common Components of Organizational Structure

*E*very organization—large or small, for-profit or not-for-profit—has a structure. Some organizations, such as General Motors or IBM, are very formalized. Others, such as small businesses, have structures that are less formalized and very simple. The organization may be described by its organizational framework, which is called the **organizational structure.** Just as we have skeletons that define our shapes, organizations have structures that define theirs. And similar to the bones, organs, and flesh that support our lives, organization structures are supported by their complexity, formalization, and centralization. (See Exhibit 6-1.) Let's introduce each of these and contrast them in a fictional scenario between you and your brother. Some background information, obviously, is in order. Your brother and you have each decided to open up a fast-food hamburger restaurant. Your brother has opted to spend $600,000 to buy into a McDonald's franchise, whereas you have decided to do it on your own. How will the structures of your brother's restaurant business differ from the structures of your business in terms of complexity, formalization, and centralization?

> **organizational structure**
> an organization's framework

Complexity

The **complexity** of an organization refers to the number of differences that exist in the organization. These differences can revolve around a variety of specialized jobs that are required to produce a good or service, the number of levels that exist in the organization, or how geographically widespread the organization is. For instance, your brother's restaurant will have a number of specialized jobs, as prescribed by the franchise agreement. There will be supervisors, store managers, day-shift and night-shift managers, cooks, wiper-uppers, and customer service representatives. Your brother will also have someone who specializes in children's birthday parties—the same person who keeps the playground equipment safe. You, on the other hand, are starting from scratch. You can develop your jobs any way you want. You can have people doing a variety of tasks and not specializing in any one aspect. In fact, you may be doing a lot of these things yourself. In such a case, the complexity at your hamburger restaurant would be low, your brother's high.

> **complexity**
> the number of differences that exist in an organization

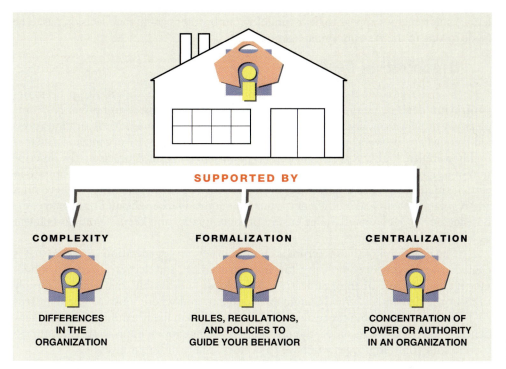

EXHIBIT 6-1
Components of a Structure

Formalization

The second component of an organization's structure is its **formalization.** Formalization refers to how many rules, regulations, and policies exist to guide your behavior. The more do's and don'ts that exist, the more formalized the organization has chosen to be. Much of the McDonald's Corporation's success has been attributed to its standardized ways of doing things. Buy a hamburger in Berlin, Germany, or Berlin, Maryland, and you'll notice something strikingly similar. The food tastes the same. People who own McDonald's franchises spend considerable time learning the McDonald's way. Cooking food, buying supplies, and even advertising all follow rigid rules. Your hamburger shop, however, is starting from scratch. It's up to you to put in place what regulations, if any, you want. And the fewer that you have, the less formalized your organization will be.

➤ **formalization**
the rules, regulations, and policies that exist to guide behavior

Centralization

The last component of organization structure, called **centralization,** describes the concentration of power or authority in an organization. Decisions can generally be made in one of two areas. First, they can be centralized decisions—that is, made primarily by management. Here, management makes all major decisions that affect your work, such as where the organization is headed, the products produced, your work hours, and how you should do your job. For example, your brother's franchise requires him to purchase napkins and other supplies from approved suppliers. Even if he might be able to get supplies cheaper elsewhere, he can't. That decision has been made for him. On the other hand, decisions can be decentralized. Decentralized decisions, though the opposite of centralized ones, do not mean that employees make all the decisions. Instead, decentralization means that those closest to the problem make the call. For example, you might have a cook in your restaurant who may refuse to accept a produce delivery because the

➤ **centralization**
a concentration of power or authority in an organization

lettuce and tomatoes appear to be rotting. In your brother's shop, that decision has to be made by one of the restaurant managers.

Organization Design

> **organization design**
> implementation of various degrees of complexity, formalization, and centralization to form an organization's structure

*W*henever someone shapes an organization's structure, we call this process **organization design.** In implementing various degrees of the three components—complexity, formalization, and centralization—a structure is formed. Most organizations fall somewhere between two extremes. The first extreme is an organization that is highly complex, highly formalized, and very centralized. This is precisely the description of a bureaucracy, as discussed in Chapter 1. Bureaucracies can be appropriate in certain situations. Where there is a greater need for tight coordination, or where rules and regulations help foster efficiency, a bureaucracy can be beneficial. For instance, the bureaucracy of McDonald's helps ensure product quality and keep overall costs lower by buying in quantity.

> **adhocracy**
> an organizational structure that is characterized as low in complexity, low in formalization, and decentralized

The other end of the spectrum is an **adhocracy,** an organization structure that is characterized as low in complexity, low in formalization, and decentralized. An adhocracy is characteristic of an organization that is loose and flexible, that changes rapidly to meet the demands of the dynamic environment, and where jobs are not standardized. Your startup hamburger restaurant would more than likely exhibit adhocratic tendencies. You need, for instance, the flexibility to change menu items to serve your customers, and your employees will have to perform many different tasks.

Rarely are organizations totally adhocratic or bureaucratic. Most organizations are somewhere between the two extremes. Most of us today would probably prefer to work in organizations that are more adhocratic than bureaucratic. Unfortunately, until the 1990s most organizations were still more bureaucratic than adhocratic. We'll look shortly at these different structures and the movement in the 1990s away from bureaucracies.

Classical concepts of organization structures were first formulated in the 1940s as a set of principles for organization design. More than six decades have passed since most of these principles were originally proposed. Given the passing of that much time and all the changes that have taken place in our society, you might think that these principles would be worthless today. Surprisingly, they're not—although they may not be as strong as they were in the middle of the last century. Nonetheless, for the most part, these classical concepts still provide valuable insights into how our organizations are designed.

We'll look at four basic classical principles that have guided organization design decisions over the years: standardized jobs, chain of command, authority and responsibility, and span of control.

Standardized Jobs

> **standardized job**
> a job broken down into a number of steps, with each step being completed by a separate individual

Standardized jobs have been around for centuries in the United States. In fact, in the 1700s the economist Adam Smith published his book *Wealth of Nations*, in which he advocated that jobs should be divided into smaller parts. A **standardized job** is a job broken down into a number of steps, with each step being completed by a separate individual. Rather than employees doing an entire activity from start to finish, individuals specialize in doing part of it rather than the entire activity. Assembly-line production, for instance, in which each worker does the same task over and over again, is an example of standardization. Likewise, the specific tasks performed by the cooks each time at your brother's McDonald's restaurant represent task standardization.

With standardized jobs, employees become experts at what they do. Standardization makes the most of the skills of employees. In most professions—medicine, retail, the arts, business—some tasks require employees to develop specialized skills. If you were engaged in every step of, say, directing a movie, you would require the skills necessary to perform both the most demanding and the least demanding jobs. The result would be that, except when performing the most highly skilled or highly sophisticated tasks, you would be working below your skill level. That's why you rarely, if ever, find a cardiac surgeon closing up a patient after surgery. Those not as skilled in open-heart surgery, or those learning the skill, are more apt to stitch and staple the patient after the surgeon has performed bypass surgery. Because skilled workers are often paid more than unskilled workers, it represents an inefficient use of resources to pay them to do easy tasks. That's why your college has a maintenance crew to periodically sweep the classroom, empty the trash, and wash the blackboards. Paying faculty to do these chores is not the best use of faculty time, nor is it money well spent.

Early proponents of standardized jobs recognized that this system of work assignment could lead to an unending source of increased productivity. That's why your brother's McDonald's restaurant uses such a system. Many other organizations responded in kind. But a good thing can be carried too far. There is a point at which standardization leads to boredom, fatigue, stress, low productivity, poor quality, increased absenteeism, and high turnover. (See Exhibit 6-2.) That's precisely the point the early human relations advocates made. (See Chapter 1.)

Chain of Command

Imagine sitting in class for some twelve to fifteen weeks, taking notes from your instructor. During this time, you notice that your professor stresses certain material that is presented in the book, as well as other material that doesn't come from the book. You reason that if your instructor spends three or so hours a week lecturing on certain topics, that

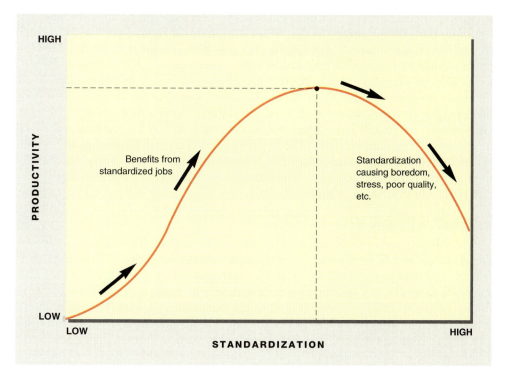

EXHIBIT 6-2
Standardized Jobs and Productivity

material will probably show up on the test. Then, come test day, you're given the exam. It has nothing to do with what was being emphasized in lectures. Furthermore, you find out that your instructor had no input into the test. All he does is lecture; someone else tests you. Is this being fair? Probably not. And early writers felt the same way about organizational design. Employees shouldn't serve more than one master.

Early management theorists argued that employees (or students, for that matter) should be responsible to one and only one person. Your brother's franchise has clear lines of authority defining who is in charge and who answers to whom. Early management theorists called this principle **chain of command.** You shouldn't report to two or more bosses. If you do, you might have to cope with conflicting demands or priorities from several supervisors.

> **chain of command**
> clear lines of authority defining who is in charge and who answers to whom

But the reality in organizations today may reflect something quite different. The flexibility that you may need to survive in your job might require you to have several supervisors. You may have key people helping you manage your restaurant. Other employees might be expected to take orders from all of them—even if at times the orders from different managers appear conflicting. The business may just demand multiple managers for certain tasks. Even in the classroom, you may see some courses being team-taught. Students, therefore, may be accountable to more than one instructor. All your instructors should have input into evaluating your work—evaluating you primarily on what you did for them. The key for your success is the degree to which your instructors communicate and collaborate. The same is true for employees. The key for their success is also the degree to which their supervisors communicate and collaborate regarding the task to be done.

Authority and Responsibility

> **authority**
> the rights inherent in a job to give orders and expect the orders to be obeyed

Authority refers to the rights inherent in a job to give orders and expect the orders to be obeyed. Your instructor, for example, has the authority to develop her syllabus and to hold you accountable to it. Her authority comes to her because of the job she holds. Both you and your brother have authority in managing your businesses. Authority relates to one's position. It ignores personal characteristics. For example, the expression "The king is dead; long live the king" illustrates the concept of authority. Whoever is king acquires the rights inherent in the king's position. When a position of authority is vacated, the person who has left the position no longer has any authority. So when the semester is over, your instructor no longer has authority over you. When your employees quit—to go to school or to work for someone else—you no longer have authority over them either.

Although authority gives you some control over things around you, it doesn't come free. Instead, where there's authority, there's responsibility. **Responsibility** refers to an obligation to do what is expected. For example, you may have the authority to require your hamburger employees to do certain tasks, but you are also responsible for giving them the tools to do their job. Asking the cook to cook without grilling utensils will only lead to low productivity and low quality of work. The two must go hand in hand. Authority with no responsibility can lead to abuse. If you have the authority to spend money in your organization, but don't have to answer to anyone for how you spend it—such as those who lent you the money—you could be using the money for things other than what was intended. That is not responsible. Likewise, being held responsible for something you don't control can create problems. That's why

> **responsibility**
> an obligation to do what is expected

UNLOCKING YOUR POTENTIAL *6-1*

Understanding Authority

*A*uthority is something most of us recognize. It gives someone the right to ask us to do something. But how do we view those requests? Here are several statements asking you to respond either "Agree" or "Disagree." Although there might be situations where you could choose either answer, don't read into the statements. Answer based on your initial reaction.

	Agree	*Disagree*
1. I do whatever my supervisor asks me to do while I'm at work.	___	___
2. If, in wartime, my commanding officer ordered me to shoot civilian men and women to protect my fellow troops, I would follow that order.	___	___
3. Pending a possible investigation by college officials, I would destroy evidence of wrongdoing if my resident assistant asked me to.	___	___
4. If before class my instructor asked me to purchase a soda for him, I would do so.	___	___
5. Even though my instructor requires a term paper for passing the course, I won't do it if I don't feel like doing it.	___	___
6. I believe that my supervisor should only ask me to do things that I find morally acceptable.	___	___
7. I do things when asked even if I think they are dumb to do.	___	___
8. If I asked people working for me to do something and they didn't, I'd consider their refusal insubordination.	___	___
9. No one has a right to tell me what to do—at work or in class.	___	___
10. I would question my supervisor if I didn't agree with a request made of me.	___	___

you sometimes get upset over class group projects—even if you picked your group—when one grade is awarded to every member of the group. Everyone in the group is responsible for completing the assignment as given by the professor. However, whether or not someone has done his or her fair share, that person still receives the same grade you do. If, on the other hand, group members had not only the responsibility for the assignment completion, but also had the authority to eliminate a poorly performing group member, then perhaps the individual's level of effort might change.

In organizations, there are generally two types of authority: line authority and staff authority. **Line authority** is the authority that entitles a supervisor to direct an individual's work. It is the classic employer–employee authority relationship that extends from the top of the organization to the worker population, following what is called the chain of command. Another type of authority, **staff authority,** is the authority in positions created to support, assist, advise, and generally reduce informational burdens of supervisors. As organizations grew larger and more complex, supervisors found that they did not have the time, expertise, or resources to get their jobs done effectively. In response, positions with staff authority were created. The president of your college, for example, can't effectively handle all the requirements of providing assistance to students, so a number of departments exist. These departments, such as health services and financial aid, are considered staff functions and the personnel in those positions primarily possess staff authority. The head of the health services department does, of

▶ **line authority**
the authority that entitles a supervisor to direct an individual's work

▶ **staff authority**
authority in positions created to support, assist, advise, and generally reduce informational burdens of supervisors

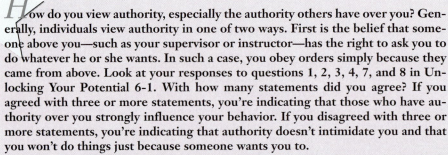

KEYS TO UNLOCKING YOUR POTENTIAL *6-1*

*H*ow do you view authority, especially the authority others have over you? Generally, individuals view authority in one of two ways. First is the belief that someone above you—such as your supervisor or instructor—has the right to ask you to do whatever he or she wants. In such a case, you obey orders simply because they came from above. Look at your responses to questions 1, 2, 3, 4, 7, and 8 in Unlocking Your Potential 6-1. With how many statements did you agree? If you agreed with three or more statements, you're indicating that those who have authority over you strongly influence your behavior. If you disagreed with three or more statements, you're indicating that authority doesn't intimidate you and that you won't do things just because someone wants you to.

The second belief regarding authority is that we won't do something simply because a boss or supervisor asked, but rather because we are willing to do it. Look at questions 5, 6, 9, and 10. If you agreed with three of the four statements, you are indicating that you have the final decision in what you choose to do. That is, you'll go so far as to disobey a request if (1) you find the request immoral, (2) you don't understand what was asked, (3) you believe that what you are being asked to do will hurt the organization in achieving its goals if you comply, or (4) you are unable to mentally and physically accept the challenge. Refusing to do something because you object to it, however, does not mean that your decision will be acceptable to your boss. You may suffer some negative consequence for your refusal. But, for you, the consequence is less objectionable for not doing what was requested than for doing what was requested.

Each of us has a range of authority acceptance. Yes, maybe you find getting the instructor a soda objectionable, but it's really no big deal. So you do it. In that case, it's not blindly accepting the instructor's request; it's just that you don't find it highly unacceptable. However, you'll more than likely refuse any request that is out of your range of acceptance and is unacceptable to you.

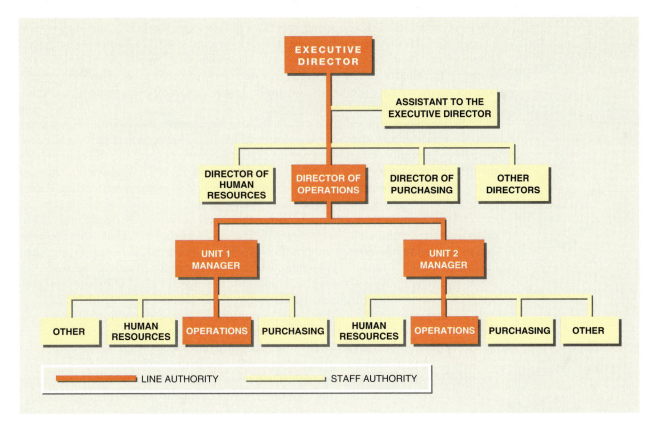

EXHIBIT 6-3
Line Versus Staff Authority

course, have line authority over her support staff, but she has only staff authority over employees outside the department. The president might also find that he is overburdened with legal and political issues. Thus, he needs an assistant. In creating the position of assistant to the president, he has created another staff authority position. Exhibit 6-3 illustrates line and staff authority.

Span of Control

How many employees can your supervisor effectively direct? Can you and your brother manage twenty-five employees each in your hamburger restaurants? Can an instructor be as effective in a large lecture hall teaching 250 students as one who teaches a class of 18? These types of questions focus on the issue of the **span of control,** the range of control or authority. Although there is no consensus on a specific number for an ideal span of control, early management writers favored small spans—typically no more than six—in order to maintain tight control. In schools, for instance, class sizes traditionally averaged in the range of eighteen to twenty-four students. But these numbers are not the same throughout the organization. Individuals at the top levels in the organization often face new and unique problems. Therefore, they need to supervise fewer people so that they can devote their attention to problem solving. At lower levels in the organization, problems that arise are often routine and recurring. Not a lot of thought has to go into solving them—the answers are usually in some manual. Accordingly, the span of control at the lower levels of an organization tends to be larger. So you as owner of a business might have three key people reporting directly to

> **span of control**
> range of control or authority

you. And each of these three people may have ten to twelve workers reporting to them. Likewise, classes that have significant lab work or one-on-one evaluation—such as biology or student-teacher supervision—may have class sizes ranging from eight to ten students. On the other hand, introductory courses in economics or psychology and courses where tests are predominantly multiple-choice can often accommodate significantly larger class sizes.

Beliefs about an ideal span of control also have changed over time. Toward the end of the last century, there was a widespread tendency for organizations to eliminate or reduce the number of middle-level managers and, thereby, increase the span of control for the remaining supervisors. For instance, back in 1992, Wal-Mart surpassed Sears as the number-one retailer in the United States. Management writer Tom Peters predicted this result a few years earlier: "Sears doesn't have a chance," he said. "A twelve-layer company can't compete with a three-layer company."[1] Peters might have exaggerated the point a bit, but it clearly reflects the fact that in recent years the pendulum has swung toward structures with wider spans of control. For example, the span of control at such companies as General Electric and Reynolds Metals has expanded to ten or twelve employees—twice the number of fifteen years ago.[2] Why the increase? Simple—it's more efficient. Just consider your college. If one faculty member can teach eighty students in one class rather than the traditional thirty to forty students per class, there's a major cost savings. With tight budgets, legislators in many states have forced state colleges to increase class size rather than hire new faculty members.

Most of you will be working in organizations with a wide span of control. Increasingly, you will be working with more people and, thus, have more interactions with others. As spans of control continue to grow throughout present-day organizations, you will be expected to deal effectively with more peers than anytime in the past. That simply means that the need for you to develop and use effective human relations skills is becoming even more important as time passes.

Grouping Employees at Work

*T*here have been debates for decades regarding the best ways for employees to be grouped. Some have focused on the efficiencies and coordination of having people who perform like activities working under the supervision of a single individual. Others felt that employees would better reach organizational goals if all people involved in producing a particular good were brought together under one roof. And there were those who said that a combination of both grouping methods might prove to be better. Realistically, no single method of grouping employees is best. Consequently, how you will be grouped will reflect a structure that best contributes to the attainment of the organization's objectives and the goals of individual supervisors. It may also be a reflection of a country's culture. Let's look, then, at three basic organizational groupings—by the job, by the product, and by a matrix approach—and identify the strengths and weaknesses of each of these grouping methods.

By Jobs Performed

One of the most popular ways to group employees is by the jobs they perform. For example, you might be part of an organization that separates jobs into engineer-

---

[1]Quoted in Jim Braham, "Money Talks," *Industry Week* (April 17, 1989), p. 23.
[2]John S. McClenahen, "Managing More People in the 90s," *Industry Week* (March 20, 1989), p. 30. See also A. Bernstein, S. Jackson, and J. Byrne, "Jack Cracks the Whip Again," *Business Week* (December 15, 1997), pp. 34–35.

The way employees are grouped in an organization will relate to the environment an organization faces. That environment need not involve simply technological changes or the uncertainty that exists. It also includes the culture of the country in which the organization is located. An organization operating overseas should group employees according to cultural characteristics in that society.*

For example, in a country where government leaders are all-powerful, decisions will more than likely be centralized. When the culture advocates many rules and regulations to direct its citizens' behavior, formalization in organizations should also be high. French and Italian organizations tend to be bureaucratic, grouping employees by the jobs they perform and coordinating and controlling the operations through high degrees of complexity, formalization, and centralization. Organizations in a country like Germany, however, group employees according to patterns with a high degree of formalization and a low level of centralization. Employees in these organizations possess the authority to make decisions that affect their work.

The extensive use of teams in a country like Japan is explainable and expected, given Japan's national culture. A society built on taking care of one another and focusing on the large group supports structures that are simpler. Teams reinforce collective responsibility. However, in India, where strong country leaders rule, teams probably wouldn't work well. Employees are accustomed to being closely supervised on the job in India. Thus more authority-dominated structures are likely to be found there.

What do these cultural variables mean to us? As we discussed in Chapter 2, "When in Rome, do as the Romans do." If we work for organizations abroad, we must adjust our level of conformity in light of the culture within the organization and the characteristics of the surrounding society. Even if we leave behind an organization that groups us in ways we prefer and thrive under, we expect others to necessarily honor our preferences in a different organization and culture. It just doesn't work that way. We need to assess the situation we are in and behave accordingly.

*Ilan Vertinsky, David K. Tse, Donald Wehrung, and Kam-hon Lee, "Organizational Design and Management Norms: A Comparative Study of Managers' Perceptions in the People's Republic of China, Hong Kong, and Canada," *Journal of Management* (December 1990), pp. 853–867.

ing, accounting, manufacturing, human resources, and purchasing departments. (See Exhibit 6-4.) These separations reflect the standardized jobs performed in each grouping. This type of structure, often the most common you'll find, can be used in all types of organizations. Only the functions change to reflect the organization's objectives and activities. For instance, a hospital might have departments devoted to research, patient care, accounting and so forth. A professional football franchise might have departments for player personnel, ticket sales, and travel and accommodations, whereas a university might have departments of education, philosophy, history and economics.

The Strengths.   The primary strength of grouping employees by the work they perform lies in the advantages that employers get from specialization. Putting like work activities together results in economies of scale. That is, repeating the same work

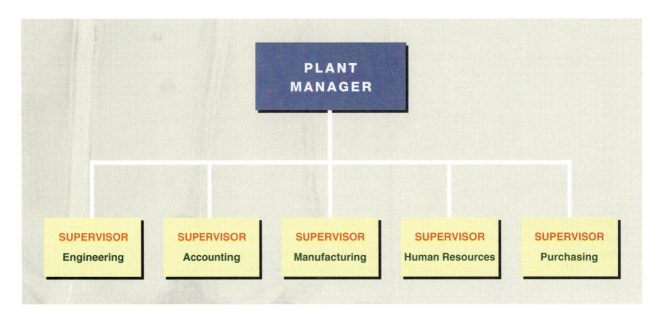

EXHIBIT 6-4

An Example of Grouping Employees by Jobs Performed

activity over and over again makes employees experts at what they do. Consequently, employees can, up to a point, become more proficient at their jobs, and thus more productive. For example, your instructors have a level of expertise in a particular field. That expertise allows them to become specialized in their fields. That knowledge base can then be taught to you. Imagine, however, if one of your instructors had to teach beginning piano, physics, geography, and history of modern culture. It's doubtful that he could be an expert in each of these areas. Accordingly, if teaching all these classes were required of him, he'd be less productive.

Grouping individuals by the work they do also helps the organization minimize duplication of jobs and equipment. If you have three employees who are responsible for unloading and storing shipped supplies, you need to provide only those employees with back braces. If all twelve of your employees were expected to do the same, you'd have to purchase extra braces. Similarly, in other organizations that group employees by the work they do, you can expect that accounting work is done only by those in accounting, sales by only those in marketing, research and development by only those in R&D, and so on. Work is done once, and only once, by a specialized group.

Finally, grouping people this way makes them more comfortable and satisfied because it gives them the opportunity to speak the same language as their peers. When employees can communicate effectively, the potential for conflicts is reduced, as is the associated stress that may accompany poor communications. In essence, grouping individuals by the job they do fosters a positive human relations atmosphere. What's more, because they speak the same language, their communications are more efficient. A group of workers who do relatively the same things can develop and use a shorthand version of communications. The group often devises its own acronyms, which facilitate the speed of communications. For instance, just look at your brother's McDonald's restaurant. Customers don't have to say "I want a Quarter Pounder with cheese, fries, and a soda" to order these. Instead, they say, "I want a Number 2 Value Meal." Everyone at McDonald's knows precisely what that is. Go to your local Blockbuster video store and ask for a Number 2, and you'll probably get a blank stare (if you're not thrown out of the store).

The Weaknesses.   There's no question that grouping people by their work has many positive things associated with it. That's the primary reason organizations have done it that way for decades. But such a structure is not without its drawbacks. The most obvious weakness is that the organization frequently loses sight of its best interests in the pursuit of group goals. That is, no one group is totally responsible for results. They become insulated and have little understanding of what people in other groups are doing. Because only top managers can generally see the whole picture, their job becomes primarily concerned with coordination. That's why there are high degrees of formalization in a bureaucracy. Furthermore, the variety of interests, perspectives, and talents that exist in different groups can result in continual conflict between them. Each tries to show how important it is. We tend to focus on what makes us look good— even if it's at the expense of another group. In business, that's the classic conflict between marketing and manufacturing. Salespeople are evaluated and rewarded on how much they sell. So they sell all they can, in any configuration that the customer wants— whether or not manufacturing can produce what is being sold or what has been promised. Instead of looking at things as members of the same organization, one lays blame on the other. That's often a lose–lose–lose situation—for the organization, its members, and its customers.

Another weakness associated with grouping individuals by the jobs they perform is that it provides little or no training for future positions of greater responsibility. If a person works in a rather narrow segment of the organization, how will he or she be in a position to ever understand what goes on elsewhere? A hamburger cook who never ran the cash register will be lost if that task is ever required. Sometimes, people can become too much of an expert, which could also be an obstacle. That's why in Japan, for example, workers are trained in everyone else's job. The issue is not that someone could jump in and do the job one day with the same level of proficiency as someone who has been doing it for years. Instead, if the situation ever arose, the replacement at least is not totally lost. It's taken some time, but that concept is starting to be used in jobs in the United States.

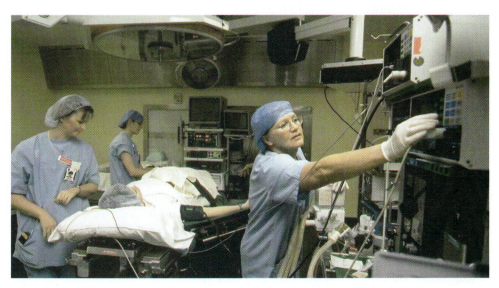

At Sweden's Kardinsla Hospital, employees are grouped by their specialties. Here an operating-room team prepares a patient for surgery. When the surgery is over, the patient will be turned over to another group of specialists—recovery room nurses.

3. Which statement about authority and responsibility is most correct?
   a. Authority and responsibility are the same.
   b. Authority refers to rights inherent in one's job. Responsibility is the obligation to do what is expected.
   c. Responsibility refers to the rights inherent in one's job to get work completed. Authority is the obligation to supervisors to do what is expected.
   d. Responsibility without authority, or authority without responsibility, is rare and can never create organizational difficulties.

4. Which one of the following is not a strength of grouping employees by the jobs they do?
   a. Grouping employees by the jobs they do helps focus work activities on organizational goals.
   b. Grouping employees by the jobs they do minimizes duplication of work activities.
   c. Grouping employees by the jobs they do enhances communication among departmental members.
   d. Grouping employees by the jobs they do creates more skilled experts among the workforce.

Finally, let's go back to the issue of efficient communication. Yes, you are more efficient using jargon with your work group, but you have to interact with others more and more in today's organizations. If you are so accustomed to speaking in your group's terms and acronyms, and continue to do so, others will be lost or confused by what you say. For example, when we talk with our peers about EEO, ERISA, ADA, PI, and the like, they understand. Such terms are second nature to us. But if your background or work group doesn't deal with Equal Employment Opportunity (EEO), the Employee Retirement and Income Security Act (ERISA), the Americans with Disabilities Act (ADA), or Programmed Instruction (PI), you won't have a clue about what's going on. Thus, to communicate effectively with others, you need to use terms that they recognize.

By Products Produced

Grouping employees by the products they produce was pioneered in the 1920s by General Motors and DuPont. This type of employee grouping is designed to foster self-contained units. Exhibit 6-5 illustrates an example of grouping people by the products they produce. Each major product area in the organization is placed under the authority of a top-level manager who is a specialist in, and responsible for, everything having to do with his or her product line. Notice, for example, in contrast to grouping employees by the jobs they perform, major work activities have been divided up to give the product supervisors considerable autonomy and control over their operations. For instance, in your hamburger restaurants, you or your brother could group people according to such product lines as beverages, side orders, and main-course items. These product-line groups could be responsible for ordering their own supplies or determining how they can be most productive. It's their little world, and they make decisions about their work activities that will help them reach their goals. Grouping people by what they produce can also be done in a service-related organization. A real estate firm may have departments for residential sales, residential rentals, commercial sales, commercial leases, and the like. Each offers a common array of services under the direction of a product or service manager.

While looking at Exhibit 6-5, you may notice something that appears familiar. When people are grouped by the products they produce, a set of autonomous little

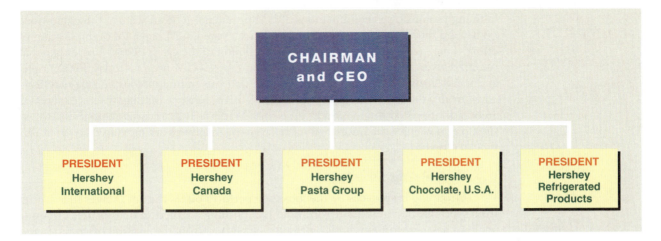

EXHIBIT 6-5

An Example of Grouping Employees by Products Produced

companies is created. Within each of these product lines is another organizational form—and it is almost always of the grouping-by-work-performed variety.

The Strengths.   The primary advantage to grouping employees by the product they produce is that such a grouping focuses on results. Product leaders have full responsibility for a product or service. It is their job to get everyone who works on the product or service to fully understand what is expected of them and what importance they play in achieving goals. Employees in such a structure must also understand that it takes each grouping of employees, working together, for these goals to be realized. For example, in your hamburger stand, your success is measured by sales and profits. If beverage supplies are not replenished, and you must tell customers that they are unavailable—even though you have the best hamburgers in town—your customers may go elsewhere, probably to your competition. Therefore, for any individual group to succeed, all groups must succeed. And that will happen only when they all work together toward a common goal. Rewards given, then, are based on how well the whole did, not any particular segment. This reduces the inherent conflict that frequently exists when employees are grouped by jobs performed.

Grouping employees by the product produced is also an excellent way to develop tomorrow's leaders. Project supervisors gain a broad range of experience in running their autonomous units. The individual responsibility and independence give them an opportunity to run an entire company (though on a smaller scale). So a large organization such as Procter & Gamble with fifteen product lines has fifteen product supervisors who are developing an overall perspective that prepares them for future higher-level positions in the organization.

The Primary Weakness.   The major disadvantage of grouping employees by the product they produce is the duplication of activities and resources. Think for a moment about General Motors. The organization has several product lines, including Pontiac, Buick, Oldsmobile, Chevrolet, GMC Trucks, Cadillac, and Geo. Each product line requires some sort of manufacturing and assembly-line operation. Is it efficient for Pontiac, Buick, and Oldsmobile, for instance, to each have an engine-manufacturing group? Couldn't one group produce the required engines for all GM cars and trucks? Couldn't a dealership sell all GM cars and trucks, as opposed to having separate dealerships (although some do sell combinations of GM products)? The answers to these questions go beyond the scope of this text. But as it once existed, GM had a lot of duplication of effort. That's part of the reason it lost $23.5 billion in the early 1990s.[3] Losses like that can make even a giant like GM change its ways. Buy a GM product today, for example, and you'll likely be given some information that the engine in your vehicle may have come from a different GM group. In the end, heavy reliance on this structure increases an organization's costs and reduces efficiency. With today's concerns about these two issues, it's no wonder that more and more large organizations are moving away from this type of structure.

By a Matrix Structure

> **matrix structure**
an organizational structure that combines the strengths of grouping employees both by jobs performed and by products produced

Grouping employees by the jobs they perform offers the advantages that accrue from specialization and standardization. Establishing a structure that focuses on product lines has a greater emphasis on results, but suffers from duplication of activities and resources. Does any structure combine the advantages of specialization with the focus and accountability that a product-line structure provides? The answer is yes, and it reflects a coordinated approach, commonly referred to as a matrix structure.[4] A **matrix structure** is an organizational structure that combines the strengths of grouping employees both by jobs performed and by products produced.

Earlier, we stated that specialization is used to gain the economies from standardization. The coordinated approach overlaps specialized job groupings with a set of project leaders who are responsible for specific products, projects, or programs within the organization. (We will use these terms—*products*, *projects*, *programs*—interchangeably, since a matrix structure can involve any of the three.) Exhibit 6-6 illustrates a matrix structure of an aerospace firm. Notice that along the top of the figure are the familiar functions of engineering, accounting, human resources management, and so forth—the specialized jobs. Along the vertical dimension, however, the various projects that the aerospace firm is currently working on have been added. Each project is directed by a project leader who staffs his or her project with people from the various departments. The addition of this vertical dimension to the functional departments, in effect, weaves together elements of both employee groupings—by the job and by the product produced. Hence the term *matrix*.

Its Unique Nature. The most unique characteristic of the matrix structure is that each employee will have at least two bosses: the departmental supervisor and the project leader. The project leader has authority over all who are part of his or her project team. The design engineering specialists, for instance, who are responsible for engineering activities on the Omega project are responsible to both the supervisor of the design engineering department and the Omega project leader. Authority is shared between these two people. Typically, this is done by giving the project leader authority over anything that relates to the project. However, decisions affecting an employee's basic employment, such as promotions, salary recommendations, and performance evaluations, remain the department supervisor's responsibility. To work effectively, project leaders and departmental supervisors must communicate regularly and coordinate the demands placed on their employees.

---

[3]Alex Taylor III, "GM's $11,000,000,000 Turnaround," *Fortune* (October 17, 1994), p. 54.
[4]See, for example, Charles Handy, *Understanding Organizations* (New York: Oxford University Press, 1993), p. 415; and Jay Galbraith, "Matrix Organization Designs: How to Combine Functional and Project Forms," *Business Horizons* (February 1971), pp. 29–40.

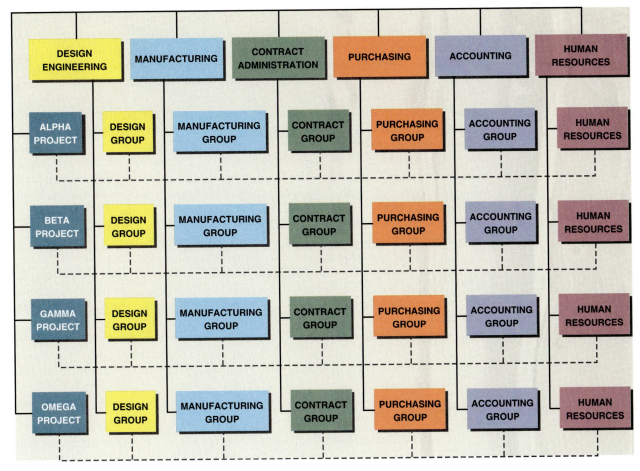

EXHIBIT 6-6

An Example of Grouping Employees by a Matrix Structure Approach

The Strengths and the Weaknesses. The primary strengths of a coordinated approach come from the two groupings of employees that form the matrix. That is, it puts specialists together, capitalizing on their expertise. But it does so in such a way that these specialists work on a number of projects, minimizing much of the duplication. A matrix also facilitates coordination of these specialists to ensure that organizational goals are achieved. And it identifies who is ultimately responsible for the activities associated with the project.

The major disadvantages of the matrix lie in the confusion it creates and its potential to foster power struggles. When the unity-of-command principle is violated, ambiguity and uncertainty significantly increase for employees. Confusion can exist over whom we actually report to. This confusion and ambiguity, in turn, plant the seeds for power struggles. Because the relationships between departmental supervisors and project leaders are not specified by rules and procedures, they need to be negotiated. This can lead to conflict among all involved parties.

Finally comes the issue of how you are regarded in a matrix. No one can question what a matrix is attempting to do. In a dynamic environment where much uncertainty exists and technology changes hourly, there's a great need for coordinating activities. But employees are not activities. Rather, there's a social aspect to work that may be overlooked. Employees often like the feeling of belonging to a group. For a lot of workers, that's the office. That's their home away from home. If that workplace they call home doesn't exist, or they're removed from it for an extended period, where do they belong? Organizations seldom pay much attention to the need for belonging experienced by employees in the work environment. And what happens when a project is done? Does the same group of workers start work on a new project? Do they go back to their respective departments? That really depends. Most people will say that if workers are good at what they do, the organization will find them a place. But that can't be guaranteed. If the work doesn't exist, and there's nothing else available after the project is complete, workers may simply be laid off. For instance, imagine the nightmare that organizations such as Westinghouse or NASA face when government funding for their projects is cut. Thousands of specialists—scientists, computer programmers, and the like—are no longer needed. Absorbing that many people in other locations in an organization is simply impossible. The only alternative that makes business sense is to cut staff.

Chances of going back to the department are also slim. Departmental duties weren't left undone while some employees were off working on a special project. Instead, the duties were either reassigned to other individuals or eliminated altogether. So there's nothing left to go back to. Consequently, once again, the chances are good that affected individuals will be separated from the organization.

So why would anyone work in a matrix when the potential for job loss is so great? They may have no choice. That's the structure some organizations have found most beneficial—for coordinating activities in a dynamic and uncertain environment and for cost-effectiveness.

Organizational Culture

Recall the discussion in Chapter 1 that every individual has something that psychologists have termed "personality." As described in Chapter 3, an individual's personality is made up of a set of relatively permanent and stable traits. When you describe

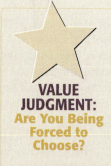

VALUE JUDGMENT: Are You Being Forced to Choose?

Those of us who work on multiple projects often face a difficult issue that never arose when we were simply grouped by our jobs and worked in a single department. That is, we no longer have the luxury of having only one boss. In fact, we may have multiple bosses throughout our workday. That means we are responsible to our departmental supervisor, who in many cases, is the individual responsible for evaluating our work and deciding on our salary increase. But simultaneous with that work relationship is the fact that we are also responsible to project leaders for specific project tasks.

So who is the more important person? Do we give our departmental supervisor's request priority because, after all, it is the supervisor who handles administrative and employee-related paperwork? Or is it our project leaders, who are involved with us day to day, who get top billing. Of course, failure to complete the required tasks on our projects could result in our being removed from the project team. That action could ultimately lead to our being terminated. Or are both bosses to be given equal priority, while we simply accept that we have to serve two masters? How do you feel about this issue?

someone as warm, innovative, relaxed, or conservative, you are describing personality traits. An organization, too, has a personality, which is called the organization's culture.

Organizational Culture refers to a system of shared values that governs the behavior of an organization's members. Just as tribal cultures have totems and taboos that dictate how each member will act toward fellow members and outsiders, organizations have cultures that govern how its members should behave. These shared values determine, in large degree, what you see and how you respond to the employer's world. (See Exhibit 6-7.)

The outcomes from the characteristics listed in Exhibit 6-7 are relatively stable and permanent over time. Just as an individual's personality is stable and permanent—if you were outgoing last month, you're likely to be outgoing next month—so, too, is an organization's culture. The fortunate aspect of understanding this culture is that many organizations help you adapt to its values. We call this adaptation process whereby individuals adapt to shared organizational values **organizational socialization.**

Socialization refers to the rituals you will face when you join an organization. For instance, when you begin a new job or get a promotion, you are required to make adjustments. You must adapt to a new environment—different work activities, a new boss, a different and most likely diverse group of co-workers, and probably a different set of standards for what constitutes good performance.[5] Although you should recognize that this socialization will go on throughout your career—within an organization as well as between organizations—the most profound adjustment occurs when you make the first move into an organization: the move from being an outsider to being an insider.

> ➤ **organizational socialization**
> a process whereby individuals adapt to shared organizational values

Organizational Structures Evolve over Time

*O*ver the years, most organizational structures provided supervisors with a means of control—whether that control was over one's authority, products or goods

---

[5]Jitendra M. Mishra and Pam Strait, "Employee Orientation: The Key to Lasting and Productive Results," *Health Care Supervisor* (March 1993), pp. 19–29; and H. Sheridan, "Culture-Change Lessons," *Industry Week* (February 17, 1997), p. 20.

Member identity	Do employees identify with the organization as a whole or with their type of job or field of expertise?
Group emphasis	Are work activities organized around groups or individuals?
People focus	Does the organization take into account how its employees are affected by its policies?
Unit integration	Are units independent of one another, or do they operate in a coordinated fashion?
Control mechanisms	Are there many rules and regulations to guide employees' behavior?
Risk tolerance	Are employees encouraged to be creative and take risks?
Reward criteria	Are rewards based on performance or nonperformance criteria?
Conflict tolerance	Are disagreements encouraged to be openly aired?
Means-ends	Does the bottom line matter most or the techniques and processes used to achieve those outcomes?
Open systems	Does the organization monitor and respond to its environment?

Source: Charles A. O'Reilly III, J. Chatman, and D. F. Cladwell, "People and Organizational Culture: A Profile Comparison Approach to Assessing Person-Organization Fit," *Academy of Management Journal* (September 1991), pp. 487–519.

EXHIBIT 6-7
Organizational Values

produced, other employees, or information. Today, however, that's not enough. Employers are constantly reminded that whatever they do must meet customers' needs. Doing what you want and expecting customers to live with your product simply won't work. Competition is too keen, and if customers don't like what you do, they'll go somewhere else. Employees, too, have become brighter and want a role in what affects them at work. They want the interaction that working in a team environment can provide. Taken together, all these factors are causing us to rethink how organizations should be designed.

Why Organization Designs Change

Throughout this chapter, and with references to earlier parts of this text, we have made the analogy that organizations are like people. Organizations have personalities we described as their culture. They also have skeletons on which a body is supported, their structures. In a perfect world where nothing ever changed, or where we had a perfect understanding of what we faced, organizations would not have to adapt. But that's not the case. The world and the things in it do change. Consequently, organizations are constantly readjusting to meet the demands facing them. It's important also to recognize that, like people, organizations evolve over time. For instance, every person comes into this world as an infant, grows through the teen years, reaches maturity and adulthood somewhere in his or her twenties, and continues until old age sets in. Growth of organizations is similar. Organizations are set up, they grow, they reach some level of stability over the years, and then they decline. But organizations, unlike humans, may not die. Rather, they usually continue their cycle. That means they change—sometimes starting the process over again.

The fascinating thing over the past decade is how quickly this organizational cycle is repeating itself. In Chapter 1, we looked at bureaucratic organizations, which have flourished for more than fifty years. But the environment in which bureaucracies prospered was more stable than it is today. As such, to respond to the ever-changing world of work, organizations must reshape themselves. Top managers in these organizations have to reconfigure the structure to make it more responsive to customers, employees, and the owners of the organization. Although a number of different structures are making their way into organizations, one element is common to most: The organizations we will work in tomorrow are more likely to be simpler structures. Let's look at how these structures are taking shape in the United States today.

Movement to a Simpler Structure

Recall our discussion in Chapter 2 regarding the challenges business faces. Two of these—downsizing and reengineering—are particularly relevant to today's changes in organization structure.[6] How? To answer, let's briefly review some facts regarding common structures. These bureaucratic designs were highly complex and formalized, and decisions were made in a centralized fashion—resulting in rigid, often massive, multilevel structures. Although they were designed to promote efficiency, they did not lend themselves to adjusting to the dynamic world around them. As a result, more emphasis today has been given to organizations that focus on structural simplicity. Let's look at what we mean by a simple structure.

If *bureaucracy* best describes most large organizations, *simple structure* best characterizes most small ones. A **simple structure** is an organizational grouping that appears to have almost no structure—one that is low in complexity, has little formalization, and has

> **simple structure**
> an organizational grouping that appears to have almost no structure—one that is low in complexity, has little formalization, and has its authority centralized in a single person

---

[6]Ronald Henkoff, "Getting beyond Downsizing," *Fortune* (January 10, 1994), pp. 58–62.

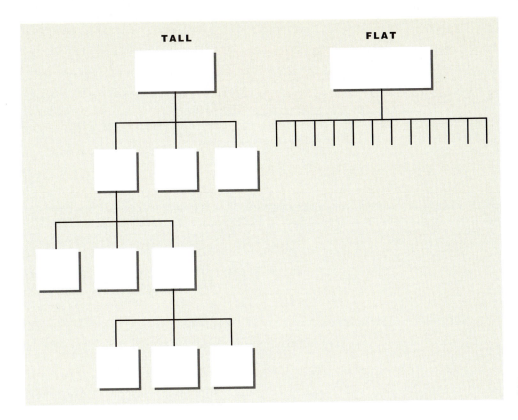

EXHIBIT 6-8
Tall Versus Flat Structures

its authority centralized in a single person. A simple structure is defined more by what it is not than by what it is. It is not an elaborate structure.[7] The simple structure is a flat organization; it usually has only two or three levels, employees who perform a variety of tasks and one individual who makes most of the decisions. (See Exhibit 6-8.)

The simple structure is most widely practiced in small businesses in which the manager and the owner are the same person (like your hamburger restaurant). This, for example, is illustrated in Exhibit 6-9, which shows an organization chart for a cosmetic retail store. Jen Singleton owns and manages this store. Although Jen employs five full-time salespeople, a cashier, and part-time weekend help, she runs the show.

The strengths of the simple structure should be obvious. Communications are efficient, it's flexible to respond to the changing environment, and accountability is clear. One major weakness is that, in the past, a simple structure was viewed as effective in only small organizations. It became increasingly inadequate as an organization grew because its low formalization and high centralization resulted in information overloads at the top. As size increased, decision making became slower and eventually came to a standstill as the single person in charge tried to continue making all the decisions. This proved to be the undoing of many small businesses. The simple structure's other weakness is that it is risky: Everything depends on one person. One heart attack, or a fatal auto accident, can destroy the organization. But these weaknesses were not necessarily the fault of the simple structure. Rather, those in charge just couldn't give up the control that they had so enjoyed.

---

[7]Henry Mintzberg, *Structure in Fives: Designing Effective Organizations* (Upper Saddle River, N.J.: Prentice-Hall, 1983), p. 157.

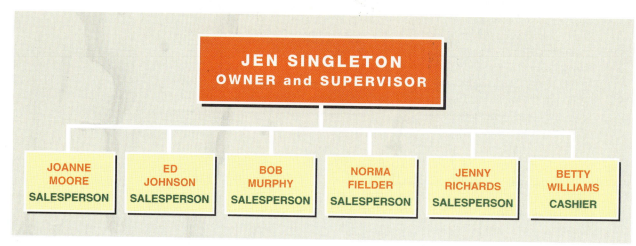

EXHIBIT 6-9
Jen Singleton's Simple Structure

Simple-Like Structures and Larger Organizations

If there has been one thing in common in yesterday's organizations, it was the rigid boundaries that separated employees from other parts of the organization. They were often specialized by the jobs they did, they rarely interacted with others in different parts of the business, and a select few ran the show. But that setup may no longer give employees the best advantage in organizations. Some of those boundaries must be broken down, giving employees more interaction with others whom they count on for getting their jobs done. In business today, we call this arrangement the horizontal structure.

> **horizontal structure**
> an employee grouping with a flat structure

The Horizontal Structure. Before we begin this discussion, let's set the record straight. A horizontal structure is really nothing new. **Horizontal structures** are simply very flat structures. Earlier, we called such flat arrangements simple structures. What's new about these, however, is that they are being used not only in small businesses, but also in giant companies such as AT&T, DuPont, General Electric, and Motorola.[8] A horizontal organization, as the term implies, means that job-related activities cut across all parts of the organization. Rather than performing specialized jobs and working in departments with people who do similar tasks, you are grouped with other employees who have skills different from yours—forming a work team. You will come together to work toward a common objective. You will be given the authority to make the necessary decisions to do the work and be held accountable for measurable outcomes.[9] That is, your jobs encompass the entire work to be completed, from beginning to end, rather than an individualized job task.[10] In essence, control will shift from those above to you, the workers.

[8]John A. Byrne, "The Horizontal Corporation," *Business Week* (December 20, 1993), pp. 76–81. For an excellent discussion of the Horizontal Organization, see F. Ostroff, *The Horizontal Organization* (New York, NY: Oxford Press, 1999).

[9]See, A. M. Townsend, S. M. DeMarie, and A. R. Hendrickson, "Virtual Technology and the Workplace of the Future," *Academy of Management Executive*, August 1998, pp. 17–28.

[10]Ruth E. Thaler-Carter, "Whither Global Leaders," *HRMagazine* (May 2000), p. 82; Leanne Atwater and David Waldman, "Accountability in 360 Degree Feedback," *HRMagazine* (May 1998), p. 96; Robert Hoffman, "Ten Reasons You Should Be Using 360-Degree Feedback," *HRMagazine* (April 1995), p. 82; and "Companies Where Employees Rate Executives," *Fortune* (December 27, 1993), p. 128.

Working in a horizontal organization will also bring about other changes for you. For instance, you can expect to be rewarded for mastering multiple skills rather than just a select few. The more you can do, the more value you add to your employers. Additionally, rather than being evaluated on the work you did, you will receive rewards based on how the team performed. Remember that group project you did for class in which you got a group grade and were upset that someone didn't do his or her fair share? Well, that's reality, and it's something that you may experience in the work world. But that, too, may change. Like your instructor who evaluates the group project, traditionally one person evaluated the work. In a horizontal organization, however, supervisory evaluations will no longer be the only evaluations. More than likely, you will be evaluated by anyone who has knowledge of your work. For instance, at General Electric, CEO Jack Welch has implemented what he calls a 360-degree appraisal process.[11] At GE, team members are evaluated by team leaders, peer members, other employees with whom they work, and even customers. This evaluation system is becoming a model for other organizations.

Horizontal Structures and You. Whenever an organization establishes its structure, one of the first orders of business is to display it in some form of chart. **Organizational charts** show reporting structures, communication flows, and who's in charge. Unfortunately, in an organizational chart grouped by the jobs people perform, workers are often shown at the very bottom of a pyramid. Employees don't need to be reminded in those instances that they are perceived as the lowest element in the organization. In fact, some organizations—such as Pepsico, which still retains multiple levels—have inverted their organizational charts to show that the employees are the number-one reason for company success. Having management at the bottom of the pyramid shows these employees what supervisors are supposed to be—a team that exists to support their work efforts.[12] The horizontal-structure organization chart takes this one step further. Having a flat structure reinforces that we are all important to the organization's success. It indicates that all employees—no matter what their job function—are equal and are working toward a common goal. If nothing else, this supports a more positive culture in which employees can be more productive.

> **organizational charts** charts that show reporting structure, communication flows, and who's in charge

Although the movement toward simpler structures brings with it many strengths and may provide an exciting work atmosphere, keep one thing in mind. Simpler structures must be used where appropriate. In some industries where efficiency of mass production is warranted, grouping employees by the jobs they perform may better serve the organization. The question raised, then, is when do the different structures work best? The answer will depend on the environment in which a company operates. And the company should respond accordingly. The result of that grouping, however, is what you should be concerned about.

Organizations group you for a particular reason. They don't implement structures haphazardly for the fun of it. It's too expensive and very difficult to make these changes. But when they do, you should learn from it. How so? Recognize what the structure is telling you as an employee. If you are grouped by the job you perform, your organization has decided that efficiency matters most. Therefore, for your career to be successful in that organization, you need to focus on being efficient and continue refining your current skills. That may mean becoming more of an expert in your chosen field, which may include getting an advanced degree. You are given clues, too, to decisions you may have to make. In such a grouping, you'll want to give greater

---

[11]Ibid.
[12]John A. Byrne, "The Horizontal Corporation," *Business Week* (December 20, 1993), p. 80.

Succeeding in a Simpler Structure

1. **Continue to demonstrate the abilities and motivation to perform multiple tasks.** Employers cannot make simpler structures work effectively if you don't have the ability to do your job. It is a two-way street; employers may offer help, but you also need to take it on yourself to learn new skills to advance your education. You also need to learn about working together, making sound decisions, and interacting well with others.

2. **Seek clarification for your assignments and the decisions you'll be allowed to make.** Involving employees may mean a number of different things to different people. Find out exactly what your boss expects, what goals are to be accomplished, and how much control you'll have over these things. Clarification now may prevent problems later.

3. **Know your range of authority**. This is too important to be left to a discussion in step 2. You need to understand what authority you have been given, how widespread that authority is, and what boundaries have been placed on you. Within your boundaries, you should be able to act freely. Outside your boundaries, you need to know what to do and whom to contact.

4. **Make sure your supervisor lets others know of this work arrangement.** One thing that can hurt you most is being given this authority and responsibility, and no one knowing about it. Your supervisor must inform others about what is occurring. In fact, you may be acting on his or her behalf in some instances. Others need to know that you have the authority to do certain things, to interact directly with them, and to seek their help. If your supervisor hasn't paved the way for you, you'll need to nudge him or her to communicate this in order for you to be effective in your job.

5. **Keep your supervisor well-informed.** Remember, this newfound authority and responsibility doesn't exist in thin air. You are actually getting it from your supervisor. And if you don't fulfill your goals, your supervisor has the ultimate authority. The buck stops with him or her. Obviously, your supervisor trusts you to do the job, but he or she still needs to know how things are going. Establish update meetings so that you can keep your supervisor informed of progress, problems, obstacles, and the like. Your success is your supervisor's success, too, so make him or her look good. In doing so, you'll probably be rewarded with expanded opportunities.

5. Which one of the following is not a disadvantage associated with a matrix structure?
   a. In a matrix structure, the unity-of-command principle is violated.
   b. In a matrix structure, power struggles may arise.
   c. In a matrix structure, there is duplication of resources.
   d. In a matrix structure, employees may face conflicting priorities.

6. Which one of the following terms is not related to the others?
   a. simple structure
   b. basic structure
   c. horizontal structure
   d. flat structure

weight to alternatives that are more cost effective or that provide greater output for a given input. Play to the strength of the structure; that's usually what organizational members are being rewarded for.

In other employee groupings, similar suggestions can be found. Being grouped by the product you produce means that the bigger picture is most important—that is, achieving organizational goals. In such a situation, you'll be interacting with others who possess skills different from yours. Learn from them. Broaden your experience and become better skilled in a variety of things. You, too, may want to continue your education here, but it probably won't be in a specialized area. Rather, it may be in a different field altogether so that you add more value to your employer. You may find yourself working more in teams, and this may take some getting used to. Be prepared to stretch yourself, learning new skills and accepting any opportunity that is provided to you.

The bottom line, however, is that no matter what type of structure you work in, you will be expected to do your very best. And that requires interacting with others.

SUMMARY

This summary corresponds to the Learning Outcomes found on page 127.

1. The components of an organization's structure are a function of the measure of its degree of complexity (the differences that exist), formalization (rules, regulations, and policies that guide behavior), and centralization (a concentration of power or authority).

2. An adhocracy is an organizational structure that is low in complexity, low in formalization, and decentralized. It is a loose structure that can be changed rapidly to meet the demands of the dynamic environment around it.

3. The four principles that guide how employees are grouped are standardized jobs, chain of command, authority and responsibility, and span of control.

4. The advantages of standardized jobs relate to economic efficiencies. Standardized jobs make efficient use of the diversity of skills that workers hold. Skills are developed through repetition and less time is wasted. The disadvantage of standardized jobs is that, in excess, they can lead to boredom, fatigue, stress, low productivity, poor quality, increased absence, and high turnover.

5. Authority is position power, the right inherent in a job to give orders and expect the orders to be obeyed. Responsibility is an obligation to do what is expected. Unless authority and responsibility are balanced, problems may arise within the organization.

6. The advantages of grouping employees by the products they produce include more focus on results to be achieved and a better means of training tomorrow's leaders. The primary disadvantage comes from its duplication of effort, which may waste valuable resources.

7. A matrix organization combines the strengths of grouping employees by the jobs they do and by the products they produce. A matrix reflects a coordinated approach—capitalizing on the expertise of employees working toward a common organizational goal while minimizing duplication of resources.

8. A simple structure is an organizational grouping that is low in complexity and has little formalization, but has authority centralized in a single person. In a simple structure, communications are more efficient, the organization is better able to respond to the changing environment, and accountability is clear.

9. Horizontal organization refers to an employee grouping where the structure is flat and work is performed in teams. These teams represent employees from across the organization who possess a variety of skills. In a horizontal structure, employees' jobs encompass the entire work to be completed—from beginning to end.

10. Flatter structures will bring about many changes for employees. They will be rewarded for mastering multiple skills, and rewards will be based on how well work teams perform. Employees can also expect changes in how they are evaluated. Instead of just a supervisor evaluating their performance, anyone who has had work contact with employees—team members, supervisors, customers—will have a say in how well they did.

REVIEWING YOUR UNDERSTANDING

1. What are complexity, formalization, and centralization, and how are they related?

2. Compare bureaucracies with adhocracies. Which structure do you believe is more efficient? More effective? Defend your position.

3. Would you rather work for a supervisor who has a wide span of control or one with a narrow span? Explain.

4. What are the benefits of grouping employees by the jobs they perform?

5. "Becoming an expert today is the kiss of death for one's career. We can become so specialized that we work ourselves into unemployment." Do you agree or disagree with the statement? Discuss.

6. Why must authority and responsibility be balanced in the workplace?

7. In which type of organization structure would you prefer to work: one where you are grouped by your job, by the product you produce, or a combination of the two? Explain your answer.

8. "Employees should not be responsible to more than one supervisor. If they are, major problems frequently occur." Do you agree or disagree with this statement? Explain your position.

9. What do you think are the most appropriate organizational values?

10. Can a simple structure work in a large organization? Explain.

11. Describe the characteristics of a horizontal structure. How do you think tomorrow's workers will accept these characteristics?

ANSWERS TO CHECKING YOUR UNDERSTANDING

1. b **2.** d **3.** b **4.** a **5.** c **6.** b

LEARNING TOGETHER

A. Trace the history of organizational structure. Select a ten-year period in time (for example, the 1950s, 1980s, or 1990s) and identify the factors that contributed to changes in organizational structure. Make a display of your research findings and share it with the class.

B. Compare the organizational structures of two large or two small businesses in your area. Write up your findings from interviews with at least two people from each organization. Draw some conclusions from your interviews—especially about why both businesses may have very different structure and about their views on human relations. Report your findings to the class.

C. In teams of two to three individuals, prepare a written list of twenty questions about organizational design based on the discussion in your text that may be used in interviews with representatives of management and labor. Then, with the guidance of your professor, contact several local organizations and schedule appointments. Summarize and report your findings to the class.

D. Each of four groups will be assigned one of the following topics: (1) standardization of jobs, (2) chain of command, (3) authority and responsibility, and (4) span of control. In your group, prepare a pro and con debate about your topic as it relates to the workplace, listing the human relations issues that present themselves as a result of the pros and cons.

Grouping Employees

Melissa, Petri, and Mark work for Rosalyn in the Grand Rapids office of International Soft Forms (ISF). ISF is a software development corporation with nearly one-hundred offices throughout the world. The Grand Rapids office is organized into three divisions. The contracts division, headed by Rosalyn, is the research and development backbone of the company. It is organized and reorganized by the projects they do (that is, work units that concentrate on specific contracts as they are awarded). The financial division handles all the accounting, payroll, grants, and contract billing and collections. The marketing division is responsible for sales, marketing, and public relations.

Melissa is a programmer. She works alone most of the time and frequently has projects that last eighteen months or more. Presently she is working on a government contract designing a forms package that will accompany income tax documentation. The project has a timeline that carries a heavy penalty if the product is not delivered by the contract date.

Petri and Mark both have software applications expertise and are working on a project for an international travel agency. They are designing a multifaceted travel package, complete with forms and publicity brochures, to promote a new cruise line that will offer luxury vacations of up to six weeks in duration. Their project timeline has been altered several times because of changes the travel agency wants to make. All the travel agency changes have been negotiated through the ISF sales staff. Petri and Mark make all decisions regarding redirection of the project that will be implemented by their fifteen-member staff.

Petri and Mark work well together because Petri has excellent creative and design skills. Mark's skills are more analytical, specific, and sequential in nature. Petri helps the staff visualize the various components of the project, while Mark assists staff in assuring that the steps are taken in sequence.

Recently another major change was negotiated and the project redirected again. Both Petri and Mark are getting frustrated with the changes, especially because some of the negotiated changes (including the timeline) are totally unrealistic. Petri and Mark met with Rosalyn to share their concerns. They were concerned about their staff experiencing frustration in the project. Mark said some of the staff are unsure of where they are going and are showing signs of stress and fatigue. A couple of the staff have asked Mark to reassign them to Melissa's project. Petri thinks the staff needs to grow up and work together. He is, however, concerned with the lack of creativity that several of the staff seem to have when they discuss the project.

Questions

1. In groups of three or four, identify what type of company structure seems to be present in the case. Defend your position to the other groups. Did all groups come up with the same answer? Why or why not?

2. Describe how the basic principles of standardization, chain of command, authority and responsibility, and span of control are used or abused in this case. For each problem area noted, suggest at least one way the situation could be improved.

3. How are employees grouped in this case? Is it the best way? Why or why not?

4. Describe the various types of authority you see in this case. Draw some conclusions about your observations.

5. Are any principles of good management being violated in this case? If so, which ones?

ORGANIZATIONAL COMMUNICATIONS

*L*earning Outcomes

After reading this chapter, you will be able to:

1. Describe the purpose of organizational communications.

2. Identify the three primary formal communications patterns.

3. Explain the concept of an open-door communication policy.

4. List five ways organizations keep their employees informed.

5. Describe why organizations provide handbooks to their employees.

6. Describe the steps of a typical organizational complaint procedure.

7. Explain the purpose of an employee suggestion program.

8. Define *grapevine*.

In Chapter 4, we introduced you to the topic of communications. In that chapter, the focus was how you communicate with others, as well as the interpersonal issues that affect this interaction. We looked at that material solely from a free exchange between you and others. Although interpersonal styles affect all of your communication efforts, we need to take that discussion one step further. Why? Because when you work in an organization, your communication efforts are going to be directly influenced by the processes the organization sets up to guide it. We call this organizational communications.

Organizational communications programs are designed to keep workers current regarding what is happening in an organization, as well as ensuring that workers are knowledgeable of the policies and procedures that affect them.[1] Whereas public relations efforts in an organization are designed to keep the public informed of what an organization does, organizational communications focus on you—its employees.[2] Communication programs serve as one basis for increasing your loyalty and commitment.[3] This is accomplished by building into the organization's culture a means through which information is free-flowing, timely, and accurate. When this exists, you have a better feeling that the organization values you. For example, imagine setting your course schedule in April for the fall semester. After carefully reviewing the classes you needed to take, you registered for course sections that would fit with your work schedule for fall. After spending a summer away from campus, you return in late Au-

> **organizational communications**
>
> programs designed to keep workers current regarding what is happening in an organization, as well as ensuring that workers are knowledgeable of the policies and procedures that affect them

---

[1]Richard G. Charlton, "The Decade of the Employee," *Public Relations Journal* (January 1990), p. 26.
[2]Ibid.
[3]Julie Foehrenback and Steve Goldfarb, "Employee Communication in the '90s: Great (er) Expectation," *Communication World* (May–June 1990), pp. 101–106.

VALUE JUDGMENT: Communicating with the Diverse Workforce

Throughout this text, we have been addressing issues that relate directly to the diversity that exists in our workforce. Although each of these areas is important for us to consider, nothing is more important to effective human relations than having formal communications in place that meet the needs of the diversified workforce. Why is this so? Simply because we have people from all nations working together in an effort to achieve organizational goals. Obviously, in many of these cases, English is not their primary language. So what are you, and your organization, supposed to do? Recognizing that a potential problem exists is the first step. Then, something must be done.

Consider what one organization did at their factory. They have workers who come from more than forty different countries. Among these employees, nineteen different primary languages are spoken. Although some speak more than one language, in order to formally communicate with all workers, the company sends all information in English, French, Portuguese, Vietnamese, and Haitian Creole.

The lesson here is quite simple. When we are responsible for some type of formal organizational communications, we must remember one of the suggestions we discussed in Chapter 4: speaking someone's language in an effort to reduce barriers to our interpersonal communications. The same holds for the information that comes from our organization. Productivity depends on it. Failing to do so will only leave some people uninformed. And we know that when that happens, the grapevine becomes more dominant than the primary source of information. That can spell disaster if it is allowed to go unchecked.

gust to begin the semester. However, as you go to your third class of the day, you are met with a notice on the classroom door that says: "The course has been canceled. Please see the department secretary." When you arrive at the department, you find out that the only open section of the class is at a day and time that conflicts with your work schedule. Because this is a prerequisite course for one you need to take next semester, you scramble to rearrange your schedule. By the time you are done, you have shuffled three courses and successfully pleaded with a co-worker to swap work schedules with you. Had you been given advance notice of this course cancellation, you might have been able to plan ahead and eliminate this last-minute scramble. You also would have been less upset and not had your perception of the academic department clouded. You feel that something should have been communicated to you before the first day of classes. Because it wasn't, you may feel that the department just doesn't care about its students. Organizational communications build trust and openness—even if the information shared is not good news.

Have such programs worked in the real world? If you were to talk to employees of Hewlett-Packard or Challenger Electrical Equipment Corporation of Allentown, Pennsylvania, you'd see that they have. For example, at Hewlett-Packard, efforts by organizational members to enhance communications have resulted in more satisfied individuals and higher employee morale.[4] Likewise, supervisors at Challenger Electrical Equipment Corporation didn't recognize the extent to which employees were upset with the lack of information sharing in the organization—until the employees tried to join a union to demonstrate their dissatisfaction.[5] The bottom line in both cases is that employees want to be included and kept informed about the things that affect them. An organization failing to do so is sitting on the proverbial time bomb. Accepting this, let's look at a few ways an organization keeps us informed.

Formal Communications Patterns

For any organization to be successful, there must be effective interpersonal exchanges by all organizational members. These exchanges bind us together as members of a group—helping us form a team. To help support this goal, companies establish patterns of communications flow. How you formally communicate in your organization, however, will often be guided by how you are grouped as well as the formality of the organization's culture. Realistically, the larger the organization, the more formalized the communications process. In most organizations, this results in three primary organizational communications patterns: from the boss to you, from you to the boss, and among you and your peers. (See Exhibit 7-1.)

From the Boss to You

Any communication that comes from your boss to you is referred to as downward communications. **Downward communications** includes any information delivered by any means to an individual from anyone who has a higher position in the organization. Information may include policies, directions, rules, and expectations. In the workplace, downward communications includes your supervisor setting work goals for you to accomplish, assigning tasks for you to do, making requests made for certain information, and the like. Remember, the authority in your boss's position gives him or her a legitimate right to run the department. Downward communications, then, helps him or her keep you informed, direct your activities, and evaluate you.

> **downward communications**
> any information delivered by any means to an individual from anyone who has a higher position in the organization

---

[4]See Brad Whitworth, "Proof at Last," *Communication World* (December 1990), pp. 28–31.
[5]Commerce Clearing House, "Challenger Meets Employee Communication Challenge with Merit Plan," *Human Resources Management: Ideas and Trends* (April 13, 1994), p. 61.

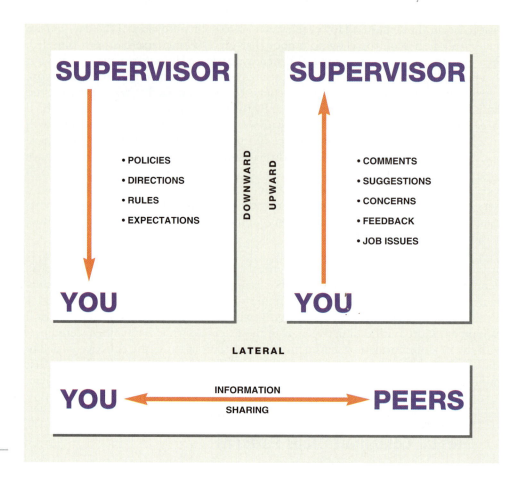

EXHIBIT 7-1
Communication Patterns

When you think about communications coming from your boss to you, you may be getting the impression that it is always verbal. That's not necessarily the case. In fact, any time your supervisor sends you a memo advising you of something that is important for you to know, he or she is using downward communications. In fact, the syllabus you received at the beginning of the semester for this course is a good example of a downward communications pattern. All the relevant information you need to be successful in the class is provided to you in that syllabus. Here, as in a work setting, downward communications acts to guide your behavior.

From You to the Boss

No supervisor can function effectively without getting some feedback from you. A supervisor can get you to do things by means of downward communications. However, for you to inform the supervisor that the task has been completed, there must be some type of feedback. That feedback from you to your supervisor is one example of **upward communications,** any information delivered by any means to an individual from anyone who has a lower position in the organization. Information may include comments, suggestions, concerns, feedback, and job issues.

Any time you talk to your supervisor about your job, you're using upward communications. Just as your professor asks questions about something you've discussed in class, your boss needs to know how things are going for you—both good and bad. For

> **upward**
> **communications**
> any information delivered
> by any means to an
> individual from anyone who
> has a lower position in the
> organization

instance, you may want to keep your supervisor informed about potential delays, quality problems, or cost overruns. You may communicate with your supervisor in these instances either to ask for input in solving the problem or simply to forewarn him or her about the events. In fact, in many organizations (such as Wal-Mart, Home Depot, American Express, and Southwest Airlines), this process is encouraged. Why? Because it provides people in power a true picture of how things really are and what can be improved in the organization.

Once again, you must understand that the extent of upward communications will depend on the organization's culture. If you work in a setting where your input is not valued, or never sought, telling your boss what you think may not be politically smart. In this case, rigid authority is driving the operation, and your upward communications will be, and probably should be, limited. On the other hand, if there's trust and respect for all organizational members, and you are permitted to participate in discussions regarding work activities, then there's a clue that upward communication is welcomed. We refer to this as an **open-door policy**—that is, a policy whereby an employee can talk with supervisors about anything at any time. In that environment, your voice will be heard.

➤ **open-door policy**
a policy whereby an employee can talk with supervisors about anything at any time

One of the interesting aspects of upward communications is that you have been practicing it in your classroom. When you seek clarification about a test question, or disagree with the answer your professor has given, you are sending information upward. So, too, are the faculty evaluations you may complete at the end of every course. Although these evaluations may be used in helping assess your professor's teaching performance, you are giving feedback. Comments about those things that you liked, need some improvement, or should change entirely are all pieces of information your instructor needs from you.

Among You and Your Peers

Today's organizations are recognizing that rigid communications patterns, like outdated machinery, keep the organization from reaching its goals. Change is happen-

KEYS TO UNLOCKING YOUR POTENTIAL *7-1*

*E*ach of the ten scenarios presented in Unlocking Your Potential 7-1 reflects a particular type of communications flow. In general, communication flows downward (from the boss to you), upward (from you to the boss), or laterally (among co-workers). Here are the correct responses to each of the ten scenarios.

- __D__   1. You receive your annual performance appraisal.
- __U__   2. You ask your professor to repeat an important definition on a subject you're discussing in class.
- __D__   3. You receive your course grade from your professor on the self-addressed stamped postcard you left when you turned in your final exam.
- __L__   4. Your project team discusses what each of you will do in your upcoming class presentation.
- __U__   5. You write a letter of recommendation in support of your professor's promotion.
- __L__   6. You ask another individual in the class to attend a guest speaker's lecture.
- __U__   7. You voice-mail your supervisor to let her know that the package she's been waiting for has arrived from Federal Express.
- __D__   8. You receive a holiday greeting card from the owner of your company.
- __D__   9. You receive a recall notice from an automaker about the potential problem with seat belt latches on the car you bought last year.
- __L__   10. Your aunt, senior vice-president of engineering for a major aerospace company, calls to wish you a happy birthday.

Extra Effort

Similar to what you may have done with determining your time-management skills (Chapter 5), track the communications you have in a given day. Jot down where the communications originated (from you or someone else) and indicate where it went (upward, downward, or lateral). Which communication pattern did you experience most? Is this a typical day for you? How effective do you believe these communications to be? Would you try something different next time to make the information flow better? Explain.

ing so fast that you don't often have the luxury of waiting for formal communications to occur. Consider this. It's ten A.M. Monday and you need some information from an individual in another department. This person has a vital piece of information that you need to complete your catalog and send it to the printer. And your deadline to turn the material over is two P.M. Dealing with this issue appears simple. Just pick up the phone and call the individual. Unfortunately, formal communications in the organization don't allow this. Instead, you must contact your supervisor, who contacts hers to deliver the message. Yet the message doesn't go from your boss's boss to the individual. Rather, it flows to him through his supervisor, too. And then this process repeats itself. Well, guess what, two P.M. comes quickly. Rigid upward and downward communications are simply inefficient for this situation. This example is an exaggeration, of course, but it wasn't that long ago that it was the norm. Fortunately, organizations have recognized that communications must be faster to be effective. To achieve this, many promote **lateral communications,** communications among peers.

> **lateral communications**
communications among peers

Lateral communications permits you to communicate with your peers no matter where they are located in the organization. It is usually supported under the belief that it is more efficient to be able to talk to a variety of people in order to get your job done. For example, let's say you gave your supervisor feedback on a new procedure he has implemented in the department (upward communications). You also told co-workers in other departments what this procedure has done to eliminate a lot of wasted paperwork (lateral communications). But you also make a point of contacting your supervisor's boss to express your satisfaction with the new procedure (open-door policy). Your communication, then, has reached all parts of the organization. And you did so in a speedy and efficient manner.

Being Informed by the Organization

*I*n the spirit of finding various vehicles to ensure that organizational communication takes place, a number of means are available to share information between your supervisor and you. The following sections discuss the five most popular ways organizations use to get information out to employees: bulletin boards, company newsletters, company-wide meetings, electronic media, and employee handbooks.

✔ Checking Your Understanding 7-1

1. Which of the following statements best reflects the purpose of organizational communications?
   a. Organizational communications are designed to promote teamwork among organizational members.
   b. Organizational communications are designed to keep organizational members up to date on organizational events and policies.
   c. Organizational communications are designed to enhance customer service efforts in the organization's goals of achieving excellence.
   d. Organizational communications are designed to formally control interpersonal communications between and among organizational members.

2. Which one of the following is not considered a formal organizational communication pattern?
   a. upward communications
   b. downward communications
   c. diagonal communications
   d. lateral communications

Bulletin Boards

A bulletin board in any organization serves several purposes in communicating with employees. A **bulletin board** is a board that contains postings on job openings, upcoming company-sponsored events, new policies, and so on and is generally centrally located in the organization where a majority of employees can see it. Bulletin boards are usually found near the main office, company cafeterias, employee lounges, or vending machine areas. Announcements are posted in these highly visible locations to better convey information from supervisors to their employees.

Organizations often allow bulletin boards to be used for employee-related activities. For example, your organization may permit you to advertise personal belongings for sale or promote a charitable event with which you are associated. Most organizations require you to get prior approval of items you wish to post on the bulletin board. Items that do not have this approval are usually removed. Some may see this as a barrier to their freedom of speech, but it's often necessary to ensure that information is appropriate and sensitive to all who may read it.

Company Newsletters

The organization's **newsletter** is designed to provide employees information about organizational activities and anything else of company interest.[6] This includes such things as problems the company may be experiencing; successes the company has enjoyed; updates on newsworthy company items (such as company-sponsored sporting events and United Way campaigns); and stories about co-workers who have received awards, are retiring, and so forth. Some of the more progressive newsletters also have sections devoted to answering questions that employees have raised. It's usually safe to believe that if one person has a question about something, several others do, too. By answering such a question in the newsletter, the company can reach a broader audience.

Company newsletters provide permanent records that can be kept and referred to at some future time. Furthermore, some information, such as technical and detailed information (for example, a change in retirement contributions), may be better communicated in this written format. Another trend in newsletters is having employees submit articles for publication.[7] This gives them an opportunity to express their views to a larger audience and foster more peer communications.

Company-Wide Meetings

Every so often, there is a need for all employees to be informed at once in a face-to-face encounter. Should the organization be facing a merger, going into a new product line, or changing its culture, for example, it may be useful for a key decision maker to address organizational members in person. In doing so, this individual can add emphasis to the changes that are occurring and answer any questions.

In addition to opening up the channels of communication for employees, **company-wide meetings** permit all organizational members to get the same information at once. This often reduces the rumors that may run wild in the organization—especially when the news has some shock appeal to it.

> ➤ **bulletin board**
> a board that contains postings on job openings, upcoming company-sponsored events, new policies, and so on and is generally centrally located in the organization where a majority of employees can see it

> ➤ **newsletter**
> a method of providing employees with information about organizational activities and anything else of company interest

> ➤ **company-wide meetings**
> meetings at which all organizational members get the same information at once

---

[6]Betty Sosnin, "Corporate Newsletters Improve Employee Morale," **HR Magazine** (June 1996), pp. 106–110.
[7]Art Durity, "Confessions of a Newsletter Editor," *Personnel* (May 1991), p. 7; see also Brubaker, op. cit.

Electronic Media

The technology that exists today serves organizational communications well. Whether it exists in the form of an interactive video or access to online information, technology is making it possible to get better information faster. Whenever an organization wishes to provide employees with up-to-date information regarding their pay and benefits, nothing serves that purpose better than **electronic media,** any technological means of enhancing communications.

Students today often take for granted what these electronic means have done for enhancing communications. For example, doing research for your term paper is much more efficient today than it was just a decade ago. Most of us who teach (and have been doing so for the past two decades) remember going through such publications as the *Social Science Index* and manually tracking the articles on a particular subject. Today, type a few keywords into an automated database system, and there are your sources with abstracts providing the overview of the article. Press a few more buttons, and you may even be able to print the entire article. The same holds for organizations. Organizations often post important information on their electronic bulletin board, and anyone with a computer has access. In some other cases, organizations may even have information available on the Internet. If you have access to the Internet, chances are that you can get much of the catalog information from your college on the World Wide Web—just another means of an organization giving accurate and timely information.

> ► **electronic media**
> any technological means of enhancing communications

Employee Handbooks

During the first few days of a new job, you were informed of a number of important facts regarding employment in the organization. This information usually centered on such things as hours of work, what is expected in terms of performance, and when payday will be. But this preliminary information is not complete. There's often so much more to absorb. Because employees usually can't learn everything by being lectured to in a four-hour orientation session, organizations provide a permanent reference guide, called the employee handbook.

An **employee handbook** is a tool that serves both you and your employer. Like your college catalog, which tells you most everything you need to know about attending and graduating from your school, a well-designed employee handbook provides important information regarding what the company is about, its history, and employee benefits.[8] The handbook, then, helps you learn about the company and what the company provides—and it does so in a way that permits you to read it at your own pace. (See Exhibit 7-2.) With this resource, questions, for instance, about benefits—such as vacation allotments and retirement programs—can be more easily answered. Exhibit 7-3 shows the scope of information available in an employee handbook.

> ► **employee handbook**
> a tool that serves both employees and employers, providing important information regarding what the company is about, its history, and employee benefits

Beyond just being a source of information, your handbook may also assist in creating a sense of security. By being thorough in its coverage, the employee handbook will address various organizational policies and work rules, which tell you exactly what is expected. For example, the handbook may express information on discipline and discharge procedures and a means of redressing disciplinary action should someone feel that it was administered unfairly. The handbook, then, serves to ensure that organizational policies are fair, equitable, and consistently applied to each organizational member.[9]

---

[8]See, for instance, David L. Barette, "What's New," *HR Magazine* (November 2000), pp. 185–188.
[9]Ibid.

EXHIBIT 7-2

Purpose of the Employee Handbook

Promoting Upward Communications

*A*ny communications system operating in an organization will be effective only if it permits information to flow upward. That means having the ability to raise concerns or complaints, as well as having an opportunity to make suggestions. Let's review these two important organizational communications activities.

Resolving Internal Disputes

➤ **internal dispute (complaint) procedure**
a way for employees to question actions that have occurred in the organization and to seek the organization's assistance in correcting the problem

An organization's **internal dispute (complaint) procedure** is a way for employees to question actions that have occurred in the organization and to seek the organization's assistance in correcting the problem. For example, if you feel that your supervisor has inappropriately evaluated your performance, or that you have been treated unfairly in regard to a promotion, raise, or job responsibility, an internal dispute process allows your issue to be heard. Typically under the direction of an employee relations (ER) specialist, your complaint is investigated and a decision is made regarding its legitimacy. Depending on the organization, an equal employment opportunity (EEO) officer may be available to investigate complaints dealing with such factors as sex, disabilities, race, or age. If there isn't an EEO officer, the employee relations representative generally handles these complaints, too.

(Effective February 2000—Carroll Tree Service)

EXHIBIT 7-3
Contents of a Sample Employee Handbook

Complaint procedures in your organization may be called different things. Yet, irrespective of its name, a complaint procedure will often follow four basic steps. (See Exhibit 7-4.) Of course, if you belong to a union, this process may be different. That's because when a union is present, the internal dispute procedure is spelled out in the labor contract. In that setting, it's called a **grievance procedure.**

grievance procedure an internal dispute procedure spelled out in a labor contract

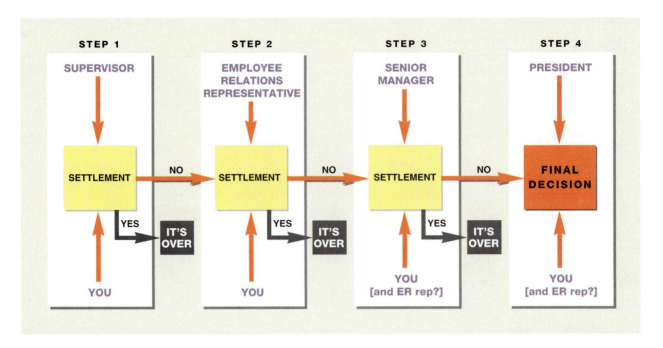

EXHIBIT 7-4

A General Organizational Complaint Procedure

Step 1: You and Your Boss.   This is generally regarded as the first step to resolving any problem. Here, you try to address the issue with your supervisor. If you are able to resolve your differences, nothing further needs to be done. That's why most organizations view this as an informal step in resolving internal disputes.

Most organizations prefer that you first contact the person who has wronged you. But that is not always possible. Depending on the problem, you may skip this step altogether. Why? If you truly fear that you'll be retaliated against, you may simply choose to go to the next level to have your complaint heard. For instance, if your supervisor is sexually harassing you, it's doubtful that telling him or her "no" again will stop the behavior. In that case, you may need other assistance.

In general, though, it's not prudent to go over your boss's head to complain. Politically, it may be unwise. For example, you should realize that going beyond your supervisor might present some risk to you. Depending on the reputation and image of your supervisor, others may give his or her decision great weight. That's not to say that your supervisor is always right. Only you can decide that for yourself. But once you involve others, the issue may get magnified. Be prepared for the fight. But don't overlook this option. You need to feel satisfied. Even if the decision is one you don't agree with, you at least need to know that you've been heard. Just don't expect that you can continue to go higher and get a decision overturned. Unless you have been denied your rights in the process or some procedural error has been made, individuals far removed from the problem are unlikely to have enough knowledge about the situation to change a decision made by your supervisor.

Therefore, common sense should dictate that you try to work out your problems with your supervisor. After all, if you can't, you always have the opportunity to go to Step 2. And it may add more credence to your issue if you can say that you've done everything you could to solve the problem between the two of you.

UNLOCKING YOUR POTENTIAL *7-2*

Using the Complaint Procedure

*E*very organization has a way, either formal or informal, to deal with problems you may encounter. When that process is formalized, support for your position may rest in part with how you use the system. Here are ten questions regarding events that may arise on your job. (If you are not currently working, think about a job you've had, or consider each situation in a classroom or college setting.) Indicate how you feel about the statement using the following: strongly agree (SA), agree (A), uncertain (U), disagree (D), strongly agree (SD).

	SA	A	U	D	SD
1. When I have a problem with my supervisor, the first thing I do is go to his or her boss and express my concern.	___	___	___	___	___
2. When raising a complaint, I accept nothing but a complete understanding of the facts.	___	___	___	___	___
3. I prefer to deal directly with my supervisor for problems that are between us.	___	___	___	___	___
4. When I have a problem, I want it investigated and a decision quickly made (one way or another).	___	___	___	___	___
5. When complaining about some event at work involving another person, I find it hard to exclude personality issues from the problem.	___	___	___	___	___
6. I realize that some problems I have at work with my supervisor can't be settled between us. Sometimes others have to get involved.	___	___	___	___	___
7. I keep good records of issues affecting me, just in case I have to document a problem at some time in the future.	___	___	___	___	___
8. In my organization, if I don't like the final decision of the owner, I can always get a lawyer to help me.	___	___	___	___	___
9. When I have a problem, I know I don't have to fight the fight alone. There's often someone in the organization who can help me.	___	___	___	___	___
10. I shouldn't complain about things at work. If I don't like something, and it bothers me a lot, I should either accept it or leave the organization.	___	___	___	___	___

Larry Detar and Carol Halstead, co-owners of Liberty Kennels in Sierra Vista, Arizona, know the importance of employee handbooks. As their organization has grown, it has become impossible to deal with employees one-on-one for every question—which is often similar for each employee. Accordingly, Larry and Carol have put together an employee handbook that describes the organization, the business direction, and what the company gives to each employee. Their handbook also identifies the tasks, conditions, and standards for each job for employees to follow.

Step 2: You and Employee Relations. If you do not get satisfaction in Step 1, you may proceed to contact your employee relations representative. This will begin the first formal step in your complaint. As part of his or her job, your ER representative will investigate the matter. That means that he or she will hear both sides of the issue, carefully analyze what data has been gathered, and make a decision.

It's important again for you to understand what may be involved in the employee relations representative's decision. This individual generally cannot overrule your supervisor's decision without the supervisor's consent unless the supervisor has violated a company policy or rule. That means that the decision cannot always be made in your favor. Even if you are right, the resolution to the problem also may be within your supervisor's discretion—whether or not it's fair to you. Nonetheless, at the end of this stage, two outcomes are possible. First, if you are satisfied with the decision and the complaint is corrected, no further action on your part is required. But if you are unhappy with what you are told, you may still have the right to take your complaint to higher levels. However, if the ER representative found no validity in your charge, he or she is not responsible for providing continued assistance to you as you take your issue forward.

Step 3: You and a Senior Manager. If you wish to further exercise your rights, the next step in the complaint procedure is to meet with a senior manager of the area (a vice-president, perhaps). Depending on the organization, this individual may decide that there's no reason for you to meet. Reviewing correspondence from what has happened in Steps 1 and 2, the senior manager may decide not to hear your case. In other cases, this individual may meet with you to hear your side of the story and explain why the decision made is appropriate.

Don't interpret this, however, to mean that Step 3 is useless. If you have new information, or if there have been procedural errors in handling your complaint, a decision can be overturned at this level. It's just unlikely that you will be able to rehash what has happened before at this level.

KEYS TO UNLOCKING YOUR POTENTIAL 7-2

Each of the ten statements presented in Unlocking Your Potential 7-2 focused on your knowledge of your organization's complaint procedure. As you have seen over the past few pages, complaint procedures typically follow a general pattern: you and your boss, you and an employee relations representative (if available), you and a senior manager, and you and the president. Given this procedure, let's see how well you understood using the process. Write down your responses (SA, A, U, D, or SD) for each of the ten statements.

Point Value

1. _____   _____
2. _____   _____
3. _____   _____
4. _____   _____
5. _____   _____
6. _____   _____
7. _____   _____
8. _____   _____
9. _____   _____
10. _____   _____

Total: _____

     For questions 1, 2, 5, 7, 8, and 10, give yourself 1 point for every "strongly agree," 2 points for "agree," 3 points for "uncertain," 4 points for "disagree," and 5 points for "strongly disagree." For questions 3, 4, 6, and 9, reverse the scoring. That is, give yourself 5 points for "strongly agree," 4 points for "agree," 3 points for "uncertain," 2 points for "disagree," and 1 point for "strongly disagree." Place your points on the lines in the second column. Add up the ten numbers and place your total in the box in the third column.

     A total of 50 points is possible on this exercise. If you scored 35 or more, congratulations! You have a good understanding of how complaint procedures operate, which can assist you in your time of need. A score of 21–34 indicates you are somewhat aware of the process but need to understand it more. You may want to review your organization's or college's complaint process in the event that you ever have to use it. A score of 20 or below indicates that you do not have much insight into handling complaints in your organization. As such, you may be overlooking a process that can help you overcome or resolve some of the organizational issues affecting you. You have the right to be able to use the complaint process. You need to understand the complaint process in your organization—if for no other reason than to protect yourself.

Extra Effort

If you haven't done so already, obtain a copy of your college's student handbook. Review the section on the student complaint procedure. How many steps are involved? Who plays a role in the process? Who is available on campus to assist you? What rights as a student do you have in the complaint process? Who has the final word?

Step 4: You and the President. The final step in the process involves taking your issue to the president. As in Step 3, the president may decide that a meeting over the issue is not appropriate. However, depending on the organization's culture, you may be given the option to voice your concern. In any case, although your rights may be protected under various state laws, any decision the president makes is often final.

Making Suggestions

Obviously, the internal dispute process focuses its attention on problems that exist between you and someone else in the organization. But there are times when you have something to say that isn't a gripe; in fact, it's offered to help out your organization. To facilitate this, your organization may have a suggestion program.

➤ **suggestion program**
a program designed to allow employees the opportunity to tell organizational members what they are doing inefficiently and what they should do to make the organization better

Like a complaint procedure, a **suggestion program** is designed to allow employees the opportunity to tell organizational members what they are doing inefficiently and what they should do to make the organization better. This information is often welcomed because it represents a point of view from someone closest to the work—identifying inefficiencies and the barriers to productive work. In many organizations, you are rewarded for your suggestions monetarily, through recognition, or both. That reward may stem from a suggestion that is good enough to implement or simply from the fact that you took the time to offer some insight. And if your organization values your upward communications, it must do whatever is possible to make it worth your while to provide the input.

As in the complaint procedure, recognize that how you make suggestions is a function of your organization's culture. If you are viewed as a know-it-all for making them, or if your supervisor sees this as an attack on how he or she runs the department, be careful when making suggestions. Although your intent is to help, this could backfire. Fortunately, you'll have a good clue about making suggestions. If the organization has suggestion boxes located throughout the workplace and makes a big to-do about what you and your co-workers have recommended, then suggestions are actively being sought. But if these are lacking or not highly visible, then you're being sent a message. Once again, your organization's culture will tell you what's appropriate and what is not.

Informal Communications: The Grapevine

*A*s humans, we have an interest in knowing most everything that is going on. Similarly, at times, we also want to share what we know with others. In fact, in this two-way process, good information passes between us fairly fast—bad information, even faster.

Let's say the star basketball player at your high school injured his ankle in a game Friday night. As he hobbled off the court, the coach and the player's parents thought it best for him to be taken for X rays immediately. Two hours later, he was home resting, in a cast up to his calf—the result of a broken ankle. At Saturday night's dance, the air was filled with talk about what had happened. Some good friends of the player who had visited him earlier reported that he had, indeed, broken his ankle and would be in a cast for up to eight weeks. Some even suggested that his basketball career might be over, for if it doesn't heal properly, they say he'll need surgery to place screws in the bone to hold it together. Come Monday morning, when school announcements are made, the news is old—the ankle was broken. Welcome to the grapevine.

➤ **grapevine**
an unofficial, unauthorized, unsupported way that communications take place in an organization

The **grapevine** is an unofficial, unauthorized, unsupported way that communications take place in an organization. Information is usually spread by word of mouth or, in today's workplace, by e-mail. The purpose of the grapevine is to get information out to organizational members as quickly as possible. To give you some

Making Suggestions

Sometimes you may have the greatest suggestion in the world, but if it can't be communicated properly, it may fall on deaf ears. Therefore, the following is recommended for properly making suggestions in an organization's suggestion program.

1. **Ask yourself, does my organization value this input?** You may find that your organization promotes receiving suggestions from employees—especially those closest to the day-to-day work. If you don't see the visible signs of this support (previously recognized individuals, company information about the program, and so on) first find out whether suggestions are welcomed. Remember, even suggestions require you to be politically smart. If suggestions are not welcomed, be careful in making them.

2. **Don't use the suggestion program to complain about something.** Suggestions you make should be given to be helpful, to fix something, or to make something better. This is not the time or the place to put something or someone down. That's best left to the complaint procedure.

3. **Frame your suggestion as corrective feedback.** Focus on the issues. Offer facts, data, and the like that others can respond to. This is probably not the time to make suggestions based on a gut reaction. They may not go very far.

4. **Do your homework.** Many suggestions get overlooked because the individual doesn't really know the facts. Thoroughly research your issue. Try to know everything about your concern as best you can. Speaking from a factual position not only gives validity to your suggestion, but also shows that it's important enough that you took the time to gather the data.

5. **Submit your suggestions according to your organization's procedure.** In organizations where formal suggestion programs operate, there may be a specified way to make suggestions. Make sure your suggestion conforms. This may include making submissions on specified forms, contacting various people, and the like.

6. **Don't hound decision makers about your suggestion.** When your suggestion is reviewed, someone will get back in touch with you. This may be for additional information or to tell you what was decided. Let this individual approach you. Calling frequently to check the status of your suggestion is counterproductive.

7. **Don't get upset if your suggestion is not adopted.** You should expect to be recognized at the very least for your input. But there's never any guarantee that your suggestion will be implemented—in part or in its entirety. That's organizational life. Usually, if your suggestion is not implemented, you can expect to be given a reason. Nonetheless, don't get frustrated over the process.

idea how the grapevine works, several years ago, a colleague and I (Dave) did an experiment (at least that's what we called this slightly mischievous activity) in a seven-thousand-member organization. These employees were located in seven buildings spread out over a twenty-five-mile radius in the Baltimore metropolitan area. We planted a story with someone that we thought would fuel the grapevine. We asked

VALUE JUDGMENT: Using the Grapevine

Effective communication in organizations is built on the assumption that appropriate and accurate information is transmitted. When this occurs, organization members are afforded the respect and dignity that factual information can deliver. But what happens if the factual information is bad news? Can using the grapevine help? Consider the following.

You have been employed by an organization for the past seven years. Throughout the employment process, many individuals remarked about the company giving Christmas bonuses. You know very well that getting such a bonus is a function of the company making money. Yet, since your arrival—as best as you can tell—bonuses are almost a certainty. In fact, you and your co-workers count on this bonus to help pay for Christmas gifts you have purchased for family and friends, or for taking that special vacation during the holiday season. Charging many of these items hasn't yet caused you concern, for the late-December bonus has always more than adequately covered the costs.

Over the years, this bonus has averaged around $1,000. You have come to view it as an infusion of cash at a time when it's needed most. Yet this year, something appears wrong. You know the company has had an off year, and profits are down. Bonuses may be in jeopardy. You've heard nothing until now—and it's approaching Thanksgiving. But you've just been told by several co-workers that they've heard that no bonuses will be given this year. They heard it from a good source that the company can't afford it. They're upset. They, like you, are counting on that money for Christmas shopping. Still, nobody's officially talking. Three weeks later, you get a letter from the company owner. In it, he confirms what you already know—the company's profits are down. But in his letter, he praises the work of the employees and talks about how he is doing everything possible to protect the Christmas bonus. He knows it's important to everyone. Consequently, he tells you that though he wishes the company could do more, employees will be given a $400 bonus this year. You, like many others, are somewhat relieved.

Later, you find out that the owner knew what the bonus would be all along. But he knew that telling you your bonus would be cut from $1,000 to $400 would cause quite a stir. So instead, he fed the grapevine with a rumor that no bonus would be coming. His rationale was that everyone would be upset that no extra money would be coming in. Then, being told several weeks later that you'd be receiving $400 would make everyone happy. It was a gamble, but one he was willing to take.

Do you believe this owner's actions were ethical? Was the grapevine used to create the outcome the owner wanted? How do you value what was done in this situation?

3. Which one of the following statements about employee handbooks is not correct?
   a. Employee handbooks serve the needs of both you and your employer.
   b. Employee handbooks represent an informal communication pattern used by your organization to keep you up to date on organizational happenings.
   c. Employee handbooks often include statements reinforcing your company's values and goals.
   d. Employee handbooks typically give you information about the benefits the company provides for employees.

4. Informal communications that exist in an organization are:
   a. commonly referred to as the grapevine.
   b. often regarded as a violation of formal communications patterns.
   c. typically inaccurate and violate an open-door policy.
   d. supported through the use of bulletin boards, newsletters, company-wide meetings, electronic media, and employee handbooks.

several individuals to write down the day and time when they received some information about our rumor topic. We waited to see how long it would take to reach all seven buildings. Much to our amazement, the message reached representatives in all seven buildings within one minute and thirty seconds. What a ripple effect we saw! We could only imagine that our rumor spread as rapidly to most other organizational members.

The biggest question raised about grapevines, however, focuses on the accuracy of the rumors. More sophisticated research on this topic has been somewhat mixed. Depending on the openness in an organization, the grapevine may be extremely accurate. In others, where the culture is more authoritative, the grapevine may not be as accurate. But even then, though the information flowing is inaccurate, some element of truth can still be found in the information. Remember the basketball player? The part about there being screws in his ankle was false, but the fact that something was wrong was right on target. Likewise, rumors about major layoffs, plant closings, and the like may be filled with inaccurate information regarding who is affected or when it may occur. Nonetheless, the fact that something is about to happen is probably on target. Because of this, many supervisors recognize that the grapevine is alive and well. And instead of spending time trying to stop it, they use it to their advantage.

SUMMARY

This summary corresponds to the Learning Outcomes found on page 155.

1. The purpose of organizational communications is to keep all employees informed of policies, events, and happenings in the organization.

2. The three primary formal communication patterns are from the boss to you (downward communications), from you to your boss (upward communications), and among you and your peers (lateral communications).

3. An open-door policy in an organization indicates that supervisors encourage employees to come to them with concerns and suggestions. Such a policy promotes upward communications.

4. Organizations may use a number of methods for keeping their employees informed. Five of the more popular methods are bulletin boards, company newsletters, company-wide meetings, electronic media, and employee handbooks.

5. Organizations provide employee handbooks to serve as one central source of information about the company and its employment policies. Most employee handbooks include introductory comments about the organization and information about what employees need to know about the workplace, their benefits, and their responsibility to the organization.

6. A typical organizational complaint (internal dispute) procedure consists of four steps: (a) you and your boss, (b) you and an employee relations representative, (c) you and a senior manager, and (d) you and the president. This process applies to most nonunionized organizations. Where unions exist, this process is defined in the labor contract and is called the grievance procedure.

7. The purpose of an employee suggestion program is to provide employees an opportunity to give constructive feedback to supervisors. This enables employees to tell organizational members what they are doing inefficiently and what they should do to make the organization better. Critical components of an organizational suggestion program are the beliefs that employees' suggestions will be heard and that those who make suggestions will be recognized for their effort.

8. The grapevine is one informal communication mechanism that exists in an organization. The grapevine frequently represents a fast and sometimes accurate source of information.

REVIEWING YOUR UNDERSTANDING

1. How are public relations efforts and organizational communications alike? How are they different?

2. In what ways does the organization's culture affect organizational communications?

3. Can an open-door communications policy succeed in an organization where downward communications dominates? Explain your position.

4. Describe how downward, upward, and lateral communications occur in your college classes.

5. Identify and describe four ways that organizations keep their employees informed.

6. Why should an organization provide its employees a handbook?

7. Describe the similarities and the differences between a complaint procedure and a suggestion program in an organization.

8. What is the grapevine, and how can it be used to benefit organizational members?

9. "Supervisors should do everything under their control to keep the grapevine to a minimum. The grapevine creates problems for most organizations and leads to employees getting false information." Do you agree or disagree with this statement? Discuss.

ANSWERS TO CHECKING YOUR UNDERSTANDING

1. b **2.** c **3.** b **4.** a

LEARNING TOGETHER

A. Discuss the statement, "Good communication results in more satisfied workers and higher employee morale."

B. Develop a set of five or six questions about methods and effectiveness of communication—formal/informal, upward/downward, open-door policy, grapevine, and so on. Interview two or three people from a company regarding their methods of communication. Draw some conclusions on why or why not each interviewee selected different methods as the most effective or most frequently used. Report your findings to your class.

C. With class members, develop a Web page to promote communications for your school. Start with a class discussion on what needs to be done, how it can be done, who needs to be involved, what permissions should be sought, who will maintain the Web page after it is created, and so on. Then divide into groups to share the work to be completed.

D. Identify the ways your school (or employer) communicates internally and externally. Draw some conclusions about the practices. Provide some suggestions (in which you would be willing to participate) to improve communications at your school (or employer). Discuss your findings with the class and modify your suggestions accordingly. Develop a plan of action and begin working on your plan.

Milano's Pizza

The team approach at Milano Brothers Pizza Factory was unsurpassed—that is, until Harrell Williams joined the team about four months ago. Harrell is having a lot of difficulty with co-workers, but is not sure why.

Harrell's supervisor, Frank Struthers, reports to Mindy Hamilton. Mindy has two other supervisors reporting to her. Mindy has meetings at 3:30 P.M. on Mondays and Fridays. Her meetings are to ensure that the full-time day and evening employees have an opportunity to interact with each other. She sends memos to her employees about promotions, changes in procedures, and customer concerns. Many of these memos are in response to both written and verbal suggestions from her employees.

Mindy believes in fostering good morale among her employees. Usually she will post a thought for the week, which focuses on some aspect of customer service. Frequently she will also post an attitude or personality booster that will get employees to think about their own behavior in building human relations skills. She encourages others to post items that promote positive actions.

At the Friday meeting she announces the employee of the week and tells why the person was selected. The franchise's bimonthly newsletter features the employees of the week. Last week Frank was selected for offering his assistance to a delivery person who had a flat tire. Frank was off duty and was on his way to a community college class when he spotted a Milano delivery person struggling with changing a tire. Frank didn't know Beth, the delivery person, but stopped to help her change her tire. He found out Beth was a new employee at one of the other Milano franchises. Mindy learned of the good deed when the franchise owner, Trudy Featherston, stopped by Mindy's store a few hours later. The word had traveled quickly from Beth to her supervisor, John, who passed the word on to his boss, Willard, whose daughter was dating Trudy's son.

Trudy Featherston visits each of her five franchises regularly. In fact, you can be assured that no more than a couple of days will go by without seeing her. She shows real concern for her employees and is always asking about their families, school, and other interests. She is a strong supporter of her employees' continuing their education. She also is a big sports fan.

When Trudy comes by, Harrell is quick to get her attention. He usually tells her about something he has done well and how he supported another employee in getting a job done. He frequently will tell her of a supervisory problem he was able to handle, to show he is helping Mindy and can be a supervisor. Harrell has some good connections for baseball tickets and frequently gets tickets to give to Trudy. Harrell wants to become a store manager.

Questions

1. Under two headings, list the types of formal and informal communications that are present in this case. Can some of the communications be both? Why or why not?

2. Discuss the pros and cons of the various types of communications at Milano's.

3. Why may Harrell be having some difficulty in his job? What can he do to change that?

4. If an internal dispute were to arise at Milano's, what process do you think would be followed? Describe the steps in the process.

5. Is there an open-door communication policy at Milano's? Explain your answer.

POWER, POLITICS, AND STATUS

Learning Outcomes

After reading this chapter, you will be able to:

1. Define *power*.

2. Contrast authority and power.

3. Identify the five power sources.

4. Describe a means of developing a power base.

5. Define *political behavior*.

6. Explain the factors that guide organizational political activities.

7. Identify seven ways of becoming politically smart.

8. Define *status*.

9. Describe why status is important in organizations.

10. Identify nine work-related status symbols.

What is it about some people that we are awestruck by them? Is it their red Mercedes convertible coming down the highway wind-blowing their hair? How about the reserved parking space provided for the select few in the organization while the rest of us have to walk several blocks from the employee parking lot? Why do we think differently of someone dressed in a $1,200 Armani suit than someone dressed in an off-the-rack suit purchased at Sears? Do we feel that someone is special because her corner office with its rich mahogany furnishings is more than six times the size of our windowless cubicle? Why doesn't she have pressboard-and-chrome furnishings like the rest of us? Are we impressed when someone can get seated immediately in a full restaurant without reservations, while we may have to wait for more than an hour? Does the fact that some individuals can get on television almost any time they have something to say give them a special presence? Or is it a platinum American Express card that is issued to individuals who charge more than $10,000 yearly and who are willing to pay its $350 annual fee?

Answers to questions like these require more than simple yes-or-no responses. Instead, they focus on a much bigger issue that is part of the American culture. That is, we do see people differently, and, because of that, we grant certain individuals special attention. Rock stars, politicians, entertainers, company presidents, surgeons, and the wealthy all have one thing in common. They possess some sort of influence over others, play the game of life exceptionally well, and have all the trimmings that say they've made it. In more appropriate terms, we call these things power, politics, and status. Power, politics, and status do not exist in a vacuum. They are factors that interact with and derive their existence within their unique environment. In this chapter we will explore the existence of power, politics, and status within the work environment. We will discuss how these three factors not only contribute to the identity of the organization but also relate to the challenges facing the organization.

Power

Power—what an amazing word in the English language. This two-syllable, five-letter word carries with it some of the most intense feelings people can have. In fact, it's almost a word we don't like to talk about. We find that discussion difficult and sometimes too personal—even more so than talking about sex. Just consider this: Often those who have power deny that they do. Those who want power will do almost anything to get it. And those who do find a way to get power will often keep their method of getting it a secret. So what is this thing we desire but won't freely talk about? Let's look at what power is, where it comes from, and how it can be developed.

What Is This Thing We Crave?

> **power**
> the ability to influence others to do the things one would like them to do

Power is the ability to influence others to do the things one would like them to do. In your life, this translates into affecting others in how they view certain events. For example, on your campus, you may be upset about the administration's decision to change the football program. Because of budget cuts and the increasing costs of athletic scholarships, the president decides that playing Division 1-A football is no longer beneficial. Instead, the college will change its football status to Division 3-A. This will mean that it will become a nonscholarship sport. Although the choice is rightfully the president's to make, you begin demonstrating your distaste with the decision. Through rallies and protests, pressure is brought on the president to rethink his position. Yet nothing changes. However, shortly after a meeting with the president and one local businessperson (someone who, by the way, is an avid fan of the college's football team), the president reverses his decision. In the end, the president was influenced by the actions of an individual outside the organization.

If you think for a moment about this example, you might assume that power belongs only to those in supervisory positions. Clearly the president of the college, or any organization for that matter, may have power. A leadership or supervisory position in the organization may give some power. That goes without question. In Chapter 6 we learned that one has authority because of his or her position in the organization. However, authority is not the same as power. Recall that authority is something granted by one's job title. It is specific to the position. Take away the position, and you take away the authority. Power, on the other hand, belongs to the person and may be independent of the job held. Most of an individual's power usually comes not from a person's position, but from something that he or she has earned or gained because of his or her personality, attitude, or situation. For example, consider your supervisor's secretary. She has very little to do with your everyday work; you report to your supervisor and take directions from him. Decisions about your workload, performance, pay increases, and so on are his. His secretary truly has no authority over you. So is it possible for her to have any power over you or influence what you do? Yes. How can that be? Simply, it's that she's close to a powerful person in the organization, your supervisor. By being your boss's gatekeeper, she often decides if and when you see the boss. Often, too, you count on her to pass information from you to your boss; therefore, she controls what your boss hears from and about you. Furthermore, it is often the secretary who actually assigns parking spots to employees or sets up the vacation schedule for workers. Now that's power!

Whenever people use their power, they're doing whatever they can to change the behaviors and attitudes of others. Yet too often, this may be negatively viewed. You may view the power of certain individuals as controlling, manipulative, or even coercive— whether or not any action takes place. For example, consider the power of a bouncer at a local nightclub near your college. The sheer size of the individual gives him power. So when he politely asks you to stop doing something, you comply. Why? Because you recognize that if you don't, things might intensify to the point where you are physically removed from the club, and that's something you want to avoid. Therefore, your behavior has been influenced not so much by what someone has done, but by what he could do.

Power, however, does not have to be negative. Some people can influence others to do good things, and it can and does happen. Parents and role models can help shape your life in a direction that will lead you to become a productive member of society. Appeals from celebrities for you to get an education, to remain drug-free, or to sponsor an undernourished child in a Third World nation use their fame and the power of the media to bring to light something beneficial. Your supervisor uses his power to keep you focused on your tasks so that the organization can achieve its goals. So, too, does your professor, when she influences you to come to class regularly.

Power is a major part of your organizational life. It's important, therefore, to understand where power comes from and how you can best use it to achieve positive outcomes.

Power Sources

One interesting aspect about power is that there's no limit on how much power can be shared in an organization. That is, as you gain power, it doesn't mean you take it away from another person. Rather, both of you have the opportunity to develop power—something you can obtain through a variety of means. So how do you develop power? According to two researchers who have studied power extensively,[1] there are

---

[1] John R. P. French, Jr., and Bertram Raven, "The Bases of Social Power," in Dorwin Cartwright, ed., *Studies in Social Power* (Ann Arbor: University of Michigan Institute for Social Research, 1959), pp. 150–167.

Legitimate power	Power that is based on an individual's formal position in the organization
Coercive power	Power that is based on the use of fear
Reward power	Power that is based on the ability to distribute anything that others value
Expert power	Power that is based on expertise, special skills, or knowledge
Referent power	Power that is based on respect from others

EXHIBIT 8-1
Types of Power

five bases of power: legitimate, coercive, reward, expert, and referent power. These sources of power are summarized in Exhibit 8-1.

➤ **legitimate power**
power that is based on an individual's formal position in the organization

Like authority, **legitimate power** is based on an individual's formal position in the organization. Because your supervisor is given the charge of supervising you, she is granted the authority to run your department. In this case, the authority implies that she has the power to directly influence your daily activities. You acknowledge that she can get you to do something simply because the chain of command dictates it. Following your supervisor's directives is a responsibility you accept when you work in an organization. Your acceptance, then, means that you will listen to and comply with her requests because she is authorized or has the right to direct your work. However, what if you or other employees choose not to accept and comply with the supervisor's directives? If the supervisor is able to get you to do what she wants, then, in addition to authority, she also has legitimate power. If she is not able to get you to do what she wants, then, even though she has authority, she does not have power. As with authority, the supervisor has legitimate power because she's appointed to a particular job; if someone takes away her job title and responsibilities, her power, too, is removed.

➤ **coercive power**
power that is based on the use of fear

A second type of power that you can gain is power based on the use of fear, **coercive power.** The actions of others are influenced simply by their need to avoid some negative consequence. In organizations, a supervisor can use coercive power to greatly influence you. Even if she never takes a negative action against you, the fact that she can discipline you or generally make your work life miserable can get you to do the things she wants. Even in college classes, you can see coercive power working. Suppose a professor notifies students that missing more than three class periods will result in their final course grade being lowered one letter. To avoid this punishment, students attend every class. Coercive power, then, has influenced the behavior of the students. Although coercive power can be and often is misused, it is also very often effective. In many situations, the use of threats has negative outcomes. Human beings don't respond well to threats. So even though students do show up for class to be counted on the roll, their minds may be elsewhere. As a result, the body count may be high, but the most important ingredient—an open mind wanting to learn—may be missing.

➤ **reward power**
power that is based on the ability to distribute anything that others value

As the adage states, you can get more flies with honey than with vinegar. So whereas coercive power gets someone to do things out of fear, **reward power** is based on the ability to distribute anything that others value; it influences behavior because of a potential for a positive outcome. Most of us like anything that has positive reinforcement associated with it. So when we work with others who have the power to give something we want, we usually comply. For instance, your supervisor has the power to evaluate your performance and recommend a pay raise. The power of that reward (the pay increase) is enough to get you to follow your supervisor's lead. Your professor can have reward power, too. Instead of penalizing those who skip classes, your professor writes exam questions that are directly related to some lecture material. Thus, by coming to class you are exposed to material that can help you get a better grade on an exam—the reward.

Although coercive power and reward power are often associated with those in supervisory positions, they need not be. Unlike legitimate power, people who do not have formal authority over you still can use coercive and reward power. For example, pledging and being accepted into a sorority or fraternity places you into a situation where current members have coercive or reward power over you. You'll often endure what they place before you in an effort to being accepted by them.

Expert power is based on expertise, special skills or knowledge. Because others perceive that you know something they don't, they are likely to accept what you say. For example, suppose you're working with several others on a major class project. Part of this project requires that you make a class presentation. You let the group know that you have access to a software program that can be used to make outstanding presentation transparencies. Because the presentation is a crucial component of your grade, your group members give you great freedom to make the transparencies for them. As such, you are able to influence them in this project.

➤ **expert power**
power that is based on expertise, special skills, or knowledge

As organizations and jobs become more technologically advanced, those who understand and can work with the technology will gain power. If you can do something that others can't, or know something others don't, you create an advantage for yourself. But be careful. Though being an expert can help you gain power, realize that this power may be short-lived. As others learn what you know, your power may be weakened.

The last type of power source, **referent power,** is based on respect from others because they believe in you. Because of their respect for you, others allow you to influence their behavior. How do you get this respect? Although there are no clear-cut ways, it comes from possessing traits that others admire. Charisma, honesty, sincerity, and empathy are all personal qualities that some people with referent power have. Because they demonstrate things you admire, you do things to please them. That's why small children often do as their parents ask—because of the admiration they have for Mom and Dad. The referent power of celebrities allows them to influence purchases. A supervisor who respects you as an individual often gets your respect in return. Accordingly, the supervisor can get you to go the extra mile—not because you're forced, but because you truly want to help. This last source of personal power is the hardest to get and keep. Yet when you think about it for a moment, it's the one based solely on positive human relations. If you deal with people properly and grant them the respect and dignity they deserve, you gain power. Play psychological games with them or abuse them in some way, and that fragile power is lost.

➤ **referent power**
power that is based on respect from others

✓ Checking Your Understanding 8-1

1. The ability to get others to do the things you'd like them to do is called:
   a. supervision
   b. compromising behavior
   c. politicking
   d. none of the above

2. Giving you an F on a term paper because you didn't properly set the top and left margins as specified by your professor in his syllabus is best reflective of:
   a. political power
   b. coercive power
   c. legitimate power
   d. negative power

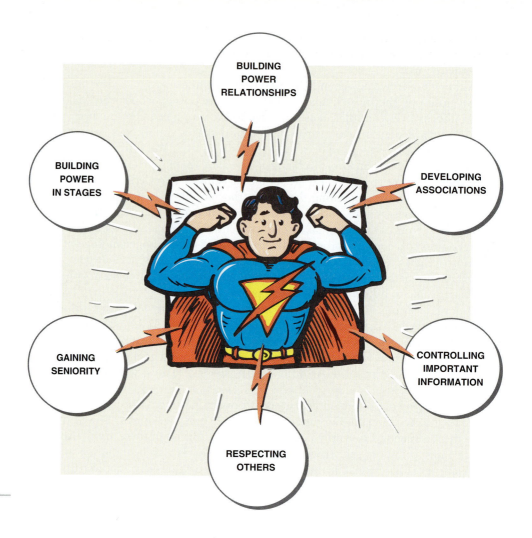

EXHIBIT 8-2
Developing Power

Developing a Power Base

One of the more difficult aspects of power is developing a plan to acquire it. For some individuals, power comes naturally. It's frequently a function of the jobs they hold. But can others do anything to develop power? The answer is yes. These include respecting others, building power relationships, developing associations, controlling important information, gaining seniority, and building power in stages.[2] (See Exhibit 8-2.) Let's look at each of these.

Respecting Others.   One of the most crucial aspects to developing power is to treat others the way you'd like to be treated. Although this concept is somewhat of a cliché, it holds a tremendous key for you. If others don't respect you (in part because you don't respect them), your power will generally be limited. They may have to do the things you ask, but that may only be a result of legitimate power. People need to know you're genuine—and that means respecting others.

Considering the great diversity that exists in the world today, you must be sensitive to others' needs. Failure to do so may only lead to problems arising between you

---

[2]See, for example, Andrew J. DuBrin, *Human Relations: A Job Oriented Approach*, 5th ed. (Upper Saddle River, N.J.: Prentice-Hall, 1992), pp. 313–314.

and others. Most of these problems can be avoided if you see the good in people, realize that most try their best, and understand that they want to do a good job.

Building Power Relationships. People who possess power often associate with others who also have power. You need to identify who these people are and do some of the same things they do.[3] If they belong to a certain health club, you may want to join, too. The idea is to make yourself visible to powerful people and let them observe you in a number of situations. That may also mean volunteering to serve on community committees where these individuals have an interest. For example, if the individuals with power in your organization are active in United Way campaigns, volunteer to serve as your department's United Way contact person. This, at the very least, will provide you the opportunity to attend meetings with these powerful people.[4]

Another suggestion often cited in building power relationships is for you to become more social. This may involve inviting those who have power to social events. This includes hosting a party for your department or entertaining several groups of individuals. Furthermore, taking someone of power to breakfast or lunch has been shown to be a good opportunity to get to know this other person and discuss items of importance to you. In fact, this has become so critical that we now refer to this as the "power lunch."

Developing Associations. We have learned from an early age that there is strength in numbers. This also applies to the world of power. When you associate with others by joining a group striving to have an influence in some situation, you become part of a coalition in which everyone's energies are brought together to form one large base of power. Whether it is the coalition's desire to change working conditions or to influence local politicians to change zoning laws, there is a common goal for all members. Through the collective action of a group of people, it is more likely that the influence will be effective.

Controlling Important Information. If you can get yourself into a position where you have access to the information other people receive, you can gain power. This is especially critical in a world where your life depends so much on information processing. Getting this information is often a function of a level of expertise you possess. For example, if you are responsible for establishing and maintaining a computer program or deciding what gets broadcast over the organization's e-mail system, you have some power that others don't.

One of the greatest means of developing this power is to continue to learn. Finding new approaches to solve old problems or creating a special process are ways of gaining a level of expertise that makes you indispensable to the organization. An engineer at 3M who patents a new adhesive gains power because he or she has become valuable to the organization.

Gaining Seniority. Somewhat related to controlling information, power can be generated by being around an organization for an extended time. People often respect individuals who have lived through the ups and downs of an organization. This experience often gives them a perspective that newcomers don't have. Staying with an organization as long as possible helps develop your power in that organization. Longevity in the organization provides you a unique perspective because you have information that others may not have.

---

[3]See, for example, Hal Lancaster, "When Your Boss Doesn't Like You, It's Detente or Departure," *The Wall Street Journal* (August 15, 1995), p. B-1.
[4]William Leonard, "Downsized and Out: Career Survival in the '90s," *HR Magazine* (June 1995), p. 90.

Building Power in Stages.   Few people go from being powerless one moment to being powerful the next. That simply does not occur in most situations. Rather, power comes in phases. As you build your power, remember that it will start slowly. You will be given opportunities to demonstrate that you can handle the power. If you pass the test, you'll more than likely be given more power.

Implied in this, however, is some understanding of what you want. If, for example, you'd like to become president of your student government association, you'll more than likely have to get involved in student matters early in your college career. As fellow students see that you have gained knowledge about things that affect students, and you have served well on several committees, they are more likely to vote you into this power position. The president of the United States is usually not occupying his first elected office; he has worked his way up to the job by building a power base along the way. Developing power in our lives is not much different. In fact, like getting elected U.S. president, power is often closely linked to the politics that exist in an organization. As such, you need to know what office politics are and how to survive them.

Dealing with Politics

> **politics**
> something one engages in when one attempts to influence the advantages and disadvantages of a situation

*P*olitics is something one engages in when one attempts to influence the advantages and disadvantages of a situation.[5] In your job, politics goes beyond normal work activities. Whenever two or more people come together for some purpose, each has some idea on what should occur. If you try to influence that situation so that it benefits you more than another or keeps others from gaining some advantage, you are playing politics. But like power, not all political behavior is negative. It doesn't have to mean manipulating a series of events, complaining about a co-worker, or sabotaging the work or reputation of another to further your career. Yet mention the word *politics* and that's what comes to mind. In fact, look at the suggestions provided earlier about gaining power. There's a fine line between appropriate behavior and politics. Sometimes doing the right thing can be viewed by some as demonstrating high ethical standards. Others, however, may view this as taking advantage of a situation and blowing your own horn. For instance, suppose that while students were taking an exam, your professor had to leave the room for an emergency. As soon as he left, you noticed fellow students blatantly cheating on the exam. Afterward, you contacted your professor and told him of the cheating that occurred during his absence. Some may congratulate you because you stood up for what was right. Others, however, may hold a different view. They know your grade is borderline. They see your behavior as trying to get on the professor's good side. After all, everyone knows that your professor constantly emphasizes having high values.

Politics plays a role in almost every organization; no organization is totally free of politics. Because resources are limited, decisions are made using less-than-perfect information. People's personalities, values, goals, and the like differ, and influencing a situation for one reason or another is bound to occur.[6] Therefore, you need to understand the political environment of your organization as well as how to properly play the political game.

Politics in Organizations

More than likely, you're well aware that office politics exists. You've seen it in almost everything you've done. You know, for instance, that to get a good course schedule

---

[5]D. Farrell and J. C. Petersen, "Patterns of Political Behavior in Organizations," *Academy of Management Review* (July 1982), p. 405.
[6]For example, see Jeffrey Pfeffer, *Power in Organizations* (Marshfield, Mass.: Pitman, 1981).

VALUE JUDGMENT: Turning In a Colleague

Imagine working in an organization with a trusted colleague. This individual has been part of your work life for several years now. When you've performed well and completed a major project, your colleague has been there to celebrate with you. More important, when you've been down in the dumps, this friend has given you advice to help you through those darkest days.

Lately, though, you feel as if your co-worker has been putting you in an uncompromising position. Several times during the last two months, he hasn't been able to complete projects—resulting in your having to add the final touches to bring them to closure. Moreover, you have covered for him when he was absent by answering his phone and making excuses regarding his whereabouts. After all, he said that he just needed to run an errand for a few minutes. You even allowed him to use your car last night because his was in the shop for repairs. This morning, while reaching into your glovebox for a napkin, you found drug paraphernalia. You concluded that a substance problem was the root of your colleague's problems. You tried talking to him earlier today about your concerns, but he wouldn't listen.

Both of you work for an organization that has a very strict substance abuse policy. Anyone suspected of abusing illegal drugs must submit to a drug test. If that test is positive, the individual is suspended with pay for sixty days. During this time, the person is required to attend a substance abuse clinic daily. At its conclusion, another drug test is administered. If the results are negative, the employee may return to work; if positive, the individual's employment is terminated.

Although you aren't sure of the extent of your co-worker's problem (even if he truly has one at all), you do know that both of you are competing for a promotion. On the one hand, you know that if you brought the work-related matters to your supervisor's attention, she would investigate the situation. She might conclude, too, that his work behavior has changed and require him to take a drug test. Even if the results of the drug test were negative, it might cast doubt on your co-worker's performance and reduce his chances for the promotion. On the other hand, this is your colleague, someone to whom you've turned for help in the past. When you really think about who's best for the promotion (not counting the performance problems of the past few months), even you have to admit he would be the better choice. He has more experience and has always been someone to whom you went for help. Furthermore, you don't have proof that what you found is truly his—maybe he was just helping another friend with his problems. As for his work, maybe he's just overloaded and needed help.

So what do you do? Do you wait a while and confirm your suspicion? Or do you talk with your supervisor now? And if it's the latter, are you taking political advantage of your colleague? What would you do in this situation?

you need to do certain things. Maybe it's influencing the person at the computer terminal to input your class schedule before others that were turned in first. Or maybe you have a good relationship with the individual who can get you into a closed class, and you do whatever you can to keep that relationship strong.

The thing to keep in mind is that organizational politics can be either constructive or destructive. If it's the latter, the situation can become vicious. And make no mistake about it, even if you are good at the destructive side of politics, someone else is

UNLOCKING YOUR POTENTIAL 8-1

Are You Political?

Are you familiar with the concept of office politics as they exist in U.S. organizations? Answer each of the following questions regarding how you view office politics by placing a check mark in the True or False box.

	True	False
1. Office politics exist because many of the rules of the game are unclear.	☐	☐
2. Office politics exist in few organizations today.	☐	☐
3. Office politics are generally destructive to the smooth operation of an organization.	☐	☐
4. Your positive image increases your political power.	☐	☐
5. Calling in favors from others is an example of a political compromise.	☐	☐
6. Your political power is often a function of the people with whom you associate.	☐	☐
7. Playing office politics is unethical.	☐	☐
8. It's politically smart not to support your supervisor if he or she is a poor performer.	☐	☐

probably better. Like gunslingers in the Old West, you are only as good as your last gunfight. At some point, it all catches up with you. Therefore, it's important to recognize what goes into your organization's politics and what you should avoid. Equally important is understanding how you can become politically smart.

Understanding the Game

Some people might take offense to referring to politics in organizations as a game. Although their point is well taken, the fact is that's really what office politics is. Some win and others lose. The point, however, should not so much be over the issue of game playing, but how you play the political game. If ever your values will be called into question, this is the time.

Whenever you enter the political arena, you should be driven by some guiding standards. For example, you must take into account three items.[7] (See Exhibit 8-3.) First, you must assess the reason why you are playing politics. If it's self-serving and goes against your department's goals, then your behavior may be unethical. Second, you must make sure that your behavior does not violate others' rights. Eavesdropping on co-workers' conversations in an effort to get information to use against them is acting unethically. Finally, if what you do results in someone being treated unfairly, then your actions may be inappropriate. This could occur, for instance, if you tell your supervisor that a co-worker is interviewing for other jobs just before she assigns one of you to a highly desirable project. At the root of these standards, guiding your political

---

[7]Based on Stephen P. Robbins and David A. DeCenzo, *Supervision Today*, 3ed. (Upper Saddle River, N.J.: Prentice-Hall, 2001), p. 405.

ARE YOU PLAYING POLITICS
FOR SELF-SERVING REASONS?

WILL YOUR POLITICAL BEHAVIOR
VIOLATE OTHERS' RIGHTS?

DO YOUR POLITICS
TREAT SOME PEOPLE UNFAIRLY?

NO — ETHICAL BEHAVIOR

YES — UNETHICAL BEHAVIOR

EXHIBIT 8-3
Political Guiding Questions

activities in an organization, are three factors: what the organization expects, the power of others, and the power you have.[8] (See Exhibit 8-4.)

Organizational Expectations. Nothing affects people's political behavior at work more than the rules and regulations organizational members have set. Remember, an organization's culture reflects its personality. This sets the stage for the values and work practices that every member is expected to demonstrate. For example, imagine the difference in political behavior in the following two settings. In the first, the organization reinforces your taking risks. Rewards you receive are based on the results you achieve—regardless of how you got them. Infighting, disagreements between co-workers, and independent work are not only accepted, but at times encouraged. Under these circumstances, you'd expect a lot of game playing or politics.

In the second organization, the opposite holds. Your rewards are based not only on how well you achieve results, but also on how you achieve them. These achievements reflect, in part, how well you work together with co-workers and how each member supports one another. In fact, the rewards are given to the group. Accordingly, if the group succeeds, you do, too. Needless to say, political game playing in this setting is somewhat minimized.

So how do you make sense out of an organization's expectations? Look at how others advance within the organization. In many cases, understanding the advancement process can best be achieved by focusing on the performance evaluation system in the organization. If the process reinforces teamwork and if you see that others who have excelled in the organization did so by working well with others, then you have a good idea of the extent of the politics you'll have to play (or refrain from) to survive. In the end, organizations do tell you what really counts.

The Power of Others. Assessing the power of others can be difficult. Clearly, you know that those who hold formal positions in the organization may have legitimate power, but that doesn't mean that they are all-powerful. For example, your supervisor has authority over you. From an authority viewpoint, he appears more powerful than you. But you've had the opportunity to work with his boss frequently and have gained

---

[8]Adapted from Stephen P. Robbins and Phillip L. Hunsaker, *Training in Interpersonal Skills: TIPS for Managing People at Work*, 2nd ed. (Upper Saddle River, N.J.: Prentice-Hall, 1996), pp. 128–130.

EXHIBIT 8-4
Political Factors

a high level of respect from him. If, because you feel that something your supervisor is doing is inappropriate or that he is taking the department in the wrong direction (and after you have discussed it with your supervisor to no avail), you go over his head, you've just landed the first punch in this political fight. Furthermore, if you've read the clues correctly and have gained some personal power with your boss's boss, you may be successful. But you're playing a game of odds, and you really don't know how things will end up. Why? Imagine that your boss's boss sides with the supervisor. Where has the power gone now? It can happen. That's why understanding the power of others and acting accordingly is such a risky venture.

The Power You Have.   The preceding discussion suggests that you have assessed your own power base, but it's too critical to leave to an assumption. Before you throw your hat into the political arena, you need to know whether you're coming from a position of strength. Maybe you don't have legitimate power. That's okay. It just indicates that you have to look at other types of power you may have. Can you generate power because of information you have or the expertise you bring to the organization? Or can you build power from associations with others? Your answers will vary and may be different in each situation. The point is that you need to know whether you're in a position to challenge another person or what he or she stands for. Just being right sometimes isn't always enough to bring the issue to a successful completion. That's why you see so many situations where a person blows the whistle on inappropriate organizational activities and ends up getting fired. In many of these cases, the individual was right and had the backing of enforcement agencies. But the powers in the organization retaliated and fired the whistle-blower. And in many cases, the courts couldn't get the person's job back.

Becoming Politically Smart: A Skills Perspective

The preceding discussion should have you wondering about surviving office politics. Although there are few clear-cut ways of not getting involved, some suggestions can be offered to help you become politically smart. These recommendations, however, are not designed to teach you how to take advantage of someone else—or a given situation. Rather, they are intended to help you develop a personal profile, which can assist you if you find yourself in a political situation.

Portraying the Proper Image.   What others think about you is important to your political success. You need to understand the organization's culture and act accordingly. Accept and demonstrate the values, norms, and behaviors that the organization wants. Doing so shows that you know what is important for organizational survival. Portraying the proper image also increases your likelihood that when you do raise an issue, others may give it more legitimacy. An outcast who's always complaining rarely gets an audience—even if he or she is right. For example, the student who nitpicks every word on a test is less likely to succeed in challenging a test question although the challenge may be accurate. "Crying wolf" often does detract from your image.

Being Loyal.   Most organizations have one cardinal rule: When representing the company or its members in a public setting, you do not make derogatory comments. You may have concerns or even seriously dislike something that is happening, but such discussions belong inside your work setting. Taking these issues public serves little useful purpose. You need to be seen as supportive of the organization. If you're not, there's little chance you'll develop support from others (especially those in power). Take faculty members who use their classes as a platform to complain about their dean's decision not to recommend tenure for a popular faculty member. It may be blowing off steam or an attempt to get you involved in supporting them, but it demonstrates their disloyalty. Imagine what would happen three months later if the dean were asked by someone in the community if he or she knew of a faculty member who wanted to earn some extra money by helping develop a training program. Do you think the dean would suggest someone who makes derogatory statements about the college? It's doubtful.

Accepting Challenging Assignments.   Most people in power positions like others who demonstrate some initiative. Maybe it's something they value in themselves and want to reward in others. Willingly and happily accepting assignments helps you develop friends in high places. If you're seen as someone who can be counted on and who doesn't complain when things don't go as expected, then you're building personal power. You're building political allies.

Compromising with Others.   Kenny Rogers sang a song several years ago called "The Gambler." Part of the lyrics said, "You've got to know when to hold 'em and know when to fold 'em." Office politics could use that as a motto. There are times when you have to force your issue. Other issues may not be that critical to you. You don't have to win every time; rather, it may be better to give in when it makes sense. By compromising, you're demonstrating that you're a team player and willing to work with others so that everyone can succeed. But you're also banking favors. When you need something, you can call in the proverbial chips.

People will generally come to your aid if you've helped them before. Call it having your back scratched after you've scratched theirs, a payback, or anything else you want. The fact is, if you help others get what is really important to them, they'll likely help you get what you want. Trade-offs are often at the root of politics. That's why we see elected officials making every effort to help those who contributed to their campaigns and supported them in getting into office.

Avoiding Tarnished Individuals.   Guilt by association—that's something you need to avoid. We all occasionally spend free time with others we like. But when one or more of those you hang out with are negatively viewed by those who hold power, you, too, may be viewed like them. You may not have given others a reason to think that way about you, but too often a connection is made between you and whom you choose as friends. After all, birds of a feather may, in fact, flock together. Accordingly, be conscious of those you call friends in the organization. If you know that some of your friends or colleagues are not seen in the best light or are perceived as trouble-makers in the organization, remove yourself from their company.

This is hardest to accomplish when one of these individuals is your good friend outside the organization. Do you turn your back on a friendship to enhance your organizational image? Or do you remain loyal to your friend and not worry about being politically smart? It's a tough decision you may have to make.

Finding a Mentor.   Nothing helps you avoid land mines more than someone who knows where the land mines are. Getting help navigating your path makes things so much safer. In organizations, this navigator is called a mentor. A **mentor** is usually a more experienced and more senior member of the organization who acts as an individual's support system within the organization. Mentors are often already part of the power group and often are able to get you exposure to the power brokers in the organization. They provide you advice on how to effectively maneuver through the system. From a political point of view, a mentor can act as a sounding board for you, providing vital suggestions and feedback on how to survive and succeed.

Mentors and Diversity.   Gaining political power and building a power base in an organization are often fostered with the help of a mentor. In the past, however, most of those who were supported by an experienced, senior member of the organization often shared something in common: They were male and they were white. But what about women and people of color? What opportunities lie ahead for them to find and get this support?

Finding or getting a mentor is rarely easy. In fact, more often than not, you are approached by the other person. But what serves as the attraction to bring the two of you together? In the past, it was something a potential mentor saw in you, which was often something he saw in himself years ago. But how can a male properly relate to a female (or individuals from different races or national origins) when there's no foundation of commonality between them? Unquestionably, these can be major issues—many of which we've highlighted in previous chapters. But organizations are attempting to bridge this gap. Many recognize that leaving it up to nature just won't work. There needs to be something in place—special programs that promote senior members taking junior members under their wing. Yet even when these programs exist, other problems may arise. For example, is the male supervisor who is mentoring a younger female employee exhibiting appropriate mentoring behavior, or is she getting special treatment because she's a woman? After all, the basis of such a relationship is an effort to further one's career. But at what point might it stop being a close, personal work relationship and cross the line into sexual harassment?

Given the potential difficulties diversity offers for mentoring, the fact remains that each of us needs this support. Therefore, if a potential mentor doesn't approach

> **mentor**
someone who is usually a more experienced and more senior member of the organization who acts as an individual's support system within the organization

you, you must make every effort to find one yourself. In either case, being mentored requires work. That effort will only be magnified when your mentor is someone who has personal attributes different from yours. In the long run, however, our human relations skills can help us make this situation positive for everyone involved.

Supporting Your Boss.   Although the preceding recommendations play critical roles in helping you become politically astute, nothing is more important than supporting your boss. Your supervisor is the person closest to you who has any power. You cannot overlook that fact. Like it or not, problems or personality conflicts with your boss can be deadly. Even if you are correct in your assertions, it's tough to successfully challenge someone who has authority over you. Organizational life has reinforced this over the years.

Problems aside, however, one of the best ways to remain politically smart is to do whatever you can to make your boss look good. It's natural for others who see you as helping them to help you when you need it. In fact, everything you do at work should be geared to helping your boss succeed. Even though your rewards may not be immediately seen, in the long run, you'll benefit. Even if your supervisor takes advantage of your generosity, others in the organization will see the work you are doing, and eventually you'll gain some personal power. That's something you may have trouble seeing every day—especially if you're irritated with the way things are going. But people who work hard and do the right things eventually get their just reward.

Status

*F*requently in organizations, individuals who have power and are politically shrewd also have the trimmings that go along with it. These outward signs of success are grouped under the heading of *status*.

What Is Status?

If there is one thing that correctly describes American culture, it is that we as a group of people are very status-conscious. We have specific rituals, play different roles, and do other things to differentiate ourselves from others. We do these things to build a position in our society in an effort to get others to recognize that we've made it. Making it, then, means having status.

KEYS TO UNLOCKING YOUR POTENTIAL *8-1*

*H*ere are the correct responses to the statements given in Unlocking Your Potential 8-1. Let's look at each.

1. Office politics exist because many of the rules of the game are unclear.	True
2. Office politics exist in few organizations today.	False
3. Office politics are generally destructive to the smooth operation of an organization.	False
4. Your positive image increases your political power.	True
5. Calling in favors from others is an example of a political compromise.	True
6. Your political power is often a function of the people with whom you associate.	True
7. Playing office politics is unethical.	False
8. It's politically smart not to support your supervisor if he or she is a poor performer.	True

The Reasons

Each of these statements was addressed in the last few pages of the text. Nonetheless, let's quickly review why the statements are either true or false. (1) True. A lack of rules and so on defines the organization's culture and member expectations (or lack thereof). (2) False. Office politics, in some form, exists in almost every organization. (3) False. Office politics can be constructive, too. (4) True. If you demonstrate the proper values and norms (image builders), others tend to give your views more legitimacy. (5) True. Helping others obtain what they want, and their helping you, is a form of compromise. (6) True. Your associations play a critical role in determining your political power; being viewed as supportive of tarnished individuals may tarnish you, too. (7) False. Office politics doesn't have to be unethical. If the political behavior isn't self-serving, doesn't violate others' rights, or doesn't treat others unfairly, it is ethical. (8) True. Although this is a difficult position to be in and will challenge all of your human relations skills, supporting a poorly performing supervisor can be viewed as associating with a tarnished individual.

Extra Effort

Contact several individuals at your university or in a local business and ask them about the advantages and disadvantages of political behavior. Ask them to describe examples of how political behavior can help promote the college's or business's goals, and ways that it can interfere with these goals.

> **status**
a social rank or the importance one has in a group

Status is a social rank or the importance one has in a group. But status is not something you give yourself. Although you may have worked hard to achieve something, having status requires at least two people. For example, if you have a high status, others must view you as having a higher ranking (in some capacity) than they do. You cannot achieve status merely by purchasing business cards at the local stationery store indicating you're president of a landscaping business. It's not something that you can necessarily buy. Rather, it's something that others grant you. Therefore, you don't achieve a level of status until others say you do.

Your status may come from a number of sources. Generally, these sources are grouped in two ways: formal and informal. Much of the discussion on power and politics, as well as authority, focused on the formal aspects of status. For instance, titles you earn do carry a certain level of prestige with them. Being elected team captain, having the lead part in your college's drama production, or winning the Heisman Trophy for your football performance elevates you in the eyes of others. Your professors, too, may have status. A professor who was chosen Professor of the Year often finds students especially interested in taking his or her class. The fact that others don't have the things you do gives you a formal status ranking.

On the other hand, status may be informally conferred on you by characteristics such as education, age, skill, or experience. Anything can have high status value if others evaluate it as such. Of course, just because high status is conferred informally does not mean that it is less important to you or that there is less agreement on whether you have

UNLOCKING YOUR POTENTIAL *8-2*

Occupational Status

*L*isted here (in alphabetical order) are twenty different occupations found in the United States. Place a check mark (left-hand column) next to those you believe to be in the top ten in terms of their prestige. Then, in the right-hand column, rank the ten occupations you checked from 1 (highest status) to 10 (lowest status).

Check If in the Top 10	*Your Ranking*
☐ Airline pilot	_____
☐ Architect	_____
☐ Astronaut	_____
☐ Biologist	_____
☐ Board member of a large corporation	_____
☐ College professor	_____
☐ College president	_____
☐ Dentist	_____
☐ Engineer	_____
☐ Environmental scientist	_____
☐ Justice of municipal court	_____
☐ Lawyer	_____
☐ Mayor of a large city	_____
☐ Minister	_____
☐ Owner of a manufacturing plant	_____
☐ Pharmacist	_____
☐ Physician	_____
☐ Priest	_____
☐ Psychiatrist	_____
☐ Surgeon	_____

it. People who know you—including those at work—have no problem placing you into status categories. And they usually agree closely on who has high, middle, or low status.

The Importance of Status. It is especially important in organizations to believe that the formal status system is fitting. That is, there should be fairness between perceived ranking and the status symbols given. If fairness is lacking, problems can arise between individuals in organizations.[9] Consider a situation where the university department chairperson of your major has an office, located in an isolated part of campus, that is smaller and not as well furnished as that of a junior faculty member in the same department. If you view importance in terms of the office and its furnishings, then you might conclude that the junior faculty member is more highly regarded than the department chair. That probably is not the case. Yet inconsistencies in status ranking have sent you the wrong message.

Status may also affect people's willingness to work hard. For instance, imagine the potential for conflict if you earn more than your supervisor. That's not as unrealistic as you may think. Your supervisor may be paid a salary and be ineligible for overtime pay. You, on the other hand, get paid on an hourly basis and, after working more than forty hours in a week, earn time and a half. If you work a lot of overtime, you could conceivably be making more money than your supervisor. If your supervisor loses sight of the goals of your unit, overtime might be stopped—just to keep your pay lower.

The problems of status inconsistency are not so much that they can place you in an uncomfortable or embarrassing situation. It's often more than just misreading what you see. Instead, it may interfere with order and consistency in your organization. You've been taught that if you perform well and excel on your job, you'll get ahead—and advancing brings with it some special privileges. But if getting ahead actually leads to losing something—whatever that may be—your willingness to continue to perform at the higher level may diminish. In that case, status is counterproductive.

Status is important to most people. But it carries with it an ethical issue. Status should not be so significant in your life that you do things just to attain it. Abusing power or politically sabotaging someone else's opportunities for status may benefit you in the short term, but it leaves a lot to be desired.

Status Sources. Where do you get status? That's a fair question, and one that's not easily answered. Although a number of personal attributes may generate a status ranking in your life, it's much more than that. Remember, because status is in the eyes of the beholder, status sources can be anything that you have that others view as having an element of importance associated with it. Nonetheless, some status sources are quite obvious. Among these are your level in the organization, working conditions, political power, authority, wealth, education, skills, abilities, age, seniority, occupation, and pay method. (See Exhibit 8-5.)

The higher the level in the organization, the more powerful and influential you are—and that's a status source very visible to all organizational members. Furthermore, some jobs exist in plush surroundings, whereas others require workers to work in extreme conditions. Wealth, whether earned or inherited, gives those with more money greater opportunities to afford the luxuries in life. Entrance into these occupations is often associated with the education, skills, and abilities you possess. Age and seniority can afford someone status. Older individuals are usually more experienced and can serve as a source of information to others. And if they are in the same organization for an extended time (seniority), they may be afforded certain privileges, such

---

[9]W. F. Whyte, "The Social Structure of the Restaurant," *American Journal of Sociology* (January 1954), pp. 302–308.

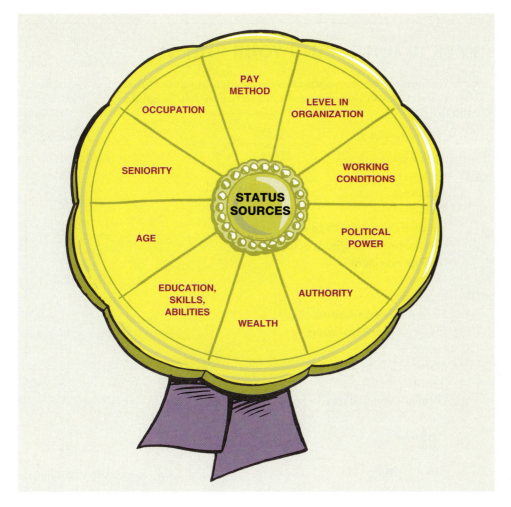

EXHIBIT 8-5
Status Sources

as bidding rights on certain jobs or preference for vacation leaves. How you are paid sends a message to others about your position and level in the organization. Certain occupations are viewed more positively than others. Salaried positions are viewed as professional jobs, and thus have a higher status associated with them than those paid on an hourly basis.

Status Symbols

We'll end this chapter with a discussion of the status symbols accumulated over a lifetime. Although these symbols—like status sources—come in a wide variety, attention can be focused on the two most common varieties: work-related status symbols and personal status symbols.

Work-Related Status Symbols. What do you get from your job that you can attribute to status? A number of **status symbols** clearly state that you have status in an organization, including such things as the size of your office, how it is furnished, club memberships the organization provides for you, your job title, how large a budget you control, the number of employees you may supervise, a personal secretary, a company automobile, and membership on special committees. (See Exhibit 8-6.)

> **status symbols**
> items that clearly state one's status in an organization

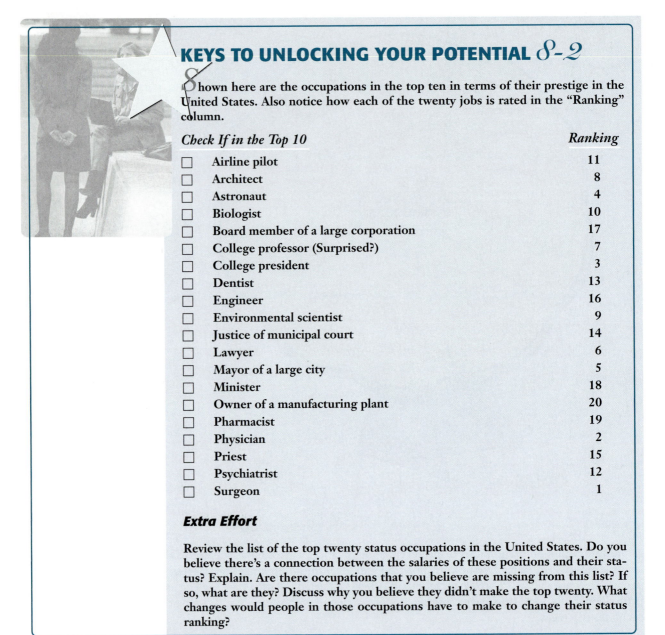

KEYS TO UNLOCKING YOUR POTENTIAL *8-2*

*S*hown here are the occupations in the top ten in terms of their prestige in the United States. Also notice how each of the twenty jobs is rated in the "Ranking" column.

Check If in the Top 10	Ranking
☐ Airline pilot	11
☐ Architect	8
☐ Astronaut	4
☐ Biologist	10
☐ Board member of a large corporation	17
☐ College professor (Surprised?)	7
☐ College president	3
☐ Dentist	13
☐ Engineer	16
☐ Environmental scientist	9
☐ Justice of municipal court	14
☐ Lawyer	6
☐ Mayor of a large city	5
☐ Minister	18
☐ Owner of a manufacturing plant	20
☐ Pharmacist	19
☐ Physician	2
☐ Priest	15
☐ Psychiatrist	12
☐ Surgeon	1

Extra Effort

Review the list of the top twenty status occupations in the United States. Do you believe there's a connection between the salaries of these positions and their status? Explain. Are there occupations that you believe are missing from this list? If so, what are they? Discuss why you believe they didn't make the top twenty. What changes would people in those occupations have to make to change their status ranking?

Source: Information regarding these rankings was supplied by research by K. Niakao and J. Treas. Their article "How U.S. Jobs Rate" was reprinted in *Industry Week* (March 1, 1993). This list and the research publication is copyrighted (© 1993) by Penlon Publishing, Inc. and is used in this book with their permission.

The size of your office (or the fact that you actually have one) has been a status symbol ever since organizations formed. It's often rumored that individuals associate office size with importance. People who have corner offices with great views, room for a lot of furniture, and maybe even a private bathroom have reached the pinnacle of status in an organization. These, at times, become the "penthouse suites" of offices and are often reserved for those who have the most impressive titles and political power. In

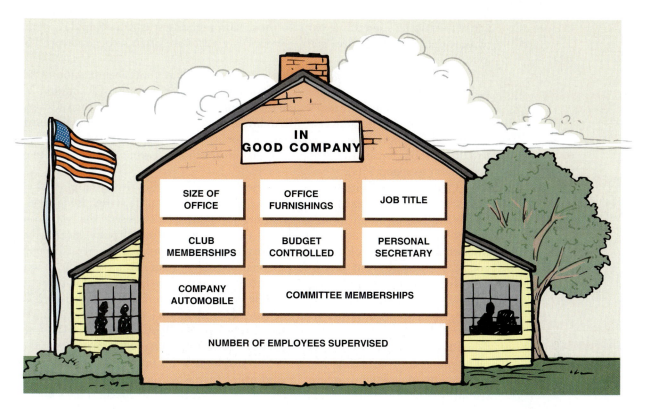

IN GOOD COMPANY

SIZE OF OFFICE	OFFICE FURNISHINGS	JOB TITLE
CLUB MEMBERSHIPS	BUDGET CONTROLLED	PERSONAL SECRETARY
COMPANY AUTOMOBILE	COMMITTEE MEMBERSHIPS	
NUMBER OF EMPLOYEES SUPERVISED		

EXHIBIT 8-6
Work-Related Status Symbols

fact, some people take office size so seriously that they even get to the point of counting ceiling tiles (because it's an easy way to determine square footage). A president may have a 450-square-foot office, a vice-president a 400-square-foot office, and so on. The square footage is really immaterial—it's the fact that those with more authority have more space.

In addition to the size of the office, status is established by how it's furnished. It is relatively easy to tell who has more status by what's in their office. Those with low status have pressboard furniture or furniture made from chrome and metal. As they ascend the status hierarchy, they get to select more expensive furnishings. But even then there are limitations. For example, a district manager may have a desk, a credenza, and a bookcase made from oak and oak veneers. But at the highest status level, the furniture is pure wood. Moreover, the wood is often a more expensive variety, such as cherry or mahogany. Additionally, these offices often have more decorations, such as signed artwork, Persian rugs, and leather chairs. Certainly your taste and preferences for decorations may differ, but it is clear in organizations which individuals have the greatest status. As an example of this, take a tour of your professor's office and then one of your college president's. See if you can verify the claim that office location and furnishings vary by status.

Another status symbol frequently seen in the work environment is the types of memberships offered to certain employees. Individuals higher in status are often given memberships to country clubs, posh health clubs, and the like. It's not that the organization is trying to rub it in the face of those with lower status; rather, it's just a means of doing something extra for those with higher status. You should recognize by now that these first three status symbol categories are often associated with your job title.

Many others may look at the budget you control as another indication of how high your status is in an organization. If you have a budget in excess of $1 million, you are perceived as having more prestige than someone who controls less than $100,000 or someone who has no budget at all. Additionally, it's not only how much you control, but also whose approval you need to spend money. If you are permitted to spend up to $50,000 without having to get approval, that means more to others than having to get permission to spend $500.

Closely aligned with how much money you control is how many employees you supervise. If your staff is bigger than mine, then you have more status. Even though there's a fallacy in simply looking at numbers, sometimes it's not seen that way. You'd probably much rather be seen as having the largest staff than having the smallest. And who could overlook the most important status symbol associated with people you may supervise: your very own personal secretary. There aren't many who work who wouldn't appreciate having a dedicated secretary to help carry out daily activities. But having a secretary work for just one individual in today's organizations is becoming the exception rather than the rule. It's just inefficient and costly to have it that way. Besides, the technology that exists today has replaced many of the traditional functions that secretaries once performed.[10] Today, you'll do much of your own typing, copying, filing, and so on. So maybe now it's more appropriate to look at the computer system you have in your office than whether you have a personal assistant. For some, however, that's not an easy adjustment to make. That's why, as some organizations downsize and replace people with technology, problems arise. Status symbols are being removed.

What about the company car? Does having a company car reflect someone's ranking? In most cases, yes. Traditionally, sales representatives are provided automobiles to use on their jobs. In many instances, the car may also be used for personal transportation. Having a company car in the first place elevates certain people in the organization. But even among those who have automobiles, there's a ranking. People who have higher status ranking generally receive a more luxurious car. Lincolns, Mercedes, Cadillacs, and BMWs, for example, are generally reserved for those at the highest levels. Midsized and midpriced sedans—such as the Taurus, Camry, or Lumina—are more frequently driven by the sales staff. Even then, there's the issue of who gets the new cars. For example, in police departments where there is a cruiser-take-home program, new vehicles don't necessarily go to the most needy. Instead, those who have seniority and rank may get the first opportunity to trade in their police cars for newer ones—giving more junior officers their hand-me-downs.

So what happens if you don't have a prestigious title or a beautiful 500-square-foot office? Furthermore, you supervise no one, do all of your own typing and copying, and drive your own clunker to and from work. Are you out of luck in the status department at work? The answer may be no. In every organization, there are special committees that are put together by people in power. These task forces are designed to work on a specific project and to make recommendations. Becoming a member of one of these teams—maybe at the request of your company president—gives you a level of prestige that others won't have. Remember several pages ago when we talked

---

[10]"Secretaries' Roles Change with Downsizing and Computer Revolution," *The Wall Street Journal* (September 26, 1995), p. A-1.

Emerson Electric's Chuck Knight has all the trappings that go along with his position as CEO of the organization. A finely furnished corner office and a beautiful view of the St. Louis, Missouri, scenery lets all who enter his office know his status in the organization.

about accepting challenging assignments? Many of those who do are often sought out to serve on these temporary committees. Being asked to serve speaks well of your political smartness and can serve as a status symbol for you.

Although most status generated will come from organizations you are associated with, some status symbols have nothing to do with work at all. Instead, they're purely a function of personal factors.

Personal Factors and Status.   Personal factors and status have one aspect in common: All of them usually revolve around money. Maybe that puts too much value on money in our lives, but it's something we can't overlook. Money enables us to have personal status symbols such as houses, cars, and clothing.

The location of the house you live in demonstrates status. After all, who doesn't know where zip code 90210 is? Living in a one-bedroom apartment in Tacoma, Washington, says something different from having a waterfront condominium overlooking Puget Sound. The size of the house is also a status factor. Large, palatial estates with plenty of room for entertaining often indicate a social standing. Vacation homes or getaway cottages in the mountains may also indicate status to others.

The cars you drive (other than company-provided cars) also tell people who you are. Driving an Audi, Chevrolet Tahoe, BMW, Infiniti, Land Rover, or Jeep Cherokee indicates that you are successful. And that translates into status. Not a lot of heads turn when I pull into valet parking in my Dodge Caravan. But how quickly that could change if I happen to be in a Ferrari one day. Even if it isn't really mine, at least for the moment, I can glow in that status symbol. Besides, how many of you rented a limousine for your high school prom to impress a date? Sure it was expensive, but it made you stand out in the crowd. And for that fleeting moment, you had achieved a status level that made you feel important.

The clothes you wear also indicate something about your status. Even magazines like *Elle* and *GQ* advertise garments using suggestions that these are the clothes that

3. Where status inconsistencies exist,
   a. organizational members experience less conflict in their group.
   b. willingness to excel may decrease.
   c. unethical behaviors decrease.
   d. all of the above

4. Which one of the following is not considered a work-related status symbol?
   a. occupation
   b. size of office
   c. budget controlled
   d. personal secretary

status-conscious people wear. Expensive, well-made clothes that are tailor-fitted clearly differentiate you from those who buy off the rack.

But let's end this discussion about status with some reality checks. Status doesn't have to be just materialistic. It can be found in the love of a good person whom you worship and adore and who loves you, too. It can take the form of having wonderful children who look up to you and gaze in awe at your every word. It's the good health that you have to awake every morning fresh and ready to experience what life delivers that day. And it's inner peace, a spiritual satisfaction that you are doing your best. Let's not forget about these valuables. After all, both you and Bill Gates (one of the richest men in the world and co-founder of Microsoft) will face at the end of your lives the reality of human mortality. And as you are frequently reminded, you can't take it with you. Enjoy power, politics, and status while you can, but never lose sight of what's really important in life.

SUMMARY

This summary corresponds to the Learning Outcomes found on page 177.

1. Power is the ability a person has to influence others to do the things he or she would like them to do.

2. Authority is based on one's position in an organization and the title he or she holds. Power, on the other hand, goes beyond authority. It is based on something about the individual—not the job he or she holds.

3. Power can be generated in a number of ways. The five most popular sources of power are legitimate power (based on an individual's formal position in the organization), coercive power (based on the use of fear), reward power (based on the ability to distribute anything that others value), expert power (based on expertise, special skills, or knowledge) and referent power (based on respect from others).

4. One can develop a power base by respecting others, building power relationships, developing associations, controlling important information, gaining seniority, and building power in stages.

5. Political behavior is something one engages in when one attempts to influence the advantages and disadvantages of a situation.

6. Several factors guide organizational political activities. These include organizational expectations (rules, regulations, and culture), the power of others, and the power one has.

7. Seven ways of becoming politically smart are portraying the proper image, being loyal, accepting challenging assignments, compromising with others, avoiding tarnished individuals, finding a mentor, and supporting the boss.

8. Status is a social rank, or the importance one has achieved in a group and how others view it.

9. Status is important in organizations because it can serve as a means for getting individuals to continue to perform at high levels. To achieve this goal, there must be fairness between one's perceived ranking and the status symbols one has.

10. Work-related status symbols, items that clearly state one's status in an organization, come in a number of varieties. Nine of the more popular work-related status symbols are the size of one's office, office furnishings, club memberships provided, job title, size of the budget one controls, number of employees supervised, a personal secretary, company automobile, and membership on special committees.

REVIEWING YOUR UNDERSTANDING

1. What is power? Would you rather have power or authority? Explain.

2. Which type(s) of power do you believe works best in organizations? Do you think that this power is appropriate for every organization? Discuss.

3. How do you develop a power base? What difficulties would you expect to encounter in developing this power?

4. What is organizational politics? Can an organization ever be totally free from office politics?

5. What situational factors lead to office politics?

6. Is it unethical to play office politics? Justify your response with examples.

7. How can you become more politically smart?

8. What is status, and why is it important to organizational members?

9. What problems arise when there are inconsistencies between status ranking and status symbols?

10. Describe the status symbols you would like to have to tell the world you have made it.

ANSWERS TO CHECKING YOUR UNDERSTANDING

1. d   **2.** b   **3.** b   **4.** a

LEARNING TOGETHER

A. You are asked to identify the best way to develop a power base. Select one of the ways you believe is the best way to develop power and gather information about the method you selected. Interview a wide range of people to get their opinion of your selected method. Be sure to listen to the pros and cons people give you. Draw some conclusions about your research. Did you change your mind about whether your method was the best way? Why or why not? Give a one-minute presentation to your class on your findings and how you might change your perception of your initial ideas on the topic, now that you have the opinions of others.

B. Interview two managers or higher-level administrators as to how they survived politics in their offices or how they viewed one of their superiors who survived politics. Characterize what you believe are the important factors that contributed to each manager's success. Give a presentation to your class on the most important lesson you learned from doing this exercise.

C. Create a scenario that might depict a very political office that has questionable ethical standards and promotes people on the basis of the way they play the game of politics. Before deciding what type of ending the scenario should have, divide into groups of four or five. Then, in your group, identify an appropriate ending. Act out (role-play) the scenario for classmates. Draw some conclusions about the exercise as to why the solution or ending of each roleplay was or was not appropriate. If the ending was not appropriate, identify ways to modify the ending to assure a positive learning experience.

D. Write an essay on your perspective of one of these statements: "Power, politics, and status may drive most people, but one should never lose sight of what's really important," or "Every organization must have politics." Debate your perspective with class members.

E. Research a prominent personality (Queen Elizabeth, Fidel Castro, Bill Gates, Richard M. De-Vos, Herb Kelleher, Cindy Crawford, Michael Jackson, O. J. Simpson, Sharon Stone, Jay Leno, Kenny G, etc.) as to how the person achieved fame, power, and status. Trace the person's life from early years and identify the one or two elements that contributed to the person's status. Share your research with your class.

CASE 8

Power and Status at Underwood Medical

Herman, Ileana, and Peter work for Dr. Gracie Markham, vice-president of external relations at Underwood Medical Center. Underwood, named after the late George Underwood III, has become known throughout the world as a specialty medical facility.

The surgeons and physicians associated with Underwood have an uncanny status with their colleagues in the medical profession. Royalty, movie personalities, high-ranking government officials, and the rich are known not only to use the facility for health care, but also to give generously to promote its medical and prestigious status.

Dr. Markham has a medical degree from a well-known medical school. She was tapped for the external relations position at Underwood because of her political acumen, social connections, and ability to attract funding sources. Her credentials are further enhanced by extremely high scholarship throughout her formal education, strong ethical standards, integrity, and concern for others.

Each of Dr. Markham's employees has good credentials to work in external relations at Underwood. All three come from modest backgrounds and have a keen respect for Dr. Markham. Each, however, views his or her relationship with Dr. Markham very differently. Herman, for example, appreciates Dr. Markham for her political and social status. He believes he can gain the power and re-spect he deserves through development of political savvy and working with the right people. Ileana believes Dr. Markham is successful because of her scholarship and because she works hard to establish high ethical standards. Ileana feels that if she works hard, she can become respected for her competence just as Dr. Markham has. Peter admires his boss for her ability to work with people. He wants to develop the personal qualities she demonstrates so he can be able to influence people the way she does.

Questions

1. Describe the types of power that seem to be sought by (a) Herman, (b) Ileana, and (c) Peter. List the elements that are important to each. What are the ends or ultimate goals each employee wants to reach? Who has the right approach? Why or why not?

2. How can Herman, Ileana, and Peter achieve the power they want? Describe some of the differences that may exist in the behavior and politics of the three employees.

3. List some of the work-related status symbols that might be sought after by (a) Herman, (b) Ileana, and (c) Peter. Are the three lists comparable? Why or why not? What conclusions can you draw from the lists you made?

4. If you were to offer some advice to Herman, Ileana, and Peter, what would it be? Did you give different advice to each? Why or why not?

part four

HUMAN BEHAVIOR IN ORGANIZATIONS

chapter

9

BEING PART OF GROUPS AND TEAMS

*L*earning Outcomes

After reading this chapter, you will be able to:

1. **Describe the difference between formal and informal groups.**

2. **Identify four types of groups.**

3. **Explain why people join groups.**

4. **Describe how roles affect your behavior in groups.**

5. **Discuss how conformity pressure affects group actions.**

6. **Discuss the advantages and disadvantages of group decision making.**

7. **Identify three consensus-building techniques.**

8. **Describe the difference between work groups and work teams.**

9. **Explain how to develop high-performance work teams.**

10. **List five ways you can contribute to a team.**

In Parts II and III we looked at human behavior and then at organizational behavior. In Part IV our emphasis will be on human behavior in the organization: being part of groups; excelling on the job; influencing others; and understanding change, conflict, and creativity.

We tend to give our best effort to those things that benefit us. We know that in our lives, we have to work—and in many cases, work hard. But we want something in return: to work with others who respect us and who can bring out the best in us. We know that things change and, at times, create problems for us. Therefore, we need to learn to deal with difficult work-related issues. Such issues are discussed in this section. Part four contains four chapters:

The behavior of individuals in groups is not the same as the sum total of each of their behaviors. This is because people tend to act differently in groups than they do when they are alone. Peer pressure and group expectations may make individuals do things in a group that they wouldn't consider doing individually. For example, even though you do not agree, you might not challenge the answer to a test question your professor just gave the class. If you think it's only you who has an issue, you may not raise your hand to disagree with what you heard. However, as some other class members begin to speak up, you, too, might add to the discussion. And as you do, others who got the question wrong are more likely to support those of you who are speaking up.

All groups, however they are formed, can serve vital purposes in your work life. But that's not to imply that groups are free of problems. Sometimes their collective action can create problems by working against the goals of the organization. How, then, do you distinguish between productive behavior when working in teams and nonproductive behavior, or those things that may create problems? The answer to that question lies in having a better understanding of group behavior.

What Is a Group?

> **group**
two or more people who come together to achieve certain objectives

A **group** is defined as two or more people who come together to achieve certain objectives. Groups to which you belong can be either formal or informal. Formal groups are work arrangements your supervisors assign to you. Your college's maintenance staff of six members is an example of a formal group. A group project your professor requires for class would also represent a formal group. In such a situation, you have specific tasks that must be accomplished—such as researching a topic, preparing a report, and giving a ten-minute presentation. In formal groups, then, your actions are defined and directed toward some organizational goal.

In contrast, informal groups are formed to fulfill a social need. For example, a number of student clubs exist at most colleges. Those of you who want to be with others who share similar interests—fraternities, sororities, student government, and the like—can join and become part of that club's activities. Informal groups at your job are also natural formations. They exist to foster a work environment that provides you some social contact with others in the organization. Sitting with friends at lunch in the cafeteria or joining the company's softball team offers you the opportunity to form friendships based on your common personal interests.

UNLOCKING YOUR POTENTIAL *9-1*

What Kinds of Groups Do You Belong To?

*G*roups, groups, groups. The term is everywhere. We may hear about people brought together to accomplish some specific purpose or about several individuals who belong to a common organization. In fact, each of us in our daily lives encounters groups constantly. Sometimes we just take them for granted; we may not even recognize that we are a part of a group. To help in developing this recognition, list all the groups that you belong to. For our purposes here, use a very general interpretation of the term *group*.

TASK

INTEREST

MADD

FUNCTION

FRIENDSHIP

Alma Mater

EXHIBIT 9-1
Types of Groups

Types of Groups

Your response to Unlocking Your Potential 9-1 provides you with some indication regarding the groups to which you belong. Generally speaking, however, you probably have identified those organizations by name. For example, you might have identified your fraternity or sorority, the church you attend, a labor union, or the organization in which you work. Although this identification is appropriate, these groups can be further classified into four types: function, task, interest, and friendship.[1] (See Exhibit 9-1.) Let's briefly look at each.

Both function and task groups are related to the formal organizational groupings of employees. A **function group** is a group formed through the formal authority relationships that exist in an organization. Typically represented in an organizational chart, function groups would include a supervisor and the employees working for him or her. For example, the chair of the English department and her seven faculty members

> **function group**
> a group formed through the formal authority relationships that exist in an organization

---

[1]Stephen P. Robbins, *Organizational Behavior: Concepts, Controversies, Applications,* 9th ed. (Upper Saddle River, N.J.: Prentice-Hall, 2001), pp. 298–299; and L. R. Sayles, "Work Group Behavior and the Larger Organization," in C. Arensburg et al., eds., *Research in Industrial Relations* (New York: Harper & Row, 1957), pp. 131–145.

would represent a function group; so, too, would the shift supervisor of Popeye's restaurant and his four crew members.

A **task group** represents a collection of people brought together to accomplish a specific task. Whereas the function group usually includes individuals who come from the same department (even though they are brought together to achieve a specific goal), task group members may be brought together from various departments in an organization. That's the main distinction between the two. For example, declining enrollments in business schools across the United States have required many business deans to form task groups to deal with the issue. But the forces marshaled don't simply come from the business departments. Instead, college recruiters, academic counselors, representatives from the registrar's office, and employees from student services are brought in to find ways to increase student enrollment.

An **interest group** consists of individuals who band together to promote a self-fulfilling interest. For example, employees coming together to approach their supervisor over their pay levels or working conditions form to protect their vested interests. Likewise, students who protest the firing of a popular yet unconventional professor have come together based on their interests. Unlike function groups, however, interest groups are generally short-lived—lasting as long as the interest or cause remains.

The final classification of groups is a friendship group. A **friendship group** is a group formed on the basis of something that members have in common, such as age, occupation, or political or military affiliation. College graduates who join the college's alumni association and become supporters of school-sponsored events would be an ex-

KEYS TO UNLOCKING YOUR POTENTIAL *9-1*

*W*hat groups do you belong to? More than likely, your response to Unlocking Your Potential 9-1 shows various associations. However, when we look at groups more closely, we find that four specific types of groups exist: function, task, interest, and friendship. To better understand your group associations, it would be beneficial to place each group into its appropriate category. Here are some examples of group categories of associations that you may have identified in Unlocking Your Potential 9-1.

Function Groups	*Task Groups*
Crew member, Wendy's day shift	Student member, University
Postal clerk	Academic Affairs
Intern, Advertising Department	Homecoming float committee
Waitress, dining room	Hugger, Special Olympics

Interest Groups	*Friendship Groups*
Students Against Drunk Driving	Club lacrosse
Community on Patrol	Church choir
Greenpeace	Youth organization
Intramural soccer team	Scouts

Now take the groups you identified and place them into the appropriate categories. Are your groups spread out among the four categories? Or do you belong to only one type of group? What does this say about you?

ample of a friendship group; so, too, would senior citizens' groups, the Civilian Conservation Corps Alumni, the Retired Airline Pilots Association, or the American Legion.

Irrespective of how groups are classified, a more fundamental question is, why do people join groups in the first place? Although there is no single rationale that can explain this uniting behavior, over the years several popular reasons have been identified.

Reasons We Join Groups

Because you likely belong to a number of groups, it's clear that different groups provide different benefits. You, as research has shown, join a group out of your needs for security, prestige, affiliation, influence, self-esteem, or goal achievement. (See Exhibit 9-2.)

Security is gained from strength of numbers. By joining a group, you can reduce the insecurity of standing alone. This results in feeling stronger, having fewer self-doubts, and being more resistant to threats. You've learned at an early age that if only one person speaks out, you may get nowhere. Let's say you work for someone who is rude and treats you poorly. If you go to him alone and raise your concern, you may be unsuccessful, and he may make matters worse for you. But if the entire staff of eight employees goes to the supervisor to give him feedback, the collective voice may have more of an effect. That's the security that being in a group provides.

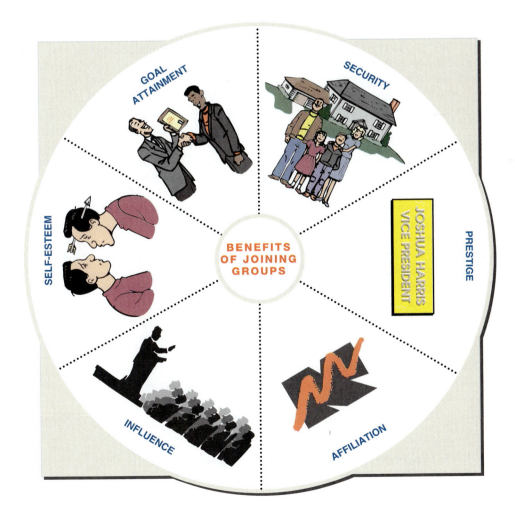

EXHIBIT 9-2

Benefits We Get from Joining Groups

Prestige indicates the stature you get from belonging to a particular group. Inclusion in a group that others view as important provides recognition and status for you. Just as elected officials, sports figures, and entertainers achieve some level of fame, being accepted into an honors class, being elected president of the student government association, or being recognized as a college athlete may elevate your prestige.

Affiliation with groups (for example, friendship groups) can fulfill your social needs. You frequently enjoy the regular interaction that comes with group membership. Because you have some common views, you can share things with others that can build lasting friendships. For instance, you may form a special bond with your college roommate that continues throughout your life. The affiliation of living together for a period while in college—with all its ups and downs—provides you that special person with whom you can share your most intimate thoughts. In a similar fashion, special relationships you build at work—someone whom you've helped or who has helped you—significantly contribute to fulfilling your need for friendships and social relations.

One of the appealing aspects of groups is that they represent a means of influencing others. What you often cannot achieve individually becomes possible through your group's action. Of course, this influence might not be sought only to make demands on others. It might be desired merely as a countermeasure to protect you from others who place unreasonable demands on you. For example, evening students might raise an issue with a college's administration that adequate academic advising hours are unavailable for those who cannot come to campus before 4:30 in the afternoon. Using their influence, they persuade the college to expand advising hours so that they, too, can be accommodated. Informal groups additionally provide opportunities for you to exercise influence over others. As a group leader, for instance, you might be able to make requests of group members and obtain their support. This is especially true when you work with volunteers—people who really don't have to do anything in the group they don't want to. Taking charge of your class's group project, for instance, and getting other group members to be committed to their work and completing assignments on time is one means of exerting influence.

Self-esteem conveys your feelings of self-worth. That is, in addition to conveying status to those outside the group, membership in a particular group can raise your feelings of self-esteem. This comes from the association of being accepted into a highly valued group. For example, being admitted into a prestigious graduate school, being hired by a noted law firm, or receiving an academic scholarship may make you feel good about what you've accomplished.

Finally, you may join a group for goal achievement. There are times when it takes more than one person to accomplish a particular task. In those cases, there is a need to bring together the talents and skills of others in order to get that task completed. The president of your college, for example, does not plan and execute all aspects of graduation. Instead, she brings together several knowledgeable people who each work on a part of the ceremony. For example, someone makes sure the facility is set up for the event and develops plans to ensure that traffic and parking problems are minimized. Others work with the faculty and students regarding caps and gowns and how they are to enter and exit the building. Another member of the group may have the task of finding a commencement speaker, whereas someone else works on catering the after-graduation reception. All in all, the intent of this group is clear—to make graduation a special day for students and their families.

Factors Influencing Our Behavior in Groups

Just as you may belong to a number of different types of groups, how you behave within each may differ. Trying to understand why you act the way you do with

1. What is the difference between a formal group and an informal one?
   a. Informal groups are often represented as work arrangements. Formal groups represent a means to foster social contact with others.
   b. Formal groups are defined as two or more people who come together to achieve certain objectives. Informal groups are defined as two or more people who come together to achieve organizational goals.
   c. Informal groups represent a means to foster social contact with others. Formal groups are often represented as work arrangements.
   d. Formal groups exist to foster a social work environment. Informal groups exist to achieve organizational goals.

2. Which one of the following was not cited as a reason people join groups?
   a. pressure
   b. security
   c. goal achievement
   d. affiliation

friends at a Saturday afternoon football game versus the way you do when on the job is best explained in terms of group roles, group norms and conformity, group cohesiveness, group size, group prestige, and group leaders. Let's take a closer look at each of these concepts.

Group Roles.   A **role** is a set of expected behaviors attributed to someone who occupies a given position in society. In your life, you play multiple roles. You adjust these roles to the group to which you belong. At work, you attempt to determine what behaviors are expected. You'll gather information about your job, get suggestions from your boss, and watch what co-workers do. These sources of information provide many clues about how you are to behave. But when you are confronted by different role expectations (what you like to do versus what your employer wants you to do), you may experience *role conflict*. For example, if you are capable of producing more than 26,000 linear feet of vinyl baseboard trim during your shift, but your work group pressures you to restrict output to 21,500 feet, there's role conflict. On the one hand, co-workers want to restrict production so that everyone has work to do, and no one gets laid off. Production supervisors, however, want to produce as much high-quality product as possible in order to meet organizational goals. This was precisely the issue faced by members of the Roppe Corporation, a company that produces rubber products in Fostoria, Ohio.[2] That role conflict continued until both groups could find a workable solution that addressed the needs of each group.

Likewise, your professor may also face a role conflict. If his colleagues want him to give out very few high grades in order to maintain the department's tough-standards reputation, and your class wants him to give out lots of high grades to enhance their grade point averages, conflict occurs. To the degree that the instructor sincerely seeks to satisfy the expectations of both his colleagues and his students, he faces role conflict.

Group Norms and Conformity.   All groups you belong to have established **norms,** acceptable standards that are shared by a group's members. In the workplace, norms dictate things such as output levels, absenteeism rates, promptness or tardiness, and the amount of socializing allowed on the job.

> **role**
> a set of expected behaviors attributed to someone who occupies a given position in society

> **norms**
> acceptable standards that are shared by a group's members

---

[2]Michael P. Cronin, "No More Clock Watchers," *Inc.* (February 1994), p. 83.

Although each group will have its own unique set of norms, common classes of norms appear in most organizations. These focus on effort and performance, dress codes, and loyalty.

Probably the most widespread norms you'll encounter relate to your levels of effort and performance. Work groups typically provide their members with very explicit cues on how hard to work, what level of output to have, when to look busy, when it's acceptable to goof off, and the like. These norms are extremely powerful in affecting your performance. They are so powerful that performance predictions that are based solely on your ability and level of personal desire often prove to be wrong.

Some organizations have formal dress codes. However, even in their absence, norms frequently develop to dictate the kind of clothing that should be worn to work. For example, norms dictate the dress code among customer service representatives at one of the nation's largest banks. Most workers who have little face-to-face customer contact may come to work dressed very casually. However, on occasion, a newly hired employee will come to work the first few days dressed up in a suit. Those who do are often teased and pressured until their dress conforms to the group's standard.

College seniors interviewing for their first postgraduate job pick up this norm quickly. Every spring on college campuses throughout the country, those interviewing for jobs can usually be spotted. They're the ones walking around in the dark gray or dark blue outfits. They are portraying the dress norms they have learned are expected in professional positions. Of course, what connotes acceptable dress in one organization may be very different from another. At Ben and Jerry's (the ice cream maker), coming to work in jeans and a tie-dyed shirt may be fashionable. That same outfit worn by a Merrill Lynch stockbroker may lead that individual to premature departure from Wall Street.

Few bosses appreciate an employee's ridiculing the organization. Making fun of how the place runs, mocking the owners or the decisions they make, or recommending to a customer that a competitor has a better, less expensive product may be grounds for a charge of insubordination. Supervisors also frown on the fact that you may be actively looking for another job—especially with a competitor. Examples such as these demonstrate what we mean by loyalty norms. A concern for demonstrating loyalty, by the way, often explains why those who aspire to bigger and better things in the organization willingly take work home at night, come in on weekends, and accept transfers to cities where they would otherwise not prefer to live. In doing so, these employees create a positive image about themselves and demonstrate loyal behavior to their supervisors. The same can be said about attending college. Very few faculty members have ever failed a student who actively sought help in the class and did extra work to demonstrate his or her commitment to learning the course material, even though he or she had problems passing the exams. In such situations, the student's commitment to actively learning was a behavior that was rewarded.

How far can you take these expected behaviors? Will you give up your individualism in order to be accepted by the group? Will you lose your identity in order to associate with the group? Obviously, answers to these questions will vary. But because many individuals have a desire to be accepted by the groups they belong to (or those they want to belong to), they are susceptible to conformity pressures. Many years ago, researcher Solomon Asch showed what effects pressure from group members can have on our judgment and attitudes.[3] In the study, groups of seven or eight people were seated in a classroom and asked to compare two cards. One card had one line. The other had three lines of varying length. As shown in Exhibit 9-3, one of the lines on the three-line card (B) was identical to the line on the other card (X). Differences in length between the other two lines (A and C) were obvious. During the experiment, each group member was to state aloud which two lines exactly matched. For the first two rounds, everyone agreed that lines X and B were the same length. However, during subsequent rounds, members of the group purposely began to give the same incorrect response, observing the response of the one individual in the group who did not know that he or she was the subject of an experiment about conformity. What do you think happened?

Surprisingly, more than a third of all individual subjects in the experiment went along with the crowd. Even though they knew the choice of the other group members

---

[3]Solomon E. Asch, "Effects of Group Pressure upon the Modification and Distortion of Judgements," in Harold Guetzkow, ed., *Groups, Leadership, and Men* (Pittsburgh, Penn.: Carnegie Press, 1951), pp. 177–190.

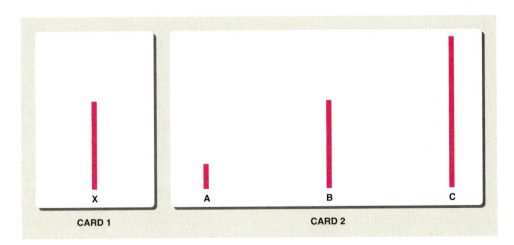

EXHIBIT 9-3
Group Conformity Study Cards

KEYS TO UNLOCKING YOUR POTENTIAL *9-2*

*E*ach of the five questions posed in Unlocking Your Potential 9-2 focuses on some aspect of facing pressures to conform. Specifically, based on your responses, you may indicate your preference for being a conformist or a nonconformist.

	Response	
Question	*Conformist*	*Nonconformist*
1.	Yes	No
2.	No	Yes
3.	Yes	No
4.	No	Yes
5.	No	Yes

So how did you do? If you're like most people, you probably lean toward the conformity side. Our culture has ingrained that position into us since an early age. Being a conformist, though, has its advantages; conversely, it may cause us some difficulties. The issue is, however, how comfortable you feel in conforming when, in fact, you prefer not to. That's something that each of us has to work out on his or her own.

was incorrect, they did not want to be different or disagree with the other group members. Research results such as these suggest that there are group norms that pressure us toward conformity. We desire to be one of the group and to avoid being visibly different. Such studies also show that when our view, which may be based on objective data, differs significantly from that of others in the group, we often will face extensive pressure to align our opinions to conform with the opinions of others.

Group Cohesiveness. Intuitively, it makes sense that groups in which there's a lot of internal disagreement and lack of cooperation are less effective in completing their tasks than groups in which individuals generally agree, cooperate, and like each other. Research on this position has focused on **group cohesiveness,** the degree to which group members are attracted to one another and share group goals. The more you are attracted to one another and the more the group's goals align with your individual goals, the greater the group's cohesiveness. As a result of this alignment of interests, you are more effective in achieving those goals.

> ➤ **group cohesiveness**
> the degree to which group members are attracted to one another and share group goals

As an example of this situation, consider a football team consisting of several star players. Individually, these players have contract terms that reward them for leading the league in certain categories—such as scoring touchdowns, pass completions, quarterback sacks, and field goals made. These may be their individual goals, but as a team, they also want to go to the championships. So they try their hardest to excel and reach their individual goals, focusing their attention on the team's standing. That's why a punter tied for the best punting average going into the last game of the season may deliberately kick a short punt to put the opponent deep into its own end of the field—knowing that such a short punt will decrease his chances for winning the title. When group cohesion is high, then, you do things that better the group's effort—even if it may lessen your individual reward. As the saying goes, in the word *team*, there is no "I."

Groups and Diversity

One of the primary advantages of working in groups is that a wide variety of opinions and perspectives can be discussed. Given this opportunity, we should expect, then, that decisions reached in group settings do become more legitimate and more widely accepted. These outcomes should be welcomed, especially given the diversity that exists in the workforce today. Decisions about how to adapt the work environment, for example, to reflect differences in people should come from all individuals who need to work together. At least that's the idea. But do groups really work this way?

Although there can be two sides to every debate, there's some startling news about how work groups and diversity mesh. For the most part, when groups of people who possess different personal characteristics are put together in a group setting, they rarely blend together as one unit. Instead, they tend to congregate primarily with others who share similar backgrounds and characteristics. For instance, women tend to associate with other women, African Americans with other African Americans, people of Hispanic ancestry with other Hispanics, and so forth. And even though organizations provide diversity training that emphasizes associating with one another and respecting the dignity and customs of all, cliques appear to be a natural phenomenon. Furthermore, there doesn't appear to be anything that the organization can do to stop these cliques from forming.

The existence of cliques, however, doesn't have to be a problem. Recognizing that people tend to gravitate toward groups where people share a common interest can explain their popularity. Such a grouping provides a supportive environment where shared feelings—based on common experiences—can be openly discussed. However, problems can occur when we allow cliques to exclude others or create separate and independent groups. We must focus our concern on this last situation.

Group Size.   The size of a group may have an effect on your behavior in a group. However, that effect depends on what criteria you are looking at.[4] For instance, imagine that you had a class project and had to coordinate the activities of fifteen of your classmates. At some point, you'd be getting in one another's way. However, if your group is trying to solve a difficult problem, a group of fifteen may work best. Why? Although there are more individuals to interact with, larger groups tend to bring richer backgrounds and experiences to the table. For instance, during the *Apollo 13* mission, when the space capsule experienced life-threatening problems, dozens of individuals at Mission Control in Houston went to work to come up with solutions. Without the multitalented skills present in that room, quite possibly Apollo 13's mission would have been a major disaster.

So what, then, is an optimal group size? Unfortunately, a specific number to be used in all cases escapes us. That number is more a function of why you're using groups in the first place. For instance, if you need a lot of input—especially from a variety of different perspectives—groups with a dozen or more individuals work best. That's why college presidents frequently involve many people from across the campus—faculty, staff, students—when they are faced with making such a major decision as closing departments because of budget cuts. Soft drink producers such as Pepsi or Coca-Cola use a large group of taste-testers to test-market their new products. Imagine them selling a product where five or fewer group members agreed on the new taste. That could prove very unfortunate. Large groups, then, are needed for assisting in fact-finding

---

[4]E. J. Thomas and C. F. Fink, "Effects of Group Size," *Psychological Bulletin* (July 1963), pp. 371–384; and Marvin E. Shaw, *Group Dynamics: The Psychology of Small Group Behavior,* 3rd ed. (New York: McGraw-Hill, 1981).

efforts. On the other hand, if the purpose of your group is to produce something, groups of approximately five to seven members tend to be more effective for taking action. Groups of this size still can draw from the differences each brings to the group, while taking discussions to conclusions more quickly.

Regardless of the number of people, you need to be aware of a problem inherent in any group. Although your productivity with five group members is generally greater than if you had only three, individual productivity of each group member declines as the group gets larger. That is, a group of five will tend to produce at a level less than five times the average individual performance. You've seen this. It happens, for instance, on a project where four of the five members of your group do the work. The fifth person may become a free rider and coast on your group's efforts. Part of the reason for this is explained by a group occurrence called social loafing.[5] **Social loafing** is a tendency for individual group members to slack off when a group as a whole is held responsible for completing a task. Social loafing occurs because the results of the group cannot be attributed to any single person. However, this event can be somewhat lessened by having mechanisms in place that also identify individual effort.

> **social loafing**
a tendency for individual group members to slack off when a group as a whole is held responsible for completing a task

> **prestige**
the distinguished grading, position, or ranking of a group

Group Prestige.   The last factor we'll identify that influences groups is a component called prestige. **Prestige** is the distinguished grading, position, or ranking of a group. Stature is derived from belonging to a particular group. Members of the Navy Seals, a hostage negotiation team in a local police department, or the work group that brings the most revenue into the company, for example, enjoy the prestige of the group with which they are associated. With high prestige comes privileges—such as top-of-the-line equipment, the latest technology upgrades, and other amenities. Prestige, however, is not something new. Rather, as far back as scientists have been able to trace human groupings, they have found distinguished rankings: tribal chiefs and their followers, nobles and peasants, the haves and the have-nots.

Group Leaders.   Earlier, we touched on the idea that group leaders can influence group members. Although that is correct, the more pressing questions are, who are these group leaders and where do group leaders come from? It depends. For example, if the group is formally established, then a group leader is usually designated. These individuals have been given certain amounts of authority and are held accountable for attaining some goal. Formal group leaders, then, may have the title of supervisor, team captain, project leader, or president.

When the group is informal, however, no one individual is officially designated as the leader. Instead, one person typically emerges to a position of influence. This individual may be informally granted the primary position by other group members because of his or her age, skills, expertise, or the like. Informal leaders, too, may emerge even when a formal leader is present. Because group members may respond to someone's personal characteristics—as opposed to the formal authority granted by one's position—someone else in the group may also be viewed as the leader. In sports, for example, though coaches or managers have the formal position, often certain star players are viewed as the true team leaders. In New York, for example, even though Joe Torre is the manager of the Yankees, many of the players—especially the younger ones—look to Derek Jeter for his insights and direction. When situations like this occur, it is crucial for the formal and informal group leaders to have similar goals. If they don't, serious conflicts may arise.

---

[5]S. J. Karau and K. D. Williams, "Social Loafing: A Meta-Analytic Review and Theoretical Integration," *Journal of Personality and Social Psychology* (October 1993), pp. 681–706.

Whoever leads the group, one fact remains. Groups are brought together for a particular purpose—and an underlying characteristic that permeates all of their activities is their ability to make decisions.

Group Decision Making

*M*any decisions, especially important decisions that have a far-reaching effect on your work activities, are made in groups. It's a rare organization that doesn't at some time use committees, task forces, review panels, study teams, or similar groups as vehicles for making decisions. Studies indicate that you'll spend almost half of your workday in meetings. Undoubtedly, a large portion of that time is involved with defining problems, arriving at solutions to those problems, and determining the means for implementing the solutions.

Advantages of Group Decision Making

Individual and group decisions each have their own set of strengths. Yet neither is ideal for all situations. Let's begin by reviewing the advantages that group decisions have over individual decisions. Decisions made in groups provide more complete information. There is often truth to the premise that two heads are better than one. Your group will bring a diversity of experience and perspectives to the decision process that, as an individual acting alone, you cannot. Groups also generate more alternatives, because they have a greater quantity and diversity of information. This is most evident when your group consists of members who represent different task specialties.

Making decisions in groups also increases the likelihood that others will accept the solution. Many individual decisions you make may fail after selecting the best alternative. That's because others may not accept your solution. It's not that your decision was wrong; it's because others were not involved. But if those who will be affected by the solution (and whose help you'll need to implement it) get to participate in your decision-making process, they will be more likely to accept the decision and to encourage others to do so. That's why local government officials have meetings inviting the community to state their views when decisions are to be made about such things as zoning regulations, building a landfill, or funding educational programs. Don't make the assumption, however, that such an open forum is a ruse to justify what you want to do. That strategy will often backfire. If you involve others in the discussions, you must consider the information you are given. It just might result in a decision that is the opposite of what you intended. For example, anyone attempting to get to Vancouver, British Columbia, will notice one major obstacle. About twenty miles out of downtown Vancouver, major highways end. The remainder of the trip involves traveling through residential neighborhoods. Although local government and business officials have suggested making traffic changes enabling easier access for tourists to reach the convention center and downtown points of interest, community members have rejected the idea. As a result, the solution the leaders wanted never materialized.

Finally, group decision making increases legitimacy. The group-decision-making process is consistent with democratic ideals, and therefore group decisions may be perceived as more legitimate than decisions you make alone. The fact that you don't consult others can create a perception that your decisions are self-serving and primarily benefit you, rather than work toward the best interests of achieving organizational goals.

Disadvantages of Group Decision Making

If groups are so good, how did the phrase "A camel is a racehorse put together by a committee" become so popular? The answer, of course, is that group decisions are not without their drawbacks. You face several major disadvantages when using groups to make decisions. First, they're time-consuming. It takes time to convene a group. Additionally, the interaction once the group is in place is frequently inefficient. The result is that your group almost always takes more time to reach a solution than you would take to make the decision alone.

You may also face a situation where one or more group members dominate the group. Members of any group are never perfectly equal. They may differ in rank, experience, knowledge about the problem, influence with other members, verbal skills, assertiveness, and the like. This creates the opportunity for some to use their advantages to dominate others in the group. Remember our discussion about conformity pressures? Some individuals may be able to get the rest of the group members to agree to their way of thinking even if they truly believe it's wrong. For example, how many employees of Philip Morris (the cigarette maker) do you believe would voice their displeasure in a meeting with the leaders of the company about the addictive nature of smoking—especially when the purpose of the meeting is to find a way to better market the products so as to increase company profits? Not many. That's because few individuals would publicly disagree with the group leaders if they thought it might cost them their jobs. Doing so may be seen as demonstrating a lack of loyalty, or worse. They may not like themselves for caving in, but they rationalize their behavior by perceiving that it's just not worth the trouble to voice an opinion.

VALUE JUDGMENT: Agreeing with the Boss

Many studies have looked at how some group members may pressure others to think as they do. Whether it's subtle coercion or not, the result is the same. These members want to dominate your views and how you see things. They also want you to agree with their decision.

This suggests a value dilemma that many of us may face. For instance, is it ethical to outwardly agree with your boss when you actually think he or she is wrong? Are those of us who give in to this pressure to conform acting unethically by claiming to agree? Are we compromising our personal standards of integrity? Or are we caught in a no-win situation? Agreeing may be the politically correct behavior at that moment, but does it represent our lack of moral character and backbone?

The pressure to give in to the majority can be very strong in any situation. Openly challenging someone in charge, seeking clarification when none was intended, or asking about questionable practices may lead to our being labeled as disloyal, lacking in commitment, or untrustworthy. Even something that is relatively minor may give us a reputation as a troublemaker.

On the other hand, going along with the group indicates that you accept their norms. In fact, doing so may solidify your membership in the group. As a result, this group may run more smoothly, as there is visible cooperation and cohesiveness among its members.

So how do you act when you disagree with the boss? Do you weigh the importance of the issue before you make your decision to speak up? If it doesn't really affect you, or you believe it really isn't wrong, do you give your nod of approval by going along with the flow? Or do you stand up for what you believe in and make your point that "the emperor has no clothes," even if it may jeopardize your standing in the group or your job? What's your view of this dilemma?

3. An advantage of group decision making is that:
   a. groups take more time to reach decisions than individuals.
   b. decisions reached increase the likelihood that others will accept the solution.
   c. differences of opinion are minimized.
   d. the likelihood of any one member dominating the discussion is reduced.

4. Which of the following words is best associated with the concept of groupthink?
   a. legitimacy
   b. conformity
   c. ambiguity
   d. responsibility

When someone dominates the group it is actually pressure being applied on group members to conform. For example, have you ever been in a situation (a meeting, a classroom, or with friends) where a number of people were sitting around discussing something, and in the course of that discussion you had something to say that ran contrary to the views of those that dominated the discussion? What did you do? Remain silent? Would you be surprised if you later learned that others shared your views and also had remained silent? If so, what you experienced is **groupthink,** a tendency to withhold unpopular views in order to give the appearance of agreement to those in charge.[6] Groupthink undermines critical-thinking efforts in groups and eventually harms the quality of final decisions.

Finally, there often is ambiguous responsibility when groups are used. Group members share responsibility, but who is actually responsible for the final outcome? If the decision was a good one, you'll often find that each member of the group takes full credit for what the group has done. You'll hear such things as "It was my suggestion that led to the solution." On the other hand, if the decision is bad, no one in the group takes ownership. After all, it was the group's fault. "Sure, if it was up to me I would have done things differently. But, hey, that's what the group decided to do!" Responsibility for some of the greatest organizational mistakes—such as the failure to abort the space shuttle *Challenger*'s liftoff because of leaking O-rings—often gets lost in the shuffle. When the decision is an individual one, it is clear who is responsible. But in a group decision, the responsibility of any single member is watered down. Sadly, some people use groups inappropriately—not to accrue the advantages that groups provide us, but simply to cover their backsides. That's not the purpose of groups.

➤ **groupthink**
a tendency to withhold unpopular views in order to give the appearance of agreement to those in charge

Using Groups Appropriately

Are group decisions better than decisions made individually? Are such decisions more effective in achieving goals? Whether groups are more effective than individuals depends on the criteria you use for defining effectiveness. For our purposes, we'll evaluate the two using four measures: accuracy, speed, creativity, and acceptance. Group decisions tend to be more accurate, and groups make better decisions than individuals.[7] That's because groups generally base their decisions on more information. But

[6]Irving L. Janus, *Victims of Groupthink* (Boston: Houghton Mifflin, 1972).
[7]Larry K. Michaelson, Warren E. Watson, and Robert H. Black, "A Realistic Test of Individual Versus Group Consensus Decision Making," *Journal of Applied Psychology* (October 1989), pp. 834–839.

don't interpret this to mean that all groups outperform every individual. Rather, group decisions have been found to be better than those that would have been reached by the average individual in the group. However, they are seldom better than the performance of the best individual.

If the timeliness of your decision matters most, then make the decision yourself. Group decision efforts are characterized by give-and-take, which consumes time. Something that may take you an instant to resolve could take a group hours to decide. Effectiveness may also mean the degree to which your solution demonstrates creativity. If a creative solution is important in reaching your goals, a group will tend to be more effective than making the decision yourself. The final criterion for effectiveness is the degree of acceptance that your final decision achieves. As previously noted, in groups you obtain input from more people. Consequently, you are more likely to generate solutions that will be more widely accepted by others.

Building Consensus.   Whenever you bring together several individuals for the purpose of making a decision, one thing is guaranteed. Unless there is severe pressure to conform, the decision you make will not be exactly what any individual wanted. Rather, the main emphasis in group processes is building consensus. **Consensus building** is an attempt to develop a solution that is acceptable to most members of a group. It means getting input from everyone involved, hashing out differences, and reaching workable compromises that everyone can support. Reaching a consensus requires sound communication skills—especially a willingness (and tolerance) to listen to different positions.

Techniques for Consensus Building.   You can use a number of group decision-making techniques to help build consensus. The more popular of these are brainstorming, using the nominal group technique, and conducting electronic meetings.

Brainstorming is a relatively simple technique for overcoming conformity pressures that may keep a group from developing creative alternatives.[8] It involves encouraging the freewheeling proposal of any and all alternatives. During this brainstorming session, no criticism is allowed. Instead, all alternatives—however weird they may appear—are recorded for later discussion and analysis. Following this process, brainstorming works well for generating many ideas.

The **nominal group** restricts discussion during the decision-making process, hence the term. Group members must be present, as in a traditional committee meeting, but they are required to operate independently. They secretly write a list of general problem areas or potential solutions to a problem. The primary advantage of this technique is that it permits the group to meet formally but does not restrict independent thinking, as so often happens in the traditional interacting group.

A more recent approach to consensus building is by meeting electronically. An electronic meeting blends the nominal group technique with sophisticated computer technology.[9] Using computer terminals, up to fifty people (from almost any location) are networked in the session. Issues are presented to group members, and responses are made via computer communication programs. Individual comments, as well as aggregate votes, are displayed on individual monitors.

> **consensus building**
> an attempt to develop a solution that is acceptable to most members of a group

> **brainstorming**
> a technique for overcoming conformity pressures that may keep a group from developing creative alternatives

> **nominal group**
> a technique used to generate many high-quality ideas while restricting interaction among group members and requiring them to operate independently

---

[8]A. F. Osborn, *Applied Imagination: Principles and Procedures of Creative Thinking* (New York: Scribner's, 1941).
[9]L. M. Bastianutti, "Blocking Electronic Brainstorms," *Journal of Applied Psychology* (February 1994), pp. 903–911.

Building Consensus

How should meetings be established that encourage frank discussion leading to consensus? Here are several steps that can be used to achieve that goal. Keep in mind, however, that although many of the steps imply that this is a meeting you are running, meetings you attend should follow a similar pattern. If they don't, at least you'll have enough information to help shape the flow of the meeting.

1. **Prepare an agenda.** An agenda defines the meeting's purpose for group members. It gives focus to why everyone is being brought together.

2. **Send the agenda to group members well in advance of the meeting.** If they have the agenda ahead of time, group members can contact you with any questions. Further, having the agenda provides ample time for everyone to adequately prepare for the meeting.

3. **Consult with group members before the meeting.** Let members know that their input is valuable, and you welcome their speaking up at the meeting when they have something to offer.

4. **Establish specific time parameters for the meeting—when it will start and end.** This helps keep the meeting on time and focused on the important matters.

5. **Maintain focused discussions during the meeting.** Items not on the agenda should not be given substantial time during the meeting. If an issue is important, maybe another meeting, with its own agenda, should be held to address that issue. Keep to the issues at hand. Losing focus will result in no consensus being achieved.

6. **Encourage and support participation by all group members.** If you have done a good job in Step 2, group members should come prepared to talk, but they still may need some encouragement at the meeting. Sometimes direct questions about what they think about the issues at hand will get them to talk.

7. **Encourage the clash of ideas.** Remember, you want as much information as possible about a topic to surface. Disagreements are acceptable. That indicates that different voices are being heard. Getting consensus means that you'll have to eventually work out the differences. Failure to do so can reduce someone's commitment at a later stage.

8. **Discourage the clash of personalities.** Disagreements can enhance the process, but they should be over issues—not over people. Differences due to disliking the personality of a group member can cause a disaster and keep consensus from being achieved.

(Continued)

(continued from page 219)

9. **Listen actively to what is being said**. In order to be objective, you need to fully understand what is being said in the session. A private discussion with one group member while someone else is talking may result in your missing an important piece of information.

10. **Look for common ground**. Focus the discussion in the direction where there is agreement. Even in hashing out differences in ideas, there often is some common ground. Build on this momentum until your consensus goals are achieved. Sometimes, however, you may have to simply agree to disagree and move forward, acknowledging the differences that exist.

11. **Bring closure by reviewing what was agreed to by the group.** Let everyone know as they prepare to leave the meeting exactly what outcome was reached. Thus, no misunderstandings should occur at a later date. Let participants know what will happen with the decision (when it will be implemented, what needs to be done to implement it, and so on).

The major advantages to electronic meetings are anonymity, honesty, and speed. All group members can anonymously type any message they want, and it will flash on the screen for all to see. Electronic meetings also allow participants to be brutally honest with no penalty. And the meeting is fast—unnecessary chitchat is eliminated, discussions stay focused, and many can contribute their ideas at once without interrupting others. Electronic meetings can be as much as 55 percent faster than traditional face-to-face meetings. For instance, Phelps Dodge Mining used this approach to cut its annual planning meeting down from several days to twelve hours. However, electronic meetings are not cure-alls. There are drawbacks. Those who type quickly can outshine those who may be good thinkers but are lousy typists. Moreover, those with the best ideas often don't get credit for them. Lack of recognition can create morale problems. Finally, the process lacks the informational richness of face-to-face interactions. These last two elements are reminiscent of scientific management, in which organizations overlook the necessary human interactions that employees need.

Work Teams

*A*lthough the discussion so far in this chapter has focused on groups, a renewed emphasis is sweeping across our organizations. We call this phenomenon work teams. **Work teams,** formal groups composed of individuals responsible for attaining a goal, are increasingly becoming the leading means around which work is being designed. Why? Because work teams typically outperform individuals when the tasks being done require multiple skills, judgment, and experience. As organizations look for ways to compete more effectively and efficiently, they are turning to work teams as a way to better use employee talents. Work teams are more flexible and thus more responsive to a changing environment than grouping employees by the jobs they perform.

Before we go on, however, let's differentiate between work groups and work teams. If you've been reading closely, you may think that the two are the same. That

> **work teams**
> formal groups composed of individuals responsible for attaining a goal

This team of Textron employees has joined forces in developing a high-tech coating that, when applied on plastic, gives it the appearance of chrome. But unlike chrome, which rusts and scratches, this coating keeps the chrome look-alike in perfect condition. Here, the Textron employees proudly display their product, which has been used on plastic grills that will be installed on Lincoln Mark VIIIs.

may appear so, but there's a fine distinction between the two.[10] All work teams are work groups, but not all work groups are work teams. In work groups, your involvement with others primarily revolves around sharing information and making decisions so that everyone can do his or her assigned jobs better—jobs that are typically independent of one another. Although you are working together, your focus still remains on getting your tasks completed. A work team, on the other hand, brings several people together in a coordinated fashion to achieve a team goal. This requires the interaction and energy of all team members, who combine their productive efforts—succeeding (or failing) as a team.

Being Part of a Work Team

Work teams usually perform one of three functions. Sometimes organizations may use your team to provide advice or solve problems. For instance, your team may be asked to recommend ways to cut costs, find ways to improve quality, or select a new piece of computer-assisted design software. Other teams you belong to may be able to make their own work-related decisions. In essence, being part of a self-directed team means you act as your own supervisor—and do the work that your supervisor typically did. That means you have the responsibility and the accountability to achieve some goal—and to police yourself. At the Hershey Chocolate Company, for example, most of the Reese's candy made is produced by a self-directed work team. After receiving a directive from the main office, this team orders its supplies, schedules its own work hours and vacations, and hires and evaluates one another. Finally, you may be part of a team that is created to make or do things. Pooled together with employees from different work areas in the organization, your team's charge is to accomplish a specific task.[11] For example, Black & Decker brought together more than eighty-five employees from design, engineering, marketing, finance, and other departments in its effort to develop some new tools for the do-it-yourself homeowner.

---

[10]M. B. Nelson, "Learning What 'Team' Really Means," *Newsweek*, July 19, 1999, p. 55.
[11]G. Taninecz, "Team Players," *Industry Week*, July 15, 1996, pp. 28–31; S. S. Brooks, "Managing Horizontal Revolution," *HRMagazine*, June 1995, pp. 52–58; and Lipnack and Stamps, *The TeamNet Factor*, pp. 14–17.

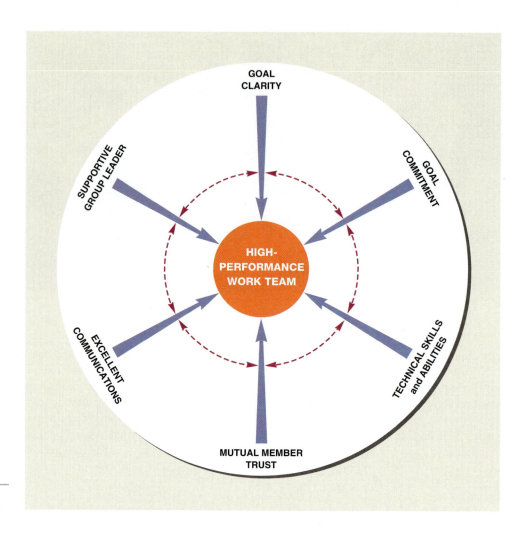

EXHIBIT 9-4

Developing a High-Performance Work Team

Developing a High-Performance Work Team

What can you do to make your team highly productive? Although there are no clear-cut do's and don'ts, some guidelines do exist. (See Exhibit 9-4.) Let's look at these.

You must ensure that your team has both a clear understanding of the goal to be achieved and a belief that the goal is important. This helps gain everyone's commitment, letting each member know what he or she is expected to accomplish and letting them understand how each will work together to achieve these goals. Commitment alone, however, is not enough. Your team must also consist of competent people. All team members must have the necessary technical skills and abilities to achieve the desired goals and the personal characteristics required to achieve excellence while working well with others. This latter point is important and cannot be overlooked. You'll find that not everyone who is technically competent has the skills to work well as a team member. In that case, you'll need to work more closely with that individual to teach him or her what is appropriate team behavior. In the event that no change takes place, you may have to remove the individual from the team.

Your team must have high mutual trust among members. That is, members must believe in each other's integrity, character, and ability. But as you probably know from personal relationships, trust is fragile. It takes a long time to build and

1. **Understand that everyone is working together.** If team members suspect that you're looking out for your own self-interest, trust will never materialize. Unless your actions show that you have taken the team's interest to heart, you'll lose all credibility.

2. **Be supportive of team members and their efforts.** Be available and approachable. Encourage and support fellow team members' ideas. Defend your team if the need arises. In essence, be a team player.

3. **Communicate with your team members.** Keep all team members informed of anything that affects them. Share relevant information you may have. Be open with them and encourage their feedback. Also be candid about your own problems and limitations.

4. **Keep confidential information private.** Confidential information shared by team members should not be disclosed to others. Don't betray others for sharing something personal with you. Someone who can't keep a secret won't build much trust with others.

5. **Be respectful of team members' ideas.** Realize that you may not always have the right answer or the best way to do things. Actively listen to what others have to say.

6. **Treat everyone as you want to be treated.** Sure, you'll be closer to some team members than others, but don't let that lead to anyone's exclusion. Give credit to a team member when it's due. Recognize anyone for a job well done. Respect others.

7. **Always do what is right.** Be steady in your daily work efforts. Letting honesty and good values drive your actions can lead to earning the trust of others.

8. **Demonstrate competence.** Develop the admiration and respect of team members by demonstrating sound technical skills and good interpersonal skills.

Source: Adapted from Fernando Bartolome, "Nobody Trusts the Boss Completely—Now What," *Harvard Business Review* (March–April 1989), pp. 135–142.

EXHIBIT 9-5

Suggestions for Building Team Trust

can easily be destroyed. (See Exhibit 9-5.) The climate of trust within your team must focus on openness, honesty, and collaboration. The presence of these promotes intense loyalty and dedication to the team. Your team will be willing to do anything that has to be done.

Not surprisingly, an effective team must have good communications. Each member must be able to convey messages—both verbal and nonverbal—in a form that is readily and clearly understood. There must be ample feedback between members to guide each other and to correct any misunderstandings. Finally, your team must have a good group leader who can help the team deal with the problems they can't resolve themselves. The leader must coach the team members by providing guidance and support.

The preceding suggestions imply a team focus in which you are the team leader. But what if that is not the case? What if, instead of having a guiding role, you are one of the team members? What, then, do you need to know to succeed? Let's look at some suggestions.

How Can You Contribute to a Team?

Being a team member is not a catchy phrase for the late 1990s. Rather, it is a way that you can expect to work with others in this new millennium. The key word here is *work*.

You should expect your team members to demand a lot from one another. In so doing, the team is encouraging harmony, which may lead to improving your group's morale. You need to encourage fellow members to excel. Developing a synergy by pushing each other to reach his or her potential not only makes the group more productive, but helps everyone grow personally. You need to respect others—even when obvious differences of opinion exist. You'll have to be accepting of others as individuals. Because you're working with people from all walks of life, there's no room for personal biases on the team. Certainly, problems will arise; they do in the best of teams. For instance, look at the heated discussions that occur between family members. When that happens, though, people often share their feelings, clear the air, and go on.

You must also recognize that what you do (or don't do) greatly affects your team. You cannot sit back and expect others to take care of you. You need to pull your own weight consistently. You need to be cooperative and lend a hand whenever necessary. This implies that you'll need to learn what other group members do so that you can perform their jobs if the need arises. Contributing to the team also means you'll need to continue your education throughout your career so as to maintain your competency in a quickly changing world. Developing new job skills (including making good decisions), enhancing your communication abilities, and improving other interpersonal skills—such as handling conflict or interviewing—can add up to helping you become a real team player.

Teams Have Problems, Too

Although teams will be more commonplace in your work life, several obstacles may keep you from becoming highly productive. Any time two or more individuals are brought together, problems tend to arise. Teams are no exceptions. You must recognize where potential problems lie in order to find ways to prevent them or reduce their effect. More often than not, the hurdles you'll face will come in one of four varieties: little direction provided, lack of support, infighting among team members, and lack of trust.

Most teams will perform poorly when they don't have adequate direction for what's expected of them. Nothing will undermine your enthusiasm for the team concept as quickly as the frustration of being on a team where the purpose, goals, or approaches are unclear. It's hard to believe that your effort will amount to anything.

As a team member, you rely on the organization for a variety of resources—people, money, and equipment. If those resources are lacking or inadequate, given what you're attempting to do, it will be difficult to reach your goals. Just imagine how effective your professor would be if there weren't an available classroom with desks or tables and chairs for you to sit in and no blackboard or overhead projector to use to illustrate subject material.

Team effectiveness will also decrease if your team has excessive infighting. Being an effective team does not imply that all members like one another. That's not the issue. Like them or not, you need to respect what others do and their roles on the team. Consequently, you must be willing to put aside petty differences in order to facilitate your goal. Closely aligned with infighting is a lack of trust. When trust is broken between some team members, they can no longer depend on one another. Sadly, if mistrust spreads and splits the entire team, there is little reason to keep the team together. When that happens, everyone loses.

Fortunately, if you know what can go wrong with your team, you can work on dealing with these difficulties. It all comes down to how important it is to you and your team to stay together. If it's worth saving, everyone involved will find a way to rebuild the team and return to more productive days. As with our families, the closeness is worth every bit of the effort it takes to make things right.

SUMMARY

This summary corresponds with the Learning Outcomes found on page 203.

1. Formal groups are assigned by supervisors in an organization. In a formal group, specific tasks must be accomplished. Informal groups are formed to fulfill a social need.

2. Four types of groups are the function group (a supervisor and employees), the task group (people brought together to accomplish a specific task), the interest group (individuals who come together to promote a self-fulfilling interest), and the friendship group (people who come together because they have something in common).

3. People join groups because of their needs for security, prestige, self-esteem, affiliation, influence, or goal achievement.

4. A role is a set of expected behaviors attributed to someone who occupies a given position in society. At any given time, individuals adjust their role behaviors to the group of which they are a part.

5. Because individuals want to be accepted by their fellow group members, they tend to go along with the flow of the group. Pressure to conform, either real or implied, can affect one's judgment and attitudes.

6. Group decision making offers certain advantages: more complete information, more alternatives, increased acceptance of a solution, and greater legitimacy. On the other hand, decision-making groups are time-consuming, can be dominated by a minority, create pressures to conform, and cloud responsibility.

7. Three ways for building consensus among group members are brainstorming, using the nominal group technique, and holding electronic meetings.

8. Involvement in a work group revolves around sharing information and making decisions that affect each member's personal job and responsibility. A work team brings several individuals together in a coordinated fashion to achieve a common goal.

9. Although no precise rules exist for developing high-performance work teams, several guidelines do exist: having a clear understanding of the goals, being committed to the goals, having team members who possess technical skills and abilities, working in an environment of mutual trust, using good communications, and having a supportive group leader.

10. Five ways you can contribute to a team are encouraging fellow team members to excel, respecting one another, recognizing how your work affects the team's goals, cooperating with team members, and continuing your education.

REVIEWING YOUR UNDERSTANDING

1. Given a choice between joining a formal or an informal group, which would you choose? Why?

2. What are four types of groups and under which circumstances is each most useful?

3. Are there benefits from joining a group? Discuss.

4. What are group roles, and how do they affect your behavior?

5. "There are times when it's appropriate for a group to put pressure on other group members to conform." Do you agree or disagree with the statement? Explain.

6. What is the optimal size of a group? Should the optimal size ever be changed? Discuss.

7. Under what conditions are group decisions better than decisions made by an individual?

8. What is groupthink, and what effect does it have on group decision making?

9. In what ways can teams be used?

10. Identify the criteria that must exist to produce a high-performance work team. What can you do to make these a reality in your team?

ANSWERS TO CHECKING YOUR UNDERSTANDING

1. c **2.** a **3.** b **4.** b

LEARNING TOGETHER

A. Brainstorming is a wonderful way to create alterative ideas. The advantage to brainstorming as a group is that more ideas are generated than any one person could probably think of on his or her own. Some of the solutions or ideas thought up may not be workable and many may be downright stupid; however, the point is that you never know when a crazy idea might revolutionize the world ("Man on the moon! Preposterous!"). Read the following scenario. Then, brainstorm by yourself with no input from your group for about five minutes. After about five minutes brainstorm out loud as a group.

You are visitors from another planet. You have landed on an extinct and lifeless planet called Earth. The year is Stardate 2389. While walking around on the surface of this once-thriving world, you and your fellow archaeology students find a potato. You must generate as many ideas as possible to determine what it is and what it might have been used for. Be creative!

Compare your answers with the group's. Were there ideas from the group that shocked you because of their general feasibility? What were the major differences between your ideas and the group's as a whole?

B. Divide into four groups: a function group, a task group, an interest group, and a friendship group. In your group, identify the characteristics that are important for your group to function well. Identify the factors or elements that could contribute to the nonfunctioning of your group. Compare your responses with other groups and identify the factors that (a) are present in all four groups and (b) are different in all groups. Discuss the reasons for your findings.

C. Individually or in a team, research and write a paper on "Getting to Consensus." Try to add an example or two from real life in which you have had a role in building consensus. Add a paragraph at the end to stress any conclusions you think are important in building consensus. Share and discuss your research with your class. If everyone did not agree with you, add another paragraph to your report to reformulate your thoughts.

D. In groups of three or four students, make a case for either (a) why group decision making is best or (b) why individual decision making is best. Prepare a one-minute debate for your class. After each of the groups has presented its case, regroup and prepare a half-minute rebuttal and present it to the class. Draw some conclusions from your debates.

E. In teams of five or more, identify ways you can contribute to team building. Also identify some of the pitfalls to team building. Discuss how you can avoid these pitfalls.

Group Efforts

In the design firm of Jaeger and Briggs, Inc., Amanda Bell has an assignment to do a large modern office design project. Her work group includes two interior designers, Raenell Adamson and Brad Legett; a design engineer, Bridget Golub; two design associates, Bob Trent and Barbara Rothstein; and two apprentices, Marty Perkins and Elaine Jaggers. The group will have two additional support staff, Joselyn Williams and Rob Herald, and a secretary, William Jones.

Amanda has made it clear to the group that the success of the project will be to work together closely. To that end, she has weekly project meetings that everyone is expected to attend. At the one- to two-hour meetings, members of the project discuss their concerns on the project. Now that the group is four months into the project, Amanda's meetings have changed dramatically. She no longer has a set agenda, as she did in the beginning, and now lets the group decide the direction. Some of the meetings are extremely useful in giving direction to the project; others are somewhat disoriented and lacking substance.

In last week's meeting, Amanda stated that some memos going out on the project are not reflecting the project direction. She said, "For example, Brad is being too specific about what we can and cannot do." A few minutes later she said, "Brad's attention to detail is very different than my style." Raenell agreed with Amanda that their styles were much more creative.

Amanda, Brad, and Raenell have been working closely together; however, Raenell's ideas are more likely to be accepted by Amanda than are Brad's. Amanda also has expressed to Brad and Raenell on several occasions that she doesn't think Bob and Marty are contributing to the group. Amanda is going to try to get them reassigned. In today's meeting, Amanda assigned to Brad what he thought was an impossible part of the project. Not only did the announcement come as quite a surprise to him, he nearly choked when Amanda said Bob and Marty would assist him.

Questions

1. What types of groups are represented in this case? Explain.

2. Discuss how the roles of each person may be affecting the behavior of others in the group.

3. Is Amanda's group a work group, a work team, or both? Explain your answer.

4. What could be done to make the design project group more effective?

5. What pressures appear to be present that are contributing to conformity in Amanda's group? What thoughts might be going through Brad's mind? Could his perceptions affect his work? Support your answers.

EXCELLING ON THE JOB

*L*earning Outcomes

After reading this chapter, you will be able to:

1. Define *motivation* and identify three main factors affecting motivation.

2. Describe how unfulfilled needs affect your behavior.

3. Explain the hierarchy of needs.

4. Identify two ways supervisors can view employees and explain the effect of each view on motivation.

5. Describe the difference between hygiene factors and motivators.

6. Identify three personality characteristics that motivate individuals at work.

7. Explain the importance of referents in motivation.

8. Describe the three components of expectancy theory.

9. Identify the five core dimensions of the job characteristics model.

10. Explain how job enrichment, job rotation, and flexible hours affect motivation.

When we hear the word *motivation*, many different thoughts come to mind. You may view yourself as motivated when you are really energized and enthusiastic about something. Getting psyched up to attend your college's championship soccer game by making banners and floats would fall into this category. This may be one accurate example of your being motivated. However, for you to more fully understand what makes you do the things you do, you also need to know what motivation isn't. Why? Because many of us incorrectly view motivation as something some have and others don't. Through the years, as we've gained more knowledge about why people do what they do, we have learned that all people have motivations, but each of us differs in what drives us. We recognize that a person's effort in response to drives reflects the situation he or she faces and that the level of motivation may change from situation to situation.

Behavior and Your Needs

Motivation can be defined as (1) a need or desire that energizes one's behavior and directs it toward a personal goal, and (2) any activity performed by another to get someone else to meet an organizational goal. Motivation includes one's willingness to exert effort to achieve organizational goals such that this effort leads to satisfying individual needs.[1] Your success as an employee in any organization depends on how well you

▶ **motivation**
(1) a need or desire that energizes one's behavior and directs it toward a personal goal, and (2) any activity performed by another to get someone else to meet an organizational goal

---

[1]See, for example, Victor H. Vroom, *Work and Motivation* (New York: Wiley, 1964).

UNLOCKING YOUR POTENTIAL *10-1*

What Do You Want from a Job (and What Does Your Boss Think)?

No one can know precisely what you are looking for in a job—that is, unless they ask. That doesn't often happen. Instead, your boss often thinks he or she knows what you want or need. Let's see how accurate your boss might be. Listed below are ten items that have often been cited in the literature as things employees want at work. In Column A, rank each item regarding what you want from 1 to 10. A ranking of 1 is the most important thing to you on the job, 2 is the second most important, and so on. In Column B, rank from 1 to 10 what you think your supervisor would say about what you want.

Column A
What I Want
(Rankings)

Column B
What My Boss
Thinks I Want (Rankings)

_____ Recognition for good work	_____
_____ Good wages	_____
_____ Employee assistance programs	_____
_____ Appropriate disciplinary procedures	_____
_____ A good work environment	_____
_____ Challenging work	_____
_____ A supervisor who's loyal to me	_____
_____ Job security	_____
_____ To participate in what affects me in my job	_____
_____ Promotion and growth opportunities	_____

How do you motivate employees? That's been a question many people have asked. Jim Rosen of Fantastic Foods, a California producer of dry soups, thinks he's found one answer. Rosen spends considerable time with employees helping build their self-esteem. He meets with employees individually, helping them identify challenging goals, encouraging creativity in their work, and providing continuous feedback. Jim Rosen has fulfilled an important need for his employees.

do your job. Realizing that your performance is a function of both your ability and your willingness to do the job, organizations must find ways to maximize your potential—ways to motivate you. But since motivation comes from within the person and relies on one's drive to satisfy individual needs, supervisors cannot directly cause anyone to do anything. What motivation becomes for my supervisors, then, is a means of affecting the environment in which I exist. If they make my environment pleasant enough for me to want to do something, then I'll behave in the appropriate manner. For instance, even the most mundane topics in a college course can be made exciting by a professor who knows how to excite students. By doing those things necessary to keep them involved and their interest stimulated, the professor is activating their learning energies—their motivation. Organizations can also create positive environments, and thus give employees opportunities to excel. Let's take a closer look at how this happens.

Why You Do What You Do

One's level of motivation is described in terms of one's outward behavior. Those of us who are highly motivated in a given situation exert a greater effort to perform some task than those who are less motivated. At work, our efforts must be focused on some organizational goal; however, not only must organizational goals be achieved but personal needs must also be met. Employees must be able to see how their work leads to something they need or want. Thus, there are three main components to motivation: effort, organizational goals, and needs. (See Exhibit 10-1.)

Effort.   Your effort in any activity is a measure of the intensity with which you approach the task. If you work in a dedicated, focused manner, your effort is high. However, if you don't really care about what you're doing, your effort is mediocre at best. But even high effort levels may not lead to positive outcomes if your effort is misplaced.

Organizational Goals.   At work, your supervisors may need to channel your effort in a direction that leads toward some organizational goal. For example, they may assign you tasks that focus directly on improving customer satisfaction. In class, the syl-

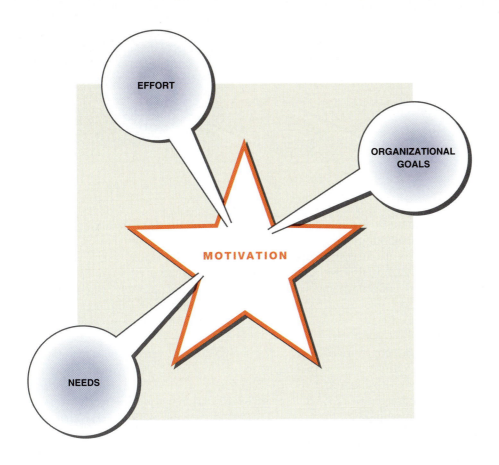

EXHIBIT 10-1

Factors Affecting Your Motivation

labus identifies course goals and tells students where effort should be placed. It makes sense that if you have to work hard (effort), you want it to count for something in the organization (meet some goal). For this to happen, though, your personal needs must also be met.

Needs.　Your needs reflect some internal process that makes certain outcomes appear attractive. Exhibit 10-2 shows the relationship between needs and behavior.

Motivation begins with an unsatisfied need. Unsatisfied needs may be anything. For instance, what if you would just love to purchase a new car? The fact that you don't have one creates an unsatisfied need. Until you do buy a new automobile, you are deprived of its pleasure and your need remains unfulfilled.

Whenever you have unsatisfied needs, you have tension. Tension, as we've come to know it, usually has a negative connotation. However, some tension is absolutely necessary for achieving personal goals. Rather than group all forms of tension into one category, let's recognize both positive and negative forms—functional and dysfunctional tension.

For motivation to occur, we must have functional tension. Functional tension creates a state of arousal for the individual, a drive. Think about what you do before final exams. You get yourself pumped up by studying long and hard—even at times pulling the proverbial all-nighter to meet a very important personal goal, performing well on an important exam. As a result of functional tension and its corresponding drive, you are well-prepared and perform at your peak level when it's time to take the

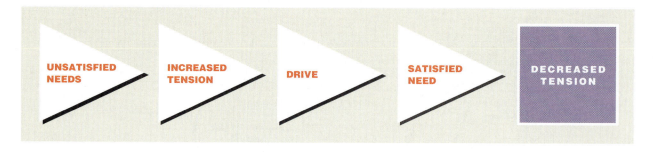

EXHIBIT 10-2

Explaining Your Behavior

final. You have an unsatisfied need (passing the exam) and the drive to fulfill it, and you will do something about it (study all night).

When efforts are successful, needs are satisfied. Satisfying needs significantly reduces or eliminates initial tension. For instance, when you work hard and save for a new car, you satisfy a need when you are able to buy one. Furthermore, when a need is satisfied, tension is reduced for that particular need, resulting in a temporary calming effect until the next need (such as purchasing a new surround-sound stereo system) becomes unsatisfied.

Therefore, it's appropriate to say that when you're motivated, you're in a state of tension. To relieve this tension, you engage in activity. The greater your tension, the greater your drive to bring about relief. Accordingly, when people see you working hard at some activity, they can conclude that you are driven by a desire to achieve some goal—and get something in return that you value. The problem, however, is that your motivation is a fragile process. Many puzzle pieces must come together at once for you to have the desire to excel. If any of the linkages shown in Exhibit 10-2 are missing, your willingness to exert energy will more than likely decrease.

You're Not Lazy, You're Just Not Motivated

Because we are dealing with human beings—people who view things in their own unique ways—a number of barriers keep employees from working hard. These obstacles can come from within themselves or from the organization in which they work. Although identifying the specific reason for an obstacle is impossible (remember, motivation is individually based), some common problems can be cited.

One of the first obstacles may be dysfunctional tension, or tension that creates a sense of hopelessness due to one's repeated failure to fulfill a need. For instance, suppose that initially you give 100 percent effort to a task, but are not able to fulfill your need. Maybe the next time around, you try even harder, but still there is no positive outcome. You keep trying and failing. At some point, you feel that this is hopeless and just give up trying.

Suppose that for the first exam in this class, you studied very hard. Unfortunately, when you got your exam back, you received a D. You're upset, but you need to pass this class. So your tension is even greater. You're doing extra things to learn this material—taping lectures and listening to them later, rewriting your lecture notes, studying with classmates, and so on. In fact, you even pull an all-nighter studying for the second exam. Yet the results are the same—a D. At this point, your passing this class is doubtful, so you stop attending. You've given up because you feel that your need won't be met. Dysfunctional tension has won.

Apathy may also be an obstacle to satisfying one's personal or organizational goals. Apathy exists when one has little or no drive in a given situation. Although you may face problems in an organization—such as recognizing you can't pass this class—you can't allow yourself to fall into the apathy trap. A positive attitude can help you see the benefits of moving forward without letting a broken spirit be a barrier to future behavior. Let's hope, too, that there are people trying to create a positive environment for you and doing whatever they can to keep you trying.

Early Motivation Theories Focused on You

*T*he 1950s was a fruitful time for the development of motivation concepts. During this period, three specific theories were formulated that are probably still the best-known explanations of motivation. These are Maslow's hierarchy of needs theory,

McGregor's Theory X and Theory Y, and Herzberg's motivation-hygiene theory. Although these theories have been heavily attacked over the years and more valid explanations of motivation have since been developed, you should know these theories for at least two reasons: (1) They represent the foundation from which contemporary theories grew, and (2) supervisors regularly use these theories and their terminology in an effort to motivate us. This latter point is critical if for no other reason than to know why people treat you the way they do.

Fulfilling Your Needs

The best-known theory of motivation is probably Abraham Maslow's **hierarchy of needs theory.**[2] The five levels of needs he proposed, arranged in hierarchical order, are depicted in Exhibit 10-3 and are briefly summarized here:

1. **Physiological needs:** food, drink, shelter, sexual satisfaction, and other bodily requirements
2. **Safety needs:** security and protection from physical and emotional harm
3. **Social needs:** affection, belonging, acceptance, and friendship
4. **Esteem needs:** internal esteem factors such as self-respect, autonomy, and achievement, and external esteem factors such as status, recognition, and attention
5. **Self-actualization needs:** growth, achieving one's potential, and self-fulfillment; the drive to become what one is capable of becoming

---

[2]Abraham Maslow, *Motivation and Personality* (New York: Harper & Row, 1954).

Margin glossary

▶ **hierarchy of needs theory**
Maslow's theory of motivation

▶ **physiological needs**
food, drink, shelter, sexual satisfaction, and other bodily requirements

▶ **safety needs**
security and protection from physical and emotional harm

▶ **social needs**
affection, belonging, acceptance, and friendship

▶ **esteem needs**
internal esteem factors such as self-respect, autonomy, and achievement and external esteem factors such as status, recognition, and attention

▶ **self-actualization needs**
growth, achieving one's potential, and self-fulfillment; the drive to become what one is capable of becoming

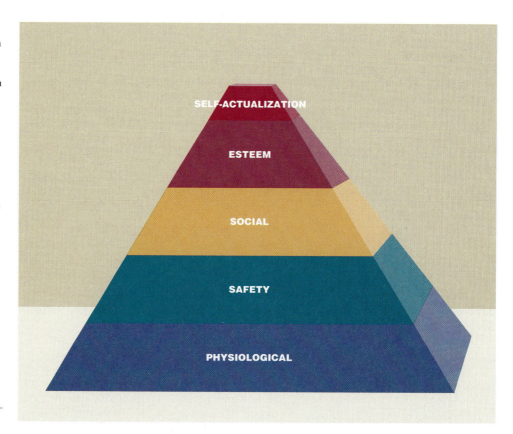

EXHIBIT 10-3
Hierarchy of Needs

From a motivation viewpoint, the theory says that although no need is ever fully satisfied, once one has substantially satisfied a need, the need is no longer a motivator. As each need is substantially satisfied and a higher need becomes dominant, one moves up the need ladder. Accordingly, if someone wants to motivate you, according to Maslow, he or she must understand where you are in the hierarchy of needs and focus on satisfying your needs at or above that level.

Maslow's hierarchy of needs theory has received wide recognition, particularly among organizational theorists. The theory is logical and easy to understand. For example, if you've just been diagnosed with terminal cancer and have been given less than six months to live, it makes sense that you won't be paying much attention to a possible promotion eighteen months from now. A lower-level need is threatened, and it now dominates your every move. But two weeks later, when you find out that the medical lab made a major mistake in the analysis of your biopsy (and second and third opinions conclude that your lump is nonmalignant, and therefore not fatal), your focus may change. You are once again very interested in that future promotion and your career growth. Makes sense, doesn't it? However, many studies attempting to validate Maslow's theory have not been able to support it. Of course, that doesn't make this theory useless. Instead, it means that maybe individuals don't move up the hierarchy exactly as Maslow proposed. It did, however, identify that they have needs. And they'll be in no position to focus their attention on the higher-order needs (social, esteem, or self-actualization) if lower-level ones are unfulfilled. That knowledge may go a long way in helping us better understand motivation.

A Supervisor's Perception of You

Although you have needs (and let's hope your boss recognizes them), the fact remains that others have a major effect on motivating you. How others see you, then, will affect how they treat you. Human relations proponent Douglas McGregor proposed two distinct views of the nature of human beings: a basically negative view, labeled **Theory X,** and a basically positive view, labeled **Theory Y.**[3] After viewing the way supervisors dealt with employees, McGregor concluded that a supervisor's view of human nature is based on a group of assumptions, either positive or negative. (See Exhibit 10-4.) These assumptions, in turn, mold his or her behavior toward employees.

What does McGregor's analysis imply about your motivation? The answer can also be expressed in the framework presented by Maslow. Theory X assumes that your physiological and safety needs are dominant. On the other hand, Theory Y assumes that needs such as social and esteem are primary. McGregor himself held to the belief that the assumptions of Theory Y were more valid than those of Theory X. Therefore, he proposed that your participation in things that directly affect you would lead to maximizing your work effort. For instance, imagine taking a class from a Theory X instructor. What would his class be like? Believing that students are immature and won't do their work, this faculty member will have rigid policies. He'll take roll every class and penalize those who don't show up. He'll require students to turn in assignments periodically throughout the semester to make sure they are not waiting until the last minute to do the work. And the list could go on. But, is this faculty member any less effective than his Theory Y colleague?

Through the years, there is no evidence to confirm that either set of assumptions is valid. Furthermore, there's no support for the belief that those who supervise you should accept Theory Y assumptions and alter their actions in an effort to motivate you more. Although common sense would dictate that you may be happier working for

> **Theory X**
> according to McGregor, a negative view of the nature of human beings

> **Theory Y**
> according to McGregor, a positive view of the nature of human beings

---

[3]Douglas McGregor, *The Human Side of Enterprise* (New York: McGraw-Hill, 1960).

If your boss views you as having Theory X tendencies, you're seen as:
- Disliking work and avoiding it whenever possible
- Having to be coerced, controlled, and threatened with punishment to get you to achieve your goals
- Shirking responsibilities and seeking formal direction
- Placing job security above everything else

So to motivate you, all your boss has to do is threaten to fire you.

If your boss views you as having Theory Y tendencies, you're seen as:
- Viewing work as being natural and an important part of your life
- Taking the initiative and being self-controlling
- Accepting of and often seeking responsibility
- Having the ability to make good decisions
- Viewing challenging work and recognition as motivators

As such, to motivate you, your boss gives you the autonomy to do your job.

EXHIBIT 10-4

Two Views of You or Your View of Others

someone who perceives you according to Theory Y, a number of effective supervisors make Theory X assumptions. For instance, if you worked for the vice-president of Toyota's U.S. marketing operations, you'd experience his crack-the-whip style. Maybe he's not making friends, but you can't overlook his success at increasing Toyota's market share in a highly competitive environment. The same can be said of the instructor described earlier. Maybe it's painful now, but there is a method to the madness. It just may be several semesters before you see why he did what he did. The point is, motivation is situational. You've got to find what works. Your parents, bosses, teachers, and friends, as well as many others in your life, know this and try to do what is best to get you to exert the effort required to accomplish personal and organizational goals. In some circles, it's even called "tough love."

The Organization's Effect on You

We know that our needs drive us to do things. That's the foundation of human behavior. Your boss also has an effect on your effort. But what can the organization do to make you want to excel? The answer to that question was offered by psychologist Frederick Herzberg and led to his **motivation-hygiene theory.**[4] Believing that one's attitude toward work can determine one's success or failure, Herzberg investigated the question, "What do you want from your job?" Exhibit 10-5 represents Herzberg's findings.

From analyzing the responses, Herzberg concluded that employees' replies would be different depending on how they felt about their jobs. As seen in Exhibit 10-5, certain characteristics were consistently related to job satisfaction (factors on the left side of the figure) and others were consistently related to job dissatisfaction (those on the right side of the figure). Things such as achievement, recognition, and responsibility were related to your satisfaction. If you feel good about your work, you tend to credit these characteristics—which are self-centered. On the other hand, if you are dissatisfied, you may tend to cite external factors such as company policy and administration, supervision, interpersonal relationships, and working conditions.

A key component of Herzberg's work was that the opposite of satisfaction is not dissatisfaction, as was traditionally believed at the time. Rather, Herzberg saw a con-

> **motivation-hygiene theory**
> Herzberg's belief that one's attitude toward work can determine one's success or failure

---

[4]Frederick Herzberg, Bernard Mausner, and Barbara Snyderman, *The Motivation to Work* (New York: Wiley, 1959).

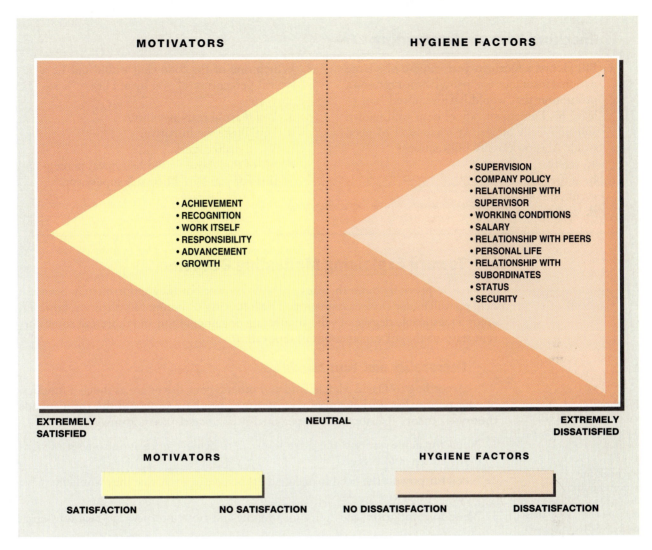

MOTIVATORS

- ACHIEVEMENT
- RECOGNITION
- WORK ITSELF
- RESPONSIBILITY
- ADVANCEMENT
- GROWTH

HYGIENE FACTORS

- SUPERVISION
- COMPANY POLICY
- RELATIONSHIP WITH SUPERVISOR
- WORKING CONDITIONS
- SALARY
- RELATIONSHIP WITH PEERS
- PERSONAL LIFE
- RELATIONSHIP WITH SUBORDINATES
- STATUS
- SECURITY

EXTREMELY SATISFIED   NEUTRAL   EXTREMELY DISSATISFIED

MOTIVATORS   **HYGIENE FACTORS**

SATISFACTION   NO SATISFACTION   NO DISSATISFACTION   DISSATISFACTION

EXHIBIT 10-5

Herzberg's Findings

tinuum; that is, the opposite of "satisfaction" is "no satisfaction," and the opposite of "dissatisfaction" is "no dissatisfaction." Accordingly, simply working for an organization where dissatisfying aspects are removed won't necessarily make your job satisfying. After all, how many of you come to class really excited because you know the ceiling won't likely fall in and crush you? Probably no one gave it a thought until we just mentioned it.

What does Herzberg say, then, about what motivates you? According to him, the factors leading to your job satisfaction are separate from those that lead to your job dissatisfaction. Therefore, supervisors who seek to eliminate factors that create job dissatisfaction can bring about peace, but not necessarily motivate you. In essence, they may be appeasing you but are not creating an environment where you may want to excel. Factors that create job dissatisfaction were characterized by Herzberg as **hygiene factors.** When these factors are adequate, you will not be dissatisfied; however, neither will you be satisfied. To motivate you, Herzberg suggested emphasizing **motivators,** factors that increase job satisfaction.

► **hygiene factors**
factors that create job dissatisfaction

► **motivators**
factors that increase job satisfaction

1. Bill Henry, a fourteen-year veteran of a large national insurance company, has just refused a promotion that would have required him to leave his hometown, where he is well known and politically active. At what level of need would Maslow classify Bill's actions?
   a. safety
   b. self-actualization
   c. physiological
   d. esteem

2. Which one of the following would not be a typical perception of you by a Theory X supervisor?
   a. You'll avoid responsibility.
   b. You'll take the initiative.
   c. You'll dislike work.
   d. All of the above would be typical perceptions of you by a Theory X supervisor.

Toward Explaining Motivating Behavior

*T*he previous three theories are well-known, but they unfortunately have not held up well under close examination. The following contemporary theories, however, enjoy a reasonable degree of valid supporting documentation and represent some current state-of-the-art explanations of motivation.

Personality and Your Needs

> **three-needs theory**
> a theory that three major personality characteristics motivate one at work

According to David McClelland and others, your drives are as much a function of your personality as they are of your desire. They have proposed the **three-needs theory**—a theory that three major personality characteristics motivate one at work:

1. **Need for achievement:** the drive to excel, to achieve in relation to a set of standards, to strive to succeed

> **need for achievement**
> the drive to excel, to achieve in relation to a set of standards, to strive to succeed

2. **Need for power:** the need to make others behave in a way that they would not have behaved otherwise

3. **Need for affiliation:** the desire for friendly and close interpersonal relationships[5]

> **need for power**
> the need to make others behave in a way that they would not have behaved otherwise

Let's look at each of these needs more closely.

Some of you have a compelling drive to succeed. You are driven by personal achievement rather than anything the organization can give you. For instance, in class, earning the A may not be important to you, but rather gaining knowledge irrespective of the course grade. In this instance, you desire to do something better (such as learning) or more efficiently than it has been done before. If you are high in this need for achievement, you'll seek situations in which you can attain personal responsibility for finding solutions to problems. You also value receiving rapid and unambiguous feedback on your performance in order to tell whether you are improving. You also like to set moderately challenging goals. However, as a high achiever, you are not a gambler; things happening by chance don't interest you. You prefer the challenge of working at a problem and accepting the personal responsibility for success or failure rather than leaving the outcome to chance. An important point is that you avoid what you perceive to be very easy or very difficult tasks.

> **need for affiliation**
> the desire for friendly and close interpersonal relationships

A need for power is the desire to have impact and to be influential. If you have a high need for power, you enjoy being in charge. You also value having the opportunity to influence others. You prefer to be in competitive and status-oriented situations.

---

[5]David C. McClelland, *The Achieving Society* (New York: Van Nostrand Reinhold, 1961).

The third need, affiliation, is your desire to be liked and accepted by others. This need, however, has received the least attention by researchers. We do know, however, that if you have a high need for affiliation, you tend to strive for friendships, prefer cooperative situations rather than competitive ones, and desire relationships involving a high degree of mutual understanding.

The point behind McClelland's theory is that you need to be in jobs that best reflect your personality. If you are high in the need for affiliation and work in a competitive environment (such as sales), your desire to excel will be affected. For example, selling insurance often requires individuals who have a high need for achievement. Of course, with proper training and experience, you can exhibit the traits that the job and the organization require. But if you're still uncomfortable, you may be changing for all the wrong reasons. Once again, understanding yourself is the foundation for your happiness.

Something for Something

You don't work in a vacuum. You constantly make comparisons of the things around you. For instance, if someone offered you $50,000 a year on your first job after graduation from college, you'd probably grab the offer and report to work enthusiastically and certainly satisfied with your pay. How would you react if you found out a month or so into the job that a co-worker—another recent graduate, your age, with comparable grades from a comparable college—was getting $70,000 a year? You would probably be upset. Even though, in absolute terms, $50,000 is a lot of money for a new graduate to make, that suddenly would not be the issue. The issue would now center on relative rewards and what you believe is fair. There is considerable evidence that you compare your effort and rewards to the effort and rewards of others in the organization. People or things to which we compare ourselves are called **referents.** As long as there is similarity between your input and outcome and the input and outcome of the referent, you'll be satisfied. An equitable situation exists—and as a rational human being, you need fairness in your life. This focus on fairness is shown in Exhibit 10-6.

> ➤ **referents**
> people or things to which we compare ourselves

YOUR INPUTS/OUTCOMES

REFERENT'S INPUTS/OUTCOMES

EXHIBIT 10-6
Focus on Fairness

Do you frequently compare your outcomes with the outcomes of others? This theory says so. In fact, you've probably been doing it for some time now in college. Think back to when your professor returned your last test. Probably one of the first things you did after looking at your grade was to ask your classmate sitting next to you what he or she got on the test. Why? He or she is now your referent. If you got a C on the exam, but didn't study as much as you should have, you'll accept the grade. But suppose your classmate studied even less and got an A. That's unfair, according to you. You know he or she didn't study, so there must be something wrong with the test. Or you rationalize that it was about time your classmate got lucky. After all, on the past two exams, you earned the higher score. What you're doing is trying to perceive equity.

As another example, think back to what you thought if you've ever been pulled over for speeding. Your heart sinks when those flashing lights come on, and you're upset when you get a ticket. But after some time, you may think, "I'm sure glad radar wasn't set up last night when I was exceeding the speed limit by another twenty miles per hour." Some you win, some you lose—but in the end, it all balances out. That's equity theory talking.

Getting What You Expect

There's no doubt that you want to be treated fairly in organizations. And you know you have a job to do. So what is needed is a way to encourage you to work hard, perform in such a way that you meet your job goals, and then get something for your

VALUE JUDGMENT: Are Some Organizational Members Overpaid?

We understand that there are pay differences in our organizations. You expect your supervisors to make more than you. That's a fact of life. And it's appropriate because they have more responsibility than you do. But at what point does this seemingly proper aspect of organizational life cross the line?

For example, top people in America's largest companies earn almost 150 times as much as the typical worker.* Some say this difference reflects an economic supply-and-demand phenomenon for high-quality talent. Paying these individuals more than one million dollars a year simply rewards them for the tremendous responsibilities and stress that go with their jobs. Besides, without them, organizational members might not be inspired to reach organizational goals.

On the other hand, some say astronomical pay packages given to selected people amount to nothing more than greed. For instance, many of these individuals had pay increases during the 1980s of more than 200 percent, whereas the average worker saw his or her salary go up by only 50 percent. And this increase was not necessarily for performance; many of the highest-paid individuals ran companies that had low profitability. Furthermore, their pay is the highest in the world. They make two or three times as much as their counterparts in Canada and Europe. In Japan, for example, top organizational members earn only seventeen times the pay of an ordinary worker—almost one-tenth what their American colleagues earn.

Does the fact that some people make exceptionally high salaries bother you? Would you feel the same if it were you who was making the money? Do you believe anyone is worth 150 times what you make? How do you value this situation?

*John Byrne, Lori Bongiorno, and Ronald Grover, "That Eye-Popping Executive Pay: Is Anybody Worth This Much?" *Business Week* (April 25, 1994), pp. 53–58.

effort. These are basic expectations of working. Fortunately, what both you and your organization are looking for can exist. It's called expectancy theory.

The idea behind **expectancy theory** is the belief that individuals will act in accord with organizational goals if they believe they'll be rewarded.[6] For instance, you'll work hard if you know that your behavior leads to a good performance evaluation, which helps your supervisor achieve departmental goals, which then leads to the organization giving you a bonus or a raise. This process is shown in Exhibit 10-7. Three connections exist in expectancy theory. These are the beliefs that if you make the effort, you'll be successful (the effort–performance linkage); if you're successful, you'll be rewarded (the performance–reward linkage); and finally, if you're rewarded, you are given something you value (attractiveness).

This might sound complex, but it really is not that difficult to see. In fact, it helps explain why, at times, we simply won't make the effort. Let's see why.

First, what do you have to do and can you do it? Unless you clearly know and understand what's expected of you and believe that you are capable of doing what's necessary, it's going to be almost impossible to succeed at a given task. Imagine that you have no idea what it takes to pass this class. You attend class, turn in assignments, and take tests, but don't know how that affects your final grade. Are you likely to work as hard under these circumstances as when you know exactly what is required? That's doubtful. Furthermore, if you learn that you need an average score of 75 percent or higher on assignments and tests to pass the course, and you think it's impossible for you to earn that average score, your effort will also suffer. You do not see a connection between effort and success.

The second connection is the belief that if you do everything you're supposed to, you'll be rewarded. If you work hard, meet all the course requirements, and earn the highest grade in the class, you expect to be given an A. But what if, just before the final term paper is due, your professor changes the requirements for an A and you will earn an A whether or not you turn in the term paper?

Without a connection between your performance and the reward, your effort level may decline; you may choose not to complete the term paper.

Finally, if you do get your reward, is it something you value? This is called the attractiveness of the reward. Suppose you've worked hard to get a pay raise. You did what was necessary, and your supervisor knows it. But instead of a nice raise, you're given an office with a window. Although this may be a valued reward for someone, it isn't for you. So your perception is that all your hard work accomplished nothing for you. Your needs haven't been met and you did not consider the reward attractive. Therefore, your effort will most likely suffer.

> **expectancy theory**
> the belief that individuals will act in accord with organizational goals if they believe they'll be rewarded

---

[6]Vroom, *Work and Motivation.*

EXHIBIT 10-7

A Process of Expectancy

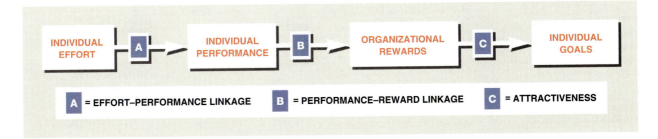

INDIVIDUAL EFFORT **A** → INDIVIDUAL PERFORMANCE **B** → ORGANIZATIONAL REWARDS **C** → INDIVIDUAL GOALS

A = EFFORT–PERFORMANCE LINKAGE **B** = PERFORMANCE–REWARD LINKAGE **C** = ATTRACTIVENESS

Designing Jobs to Meet Your Needs

*M*otivating you as an individual may be an easy task if your supervisor has to worry about only you. But when his or her staff gets bigger, or the organization as a whole is large, paying individual attention to you is more difficult. That's not to say that it can't be done. In fact, it's encouraged. Consequently, in an effort to motivate many employees at once, organizations often implement several programs. These include making your job more meaningful, breaking up monotony and giving you more control of your work schedule, and offering you a flexible reward system. Let's talk about each of these.

Having a More Meaningful Job

Many theories of motivation imply that for you to be satisfied in your job, that job must be meaningful to you. In theory, that sounds appropriate. But what does the word *meaningful* imply? To answer this question, researchers isolated those job factors that had an effect on your productivity, motivation, and satisfaction.[7] They called their work the job characteristics model.[8]

Five core characteristics or dimensions—skill variety, task identity, task significance, autonomy, and feedback—represent the **job characteristics model.** These five core characteristics are listed here and presented in Exhibit 10-8.

> **job characteristics model**
> a motivation model represented by five core characteristics or dimensions—skill variety, task identity, task significance, autonomy, and feedback

1. *Skill variety*—the variety in a job that lets you use different skills and talents
2. *Task identity*—the opportunity for you to complete the whole job or an identifiable piece of work
3. *Task significance*—the effect your job has on the lives or work of other people
4. *Autonomy*—the freedom and independence you have in scheduling the work and in determining the procedures to be used in carrying it out
5. *Feedback*—getting direct and clear information about your performance

---

[7]See, for example, Shaul Fox and Gerald Feldman, "Attention State and Critical Psychological States as Mediators Return Job Dimension and Job Outcomes," *Human Relations*, Vol. 41, No. 3 (March 1988), pp. 229–245.

[8]J. Richard Hackman and Greg R. Oldham, "Development of the Job Diagnostic Survey," *Journal of Applied Psychology* (April 1975), pp. 159–170.

EXHIBIT 10-8
The Job Characteristics Model
Source: J. Richard Hackman and J. Lloyd Suttle (eds.), *Improving Life at Work* (Glenview, Ill.: Scott, Foresman and Co., 1977). Used with permission of authors.

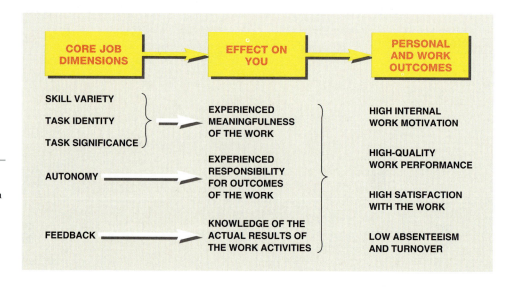

Enriched Jobs and You

*E*ach of us differs in what we like and want from our jobs. Here are twelve pairs of statements. For each, check the statement that best reflects how you feel. You must choose one or the other. Assume that in each pair, all other things are equal on the job.

I prefer	*or*	*I prefer*
1a. A job that offers little or no challenge		1b. A job that requires me to be isolated from co-workers
2a. A job that pays well		2b. A job that gives me opportunities to be creative
3a. A job that lets me make important decisions		3b. A job where I work with pleasant people
4a. A job with little security		4b. A job where I have little opportunity to make decisions
5a. A job where I am given responsibility because of the good work I do		5b. A job where I am given responsibility because I have seniority
6a. A job where my supervisor is highly critical of my work		6b. A job that doesn't use much of my talent
7a. A routine job		7b. A job with unfriendly co-workers
8a. A job where my supervisor respects me		8b. A job that gives me a chance to learn
9a. A job that gives me a chance to grow professionally		9b. A job with excellent vacation benefits
10a. A job in which I could be laid off		10b. A job with little challenge to it
11a. A job with little chance to think for myself		11b. A job with poor working conditions
12a. A job requiring teamwork		12b. A job that lets me use my talents fully

Notice how the first three dimensions—skill variety, task identity, and task significance—combine to create meaningful work for you. Specifically, if your job has these characteristics, your job will often be viewed as more important, valuable, and worthwhile. Notice, too, that when you have autonomy, you get a feeling of responsibility for the results. And if your supervisor gives you feedback, you'll know how well you're performing. The more that these conditions are present, the greater will be your motivation, performance, and satisfaction.

One of the more popular ways of increasing your motivation is to have your job enriched. **Job enrichment** allows employees to assume some of the tasks typically done by their supervisor. Enrichment requires that employees have more input into the planning and controlling of their work, usually with less supervision. It also means giving them an opportunity to evaluate their performance themselves. These aspects are precisely what the job characteristics model advocates. In addition, we can say that

> ➤ **job enrichment**
> a method of increasing motivation by allowing employees to assume some of the tasks typically done by their supervisor

▶ quality of work life (QWL)
the degree to which workers are motivated, supported, and encouraged by their work environment

these factors offer, in part, a better **quality of work life (QWL),** the degree to which workers are motivated, supported, and encouraged by their work environment. However, job enrichment will be successful only if employees find that their needs are met by the enrichment. If you did not want increased responsibility, for example, then having your responsibility increased will not have the desired effect. Consequently, if you see enrichment as merely having more to do, it's not going to be something you welcome. Successful job enrichment, then, depends on what you want from a job.

Breaking Up the Monotony and Giving More Control

Sometimes it isn't possible to enrich your job, because the formal requirements in the organization don't allow it. But that's not to say that something can't be done. Even in the extreme cases, organizations can break your monotony by rotating you to different jobs. **Job rotation** is a motivational strategy that allows one to diversify activities and offset boredom.

▶ job rotation
a motivational strategy that allows one to diversify activities and offset boredom

Horizontal job transfers can break up the boredom inherent in almost any job after your skills have been refined and the newness of the job has worn off. In some cases, this may be after only a few weeks, whereas in other cases, it may be after years. Opportunities to learn new skills, change supervisors, relocate, or make new job acquaintances can deter or slow the onset of boredom from jobs that have become habitual. Job rotation, therefore, can renew your enthusiasm for learning and motivate you to better performance. And in today's dynamic world of work, where you need multiple skills, job rotation can help you build a solid skills foundation.

Another approach toward increasing your work freedom is called *flextime*. Flexible work arrangements exist in about 40 percent of all organizations in the United

KEYS TO UNLOCKING YOUR POTENTIAL *10-2*

*U*nlocking Your Potential 10-2 was designed to identify how likely you are to find an enriched job motivating. To determine this, we'll look at your responses to the twelve pairs of statements. Statements that reflect a strong inclination for an enriched job are as follows: 1b, 2b, 3a, 4a, 5a, 6a, 7b, 8b, 9a, 10a, 11b, and 12b. Count the number of correct enriched responses you checked. If you checked seven or more such statements, you are indicating that an enriched job may create a motivating environment for you. In this case, you also may be indicating a tendency for working in an organization where Theory Y views are held. Selecting fewer than four enriched statements indicates that you prefer a job that is well-defined and has fewer uncertainties. This may indicate that you like to receive direction and are not a risk taker. If you checked five, six, or seven enriched statements, you are uncertain about what you'd prefer. You are showing some tendency for working in an enriched job, but still like being given specific directions.

Extra Effort

Given your views about an enriched job, think about what kind of organization can meet your needs. Describe what that organization and its culture are like. Where do you expect to find this organization? What kind of supervisor do you expect? Do you believe your views may change over the next five years? Explain.

Source: Adapted from J. R. Hackman and G. R. Oldham, *The Job Diagnostics Survey: The Instrument for the Diagnosis of Jobs and Evaluation of Job Redesign Projects, Technical Reports No. 4* (New Haven, Conn.: Yale University, Department of Administrative Sciences, 1974). Used with permission.

States—including American Express, IBM, Levi Strauss, PepsiCo, and the federal government.[9] **Flextime** is a system whereby employees are required to work a specific number of hours a week, but are free to vary the hours of work (often within certain limits). For example, you may be required to be present from ten A.M. to three P.M. Yet because the office opens at seven A.M. and closes at six P.M., you can schedule the rest of your day in a way that best fits you. So, for instance, if you like to get to work early and leave before the rush-hour traffic, you may choose to be at work at seven A.M. and work until three P.M. A co-worker who likes to sleep late in the mornings may choose to arrive at ten A.M. and leave at six P.M.

▶ **flextime**
a system whereby employees are required to work a specific number of hours a week, but are free to vary the hours of work

Offering a Flexible Reward System

When an employer rewards you, one of the considerations is giving you something that you desire and that matches your performance level. The organization tries to find the fine line between overrewarding you (remember that equity theory discourages this, too) and having you quit because you are not being rewarded enough. In the past, employers simply tried to achieve this goal by providing all employees with the same rewards, such as an employer-subsidized cafeteria. Each of you got this whether or not you wanted it or needed it or used it. Unfortunately, this reward system just was not effective. It benefited neither the organization (because costs were too great) nor employees (because they didn't get what they really wanted). The good news, however, is that organizations are beginning to recognize the benefit of letting employees choose their rewards while helping them curb increasing costs.

Flexible reward systems usually include flexible pay programs as well. The basis of a flexible pay program is to give employees the freedom to make individual choices. For example, suppose that based on your performance, your supervisor has recommended that you receive a 7 percent raise. If your salary is $28,000, you have earned an additional $1,960. Do you want this money all in salary? Or would you like to buy some extra vacation time, obtain better health insurance coverage, make an additional retirement contribution, or do something else? The decision is yours as long as the total cost does not exceed $1,960. What you want is what you get.

The freedom you have under a flexible pay program will depend on the organization you work for. Whereas some permit you to decide how you receive your total salary, many others focus primarily on your benefits. In this case, companies have what they call *open enrollment* each year. During this time, you have the opportunity to select the benefits you'd like for the coming year. Some may give you total freedom in determining exactly how your pay and benefits are given. Others may limit your choices in order to ensure that you have some basic benefit coverage. For instance, in this latter case, imagine that your employer gave you the option of spending all your benefit dollars on whatever you wanted. Being young, single, and in good health might lead you to believe that buying life insurance is a waste of money. Although your assumptions are somewhat correct, sadly, young people do die tragically. Even though it really won't be your worry, your family will have to bury you. Funerals cost money, and they get more expensive each year. And no benefit administrator wants to tell your family that you gave up your life insurance for an extra day off. As a result, your organization may give you less money to spend and provide you a basic life insurance policy.

The flexibility in rewards can extend to other aspects of your job. Although this discussion has dealt with rewards based on your performance appraisal, this same sys-

---

[9]A. R. Hochschild, "When Work Becomes Home and Home Becomes Work," *California Management Review*, Summer 1997, p. 85; and K. B. Hignite, "Hip Benefits," *Association Management*, February 1999, pp. 47–51.

tem can be used for other rewards. For example, if your work leads to some recognition by your supervisor and you are given a reward, you should have the opportunity to choose what you want. Although a dollar limit will be placed on the value of the reward, being able to select exactly what you want helps fulfill your needs.

Why are flexible pay and benefit programs motivational? Many reasons have been cited, one of the main reasons being that these programs allow you to get what you want. You and a co-worker can both have your needs met while receiving two entirely different things from your employer. Flexible programs recognize that differences exist in the needs and wants of employees and operate in such a way that workers can tailor their rewards to meet their individual needs.

Some Rewards Don't Cost Money

Most of us fall into a trap when we think of organizational rewards. That trap is that our rewards must be material things. The fact is, though the world we live in revolves around money, some of the best rewards we can get are free. Many of these come in the form of positive reinforcement. One aspect that greatly affects our behavior is how others reinforce us. Working for a boss who makes you feel special, recognizes your efforts, and gives you that pat on the back can go a long way in making you feel good about your work. As with the professor who takes the time to work with you and engage you in conversation because he or she cares about you and your career, positive reinforcement can act as a means of encouraging your effort.

Sadly, some supervisors (and teachers) just don't understand the potential of positive reinforcement and are losing out on developing a highly energized workforce. Sooner or later, employee (and student) behavior adjusts to their perceptions. For instance, if you work for someone who never praises your work because he thinks you're an incompetent employee, you may start believing that his opinion is true. Accordingly, your productivity will begin to suffer since you have no desire to give 100 percent. But your supervisor won't be really upset. After all, that's exactly what he or she expected from you.

On the other hand, a supervisor who recognizes and rewards you for being an outstanding employee creates a positive environment in which you can excel. His continuously working with you, reinforcing the good things you do, and telling you how important you are to the department all lead to your higher level of effort. Once again, you're more likely to work harder for someone who thinks you're a good person than someone who views you as a pain in the neck. How many times have you heard about athletes with mediocre talent winning championships under the guidance of a highly motivating coach? Is it that the team members are better players than their opponents? Probably not. The difference is that the winning athletes play for a coach who believes in them, and they therefore give everything they have in return. Kindness, caring, and treating people right makes the difference—and these things are free.

Checking Your Understanding *10-2*

3. The importance you place on a potential outcome is best reflective of:
   a. attractiveness
   b. the performance–reward link
   c. the effort–performance reward
   d. expectancy theory

4. If, in an automobile assembly plant, you put fenders on a car one month, hoods the next, and taillights the following month, you are experiencing:
   a. job enrichment
   b. job rotation
   c. flextime
   d. none of the above

Knowing When You're Motivated

*U*ntil now, we've been talking about what your employer can do to motivate you. We understand now why you behave the way you do. We also recognize the role your needs play in encouraging your effort and how your organization and supervisor can do things to make you want to excel. The biggest issue, however, is how we know when you're motivated. Surely you know when you're motivated; you've got that something inside you that tells you. But how do the rest of us know when you're motivated? Of course, we could ask you, but—if you've been reading this text closely—even if you're unhappy about something, you may still project a positive mental attitude. Unfortunately, that can mask your real feelings. So how do we know? If you believe in Maslow and you've just self-actualized, does a light go on? Could others around you spot it and say, "Hey, you've just become all you can be"? Obviously, it's not that clear-cut. The same holds for your supervisor. Just what is it that tells your boss you're giving your best effort and are satisfied with your job? The answer to that question lies in a concept called your morale.

Morale in an organization is a measure of how happy and satisfied you are with the way things are going on your job. Although morale, like motivation, is not easily defined, morale represents your attitude—and ultimately your behavior. In your class, for instance, you can easily spot morale. If your class has seventy-five individuals enrolled, yet only thirty show up regularly, it's safe to say that the other forty-five aren't happy with something in the class. Maybe they don't like the way your professor lectures or the exercises you participate in. Maybe coming to class doesn't help them pass, and they can get all they need by reading the book and taking tests. Whatever the reason, their behavior tells the professor everything he or she needs to know. The same holds for your supervisors. But morale is reflected in more than just your attendance. It also is revealed by such things as how much work you accomplish, how frequently you're absent, and how likely you are to leave the organization.

If I'm Happy, I'm Productive

There's been a raging debate for decades about happy workers and productivity. Although there are good arguments on both sides, the fact remains that if you're not happy, you'll be less productive than if you were. When morale is low, you tend to do only what is required; after all, you'd rather not get fired. But since you are upset at something, you don't want to give any extra effort. Whether happy people are productive or whether productive people are happy really isn't your concern. The issue for you is that when you are happy, you increase your productivity.

Your supervisor keeps track of productivity. Although productivity swings may not be a morale issue, any significant change in what work is getting done should be investigated. For example, your supervisor may find that your productivity changed shortly after the organization implemented a new policy on lunch hours. Being dissatisfied with the new policy, you demonstrated that you're upset by accomplishing less work. It may not have been your intention to exert less effort, but because you were not notified of the changes and don't fully understand them, you spend more time talking with co-workers than before. By monitoring your productivity, observing your morale, and communicating with you, your supervisor can improve both your level of job satisfaction and your productivity.

I'm Not Feeling Well Today

As an employee, you've learned that you can do a number of things to show your displeasure with the organization. If you're unmotivated, you often find an excuse for

Are You Getting the Most from Your Job?

What we know about motivation can help us identify specific areas that, if present, help create that positive environment in which you excel. Here are the most widely recognized foundational aspects that should exist in your job to enable you to exert high energy levels.

1. **Does your boss recognize individual differences?** Almost every contemporary motivation theory recognizes that you are different from other employees. You have different needs. Furthermore, you differ in terms of attitudes, personality, and other important individual variables. If your boss doesn't know what you want, you need to tell him or her.

2. **Are you matched to your job?** A great deal of evidence shows the motivational benefits of carefully matching you to your job. If you lack the necessary skills, you obviously won't perform well. Although the employment process is designed to make this match between employee and job skills, sometimes errors occur. Therefore, if you're dissatisfied, you need to look at yourself and find out whether this job is really what you want to do.

3. **Have you set goals?** You should have specific goals set for your job. If they don't exist, ask to meet with your supervisor to mutually establish them. Furthermore, you should be getting feedback on how well you are doing in pursuit of those goals.

4. **Are your goals attainable?** If you consider the goals that you've set as unattainable, chances are you'll give little effort. When setting goals, set realistic ones that you feel confident you can accomplish. But don't fool yourself into setting ones that are too easy. They also do little to motivate you.

5. **Are your rewards individualized?** Because employees have different needs, your rewards should be tailored to your individual needs. If they are not, you may lose your momentum. Sometimes supervisors don't know precisely what you want or have little control over the rewards. In either case, you need to let your supervisor know what's important to you and let him or her attempt to get you that reward for performing well.

6. **Is your reward performance-based?** Whatever you get from the organization, expect it to be performance-based. Anything short of this reinforces the wrong thing. Your key rewards, such as pay increases and promotions, should be given for the attainment of your specific goals.

7. **Is your reward system equitable?** No matter how delighted you may be with a reward, if you feel that someone else got something he or she didn't deserve, you'll likely be upset. Sometimes life's not fair; other times you misinterpret a situation. Recognize that differences will exist. These may be explained in terms of your experience, ability, effort, or other factors.

8. **Is money used as a motivator?** It's easy for your organization to get so caught up in setting goals, creating interesting jobs, and providing opportunities for you that it forgets that money is a major reason you work. Recognition is nice, but it doesn't put food on the table or shoes on your kids. If your organization isn't using money to motivate you, there may be a problem. But remember, money shouldn't be the only motivator.

why you can't come to work. One of them is calling in sick when you're not sick. You'd rather sleep late than face your boss today. And by calling in sick, you're telling your supervisor something is wrong. Whether or not he or she picks up on the cue is unknown. But it's a clear indication that morale is low. Why do you think New York City police officers come down with a strange case of "blue flu" when their negotiations with city officials break down? When they feel they're not appreciated, and their morale is low, they simply withhold their effort altogether. Not surprisingly, when the issues are resolved, they get better and return to work.

Take This Job and Shove It

Every organization expects some people to quit each year. But when people quit more frequently than expected (turnover is high), it's an indication that morale is low. You've got good skills to sell to an organization. You do good work. So when the organization doesn't provide an environment in which you can excel or the rewards you're looking for, you begin looking for employment elsewhere. As soon as you find something better, you submit your letter of resignation.

The grass may not be greener in another organization. Yet, knowing what you know about your current company and the lack of respect you get, moving on is understandable. You even see this in a class you're taking when students drop at midterm. Rather than putting up with whatever is dissatisfying them in the class, they stop going to the class and start it all over next semester (frequently with another instructor). If your supervisor, like your professor, sees a number of people quitting over a short time, he or she should recognize that a morale problem might exist.

A Final Word

So much can affect your motivation that it's often hard to put a finger directly on it. Yet there's no doubt that we give others clues about how we feel. If we are truly motivated, we exhibit energy-filled behaviors. We accomplish things, we are happier with what we are doing, and we are getting what we want in return.

So much of this motivation, however, doesn't exist in a vacuum. Rather, it's a function of how those in charge of us influence us. This influence, especially where there's no direct control over our work lives, is called leadership. And that's the subject of our next chapter.

SUMMARY

This summary corresponds to the Learning Outcomes found on page 228.

1. Motivation is (1) a need or desire that energizes one's behavior and directs it toward a personal goal, and (2) any activity performed by another to get someone else to meet an organizational goal. The three main components of motivation are effort, organizational goals, and needs.

2. Unfulfilled needs create tension for us. This tension causes us to behave in a particular manner. Our behavior is guided toward fulfilling our need, which in turn reduces our tension.

3. The hierarchy of needs consists of five independent steps: physiological needs, safety needs, social needs, esteem needs, and self-actualization needs. In this theory of motivation, each lower-level need must be substantially satisfied before one moves up to the next level.

4. Supervisors can view employees in one of two ways. One view is basically negative (Theory X) and assumes that employees dislike work and have to be coerced to do things. The other view is positive (Theory Y) and assumes that employees view work as a part of life, take initiative, and accept responsibility.

5. Motivating factors (such as challenging work, responsibility, and advancement), when present, will motivate. If they are lacking, however, they will not demotivate. Hygiene factors (supervision, pay, and working conditions), on the other hand, can't motivate if present. However, if they are lacking, they demotivate.

6. Three personality characteristics that motivate us are the need for achievement (the drive to excel), the need for power (making others behave the way we want), and the need for affiliation (the desire for friendly relationships).

7. Referents are people or things to which we compare ourselves. As we attempt to equate our inputs and outcomes, we look at our rewards as they relate to what others receive.

8. The three components of expectancy theory are the effort–performance linkage (believing that if you work hard, you'll be a successful performer); the performance–reward linkage (believing that if you perform successfully, you'll be rewarded); and attractiveness (believing that the reward you get has value to you).

9. The five core job dimensions are skill variety (the variety in your job), task identity (the ability to complete the whole job), task significance (the effect your job has on the lives or work of other people), autonomy (the freedom you have), and feedback (getting direct information about your performance).

10. Each of us has different needs. For instance, some of us desire more autonomy in our jobs, the ability to expand our skills, or more control over our work hours. Job enrichment allows you to do some of the work once done by your supervisor—giving you more autonomy. Job rotation allows you to diversify your work activities to increase your skill exposure. Flexible hours allow you to set your work schedule around some common hours all employees may be expected to work.

REVIEWING YOUR UNDERSTANDING

1. How is your motivation different when you are employed by an organization?

2. Can someone ever be too motivated? Discuss.

3. How is money viewed in (a) the hierarchy of needs theory, (b) the motivation-hygiene theory, and (c) expectancy theory?

4. What effect would there be on your motivation if, in a work setting, motivating factors are present, but at the same time, hygiene factors are lacking?

5. Describe a type of job where you believe Theory X assumptions are appropriate. Describe a type of job where you believe Theory Y assumptions are appropriate.

6. What are the three needs in the three-needs theory? Describe a situation in which one of these needs has motivated you.

7. "Employees will always compare what they make with others in an organization. As such, it is better for a company to have policies on pay secrecy so employees won't disclose their salaries." Do you agree or disagree with this statement? Explain.

8. How can job enrichment and job rotation help motivate you?

9. Describe how flextime may help motivate a diverse workforce.

10. Explain how others' opinions and expectations of you affect your behavior.

ANSWERS TO CHECKING YOUR UNDERSTANDING

1. d **2.** b **3.** a **4.** b

LEARNING TOGETHER

A. Following is a list of motivators. Individually rank them in order of importance to you (1 is most important; 11 is least important). Afterward, form groups and discuss the differences and similarities among the members' rankings. Were there any differences based upon gender, age, or race?

_____ status

_____ friendship

_____ peace of mind

_____ religion

_____ money

_____ family

_____ personal freedom

_____ education

_____ free time

_____ influence over others

_____ sex

B. Here is a story about two loggers. They were both hired at the same wage, did not have any production quotas, and were treated the same in all ways. The only difference in their jobs was that one logger was given a sharp axe and the other was given a blunt axe. Both loggers knew that the blunt axe could not possibly be used to fell a tree. However, both loggers joked about the situation and started to work. They worked side by side, day after day, until one day the second logger walked off the job. Describe the factors that influenced the action in this situation. Address the three components that make up the definition of motivation. Summarize your percep-

tions of this situation and share your ideas with classmates.

C. Make a bulletin board showing the five core dimensions of the job characteristics model. Clip news articles from newspapers and magazines that support each of the dimensions. If you have difficulty finding a pictorial example of any of the core dimensions, write up an interesting vignette or description of a real-life situation that provides an example of the dimension. Be creative in your display.

D. In groups of three or four students, identify things that you feel will contribute to a meaningful job. Even if you don't agree with some of your classmates' suggestions, list all ideas. When all members of the group appear to have exhausted ideas for the list, compare the lists of all the groups and add any ideas that were not included in your original group list. Then, individually, place a plus (+) by each item that you strongly feel will contribute to a meaningful job for you. Place a minus (−) by each item that you strongly feel will be negative in your ideal job. Unmarked items will be considered neutral. Write a summary paragraph about the type of job you will find meaningful based on the way you identified the positive, negative, and neutral items of the list. What did you learn from this exercise? Keep your list in a permanent place and reevaluate the list each year.

E. Describe the type of reward system you think can be used in any type of business. Identify the benefits for (a) the employees, (b) the employer, and (c) the customers. Are there any drawbacks? If so, what are they and how can you turn them into positives? Share your findings with classmates.

Then, with classmates, debate the pros and cons of the reward system you selected. If your classmates presented some new ideas to you, consider how your reward system may be altered. Write a paragraph about why some things, such as a reward system, are sometimes difficult to identify and implement because the needs of many types of people may need to be accommodated or considered.

CASE 10

Motivating Mildred

Mildred Richardson is about as depressed as she has ever been with her job. Her job doesn't seem to be going anywhere—it is the same today as it was yesterday and probably will be the same tomorrow. She also doesn't understand why she and her boss, Kenny Perkins, don't seem to communicate very well. Mildred goes to work each day (although she has called in ill more and more frequently over the past two years), is always on time, does her work with little supervision, is productive and punctual with her work, and keeps her workstation neat and tidy. She doesn't bother other employees so they can get their work done. She doesn't participate in gossip around the office—in fact, she doesn't really interact with anyone at work except, when necessary, with her boss.

Several of Mildred's co-workers have established a bowling league, but when they asked Mildred if she was interested, they seemed relieved when she said no. Mildred used to be a good bowler, but she has never shared that with her co-workers. Some of Mildred's co-workers also go jogging together, an activity Mildred does daily by herself. Mildred feels that work and social activities don't mix. She does her work, takes her breaks (usually she reads in a corner of the company lunchroom), and goes home. Each evening she tries to identify why she is so depressed. She is sure it is her job that is depressing her, because her job is basically doing the same thing day in and day out and she never gets raises.

Sometimes she thinks about having Kathleen's job—Kathleen always has new projects. It almost seems like she comes up with new things to do and she gives the concept of flextime new meaning. Her workstation usually is very messy, but she usually gets her work done just in time. Her work must be good because Kenny praises her a lot. She seems to be as happy in doing the mundane things as she is in attacking new projects. She likes to talk—maybe too much—and knows all the office gossip. She seems to be having a great time on the bowling league, although she definitely is not good at it. Mildred knows that Kathleen has had several raises.

Questions

1. Identify some of the factors that you believe are contributing to Mildred's unhappiness. State what you believe could be ways for Mildred to be happier in relation to (a) job success, (b) job motivation, (c) job enrichment, and (d) other factors that may be influencing her work.

2. Describe how expectancy theory is or is not working for (a) Mildred and (b) Kathleen. Would Mildred be happier if she adopted Kathleen's attitude and style? Why or why not?

3. What role should Kenny play, if any, in helping Mildred eliminate her depression? Is there a way he could help Mildred through the three personality characteristics (the need for achievement, the need for power, and the need for affiliation)? If so, how?

4. What referents are present in this case? Explain. What others might be implemented for the entire office?

5. In groups of three or four, discuss the core dimensions of the job characteristics model that may be contributing to Kathleen's success. Identify the items within each of the core dimensions that may be helpful to Mildred. Might these contribute to Mildred's happiness? Why or why not?

INFLUENCING OTHERS

*L*earning Outcomes

After reading this chapter, you will be able to:

1. Define *leadership* and describe the difference between a leader and a supervisor.

2. Explain why having a leader may not be important.

3. Identify the traits of a successful leader.

4. Define *charisma* and its key components.

5. Describe four skills required of leaders.

6. Differentiate between task-centered and people-centered leadership behaviors.

7. Identify and describe three types of participative leadership styles.

8. Explain situational leadership.

9. Describe the leadership style differences between men and women.

10. Contrast transactional and transformational leadership.

Understanding Leadership

➤ **leadership**
the ability to influence others to act in a particular way

Leadership is the ability to influence others to act in a particular way. Through direction, encouragement, sensitivity, consideration, and support, a leader inspires his or her followers to accept challenges and achieve goals that may be viewed as difficult to achieve. A leader sees and can get the best out of others—helping them develop a sense of personal and professional accomplishment. As a result, a leader builds a goal attainment commitment among those being led, as well as a strong desire for them to continue following.

When we think of leaders, however, we often view them as individuals who are in charge of us. These include, for instance, our supervisors, professors, and anyone else who holds a position of power over us. Obviously, through their actions, these types of individuals may influence us. Yet leadership goes beyond formal positions. In fact, sometimes this person of power isn't around, yet leadership may still exist. Let's look at these two issues.

UNLOCKING YOUR POTENTIAL *11-1*

Are You Leadership Material?

Here are fourteen statements designed to provide some insight into your leadership potential. Answer each question by selecting one of the three responses: "Always," "Sometimes," or "Rarely." Indicate your choice with a check mark. Be sure to select the response that best fits how you feel about yourself.

	Always	*Sometimes*	*Rarely*
1. I'm a good listener.	☐	☐	☐
2. I'm accessible to other people.	☐	☐	☐
3. I'm decisive in making decisions.	☐	☐	☐
4. I'm gracious when I interact with others.	☐	☐	☐
5. I keep it simple whenever possible.	☐	☐	☐
6. I'm optimistic about the future.	☐	☐	☐
7. I give credit to those who deserve credit.	☐	☐	☐
8. I confront problems when they arise.	☐	☐	☐
9. I speak directly so that others can understand me.	☐	☐	☐
10. I acknowledge mistakes I make.	☐	☐	☐
11. I have a "can do" attitude.	☐	☐	☐
12. I'm enthusiastic about work and life.	☐	☐	☐
13. I seek to associate myself with other competent individuals.	☐	☐	☐
14. I have a positive attitude.	☐	☐	☐

Source: Developed using information from Pryor Resources, Inc., P.O. Box 2951, Shawnee Mission, KS 66201. Reprinted with permission.

Are All Those Who Supervise Us Leaders?

Let's begin by clarifying the distinction between those who supervise others and those we call leaders. Often, the two descriptions are used to mean the same thing, but they are not.

Those who supervise others are appointed by the organization. They have legitimate power that allows them to reward and punish their employees. Their ability to influence employees is based on the formal authority inherent in their positions. In contrast, leaders may either be appointed or emerge informally from within a group. Leaders can influence others to perform beyond the actions dictated by formal authority.

Should all those who supervise others be leaders? Conversely, should all leaders be individuals who formally direct the activities of others? Because no one yet has been able to demonstrate through research or logical argument that leadership ability is a hindrance to those who supervise, we can state that anyone who supervises employees should ideally be a leader. However, not all leaders necessarily have other supervisory capabilities, and thus not all should have formal authority. Therefore, when we refer to a leader in this chapter, we will be talking about anyone who is able to influence others.

Can There Ever Be No Leader?

Given that our supervisors should ideally be leaders, we would expect leadership to be present. But that simply may not be the case. Although an individual with formal authority may oversee our activities, leadership may be lacking. So can we survive if there is no leadership? The answer is yes. In fact, leadership may not always be important. Research studies have concluded that in many situations, a leader's behavior may be irrelevant to goal attainment; that is, certain individual, job, and organizational factors can act as substitutes for leadership. As a result, the person in charge has little influence on others.[1]

For instance, employee characteristics such as experience, skill levels and training, professional orientation, or the need for autonomy can neutralize the effect of leadership. These characteristics can replace the need for a leader's support. The drive to succeed in these cases comes from within. No external stimulus, therefore, is needed. Similarly, jobs that are well-defined and routine require less leadership influence. In this case, one knows explicitly what is expected and how it is to be done. It generally doesn't take an inspirational leader to enforce compliance. Jobs that are intrinsically satisfying may also place fewer demands on the need to be influenced. Again, the internally satisfying job provides the influence to excel. Finally, such organizational characteristics as explicit and formalized goals, rigid rules and procedures, and cohesive work groups can act in the place of formal leadership.

Although the previous paragraph correctly cites instances where leadership is irrelevant, don't take this to mean that leadership is not important in today's world of work. That simply would be an incorrect assumption. Rather, recognize that these substitutions for leadership are the exceptions. In most organizations, leadership is critical for organizational survival. Therefore, we want to spend the rest of this chapter looking at what makes a good leader and at the kinds of things leaders do.

---

[1]For example, see Jon P. Howell, D. E. Bowen, Peter W. Dorfman, Steven Kerr, & Philip M. Podsakoff, "Substitutes for Leadership: Effective Alternatives to Ineffective Leadership," *Organizational Dynamics* (Summer 1990), pp. 21–38.

Are Some People Born to Lead?

*A*sk the average person on the street what comes to mind when he or she thinks of leadership. You're likely to get a list of qualities such as intelligence, charm, decisiveness, enthusiasm, strength, bravery, integrity, and self-confidence. In fact, these are probably some of the same characteristics you might list if you were asked that question. The responses that we get, in essence, represent leadership traits. The search for **leadership traits,** or characteristics that separate leaders from nonleaders, though done in a more sophisticated manner than an out-on-the-street survey, dominated the early research efforts in the study of leadership.

> **leadership traits**
> characteristics that separate leaders from nonleaders

Is it possible to isolate one or more traits in individuals who are generally acknowledged to be able to influence others—people such as Oprah Winfrey, Jack Welch, Martin Luther King, or Carly Fiorina—that nonleaders do not possess? You may agree that these individuals meet the fundamental definition of a leader, but they represent individuals with completely different characteristics from nonleaders. If the concept of leadership traits were to prove valid, there would have to be identifiable characteristics with which all leaders are born.

Traits of Successful Leaders

Research efforts at isolating specific traits resulted in a number of dead ends. Attempts failed to identify a set of traits that would always differentiate leaders from followers and effective leaders from ineffective leaders. Perhaps it was a bit optimistic to believe that a set of consistent and unique personality traits could apply across the board to all effective leaders, whether they influenced others in such organizations as Microsoft, the San Francisco 49ers, the archdiocese of Chicago, Merry Maids, Kaiser Permanente, or Nissan.

However, attempts to identify traits consistently associated with those who are successful in influencing others have been more promising. For example, six traits on which leaders are seen to differ from nonleaders are drive, desire to influence others, honesty and moral character, self-confidence, intelligence, and relevant knowledge.[2] (See Exhibit 11-1.)

A person's drive reflects his or her desire to exert a high level of effort given to a task. This type of individual often has a strong need to achieve and excel in what he or she does. An ambitious person, this leader demonstrates high energy levels in his or her endless persistence in all activities. Furthermore, a person who has this drive frequently shows a willingness to take initiative. Leaders have a clear desire to influence others. Often, this desire to lead is viewed as a part of one's willingness to accept responsibility for a variety of tasks. A leader also builds trusting relationships with those he or she influences. This is done by being truthful and by showing a high consistency between spoken words and actions. In other words, others are more apt to be influenced by someone whom they view as honest and having high moral character.

A person who leads also shows self-confidence in order to convince others of the correctness of goals and decisions. Followers, it has been shown, prefer to be influenced by individuals who are free of self-doubt. In other words, people are influenced more by someone who has a strong belief as opposed to someone who frequently waffles on decisions made. Influencing others requires a level of intelligence, too. To successfully influence others, one needs to be able to gather, synthesize, and interpret a lot of information. He or she must also be able to solve problems, make good decisions, and cre-

---

[2]Shelly A. Kirkpatrick & Edwin A. Locke, "Leadership: Do Traits Matter?" *Academy of Management Executive* (May 1991), pp. 48–60.

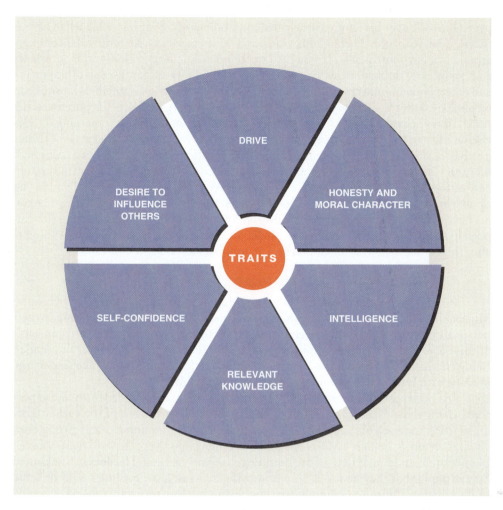

EXHIBIT 11-1
Leadership Traits

ate a vision (a plan) and communicate it in such a way that others understand it. Many of these intelligence requirements come from one's education and experience. Finally, an effective leader has a high degree of relevant knowledge about the organization and its people. This in-depth knowledge helps the leader make well-informed decisions as well as understand the implications those decisions have for others in the organization.

An Example

Anyone who has ever watched cable television, seen the Atlanta Braves in a post-season playoff baseball game, or followed the meteoric rise of Turner Network Television has probably heard the name of Ted Turner. In an American tradition, he is viewed as the epitome of leadership. Let's look at how he earned that reputation.

Each morning he is greeted by a sign on his desk. That sign reads, "Either lead, follow, or get out of the way." In Turner's case, it's clear that he has chosen to lead. He has spent his entire adult life with a drive to take one bold risk after another—and succeeded when all the experts seemed assured that he'd fail.[3] Ted's ability to see opportunities that others haven't and to boldly go for the victory has differentiated him from many of his

---

[3]See, for example, Subrata N. Chakravarty, "What New Worlds To Conquer?" *Forbes* (January 1993), pp. 82–87.

peers. He took over his family's nearly bankrupt billboard business in 1963 when he was twenty-four years old. Through his vision and business smarts, he turned the company around in a few short years. He bought a small independent television station in Atlanta and confidently dubbed it the "Superstation." Building on his knowledge of the media and entertainment industries, he and his employees combined new satellite transmission technology with the unexploited cable television market. A year later, he purchased the Atlanta Braves baseball team, then perennial losers, so that he'd have something to televise on his station besides old reruns of *Leave It to Beaver* and *Father Knows Best.* Turner gambled everything when he ventured into a twenty-four-hour news station. Although his critics laughed at his unconventional idea, it's Ted who's laughing now with the success of the highly praised Cable News Network (CNN). And he proved them wrong again when he bought the rights to classic movies, colorizing them and showing them on his newly created Turner Network Television. In the end, Turner Broadcasting (his Superstation vision) became a runaway media and entertainment success and a sought-after merger partner, as it developed into an multi-billion dollar empire.[4]

A Special Characteristic: Charisma

What do people like Johnnie Cochran, Mary Kay Ash, Hillary Rodham Clinton, Michael Jordan, and Howard Stern have in common? They all have something in their personality construct that's called charisma. **Charisma** is a magnetism that inspires followers to go the extra mile to reach goals that are perceived as difficult or unpopular. Being charismatic, however, is not attributed to a single factor. Instead, like leadership, it evolves from one's possession of several characteristics.[5]

> **charisma**
> a magnetism that inspires followers to go the extra mile to reach goals that are perceived as difficult or unpopular

Over the past two decades, several authors have attempted to identify those personal characteristics associated with the charismatic leader. Some of the earlier writings focused on such attributes as one's confidence level, dominance, and strong convictions in one's beliefs.[6] More charismatic dimensions were added when Warren Bennis, after studying ninety of the most effective and successful leaders in the United States, found that they had four common competencies: a compelling vision or sense of purpose, an ability to communicate that vision in clear terms that followers could readily understand, a demonstrated consistency and focus in the pursuit of that vision, and an understanding of their own strengths.[7]

The most recent and comprehensive analysis, however, has been completed by two researchers from McGill University in Canada.[8] (See Exhibit 11-2.) Among their conclusions, they propose that charismatic leaders have an idealized goal that they want to achieve and are able to communicate to others in a way that they can understand it. That goal, however, is something much different from the status quo. It's a better state for the future, something that will significantly improve the way things are. Of course, the charismatic leader has a strong personal commitment to achieving that goal. This leadership trait also includes behaving in a way that is viewed as unconventional or, at best, out of the ordinary. That is, a charismatic leader often does things

---

[4]Stanley Bing, "The Smartest and Dumbest Moves of 1995," *Fortune* (January 15, 1996), p. 84; and "Ted Turner Emerges in a Different Light," *U.S. News & World Report* (September 11, 1995), pp. 48–51.

[5]What Exactly Is Charisma?" *Fortune*, January 15, 1996, pp. 68–75. See B. Shamir, E. Zakay, E. Breinin, and M. Popper, "Correlates of Charismatic Leader Behavior in Military Units: Subordinates' Attitudes, Unit Characteristics, and Superiors' Appraisals of Leader Performance," *Academy of Management Journal*, August 1998, pp. 387–409.

[6]Robert J. House, "A 1976 Theory of Charismatic Leadership," in J. G. Hunt & L. L. Larson, eds., *Leadership: The Cutting Edge* (Carbondale: Southern Illinois University Press, 1977), pp. 189–207.

[7]Warren Bennis, "The 4 Competencies of Leadership," *Training and Development Journal* (August 1984), pp. 15–19; see also Marshall Loeb, "Where Leaders Come From," *Fortune* (September 19, 1994), p. 241.

[8]Jay A. Conger & R. N. Kanungo, "Behavioral Dimensions of Charismatic Leadership," in J. A. Conger, R. N. Kanungo, & Associates, *Charismatic Leadership* (San Francisco: Jossey-Bass, 1988), p. 79.

1. *Idealized goal.* Charismatic leaders have vision that proposes a future better than the status quo. The greater the disparity between this idealized goal and the status quo, the more likely that followers will attribute extraordinary vision to the leader.

2. *Ability to help others understand the goal.* Charismatic leaders can clarify and state the vision in terms that are understandable to others. This explanation demonstrates an understanding of the followers' needs and acts as a motivating force.

3. *Strong convictions about their goals.* Charismatic leaders are perceived as being strongly committed and willing to take on high personal risk, incur high costs, and engage in self-sacrifice to achieve their vision.

4. *Unconventional behavior.* Charismatic leaders engage in behavior that is perceived as being novel, out of the ordinary, and counter to norms. When successful, these behaviors evoke surprise and admiration in followers.

5. *Assertiveness and self-confidence.* Charismatic leaders have complete confidence in their judgment and ability.

6. *Appearance as a change agent.* They are perceived as agents of radical change rather than as caretakers of the status quo.

Source: Based on Jay A. Conger and R. N. Kanungo, "Behavioral Dimensions of Charismatic Leadership," in Jay A. Conger and R. N. Kanungo, and Associates, *Charismatic Leadership* (San Francisco: Jossey-Bass, 1988), p. 91.

EXHIBIT 11-2
Key Characteristics of Charismatic Leaders

that come as a surprise to his or her followers. Herb Kelleher, CEO of Southwest Airlines, typifies this outrageous behavior. For instance, he's been known to appear in public dressed as the Easter Bunny. If that seems tame, consider the unconventional nature of his public address. At a speech at an exclusive Manhattan hotel delivered to members of a professional aviation society, for example, Kelleher began his talk by addressing two of the things he's proudest of. First, he said, he's "good at projectile vomiting." Naturally, his second momentous event was the fact that he's "never had a really serious venereal disease."[9] Not your typical start to a state-of-the-business speech.

A charismatic leader is also assertive and self-confident. As noted earlier, it is not surprising that a charismatic leader would have these traits. The individual's personal commitment to activities and ability to convince others that he or she is leading them in the right direction provide followers with a sense that the leader knows best. After all, how many employees of a major airline would dare exhibit many of the clowning antics of their counterparts at Southwest? Few, unless their CEO, like Kelleher, believes that workers will be more productive in a fun-filled work environment.

Finally, a charismatic leader is often perceived as an agent of radical change. His or her refusal to be satisfied with the status quo means that everything is open for change. In the end, the vision, conviction, and unconventional nature of doing things lead to an admiration by the followers—and success for the charismatic leader.

What can be said about the charismatic leader's effect on his or her followers? There is increasing evidence that a strong link exists between charismatic leadership and high performance and satisfaction among followers.[10] That is, people working for charismatic leaders are motivated to exert extra work effort and, because they like their leader, express greater satisfaction.

---

[9]Kenneth Labich, "Herb Kelleher: America's Best CEO," *Fortune* (May 2, 1994), p. 45.

[10]D. A. Waldman and F. J. Yammarino, "CEO Charismatic Leadership: Levels-of-Management and Levels-of-Analysis Effects," *Academy of Management Review*, May 1998, pp. 266–285; R. J. House, J. Woycke, and E. M. Fodor, "Charismatic and Non-charismatic Leaders: Differences in Behavior and Effectiveness," in Conger, Kanungo, *Charismatic Leadership*, pp. 103–04; and B. R. Agle and J. A. Sonnenfeld, "Charismatic Chief Executive Officers: Are They More Effective? An Empirical Test of Charismatic Leadership Theory," in D. P. Moore, ed., *Academy of Management Best Papers Proceedings* 1994, August 14–17, 1994), pp. 2–6.

KEYS TO UNLOCKING YOUR POTENTIAL *11-1*

*R*eturn to Unlocking Your Potential 11-1 and count the number of check marks in each column. That is, count the number of times you chose "Always," "Sometimes," and "Rarely." The total number of check marks should equal 14.

Step 1: Place your counts in the following boxes:

Number of "Always" responses	=	☐
Number of "Sometimes" responses	=	☐
Number of "Rarely" responses	=	☐
	Total =	14

Step 2: Multiply as follows:

Multiply the number of "Always" responses by 5	=	☐ A
Multiply the number of "Sometimes" responses by 3	=	☐ B
Multiply the number of "Rarely" responses by 1	=	☐ C

Step 3: Total your multiplied scores:

Add the numbers in boxes A, B, and C. Place your total in box D. ☐ D

Feedback Time

If your score in box D is 50 or greater, you have demonstrated that you have a great deal of leadership ability. This may be due to traits you were born with or behaviors you've learned throughout your life so far. Keep up the good work.

A score of 30 to 49 indicates you possess the foundation to be a leader but need to work on further refining and developing some of your skills.

A score below 30 indicates that you are not exhibiting many of the leadership behaviors that could make you more effective. Look at those instances in Unlocking Your Potential where you chose "Rarely." Why do you rarely exhibit these behaviors? Is it the situation you are facing, or is it related to other factors? The first step in becoming a more effective leader is understanding where your development needs are and then developing an action plan to overcome them.

Extra Effort

Many colleges offer students an opportunity to learn more about themselves through various assessments. Take any that are available regarding your leadership abilities. The more information you can get about yourself, the better you are able to validate your behaviors. Furthermore, you can use a tool discussed earlier, the Johari Window; ask those around you—supervisors, faculty members, peers—for some feedback about your leadership abilities. Ask them what they feel you do well in and what are the areas in which you could improve.

Source: Developed using information from Pryor Resources, Inc., P.O. Box 2951, Shawnee Mission, KS 66201. Reprinted with permission.

1. Which one of the following statements about leadership is false?
   a. Sometimes formal leadership is irrelevant.
   b. All supervisors should be leaders.
   c. Leadership is the ability to influence others.
   d. All leaders should be supervisors.

2. Which one of the following is true about leadership traits?
   a. Leadership traits can be taught to individuals to help make them more effective leaders.
   b. Trait theories of leadership have been successful in explaining what always differentiates leaders from nonleaders.

   c. Effective leaders often possess such traits as self-confidence, the drive to excel, and relevant knowledge.
   d. Effective leaders must often compromise their values to be successful.

3. Which one of the following characteristics is not associated with a charismatic leader?
   a. a strong reliance on his or her ability to influence others
   b. a future vision of the organization
   c. a strong commitment to the status quo
   d. being an agent of radical change

Although over the years traits of successful leaders have been identified, these traits alone do not entirely explain leadership effectiveness. If they did, you'd be identified as a leader right from birth. Although you may have been the natural line leader in kindergarten—exhibiting your influencing abilities at an early age—leading requires more. That's because the problem with focusing solely on traits is that it ignores the skills leaders must have, as well as the behaviors they must demonstrate in a number of situations. Fortunately, these latter two—skills and behaviors—are both learned. Therefore, it is more correct to say that leaders are made.

How Do I Become a Leader?

*W*hether or not you hold a formal position of authority over others, you can be in a position where you are able to influence others. Becoming a leader, however, requires certain skills (as well as many of the traits already described): technical, conceptual, networking, and human relations skills.

Technical Skills

Rarely can you influence others when you have absolutely no idea of what they are doing. Although people may respect you as a person, when it comes to influencing them, they would like to believe that you have the experience to make recommendations. This experience generally comes from your technical skills.

Technical skills are the tools, procedures, and techniques that are unique to your specialized situation. You need to master your job in your attempt to be viewed as a source of help—the expert. As a leader, others generally won't come to you unless they need assistance. It's often the exceptions that they can't or are ill-equipped to handle. That's when they'll look to you for guidance. For example, suppose you are active in student government at your college. Frequently, your input is sought on a variety of changes taking place. Many of these, however, have some financial effect on the student government's treasury. Accordingly, you are frequently asked to provide the administration some cost–benefit analysis. Understanding this technical skill, you are

In 2001, no list of charismatic leaders would have been complete without the names of Herb Kelleher, Linda Wachner, Colin Powell, or Jack Welch. They personified the contemporary idea of charisma in organizations. But are these individuals authentically charismatic figures or self-created images?

It's customary for leaders to employ a public relations firm or have public relations specialists on staff to shape and refine their image. Herb Kelleher, CEO of Southwest Airlines, has promoted the vision of the comedic yet take-charge executive who is determined to make his airlines number one in the business. Linda Wachner, CEO of Warnaco and Authentic Fitness, has built a reputation as a tough, highly energetic businesswoman who will punch it out with the best of them. Colin Powell, retired four-star general and Secretary of State in the George W. Bush administration, has worked hard selling his book and getting involved in the political arena after his illustrious military career. Jack Welch, CEO of General Electric, relishes his reputation for reshaping General Electric by buying and selling dozens of businesses.

One view of these individuals is that they are authentically charismatic leaders whose actions and achievements have caught the fancy of the media. This view assumes that these leaders couldn't hide their charismatic qualities. It was just a matter of time before they were found out and gained the public's eye. Another view—certainly a more cynical one—proposes that these individuals consciously created an image that they wanted to project and then purposely went about doing things that would draw attention to it and confirm that image. They are not inherently charismatic individuals but rather highly astute manipulators of symbols, circumstances and the media. In support of this latter position, one can identify leaders such as Sandra Kurtzig at Ask Computer Systems, Max DePree at Herman Miller, and Chuck Knight at Emerson Electric, who are widely viewed as charismatic in their firms and industries but relatively unknown in the popular press.

Is charismatic leadership an inherent quality within a person, a label thrust on an individual, or a purposely and carefully molded image? If charisma can be obtained from the media, is it unethical for a person to engage in practices whose primary purposes are to create or enhance this perception? Is it unethical to create charisma? What do you think?

able to comply. But imagine that you didn't. You'd constantly have to ask someone else for the information. And when you got it, you might be unable to adequately explain it to the person requesting it. At some point, people might simply go around you and talk directly to the source of the technical information. When that happens, you've lost some of your influence.

Emphasizing technical skills related to your job cannot be overstated. That's because the issue of technical skills parallels our discussion of expert (or information) power. Those in the know do influence others. If you want followers to have confidence in your advice and the direction you give, they must perceive you as technically competent.

Conceptual Skills

Conceptual skills refer to your mental ability to coordinate a variety of interests and activities. It means having the ability to think in the abstract, analyzing lots of information and making connections between the data. Earlier, we described an effective leader as someone who could create a vision. To do this requires one to think critically and be able to conceptualize how things could be.

Thinking conceptually is not as easy as you may believe—and for some, it may be impossible. That's because to think conceptually, you must look at the big picture. Too many times, we get caught up in the daily grind, focusing our attention on the minute details—not that focusing on details isn't important; without it, little would be accomplished. But setting long-term directions requires you to think about the future and to deal with the uncertainty and risks of the unknown. To be a good leader, then, you must be able to make some sense out of chaos and envision what can be.

Networking Skills

Networking skills refer to your ability to socialize and interact with outsiders—those not associated with your unit. As a leader, it's understood you cannot do everything by yourself. Obviously, if you could, you'd be not a leader but rather a super-worker. Therefore, you need to know where to go to get the things your followers need. This may mean fighting for more resources or establishing relationships outside your area that will provide some benefit to your followers. Networking means having good political skills. That's a point that shouldn't be overlooked.

Your followers will often look to you to provide what they need to do an excellent job. If they can depend on you for providing the tools (or running the interference they need), you'll once again inspire a level of confidence in your followers. For example, suppose that on the day your project team needed a last-minute transparency for a class presentation, it appeared hopeless that one could be completed on time. But your good working relationship with a departmental secretary saved the day as you politely asked her to help out your group. Your followers, too, will more likely respond better if they know you're willing to fight for them. Instead of finding a hundred reasons why they can't do something, together you find one way that something different can be tried. You somehow muster the necessary resources and defend what your people are doing. In challenging followers to go beyond what they think they are capable of achieving, however, you know that mistakes will be made. When they do make mistakes, you view them as a learning experience—something from which to grow.

Human Relations Skills

Human relations skills focus on your ability to work with, understand, and motivate those around you. We have highlighted these skills throughout this book. Good human relations skills require you to be able to effectively communicate—especially your vision—with your followers and those outside your unit. It also means listening to what they have to say. A good leader is not a know-it-all but rather someone who freely accepts and encourages involvement from his or her followers.

Human relations skills are the people skills that are frequently talked about in organizations: coaching, facilitating, and supporting others around you;[11] understanding yourself and being confident in your abilities; honesty in dealing with others and the values by which you live; and confidence in knowing that by helping others succeed—and

---

[11]See, for example, Susan Camminiti, "What Team Leaders Need To Know," *Fortune* (February 20, 1995), pp. 93–100.

Becoming an Effective Leader

1. **Project self-confidence.** Being self-confident can be infectious. When others witness your confidence in an activity, they are more likely to buy into your plans of action.

2. **Be positive.** People like to be around and be led by those who are positive and enthusiastic. This creates energy and a productive atmosphere.

3. **Act honestly.** Being honest and having high moral character helps build trusting relationships among others. Tell the truth, respect others, and admit when you make mistakes.

4. **Build a relevant knowledge base.** When you are a leader, followers turn to you for information and assistance. You need to be in a position to answer their questions correctly. In a work setting, it means understanding your employees' jobs and the goals that they are to achieve. Be honest; when you don't know something, don't fake it. Let the individual know you don't know but that you will quickly obtain a response. Networking skills can assist you in this area.

5. **Be consistent.** Changing your mind frequently about issues or decisions you've made may reflect your lack of confidence or that you can't be trusted. Whatever you do, stick to it. That doesn't mean you can never change. If situations dictate it, then make the change. But be sure to explain to others why you did what you did.

6. **Understand your followers.** Everyone has needs that they are trying to fulfill. Knowing your followers' needs is one of the first steps in helping them achieve their personal goals. Capitalizing on their strengths and helping them overcome their weaknesses can help you achieve your organizational goals.

7. **Protect your followers.** No matter what the situation is, you must be viewed as someone who protects his or her followers. You must support them, praise them to outsiders, and shelter them from attacks from others. If you don't, followers will lose confidence in your leadership abilities. Protecting followers doesn't mean that you overlook any serious infractions. You do, however, deal with the individual about the issue.

8. **Be a good role model.** There's an adage that says as a leader, "you've got to walk the talk." You can say all you want, but it's your behavior that followers will see. If you ask followers to do something, yet you do something else, you'll rarely get the behaviors you want. Don't ask followers to do as you say; ask them to do as you do.

9. **Reward the contributions of others.** Being a good leader means letting your followers have the credit for all the good things that occur. It also means taking the blame for things that don't work out well. Be sincere in recognizing what your followers have done and in celebrating their achievements. Constantly let them know that you appreciate all they do for making things happen.

Source: Adapted from Stephen P. Robbins, *Supervision Today* (Upper Saddle River, N.J.: Prentice-Hall, 1995), pp. 333–334.

letting them get the credit for their work—you're doing the right thing for them, the organization, and yourself. Moreover, if you fail as a leader, it most likely won't be because you lack technical skills; rather, it's more likely that your followers—as well as others—have lost respect for you because of your lack of human relations skills. If that ever happens, your ability to influence others will be seriously impaired.

One of the interesting aspects of leadership is that traits and skills are difficult for followers to detect. As a result, followers define your leadership by the behaviors they see in you. As the adage goes, "actions speak louder than words." It's what you do that matters. Therefore, you need to understand leadership behaviors.

Leadership Behaviors and Styles

*T*he inability to explain leadership solely from traits and skills has led researchers to look at the behaviors and styles that specific leaders exhibited. Researchers wondered whether there was something unique in the behavior of effective leaders and

Are leaders born, or can individuals be trained to be leaders? The U.S. Army believes it's the latter. Potential military leaders are taught sixteen leadership dimensions at its six-week Advance Camp in either Fort Bragg, North Carolina, or Fort Lewis, Washington. Focusing on such areas as taking initiative, sensitivity toward others, and organizational communications, leadership candidates are exposed to a variety of situations—some of which focus on learning to be a good follower. Here, an individual is taking part in the rope exercise: When she is centered over the lake some forty feet below her, she will be asked to drop into the water. Those who can't successfully complete such exercises—because of a lack of one of the sixteen dimensions, or fear—are washed out of the program.

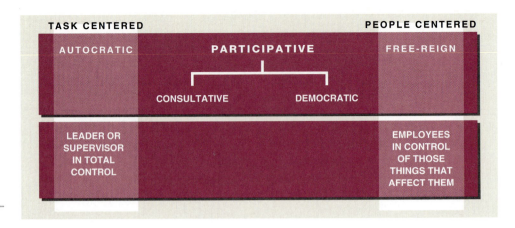

TASK CENTERED			PEOPLE CENTERED
AUTOCRATIC	**PARTICIPATIVE**		FREE-REIGN
	CONSULTATIVE	DEMOCRATIC	
LEADER OR SUPERVISOR IN TOTAL CONTROL			EMPLOYEES IN CONTROL OF THOSE THINGS THAT AFFECT THEM

EXHIBIT 11-3
Leadership Behaviors

the style in which they practiced their craft. For example, do leaders tend to be more participative than autocratic?

A number of studies looked at behavioral styles. The most comprehensive and replicated of the behavioral theories resulted from research that began at Ohio State University in the late 1940s.[12] This study (as well as others) sought to identify independent dimensions of leader behavior. Beginning with more than one thousand dimensions, researchers eventually narrowed the list down to two categories that accounted for most of the leadership behavior described by employees. These are best identified as task-centered and people-centered behaviors.[13] (See Exhibit 11-3.)

Task-Centered Behavior

A **task-centered leader** is an individual who has a strong tendency to emphasize the technical or task aspects of the job. This individual's major concern is ensuring that employees know precisely what is expected of them and providing any guidance necessary for goals to be met. Followers are often viewed as a means to an end; that is, in order to achieve these goals, employees have to do their job. As long as they do what is expected, this leader is happy.

But calling a task-centered person a leader may be somewhat of a misnomer. This individual may not lead in the classic sense but simply ensure compliance with stated rules, regulations, and production goals. In motivational terms, a task-centered leader frequently exhibits a Theory X or an autocratic (authoritarian) leadership style.

An **autocratic leader** is someone who can best be described as a taskmaster. This individual leaves no doubt about who's in charge and who has the authority and power in the group. He or she makes all the decisions affecting the group and tells others what to do. This telling frequently occurs in the form of orders—mandates that are expected to be followed. Failure to obey these orders usually results in some negative reinforcement at the hands of the authoritarian leader.

Obviously, autocratic leadership is inappropriate in today's organization. Right? Well, maybe not. There are leaders in all types of organizations—business, government, and the military—that have found the autocratic style to work best. Consider

> **task-centered leader**
> a leader who has a strong tendency to emphasize the technical or task aspects of the job

> **autocratic leader**
> someone who can best be described as a taskmaster

---

[12]Ralph M. Stogdill & Alvin E. Coons, eds., *Leader Behavior: Its Description and Measurement*, Research Monograph no. 88 (Columbus: Ohio State University, Bureau of Business Research, 1951).

[13]Ibid.; see also R. Kahn & D. Katz, "Leadership Practices in Relation to Productivity and Morale," in D. Cartwright & A. Zander, eds., *Group Dynamics: Research and Theory*, 2nd ed. (Elmsford, N.Y.: Row, Paterson, 1960).

Linda Wachner, CEO of Warnaco and Authentic Fitness, makers of intimate apparel (for example, Christian Dior, Chaps, Olga, and Speedo).[14] Simply, Linda doesn't take anything from anyone. She's known at times to be a combative, ruthless taskmaster. Choice four-letter words fill her vocabulary. Her motto is "Do it now" and "If you can't or don't like it, leave." As a result of her autocratic leadership, Linda Wachner is viewed as demanding, stubborn, and a person who just can't be pleased. Yet she's also seen as running a very successful company, more than doubling stock prices since she became CEO a few years ago and delivering a 43 percent return on investment each year. Wachner is still going strong!

People-Centered Behaviors

A **people-centered leader** is someone who emphasizes interpersonal relations with followers. This leader takes a personal interest in the needs of his or her followers and is concerned for their welfare. Interactions between this leader and followers are characterized as trusting, friendly, and supportive. Furthermore, a people-centered leader is very sensitive to the concerns and feelings of followers. Likewise, from a motivational point of view, a people-centered leader exhibits more Theory Y orientations. As a result, this individual often exhibits a participative (democratic) leadership style.

A **participative leadership style** is one where input from followers is actively sought for many of the activities in the organization. For instance, this would mean that establishing plans, solving problems, and making decisions are not done in isolation. Instead, the entire group participates. The only question that really remains is who has the final say. That is, participative leadership can be viewed from two perspectives. First is one where the leader seeks input and hears the concerns and issues of the followers but makes the final decision himself or herself. In this capacity, the leader is using the input as an information-seeking exercise. We call this style **consultative participative leadership.** On the other hand, a participative leader may allow the followers to have a say in what is decided. This is referred to as **democratic participative leadership.**

Beyond participative leadership, there is one other behavioral leadership style. This is often referred to as free-rein leadership. A **free-rein (*laissez-faire*) leader** is someone who gives followers total autonomy to make the decisions that will affect them. After overall objectives and general guidelines have been established, the followers are free to establish their own plans for achieving their goals. But this is not meant to imply that there's a lack of leadership. Rather, it implies that the leader is removed from the day-to-day activities of the followers but is always available to deal with the exceptions.

And the Winner Is

In today's organizations, many individuals would more than likely prefer to associate themselves with, or behave in a manner that is consistent with, a people-centered leadership style. But just because this style appears friendlier, we cannot make a sweeping generalization that people-centered leadership styles lead to more effective leadership. There has been very little success in identifying consistent relationships between patterns of leadership behavior and successful organizational performance. Results

> **people-centered leader**
> someone who emphasizes interpersonal relations with followers

> **participative leadership**
> a leadership style where input from followers is actively sought for many of the activities in the organization

> **consultative participative leadership**
> a leadership style in which the leader uses the input of followers as an information-seeking exercise

> **democratic participative leadership**
> a leadership style in which the leader allows followers a say in what is decided

> **free-rein leader**
> someone who gives followers total autonomy to make the decisions that will affect them

[14]Based on Marie Mallory, "What Do Women Want? Warnaco's Linda Wachner Knows," *U.S. News & World Report* (November 6, 1995), p. 75; Susan Caminiti, "America's Most Successful Businesswoman," *Fortune* (June 15, 1992), pp. 102–108; Maggie Mahar, "The Measure of Success," *Working Woman* (May 1992), pp. 70–77; and David W. Johnson, "Leaders of Corporate Change," *Fortune* (December 14, 1992), pp. 106–107.

vary. In some cases, people-centered styles generated both high productivity and high follower satisfaction. However, in others, followers were happy, but productivity suffered. What sometimes is overlooked in trying to pinpoint one style over the other are the situational factors that influence effective leadership.

Effective Leadership

*I*t became increasingly clear to those studying leadership that predicting leadership success involved something more complex than isolating a few traits or preferable behaviors. The failure to find answers led to a new focus on situational influences. The relationship between leadership style and effectiveness suggested that under condition A, style X would be appropriate, whereas style Y would be more suitable for condition B, and style Z for condition C. But what were conditions A, B, C, and so forth? It was one thing to say that leadership effectiveness depended on the situation and another to be able to isolate those situational conditions.

The Building Block Models

Several approaches to isolating key situational variables have proved more successful than others and, as a result, have gained wider recognition.[15] The first comprehensive model, developed by Fred Fiedler, a professor at the University of Washington, proposed that effective leadership was a function of a proper match between the leader's style of interacting with followers and the degree to which the situation gives control and influence to the leader.[16] According to Fiedler, a leader's style could be identified based on the leader's description of an individual with whom he or she least enjoyed working. For example, a leader who described this person in favorable terms indicated the leader was interested in good relationships. Accordingly, that leader's style would tend to be more people-centered. Similarly, describing this least-preferred individual in unfavorable terms indicated more of a task-centered style. Fiedler felt that one's style was fixed. Using three situational factors (respect for followers, structured jobs, and influence over the employment process), he identified eight situations where either the task-centered or people-centered style would work best. Situational factors would dictate which leadership style would be more effective. (See Exhibit 11-4.)

One of the more respected approaches to situational leadership was developed by Robert House.[17] The basis of this model is that it's the leader's job to assist his or her followers in attaining their goals. This is done by providing the necessary direction or support to ensure that their goals are compatible with the overall objectives of the group or organization. The leader clarifies the path to help followers get from where they are to a point where they've achieved their goals—assisting them by reducing potential roadblocks and pitfalls.

The style of leadership, according to House, will depend on two factors: the follower and the task. For example, when a follower has the experience and is responsible for a well-defined task, a people-centered style will work best. However, if experience is lacking or the job is unstructured, a more task-oriented style is appropriate.

---

[15]For a good review of the Fiedler Contingency Model, Path-Goal Theory, and Leader-Participation Model, see Stephen P. Robbins & David A. De Cenzo, *Fundamentals of Management* (Upper Saddle River, N.J.: Prentice-Hall, 1995), pp. 300–306.

[16]Fred E. Fiedler, *A Theory of Leadership Effectiveness* (New York: McGraw-Hill, 1967).

[17]Robert J. House & Terrence R. Mitchell, "Path-Goal Theory of Leadership," *Journal of Contemporary Business* (Autumn 1974), pp. 81–97.

Situational Factors	I	II	III	IV	V	VI	VII	VIII
Respect for followers	Good	Good	Good	Good	Poor	Poor	Poor	Poor
Structured jobs	High	High	Low	Low	High	High	Low	Low
Influence over employment process	Strong	Weak	Strong	Weak	Strong	Weak	Strong	Weak
Preferred leader behavior	Task-centered	Task-centered	Task-centered	People-centered	People-centered	People-centered	Task-centered	Task-centered

EXHIBIT 11-4

Fiedler's Leadership Findings

That's because followers in this instance need more direction. The fundamental issue, then, is to adjust one's leadership style to the needs of followers.

Applying the Concepts: A Situational Approach

Another model of leadership, situational leadership, was proposed several years ago by Paul Hersey and Kenneth Blanchard, one that adjusts leadership styles to specific situations.[18] **Situational leadership** is a model that adjusts leadership style to the maturity level of the follower for a given set of tasks. Situational leadership seemingly makes sense and has been encouraged today in such organizations as BankAmerica and the military.[19] (See Exhibit 11-5.)

Although Hersey and Blanchard's model is similar in nature to Fiedler's theory, a couple of differences are worth noting. First, situational leadership places much attention on the **readiness of followers.** Readiness, in this context, refers to how able and willing a follower is to complete a task. (A point should be made here that "unwillingness" in this model is not the same as being insubordinate.) Hersey and Blanchard have identified four stages of follower readiness:

R1: A follower is both unable and unwilling to do a job.

R2: A follower is unable to do the job but willing to perform the necessary tasks.

R3: A follower is able to do the job but unwilling to be told by a leader what to do.

R4: A follower is both able and willing to do the job.

A second component of the model focuses on what the leader does. Given where a follower is in terms of readiness level, a leader exhibits a certain behavior. But behavior in this model is best reflective of the type of communication taking place. That is, task behavior can be seen as one-way communication: from the leader to the follower. Relationship behavior, on the other hand, reflects two-way communication: between the leader and the follower. Given that high and low degrees of these two behaviors can exist, Hersey and Blanchard identified four specific leadership styles based on the readiness of the follower: telling, selling, participating, and delegating. Let's see how this model works by going through an example of your first day on a job.

When you first arrive on your new job, you're anxious. You're uncertain about what you're getting into and the responsibilities of your job. Clearly, the employment process should have worked well in properly matching you to the job and orienting you

▶ **situational leadership**
a leadership model that adjusts leadership style to the maturity level of the follower for a given set of tasks

▶ **readiness of followers**
how able and willing a follower is to complete a task

---

[18]Paul Hersey & Kenneth H. Blanchard, *Management of Organizational Behavior: Utilizing Human Resources,* 5th ed. (Upper Saddle River, N.J.: Prentice-Hall, 1988).

[19]Ibid., p. 171. Those who wish to look at both sides of the debate on the validity of situational leadership are encouraged to read W. R. Norris & R. P Vecchio, "Situational Leadership Theory: A Replication," *Group and Organization Management* (September), pp. 331–342; and W. Blank, J. R. Weitzel, & S. G. Green, "A Test of the Situational Leadership Theory," *Personnel Psychology* (Autumn 1990), pp. 579–597.

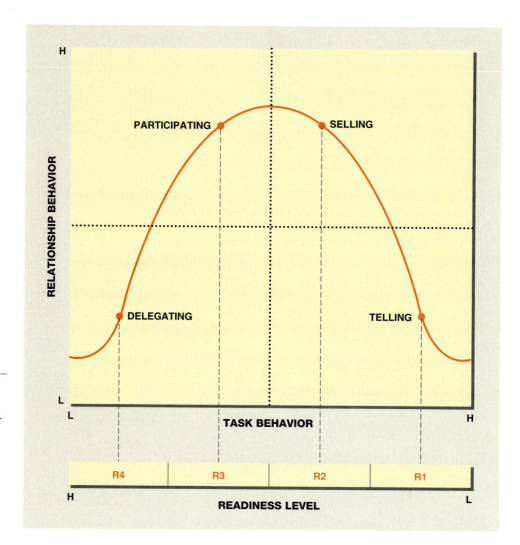

EXHIBIT 11-5
Situational Leadership

Source: P. Hersey and K. H. Blanchard, *Management of Organizational Behavior: Utilizing Human Resources,* 5th ed. (Upper Saddle River, N.J.: Prentice Hall, 1988). Used by permission from Ronald Campbell, President, Leadership Studies, Escondido, Calif.

to the organization. But the honeymoon is over, and it's time to start what you were hired to do. Imagine if you were just given a list of tasks to complete and nothing else. You'd probably have some difficulty. Why? Because at this time, you're immature (R1). It's doubtful that you even know the right questions to ask. Communications between you and your supervisor, then, need to be one-way. You need to be told what to do, to be given specific directions by your supervisor. According to situational leadership, then, at this stage, you will respond best to a telling style of leadership. But you don't stay at R1 forever. After being told what to do and getting more familiar with your job, you mature—to R2.

At the R2 stage of work development, you are becoming more involved in your job, but you still lack some ability. You're not fully trained yet. But you are starting to ask questions about why certain things are done. Even though your heart may be in the right place, you may not fully understand why certain things have to be done as your supervisor tells you. Accordingly, your supervisor must sell to get you to accept what he or she feels is necessary. The point here is that high degrees of both one-way and two-way communication are happening simultaneously.

At some point, you have become the expert on your job (R3). You know it better than anybody else. And you're beginning to put your special mark on things. You no longer need to be told or sold by your supervisor. But your supervisor still needs to be involved in what you're doing. You're just not to the point yet where he or she feels comfortable with leaving you totally alone. That's not an insult. It's just that your supervisor recognizes that you still have some developing to do. As you can imagine, this may create problems between the two of you. Accordingly, the leader may best deal with this situation by being supportive of you and not being overly task-centered. Hersey and Blanchard refer to this as a participating style of leadership.

Finally, you have fully developed on your job, have the trust of your supervisor and can do what you are asked with little, if any, direction (R4). In this situation, the delegating stage of leadership, you basically need to be left alone. Your supervisor simply assigns the tasks and leaves you alone to do your job. He or she knows from your previous performance that you can and will get the job done. And if you need help, the supervisor is always available to deal with the exceptions.

An important aspect of situational leadership is that you can be in all four quadrants at once. To be led properly, your supervisor must be able to exhibit the correct leadership style given what you need. For instance, if you are at stage R4 and get a new assignment, your supervisor cannot assume that you're automatically at R4 for the new task. That simply may not be true. In fact, you may need to be clearly directed, and that implies a telling style of leadership. If your supervisor does not tell you, there may be problems. On the other hand, if you've been at R4 for some time and get some additional assignments that require a telling style, problems will arise if you're treated like an R1 employee on all aspects of your job. All of a sudden, you're being told how to do what you've been doing for many months or years now. Your supervisor's behavior can imply that you weren't doing your job properly, which isn't true. The point is that you need to experience a style of leadership consistent with your abilities for a given set of tasks.

Leadership and the Global Village

Situational leadership theories are helping us better understand how to be more effective leaders. The basis of these theories is that a leader must adjust his or her style to reflect the situation—the organization, the job, and the follower. As such, no one style is preferred in all situations. Implied in this discussion of a situational nature is

✓ Checking Your Understanding *11-2*

4. The ability to coordinate a variety of interests and activities is best reflective of which leadership skill?
   a. technical
   b. conceptual
   c. networking
   d. human relations

5. A leader who gets input from his or her staff but makes the decision himself or herself would be classified as:
   a. an autocratic leader
   b. a democratic participative leader

   c. a free-rein leader
   d. a consultative participative leader

6. According to situational leadership, when a follower is both unable and unwilling to perform the duties of his or her job, which leadership style would work best?
   a. delegating
   b. selling
   c. telling
   d. participating

the reality that in the global village, leadership styles must also be adapted to reflect the culture of the country and its citizens.

For example, in countries like Japan, Greece, or Mexico, where collectivism (looking out for the good of all members of the group) is high, an autocratic style of leadership generally will not be effective. Rather, because of the democratic nature of people in organizations and their desire to have a say in those things that affect them, a participative leadership style will work better. Power distance (the unequal distribution of power) is another cultural variable that can provide some clues to an appropriate leadership style. In countries like Venezuela, India, and Singapore, where power distance is high (power is unequal and in the hands of a select few), an autocratic leadership style may generate more results. On the other hand, when power distance is low, such as in England and Sweden, a more participative, people-centered style of leadership is more effective.

Given this discussion, and your understanding of U.S. culture, what style of leadership do you believe would be more effective in the United States? Why?

Leadership Issues Today

We finish this chapter by looking at two current issues surrounding leadership: differences in leadership styles based on gender, and differences between transactional leaders and transformational leaders.

Do Men and Women Lead Differently?

Are there differences in leadership styles based on gender? Are men more effective leaders, or does that honor belong to women? Even asking these questions is certain to evoke emotions on both sides of the debate. But before we attempt to respond

---

UNLOCKING YOUR POTENTIAL *11-2*

Gender Differences in Leadership

Here is a list of leadership styles. Place a check mark in the appropriate box based on whether you believe the leadership style is more often associated with men or women.

Whose Preferred Style Is This?	Men's	Women's
I lead by:		
1. Using a participative style	☐	☐
2. Directing others in what to do	☐	☐
3. Using formal authority	☐	☐
4. Sharing power and information	☐	☐
5. Rewarding good performance and punishing poor performance	☐	☐
6. Relying on charisma	☐	☐
7. Focusing on continuing relationships	☐	☐
8. Focusing on winning versus losing	☐	☐
9. Enhancing a follower's self-worth	☐	☐
10. Clarifying roles and task requirements	☐	☐

---

to these questions, let's lay out one important fact. Although we want to know whether women and men lead differently, the realization is that the two sexes are more alike in how they lead.[20] Much of this similarity is based on the fact that leaders, in spite of gender, perform similar activities in influencing others. That's their job, and both sexes do it equally well. But let's not paint this as a perfect picture where everything is the same. There are some differences.

The most common difference lies in leadership styles. Women tend to lead using a democratic style. This implies that they encourage participation of their followers and are willing to share their positional power with others. In addition, women tend to influence others best through their charisma, expertise, contacts, and interpersonal skills.[21] Men, on the other hand, tend to use a task-centered leadership style. Their di-

---

[20]Gary N. Powell, *Women and Men in Management*, 2nd ed. (Thousand Oaks, Calif.: Sage, 1993).
[21]Stephen P. Robbins, *Organizational Behavior: Concepts, Controversies, and Applications*, 7th ed. (Upper Saddle River, N.J.: Prentice-Hall, 1996), p. 441.

KEYS TO UNLOCKING YOUR POTENTIAL *11-2*

Now that you've had a chance to read the material on the potential differences between men and women in their leadership styles, let's look at the responses to Unlocking Your Potential 11-2. Before you do, however, remember that both men and women are more than capable of using all leadership styles. That is, men can exhibit behaviors and use styles that have traditionally been viewed as a more feminine style. The reverse is also true given a specific situation. Nonetheless, the evidence has shown that though there are many similarities between the two groups, some style differences do exist.

Whose Preferred Style Is This?

I lead by:

	Men's	Women's
1. Using a participative style	☐	☑
2. Directing others in what to do	☑	☐
3. Using formal authority	☑	☐
4. Sharing power and information	☐	☑
5. Rewarding good performance and punishing poor performance	☑	☐
6. Relying on charisma	☐	☑
7. Focusing on continuing relationships	☐	☑
8. Focusing on winning versus losing	☑	☐
9. Enhancing a follower's self-worth	☑	☐
10. Clarifying roles and task requirements	☑	☐

Extra Effort

Go to the library and find two or three recent articles that discuss the issue of gender differences in leadership. Summarize these articles. Then respond to the following: Do you believe that in today's organizations, both masculine and feminine approaches to leadership are equally important? Discuss. Also explain how the situation one faces may affect one's leadership style.

recting of activities and reliance on positional power to control the organization's activities tend to dominate how they influence others. But surprisingly, even this difference is blurred. All things considered, when a woman leads in a traditionally male-dominated job (such as police officer), she tends to lead in a manner that is more task-centered.[22]

Further compounding this issue are the changing roles of leaders in today's organizations. With more emphasis on teams, employee involvement, and interpersonal skills, democratic leadership styles are more in demand. Leaders need to be more sensitive to their followers' needs, be more open in their communications, and build more trusting relationships. Ironically, many of these are behaviors that women have typically grown up developing.

Transactional and Transformational Leaders

The second issue is the interest in differentiating transformational leaders from transactional leaders.[23] As you'll see, because transformational leaders are also charismatic, there is some overlap between this topic and the earlier discussion on charismatic traits.

> **transactional leaders**
leaders who motivate their followers in the direction of established goals by clarifying role and task requirements

Most of the leadership models address **transactional leaders.** These leaders guide or motivate their followers in the direction of established goals by clarifying role and task requirements. But another type of leader inspires followers to transcend their own self-interests for the good of the organization and is capable of having a profound and extraordinary effect on his or her followers. These **transformational leaders** pay attention to the concerns and developmental needs of individual followers; they change followers' awareness of issues by helping them look at old problems in new ways; and they are able to excite, arouse, and inspire followers to put out extra effort to achieve group goals.

> **transformational leaders**
leaders who pay attention to the concerns and developmental needs of individual followers; change followers' awareness of issues by helping them look at old problems in new ways; and are able to excite, arouse, and inspire followers to put out extra effort to achieve group goals

Transactional and transformational leadership should not be viewed as opposing approaches to getting things done.[24] Transformational leadership is built on top of transactional leadership. Transformational leadership produces levels of follower effort and performance that go beyond what would occur with a transactional approach alone.

Moreover, transformational leadership is more than charisma. "The purely charismatic [leader] may want followers to adopt the charismatic's world view and go no further. The transformational leader will attempt to instill in followers the ability to question not only established views but eventually those established by the leader."[25]

The evidence supporting the superiority of transformational leadership to the transactional variety is overwhelmingly impressive. In summary, it indicates that transformational leadership leads to lower turnover rates, higher productivity, and higher employee satisfaction.[26]

---

[22]Ibid.

[23]B. M. Bass, "From Transactional to Transformational Leadership: Learning to Share the Vision," *Organizational Dynamics* (Winter 1990), pp. 19–31.

[24]See, for example, J. Seitzer & B. M. Bass, "Transformational Leadership: Beyond Initiation and Consideration," *Journal of Management* (December 1990), pp. 693–703.

[25]B. J. Avolio & B. M. Bass, "Transformational Leadership, Charisma and Beyond," working paper, School of Management, State University of New York, Binghamton (1995), p. 14.

[26]B. M. Bass & B. J. Avolio, "Developing Transformational Leadership: 1992 and Beyond," *Journal of European Industrial Training* (January 1990), p. 23.

SUMMARY

This summary corresponds to the Learning Outcomes on page 253.

1. Leadership is the ability to influence others to act in a particular way. The main difference between a leader and a supervisor is that a supervisor is appointed. A supervisor has legitimate power that allows him or her to reward and punish. A supervisor's ability to influence is founded on the formal authority inherent in his or her position. In contrast, a leader may either be appointed or emerge from within a group. A leader can influence others to perform beyond the actions dictated by formal authority.

2. A formal leader might not be important when certain individual, job, and organizational factors act as substitutes. Individual factors include one's experience, skill levels and training, professional orientation, or the need for autonomy; job factors include jobs that are well-defined and routine; organizational factors include formalized goals, rigid rules and procedures, and cohesive work groups.

3. Leaders have been found to differ from nonleaders in six traits: drive, desire to influence others, honesty and moral character, self-confidence, intelligence, and relevant knowledge. However, possession of these traits is no guarantee of leadership.

4. Charisma is a magnetism that inspires followers to go the extra mile to reach goals that are perceived as difficult or unpopular. Charismatic leaders are self-confident, possess a vision of a better future, have a strong belief in that vision, engage in unconventional behaviors, and are perceived as agents of radical change.

5. The four skills necessary in becoming an effective leader are technical skills (tools, procedures, and techniques that are unique to a specialized situation), conceptual skills (the mental ability to coordinate a variety of interests and activities), networking skills (the ability to socialize and interact with those outside your unit), and human relations skills (the ability to work with, understand, and motivate others).

6. Task-centered leadership behaviors focus on the technical or task aspects of a job. People-centered leadership behaviors focus on interpersonal relations among the followers.

7. The three types of participative leadership styles are consultive (seeking input from followers), democratic (giving followers a role in making decisions), and free-rein (giving followers total autonomy to make the decisions that affect them).

8. Situational leadership involves adjusting one's leadership style to the readiness level of the follower for a given set of tasks. Given a follower's ability and willingness to do a specific job, a situational leader will use one of four leadership styles: telling, selling, participating, or delegating.

9. Although there are some differences, men and women are more alike than different in how they lead. The differences that do exist lie in leadership styles. Women tend to rely on charisma, expertise, and interpersonal skills to influence others. Men, on the other hand, tend to use positional power to direct and control organizational activities.

10. Transactional leaders guide their followers in the direction of established goals by clarifying role and task requirements. Transformational leaders, on the other hand, inspire followers to better their own self-interests for the good of the organization. As a result, transformational leaders are capable of having a profound and extraordinary effect on their followers.

REVIEWING YOUR UNDERSTANDING

1. "All supervisors should be leaders, but not all leaders should be supervisors." Do you agree or disagree with this statement? Support your position.

2. What traits do successful leaders possess? Does not having these traits mean that one cannot be a leader? Explain.

3. What is charismatic leadership? Is it always important in an organization? Discuss.

4. Identify and describe four important skills leaders should possess.

5. What's the difference between a task-centered and a people-centered leader? For which one would you prefer to work? Explain.

6. Compare and contrast consultative, democratic, and free-rein styles of participative leadership.

7. How does situational leadership work?

8. How could a professor apply situational leadership in a classroom setting?

9. Compare and contrast transactional and transformational leaders. Give an example where both would be more appropriate.

10. "Given the emphasis on caring for followers, women may be more effective leaders." Do you agree or disagree? Support your position.

ANSWERS TO CHECKING YOUR UNDERSTANDING

1. d **2.** c **3.** c **4.** b **5.** d **6.** c

LEARNING TOGETHER

A. In groups of four or five, identify the characteristics of people you like as leaders. Combine the traits into one list. Share with the other groups in the class.

B. Debate the need for participative leadership in an organization. Then contrast the differences between consultative participative leadership, democratic participative leadership, and free-rein leadership. Under which leadership style would you most likely give the best performance? Which leadership style do you believe you may have developed? Write one or two paragraphs to address these questions.

C. Make a display for your classroom based on Hersey and Blanchard's situational leadership model. Design an informative brochure that creates interest in and provides an explanation for the model. The brochure should be properly documented to identify the ideas belonging to Hersey and Blanchard. Include the brochure with your display to enable individuals to have a take-home reminder of the model. Present the model to your class.

D. Prepare an oral presentation about one of the leadership gurus. When you present your findings to your classmates, have at least three visuals to make your presentation more interesting. Also prepare a summary sheet of your findings to share with your classmates.

Leading Whistle Laundry

Angela Saenz is the manager of one of eighteen Whistle Laundry & Dry Cleaners. She has had the opportunity to attend a variety of leadership seminars and workshops over the six years she has managed her store. She also has encouraged her two supervisors, Uri and Horace, to attend some of the seminars with her. Uri is usually enthusiastic about the opportunity, but Horace thinks it is a waste of time. Uri thinks the investment in making people happy at their jobs is well worth the effort. Horace feels the cleaners have a job to do and his employees should just do it or go find employment elsewhere. Both Uri and Horace speak a second language, which they find useful in supervising many of their non-English speaking employees.

Angela thinks that possibly she needs to consider sending Horace to a different type of seminar than she and Uri usually attend. From reading the local newspaper, she noticed that there were two seminars coming up in the next couple of weeks. One is a Situational Supervisory Skills seminar being offered by a team of Blanchard proponents. The other is a Task-Centered vs. People-Oriented Leadership seminar.

In the meantime, Angela has been looking at another seminar flyer she received from the Ideal Leadership Group (ILG). The ILG flyers advertise an upcoming program on developing traits needed by every successful leader, charismatic leadership for men and women, and participative leadership in a diverse, competitive marketplace. She notes that both men and women will be presenting at the ILG seminar.

Questions

1. Describe what you believe Angela or her supervisors might learn from (a) the Blanchard seminar, (b) the Task-People seminar, and (c) the ILG seminar. Which one might be best for Horace? Why?

2. Do you think (a) Angela, (b) Uri, and (c) Horace are effective leaders? Why or why not? What factors or characteristics contribute to your assessment of the leadership ability of each supervisor?

3. List the successful leadership traits that you believe are essential for Angela and her two supervisors. Support your answers.

4. Why is Angela interested in the fact that both men and women will be presenting at the ILG seminar? Do you believe she might learn something different from a male versus a female presenter on the topic of leadership? Why or why not?

5. Might any factors inherent in the cleaning business suggest that transactional versus transformational leadership would be better for the business? Why or why not?

CHANGE, CONFLICT, AND CREATIVITY

*L*earning Outcomes

After reading this chapter, you will be able to:

1. Identify the causes of change.

2. Explain why individuals sometimes resist change.

3. Explain the purpose and the focus of organization development.

4. Define *conflict* and explain three different views of conflict.

5. Describe five popular conflict-handling styles and state under what circumstances each style is most appropriate.

6. List three ways one can stimulate conflict.

7. Explain what is meant by creativity.

8. Differentiate between inspiration and innovation.

An Introduction to Change

C**hange:** to alter, transform, or convert. If it weren't for change, your life, especially at work, would be relatively simpler. Planning ahead would be no problem because tomorrow would be no different from today. The issue of finding a steady job would be solved. Since the environment would be free from uncertainty, there would be no need for the job market to readjust or adapt. A job that you have today will still be around years from now. Similarly, making a decision would be dramatically simplified because the outcome of each of our choices could be predicted with almost certain accuracy. It would indeed simplify your life if, for example, technology didn't change and require you to learn how to operate a new piece of equipment. So too would your life be made simpler if government regulations, such as tax laws, were never modified.

However, change is a reality. It's here to stay, and it's constant. That's true in your personal life as well as in your organizational life. Handling change, then, is important for you to understand. In the first part of this chapter we'll look at the key issues related to dealing with change.

➤ **Change**
to alter, transform, or convert

What Causes Change?

In Chapter 2, we pointed out that both external and internal forces affect us in our organizations. Many of these same forces also bring about the need for change. Let's look at these factors that can create the need for change. (See Exhibit 12-1.)

The External Forces.   The external forces that create the need for change come from various sources. These include the marketplace, government regulations, technology, and economic changes.

In recent years, for example, the marketplace has affected organizations such as Mercedes and Domino's by introducing new competition. Mercedes now has upscale Japanese cars produced by Lexus and Infiniti to compete against, and Domino's must now contend with Little Caesar's, which recently moved into the home-delivery market.

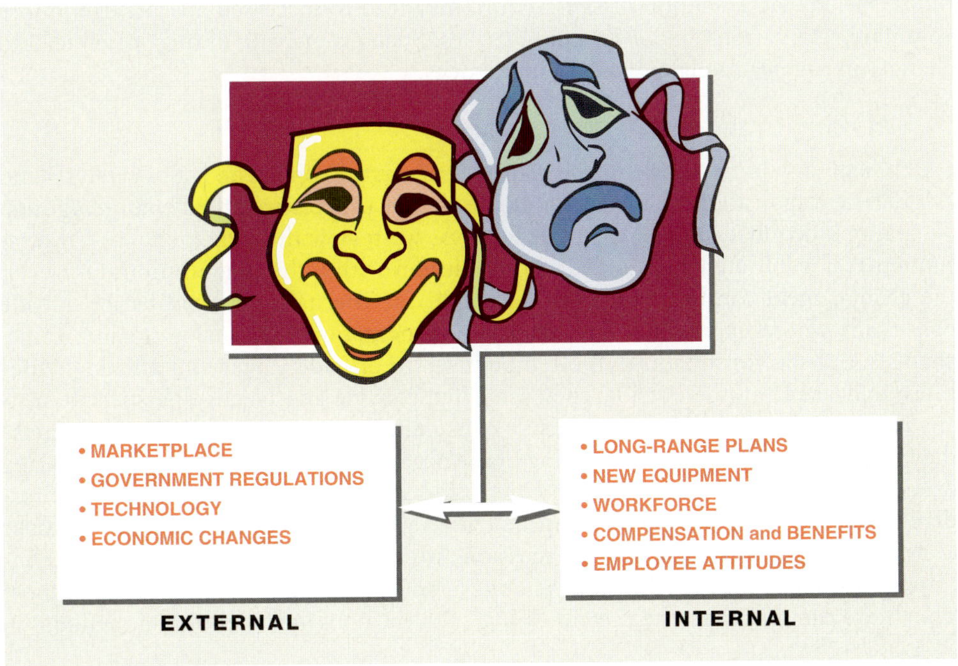

- **MARKETPLACE**
- **GOVERNMENT REGULATIONS**
- **TECHNOLOGY**
- **ECONOMIC CHANGES**

- **LONG-RANGE PLANS**
- **NEW EQUIPMENT**
- **WORKFORCE**
- **COMPENSATION and BENEFITS**
- **EMPLOYEE ATTITUDES**

EXTERNAL   **INTERNAL**

EXHIBIT 12-1
Forces of Change

Government regulations are a frequent impetus for change. The passage of a major tax revision in 1986, which included the phasing out of interest deductibility except for home mortgages, created huge opportunities to sell home equity loans for firms like Citicorp and NationsBank almost overnight. In 1990, the passage of the Americans with Disabilities Act required thousands of businesses to widen doorways, reconfigure restrooms, add ramps, and take other actions to improve accessibility.

Technology also creates the need for change. Recent developments in sophisticated and extremely expensive diagnostic equipment, such as magnetic resonance imaging (MRI) equipment, have created significant economies of scale for hospitals and medical centers. The assembly line in many industries is undergoing dramatic changes as human labor is being replaced with advanced mechanical robots. Even colleges are feeling the effect of technology since a number of schools have converted to the virtual classroom.

Economic changes, of course, affect almost all organizations. The dramatic drop in Japanese real estate prices during the early 1990s forced many of Japan's largest companies to sell off assets and cut back ambitious growth plans. Meanwhile, in the United States, record low interest rates in 1992, early 1993, and early 1996 stimulated an unprecedented demand for the services of mortgage loan brokers.

The Internal Forces. In addition to the external forces noted, internal forces can also stimulate the need for change. These internal forces tend to originate primarily from the internal operations of an organization or from the influence of external changes.

When an organization modifies its long-range plans, it often introduces a host of changes. For example, when L'Oreal (the cosmetics maker) developed a new strategy of competing more aggressively in mass merchandising markets, the organizational members had to change how the business operated.[1] The introduction of new equipment represents another internal force for change. For instance, your job may be redesigned and therefore require you to undergo training to operate the new equipment. An organization's workforce is rarely static. Its composition changes in terms of age, education, sex, nationality, and so forth. The compensation and benefits systems might also need to be reworked to reflect the needs of a diverse workforce. Employee attitudes, such as increased job dissatisfaction, may lead to increased absenteeism, more voluntary resignations, and even union strikes. Such events will, in turn, often lead to changes in organizational policies and practices.

Making Changes in Organizations

Changes within an organization need a catalyst. People who act as catalysts and assume the responsibility for influencing the change process are called **change agents.**

> **Change agents**
> people who act as catalysts and assume the responsibility for influencing the change process

Any individual can be a change agent. As we review the topic of change, we assume that it is initiated and carried out by a leader within the organization. However, the change agent can be anyone—for example, an internal staff specialist or outside consultant whose expertise is in change implementation. For major organizational changes, outside consultants will often be hired to provide advice and assistance. Because they are from the outside, they can often provide an objective perspective usually lacking in insiders. However, outside consultants may be at a disadvantage because they have an inadequate understanding of the organization's history, culture, operating procedures, and employees. Outside consultants are also prone to initiate more drastic changes than insiders—which can be either a benefit or a disadvantage—because they do not have to live with the repercussions after the change is implemented. In contrast, internal individuals who act as change agents may be more thoughtful (and possibly more cautious) because they must live with the consequences of their actions.

---

[1]Stewart Toy, "Can the Queen of Cosmetics Keep Her Crown?" *Business Week* (January 17, 1994), pp. 90–92.

UNLOCKING YOUR POTENTIAL *12-1*

Are You Open to Change?

*I*ndicate the degree to which you agree or disagree with the following twenty statements by checking the appropriate box. You'll notice that many of these statements are open-ended and could mean many things. Interpret them as you wish. Then, use the following choices in selecting your response: (A) generally agree with the statement, (N) neither agree nor disagree with the statement, or (D) generally disagree with the statement.

	A	N	D
1. In a dynamic world, I rely on trusted leaders to keep me informed.	☐	☐	☐
2. I get upset when individuals won't admit they've made mistakes.	☐	☐	☐
3. I think there are two types of people in this world: those who are truthful and those who are not.	☐	☐	☐
4. I feel people don't recognize what's best for them.	☐	☐	☐
5. I believe that of all the beliefs in the world, only one is correct.	☐	☐	☐
6. I believe the best form of government is a democracy run by intelligent people.	☐	☐	☐
7. I think everyone's goal in life is to do something important.	☐	☐	☐
8. I prefer having someone tell me how to solve my problems to solving them myself.	☐	☐	☐
9. I think the majority of information I get each day is useless.	☐	☐	☐
10. Given the events of today, I think the human race is becoming helpless and could be doomed.	☐	☐	☐
11. I feel a meaningful life is achieved only by a dedication to an important cause.	☐	☐	☐
12. I think people today do not care about anyone but their immediate family.	☐	☐	☐
13. I believe compromising with someone who has a differing view on something I view as important reflects a weakness in me.	☐	☐	☐
14. I reserve passing judgment on issues until I have gathered all the information I can.	☐	☐	☐
15. I think the future will bring a better, more peaceful world.	☐	☐	☐
16. I believe the United States is different from every other country in the world.	☐	☐	☐
17. I frequently repeat my position to others to make sure they fully understand what I am saying.	☐	☐	☐
18. My goal in life is to achieve notoriety.	☐	☐	☐
19. I feel some restriction of free speech is necessary to keep peace.	☐	☐	☐
20. I think it's better to fight for what I believe in even though the fight might get the best of me.	☐	☐	☐

Source: Adapted from V. C. Troldahl and F. A. Powell, "A Short-Form Dogmatism Scale for Use in Field Studies," *Social Forces* (December 1965), p. 213.

Two Processes of Change

We often use two very different metaphors to clarify the change process.[2] One envisions the organization as a large ship crossing a calm sea. The ship's captain and crew know exactly where they're going because they've made the trip many times before. Change surfaces as the occasional storm, a brief distraction in an otherwise calm and predictable trip.

In the other metaphor, the organization is seen as a small raft navigating a raging river with uninterrupted whitewater rapids. Aboard the raft are half a dozen people who've never worked together before, who are totally unfamiliar with the river, who are unsure of their eventual destination, and, as if things weren't bad enough, who are traveling in the pitch dark of night. In the whitewater rapids metaphor, change is a natural state and managing change is a continual process.

These two metaphors present very different approaches to understanding and responding to change. Let's take a closer look at each one.

Calm Waters Change.   Until very recently, the calm waters metaphor dominated most people's view of change. It is best illustrated in Kurt Lewin's three-step description of the change process.[3] (See Exhibit 12-2.) According to Lewin, successful change requires unfreezing a current activity, changing to something new, and then refreezing the new change to make it permanent.

Organizations can unfreeze something you've been doing in one of three ways. First, a supervisor can use driving forces to direct your behavior away from some current state. This could be achieved, for instance, if you are rewarded for learning new skills or held responsible for producing a high-quality product. A supervisor could also reduce restraining forces you face. These are things that hinder your movement from a current activity. For example, your supervisor may no longer require you to obtain permission before refunding a customer's money, or may provide more sophisticated equipment so that your quality can increase. Finally, your supervisor may use both driving forces and restraining forces together.

Once unfreezing has been accomplished, the organization can implement the change. However, the mere introduction of change does not ensure that it will take hold. The new situation, therefore, needs to be refrozen so that it can be sustained over time. Unless this last step is attended to, there is a strong chance that the change will

[2]The idea for these metaphors comes from Peter B. Vaill, *Managing as a Performing Art: New Ideas for a World of Chaotic Change* (San Francisco: Jossey-Bass, 1989).
[3]Kurt Lewin, *Field Theory in Social Science* (New York: Harper & Row, 1951).

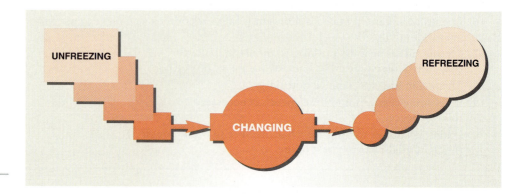

EXHIBIT 12-2
Lewin's Change Process

be short-lived, and you will revert to the previous state. The objective of refreezing, then, is to stabilize the new situation by balancing the driving and restraining forces.

Note how Lewin's three-step process treats change as a break in an organization's balanced state. The status quo has been disturbed and change is necessary to establish a new equilibrium state. This view might have been appropriate to the relatively calm environment that most organizations faced in the 1950s, 1960s, and early 1970s. But the calm waters analogy is increasingly obsolete as a way to describe the kinds of seas that you often have to navigate.

Whitewater Rapids Change.   The whitewater rapids concept of change takes into consideration that your surroundings are both uncertain and dynamic. To get a feeling for this kind of change, imagine that you are attending a college in which courses vary in length. Unfortunately, when you sign up, you don't know how long a course will last. It might go for two weeks or thirty weeks. Furthermore, your instructor can end the course any time he or she wants with no prior warning. If that isn't bad enough, the length of the class changes each time it meets—sometimes it lasts twenty minutes, whereas other times it runs for three hours. Oh yes, there's one more thing. The exams are all unannounced, so you have to be ready for a test at any time. To succeed in this college, you would have to be incredibly flexible and be able to respond quickly to every changing condition. If you're too structured or slow on your feet, you may not survive.

You must accept that the change you'll face on your job may be similar to the college example. The stability and predictability of the calm water metaphor are nonexistent. Disruptions in the status quo are not occasional, temporary, and followed by a return to calm waters. Rather, you may never get out of the rapids. You may face constant change and events bordering on chaos. As a result, you're being forced to play a game you've never played before—a game dominated by rules that are being created as the game progresses.[4]

Prepare to Go Rafting.   Not everyone will face a world of constant and chaotic change. But the set of individuals who don't is dwindling rapidly.

Employees in such industries as high-fashion apparel and computer software have long confronted a world of whitewater rapids. These individuals used to look with envy at their counterparts in industries such as auto manufacturing, oil exploration, banking, publishing, telecommunications, and air transportation, who historically faced a stable and predictable environment. That might have been true in the 1960s, but it's not true in the 2000s.

Few individuals can treat change as the occasional disturbance in an otherwise peaceful world. That may place you at great risk. Too much is changing too fast for you to be nonchalant toward change. As business writer Tom Peters has aptly noted, the old saying "If it ain't broke, don't fix it" no longer applies. In its place, he suggests "If it ain't broke, you just haven't looked hard enough. Fix it anyway."[5] Of course, what Peters is saying is consistent with current reengineering trends. Recall from the discussion of reengineering in Chapter 2 that you need to rethink all the activities and processes in an organization. The quantum change that is required to be successful in today's global marketplace cannot be overstated.

---

[4]For a good overview of this chaotic organization, see Tom Peters, *Thriving on Chaos* (New York: Knopf, 1987).

[5]Ibid., p. 3.

However, change can be a threat to you. It can also be a threat to those around you. Inertia can build up that propels a resistance to any change, even if that change might be beneficial. Let's look at why this may happen.

Why You May Fear Change

It has been said that most people hate any change that doesn't jingle in their pockets. This awareness of resistance to change is well-documented.[6] But why do you resist change? You're likely to resist change for three reasons: uncertainty, concern over personal loss, and the belief that the change is not in your organization's best interest.[7] (See Exhibit 12-3.)

Changes substitute ambiguity and uncertainty for the known. Regardless of how much you may dislike some of the work associated with attending college, at least you know the ropes. You understand what is expected of you. When you leave college and venture out into the working world in pursuit of your career, regardless of how eager you are to get out of college, you will have to trade the known for the unknown. Even something as simple as a road detour can bring about ambiguity. Your routine is now changed. And if you must take roads that you've not traveled before, uncertainty about reaching your destination in a timely fashion increases.

The second cause of resistance is the fear of losing something you already possess. Change threatens the investment you have already made in the current state of activities. The more you have invested in the current system, the more you may resist change. Why? You may fear the loss of status, money, authority, friendships, personal convenience, or other benefits that you value.

A final cause of resistance is your belief that the change is incompatible with the goals and best interests of the organization. If you feel that a new job procedure proposed by a change agent will reduce your productivity or product quality, you'll more than

---

[6]See, for example, Barry M. Staw, "Counterforces to Change," in Paul S. Goodman and Associates, eds., *Change in Organizations* (San Francisco: Jossey-Bass, 1982), pp. 87–121.

[7]John P. Kotter & Leonard A. Schlesinger, "Choosing Strategies for Change," *Harvard Business Review* (March–April 1979), pp. 107–109.

EXHIBIT 12-3
Why People Fear Change

KEYS TO UNLOCKING YOUR POTENTIAL *12-1*

Change, as you have been reading in this section of the chapter, is something you'll continuously face. How you deal with change, however, often reflects how receptive you are to new ideas. Your perception of change and the events surrounding it will affect your attitude and how you deal with a changing world. Unlocking Your Potential 12-1 was designed to reveal how open you are to change you may face.

To determine your openness to change, you need to determine your openness score. Count the number of times you checked A. Place that count in Box A. Do the same for the N and D responses you checked. Place those counts into Boxes N and D, respectively.

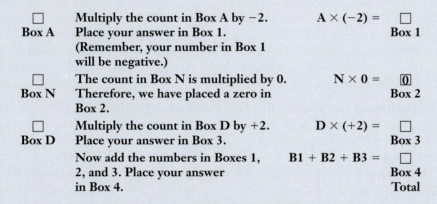

☐
Box A — Multiply the count in Box A by −2. Place your answer in Box 1. (Remember, your number in Box 1 will be negative.) $A \times (-2) = $ ☐ Box 1

☐
Box N — The count in Box N is multiplied by 0. Therefore, we have placed a zero in Box 2. $N \times 0 = $ [0] Box 2

☐
Box D — Multiply the count in Box D by +2. Place your answer in Box 3. $D \times (+2) = $ ☐ Box 3

Now add the numbers in Boxes 1, 2, and 3. Place your answer in Box 4. $B1 + B2 + B3 = $ ☐ Box 4 Total

Your total in Box 4 can be positive, zero, or negative. Scores of +20 to +40 indicate you are very open to the change that occurs around you. You see the value in change and have a positive attitude toward it. Scores of −18 to +18 indicate you are uncertain about change. You see some things changing as beneficial, but others you do not. You want to see the logic of the change before you decide whether it's appropriate. Finally, a score of −20 to −40 indicates that you are not open to change and may resist it. You prefer things to remain as they are. You prefer any change you experience to be subtle, gradual, and relatively unnoticeable.

Extra Effort

Do you feel your result for Unlocking Your Potential 12-1 is accurate? Why or why not? What advantages do you see for being very receptive to change? For being open, but cautious? For resisting change?

---

likely resist the change. In this case, however, if you can express your resistance positively and substantiate its effect, your resistance can be beneficial to the organization.

Given the likelihood that individuals will resist change, what can one expect a leader to do to help make the change more positive? People who make a living in bringing about change and those who write about it recommend the following.[8] A leader should create an environment where one can freely talk about the fears of what the

---

[8]Ibid.

change will create. In doing so, he or she can get a better understanding of what's really bothering the individual and begin to find a way to lessen the fear. Individuals need to know why the change is necessary. Even if it's initially hard to embrace, the more information one gets regarding the rationale behind the change, the more accepting he or she may be of the change. But probably the most important way is for a leader to involve others in the decisions that are being made regarding the change. More often than not, people will fight having change thrust down their throats. But having the opportunity to participate in the process not only can help reduce the fears, but also increase the chances that individuals will support the change after it's implemented.

Planned Change: Organization Development

Not all change you'll experience in an organization happens by chance. Sometimes the organization makes a concerted effort to alter some aspect of the organization. This could include how work is done (systems and process focus), the equipment used (technical focus), or dealing with a work group (people focus). Because whatever happens in the organization—such as new directions of technical advancements—ultimately affects organizational members, the people focus gets the most attention. Efforts to assist organizational members with the planned change are referred to as organization development.

> ➤ **Organization development (OD)**
> an organizational activity designed to facilitate long-term organization-wide changes

Organization Development.   **Organization development (OD)** is an organizational activity designed to facilitate long-term organization-wide changes. Its focus is to constructively change the attitudes and values of organizational members so that they can more readily adapt to and be more effective in achieving the new directions of the organization. When OD efforts are planned, organization leaders are, in essence, attempting to change the organization's culture. However, one of the fundamental issues behind organization development is its reliance on your participation in an effort to foster an environment where open communications and trust exist.[9] Those involved in OD efforts acknowledge that change can create stress for you. As such, OD attempts to involve you in the things that will affect your job and seek your input about how the change is affecting you.

OD Techniques.   Included among the more popular OD efforts in organizations are three techniques that rely heavily on group interactions and cooperation: survey feedback, team building, and intergroup development.

Survey feedback efforts are designed to assess your attitude about the change you're encountering. Similar to organizational surveys, survey feedback efforts are designed to identify your perceptions of the change taking place. You are generally asked to respond to a specific set of questions (or you may be interviewed in person) regarding how you view such organizational activities as decision making; leadership; communication effectiveness; and satisfaction with your job, supervisor, and co-workers. The data the change agent obtains are used to clarify problems that you may be facing. As a result of this identification, the change agent can take some action to remedy the problems.

Organizations are made up of individuals working together to achieve some goals. Since you are frequently required to interact with peers, a primary effort of OD is to help your group become a team. Team building is generally an activity that helps your group set goals, develop positive interpersonal relationships, and clarify the roles and responsibilities of each team member. However, not all of these activities may be

---

[9]Robert T. Golembiewski, *Organization Development: Ideas and Issues* (New Brunswick, N.J.: Transaction Books, Rutgers University, 1989).

✓ Checking Your Understanding 12-1

1. Which one of the following is regarded as an internal force for change?
   a. technology
   b. long-range plans
   c. government regulations
   d. all of the above

2. Which one of the following statements is most correct regarding external change agents?
   a. External change agents usually have an advantage in that they understand the organization's culture and operating procedures.
   b. External change agents are less likely to initiate drastic change than their internal counterparts.
   c. External change agents focus more on the calm waters view of change.
   d. External change agents, more so than their internal counterparts, usually have an objective perspective of the changes needed in an organization.

3. The view of change that takes into account both the uncertainty and the dynamic nature of the environment is called the:
   a. whitewater rapids view of change
   b. dynamic view of change in an uncertain environment
   c. calm waters view of change
   d. none of the above

4. Which one of the following is not a reason you may resist change?
   a. the belief that change is not in your organization's best interest
   b. minimal changes caused by external and internal forces
   c. uncertainty
   d. the concern over personal loss

5. Planned change in an organization refers best to an action called an:
   a. organization change effort
   b. organization restructuring effort
   c. organization chaos effort
   d. organization development effort

emphasized. There may be no need to address each area because your group may agree about and understand what is expected of you. Regardless, team building's primary focus is to increase your group's trust and openness toward one another.

Whereas team building focuses its efforts on helping your work group become more cohesive, intergroup development attempts to achieve the same results among different work groups. That is, intergroup development attempts to change attitudes, stereotypes, and perceptions that your group may have for another. Doing so can achieve better coordination among the various groups.

Although a number of techniques can help different groups become more cohesive, the most dominant technique is to help the parties resolve their conflicts.[10] That is, the change agent attempts to get your group and others to see the similarities and differences that exist between you and to focus on how the differences can be overcome.

Conflict

*W*henever two people come together, there are bound to be disagreements at times. That's natural. However, sometimes these differences can grow to enormous proportions where they become detrimental to the involved parties and the organization. When that occurs, conflict is present. The ability to effectively deal with conflict is undoubtedly one of the most important skills you should possess.

---

[10]R. Wayne Pace, Phillip C. Smith, & Gordon E. Mills, *Human Resource Development* (Upper Saddle River, N.J.: Prentice-Hall, 1991), p. 131.

Three Views of Conflict

► **Conflict**
the perceived differences between individuals that result in some form of interference or opposition

The term **conflict** reflects the perceived differences between individuals that result in some form of interference or opposition. Whether the differences are real or not is irrelevant. If you perceive that differences exist, then conflict exists. Over the years, three differing views have evolved toward explaining conflict in organizations:[11] the traditional, human relations, and stimulating views of conflict.

► **Traditional view of conflict**
a view that all conflict is bad and has a negative effect on organizations and their members

In the **traditional view of conflict,** all conflict is bad and has a negative effect on organizations and their members. In this view, conflict is seen as being destructive. Therefore, it is to be avoided at all costs. The **human relations view of conflict,** on the other hand, argues that conflict is a natural and inevitable outcome in any organization. Accordingly, conflict need not be harmful, but rather has the potential to be a positive force in contributing to an organization's performance. Therefore, conflict should be accepted and capitalized on whenever possible. The third and most recent perspective, the **stimulating view of conflict,** proposes not only that conflict can be a positive force in an organization, but also that some conflict is absolutely necessary for organizational members to perform effectively. This view encourages conflict on the grounds that peaceful, harmonious organizations become rigid and stagnant. When that happens, organizational members fail to recognize any need for change. The stimulating view of conflict does not propose that all conflict is good; rather, it implies that some conflict supports the goals of the organization and its members. Therefore, the stimulating view of conflict separates conflict into constructive and destructive forms.

► **Human relations view of conflict**
a view that conflict is a natural and inevitable outcome in any organization

► **Stimulating view of conflict**
a view that encourages conflict on the grounds that peaceful, harmonious organizations become rigid and stagnant

Of course, it is one thing to argue that conflict can be constructive, but how do you tell whether conflict is valuable? Unfortunately, the answer is neither clear nor precise. You cannot classify a type of conflict as constructive or destructive under all conditions. The type and level of conflict that helps you promote a healthy and positive environment for some individuals may, for others, be highly dysfunctional. The constructive nature of conflict, therefore, is a matter of judgment. Exhibit 12-4 illustrates the challenge you face. You want to create an environment within your group in which conflict is healthy but not allowed to be disruptive. Neither too little nor too much conflict is desirable. You should stimulate conflict to gain the full benefits of its valuable properties, yet reduce its level when it becomes a disruptive force. Because no one has found a precise way of assessing whether a given conflict level is valuable, you must use your judgment to decide whether conflict levels are optimal, too high, or too low.

If you find that the conflict is creating problems, what can you do? In the following sections, let's review some conflict-resolution skills. Essentially, you need to understand the situation that has created the conflict and to be aware of conflict-handling strategies.

Conflict-Handling Skills

Handling conflict requires you to understand the situation you are facing. Although no two situations are the same, you can use some suggestions to decide how to deal with the issue.

Pick Your Battles.   Not every conflict justifies your attention. Some might be uncontrollable, or not worth your time and effort to resolve. Although doing nothing

---

[11]For an extended discussion of three views of conflict, see Stephen P. Robbins, *Managing Organizational Conflict: A Nontraditional Approach* (Upper Saddle River, N.J.: Prentice-Hall, 1974), pp. 11–14.

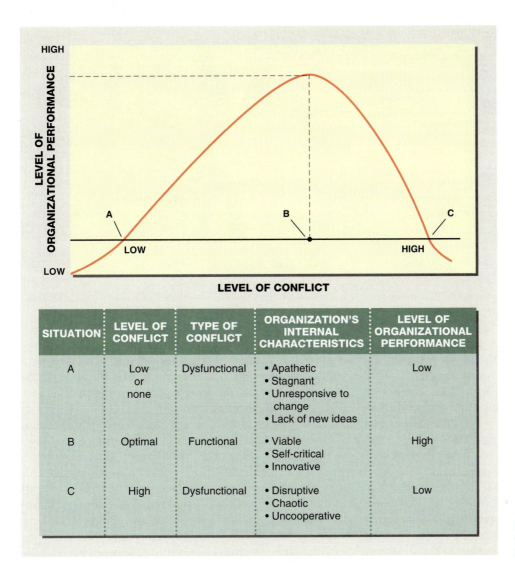

SITUATION	LEVEL OF CONFLICT	TYPE OF CONFLICT	ORGANIZATION'S INTERNAL CHARACTERISTICS	LEVEL OF ORGANIZATIONAL PERFORMANCE
A	Low or none	Dysfunctional	• Apathetic • Stagnant • Unresponsive to change • Lack of new ideas	Low
B	Optimal	Functional	• Viable • Self-critical • Innovative	High
C	High	Dysfunctional	• Disruptive • Chaotic • Uncooperative	Low

EXHIBIT 12-4
Conflict and Group Performance

might appear to be a cop-out, it can sometimes be the most appropriate response. For example, when antagonisms are deeply rooted, when one or both parties wish to prolong a conflict, or when emotions run so high that constructive interaction is impossible, your efforts to manage the conflict are unlikely to meet with much success.

You can improve your overall effectiveness and your conflict-management skills in particular by avoiding trivial conflicts. Choose your battles judiciously, saving your efforts for the ones that count.

Know Who Is Involved.   If you choose to confront a conflict situation, it's important that you take the time to get to know the key players. Who is involved in the conflict? What interests does each party represent? What are each player's values, personality, feelings, and resources? Your chances of success in handling a conflict will be greatly enhanced if you can view the conflict situation through the eyes of the conflicting parties.

Frustration, anxiety, conflict. Auto accidents are a primary cause of all of these. And if the accident weren't confrontation enough, the ensuing hassles with insurance companies can be disastrous. Progressive Corporation, a Cleveland-based auto insurance company, wants to change that perception. Through timely handling of auto insurance claims and an emphasis on quality service, Progressive has helped reduce the conflict many of its clients face.

Determine the Conflict Source.   Conflicts don't pop up out of thin air. They usually happen as a result of someone's cause. Because your approach to resolving a conflict is likely to be determined largely by its causes, you need to determine the source of the conflict. Although conflict causes vary, you'll probably find that they result from communication differences or personal differences.[12]

Communication differences are disagreements arising from semantic difficulties, misunderstandings, or noise in the communication channels. These differences, however, are often perceived to be the result of a lack of communication. That, however, is generally not the case. Don't make the mistake of equating good communication with having others agree with your views. What you might interpret as an interpersonal conflict based on poor communication may more likely be caused by different role requirements, goals, personalities, value systems, or similar factors—not solely communications.

The second conflict source is personal differences. Conflicts can evolve out of individual idiosyncrasies and personal value systems. The chemistry between you and another person may make it hard for you to work together. Personal factors such as background, education, experience, and training mold you into a unique personality with a particular set of values. These personal differences can create conflict.

Respond to the Conflict.   Although you have the ability to vary your conflict response according to the situation, you generally have a preferred style for handling conflicts.[13] This preferred style generally depends on how cooperative and assertive you are. Cooperativeness, in this context, is the degree to which you attempt to ease the conflict by satisfying the other person's concerns. On the other hand, assertiveness is the degree to which you attempt to rectify the conflict to satisfy your concerns. Based on your preference, five conflict-handling techniques are available to you:[14] avoiding (unassertive and uncooperative), accommodating (unassertive and cooperative), forc-

---

[12]Ibid., pp. 31–55.

[13]Ralph H. Kilmann & Kenneth W. Thomas, "Developing a Forced-Choice Measure of Conflict Handling Behavior: The MODE Instrument," *Educational and Psychological Measurement* (Summer 1977), pp. 309–325.

[14]Kenneth W. Thomas, "Conflict and Conflict Management," in Marvin Dunnette, ed., *Handbook of Industrial and Organizational Psychology* (Chicago: Rand McNally, 1976), pp. 889–935.

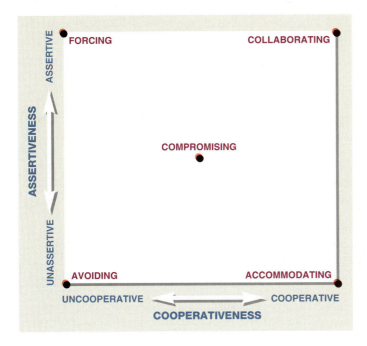

EXHIBIT 12-5
Conflict-Handling Styles
Source: Kenneth Thomas, "Conflict and Negotiation Processes in Organizations," in M. D. Dunnette and L. M. Hough, eds., *Handbook of Industrial and Organizational Psychology*, 2nd ed., vol. 3 (Palo Alto, Calif.: Consulting Psychologists Press, 1992), p. 668. Used with permission.

ing (assertive and uncooperative), compromising (somewhat assertive and cooperative), and collaborating (assertive and cooperative). (See Exhibit 12-5.) Each style has particular strengths and weaknesses, and no one option is ideal for every situation. You should consider each a tool in your conflict-handling tool chest. Though you might be better at using some tools than others, you should know what each style can do and when each is likely to be most effective. The question raised, then, is under what circumstances should you use a particular style?

As we noted, not every conflict requires an assertive action. Sometimes your best course of action is simply **avoiding**—that is, withdrawing from or suppressing a conflict. Avoidance is most desirable when the conflict is trivial, when emotions are running high and time is needed to cool them down, or when a more assertive action may create bigger problems for you.

Accommodating is maintaining harmonious relationships by placing another's needs and concerns above one's own. You might, for example, yield to another person's position on an issue. This option is most viable when the issue under dispute isn't that important to you or when you want to build up credits and possibly your power base for later issues.

Forcing is satisfying one's own needs at the expense of another party. In organizations, this is most often illustrated by someone using his or her formal authority to resolve a dispute. Forcing works well when you need a quick resolution on important issues where unpopular actions must be taken and when commitment by others to your solution is not critical.

Compromising means two or more individuals giving up something of value to achieve a common goal or to arrive at a decision. Compromise can be an optimum strategy when the two of you are about equal in power, when it is desirable to achieve a temporary solution to a complex issue, or when time pressures demand an expedient solution.

The ultimate win-win solution is **collaborating,** all parties in conflict seeking to satisfy their collective interests. It is typically characterized by open and honest discussion, active listening to understand differences, and careful deliberation over a full

➤ **Avoiding**
withdrawing from or suppressing a conflict

➤ **Accommodating**
maintaining harmonious relationships by placing another's needs and concerns above one's own

➤ **Forcing**
satisfying one's own needs at the expense of another party

➤ **Compromising**
two or more individuals giving up something of value to achieve a common goal or to arrive at a decision

➤ **Collaborating**
all parties in conflict seeking to satisfy their collective interests

range of alternatives to find a solution that is advantageous to everyone. Collaborating is the best conflict option when time pressures are minimal, when all involved seriously want a win-win solution, or when the issue faced is too important to be compromised.

VALUE JUDGMENT: Creating Conflict

So far it's been a rewarding and successful semester for you. You have been working hard, and it shows in the grades you've been earning. You're hoping that this will be your best semester yet. And for the most part, you're in control of that outcome.

However, one thing has been bugging you. In this one class, one-third of your grade comes from a major group project. You remember that at the beginning of the course, your instructor gave students the option to select their group themselves. As a result, you chose to work with your friend and three other class members. Although the group project appeared challenging and time-consuming, you had confidence that, collectively, the group could excel—as long as everyone pulled his or her own weight. When your instructor explained the project, one aspect of the assignment intrigued you: At any time during the course, a majority of project members could petition the professor to have someone removed from the group. The primary condition behind the removal request had to be project-effort related. For instance, dismissal could result if someone continually missed group meetings, did not turn in his or her assignments, or did not perform at a level consistent with the group's goals. Removal also meant that the departing team member had to complete a similar, but independent, assignment. Furthermore, the individual's assignment would be graded consistent with the requirements and standards used for group projects. But, once graded, a one-letter-grade penalty would be imposed.

For the first several weeks of your project, the five of you met frequently. The group laid out its project goals, assigned tasks to team members, and developed timetables. Your friend, however, didn't participate much and often had an excuse why he needed to leave early. He turned all his materials in to you. You felt, however, as though little effort went into his work. So before other group members saw it, you would rework the material and bring it up to the quality of the rest of the work. Consequently, they have no idea of what's going on between you and your friend. But you are tiring of this situation. You are doing twice the work. You feel that something has to be done—and done now. On one hand, you want to call your friend and tell him that the group is upset with his effort and commitment to the class project. You want to say that this was to be a team effort and that he isn't holding up his end of the bargain. And, if your friend doesn't make significant improvement, you will take a letter to your professor asking that he be removed from the group.

On the other hand, you don't speak for the group. The other three members don't know about this conflict between you and your friend. Furthermore, you don't want to issue a threat. The desired outcome may not be achieved. In fact, it could create other problems. For example, if you are successful in getting group support for the removal, it's you who'll probably have to pick up your friend's assigned duties. Refining your friend's work may be a better option than having to do it all yourself.

What would you do? Confront your friend and stimulate a situation where he'll make the effort? Or say nothing and let things continue as they are?

Stimulating Conflict

What about the other side of conflict—situations that may require you to stimulate conflict? The notion of stimulating conflict is often difficult to accept because conflict has such a negative connotation, and the idea of purposely creating conflict seems to be inconsistent with good human relations. Few of us personally enjoy being in conflict situations. Yet the evidence demonstrates that in some situations, an increase in conflict is constructive.[15] These may include situations where there's a high resistance to change or where consensus and compromise are used even though another conflict-handling style would better support attaining organizational goals. So how do you stimulate conflict? Here are some suggestions for you to consider.[16]

The initial step in stimulating conflict is for you to convey a message to others that conflict has its legitimate place. And then you visibly support your message. For example, someone who challenges the status quo, suggests new ideas, offers different opinions, or demonstrates original thinking needs to be rewarded in some form.

Ambiguous messages—such as "There will be unannounced quizzes in this class"—also encourage conflict. Such messages can reduce apathy and stimulate new ideas—both positive outcomes that result from increased conflict. For your professor, this positive outcome comes from the fact that you'll come to class more prepared just in case a quiz is given any particular day. That preparedness translates into learning.

Finally, you could become a devil's advocate. Being a devil's advocate means that you purposely present arguments that run counter to those proposed by other individuals in your group. You play the role of the critic, even to the point of arguing against positions with which you may actually agree. You are helping change the "that's the way it's always done" mentality. But there's a risk to being a devil's advocate. Others in your group may view what you are doing as game playing or feel that your comments are wasting the group's time.

Whatever conflict-stimulating technique you may use, you must keep one thing in mind. Use it wisely and appropriately so that it doesn't backfire. Achieving that goal may lead you to search for creative ideas.

---

[15]Dean Tjosvold & David W. Johnson, *Productive Conflict Management Perspectives for Organizations* (New York: Irvington, 1983).
[16]Robbins, *Managing Organizational Conflict*, pp. 78–89.

Checking Your Understanding *12-2*

6. The view of conflict that holds conflict as a natural and inevitable organizational outcome is the _____ view of conflict.
   a. stimulating
   b. traditional
   c. human relations
   d. calm waters

7. The _____ style of conflict handling works well when you need a quick resolution to an important issue.

a. compromising
b. avoiding
c. collaborating
d. none of the above

8. Which of the following is not considered a conflict-stimulating technique?
   a. playing the role of devil's advocate
   b. using a forcing conflict-handling style
   c. providing ambiguous messages
   d. supporting constructive conflict

Creativity

➤ **Creativity**
the ability to combine ideas
in a unique way and to
make unusual associations
between them

Creativity is the ability to combine ideas in a unique way and to make unusual associations between them. For example, when Nolan Bushnell thought that combining television and playing games might be of interest to the American public, he turned his idea into a $100 million video invention.[17] Or when chefs combine ingredients usually not combined (such as chocolate and chili peppers) to make a mouth-watering dish, they are being creative. Each of us has the ability to be creative, yet some of us use our creativity more than others. Although the characteristics of creative people are sometimes difficult to describe, creative people do share certain attributes. These are presented in Exhibit 12-6. How many of these traits do you see in yourself?

Teaching someone to become more creative is difficult at best. Some believe that creativity is inborn, whereas others believe that, with training, anyone can be creative. How you get creativity is probably not as important as using it. Let's look at a fourfold creative process consisting of perception, incubation, inspiration, and innovation.[18]

Perception involves how you see things. Just as with an oasis in the desert, you see things that may or may not be real. Being creative means that you see things from a different perspective. That is, you may see a solution to a problem that others cannot or will not see. For example, President Kennedy saw a future in space travel. Back in 1960, when he proposed putting a man on the moon by the end of the decade, many thought it was impossible. Going from perception to reality, however, doesn't occur instantaneously. Instead, ideas go though a process of incubation. Just like the hen that sits atop her eggs waiting for them to hatch, you need to sit on your ideas. This doesn't mean, however, sitting and doing nothing. Rather, during this incubation period, you collect data that are stored, retrieved, studied, reshaped, and finally molded into something new.

Think, for a moment, to a time when you struggled for an answer on a test. Although you tried hard to jog your memory, nothing worked. You might even have seen the page in your text or your class notes where the answer was. But to no avail. Then suddenly, like a flash of light, the answer popped into your head. You found it.

---

[17]Jimmy Calano & Jeff Salzman, "Ten Ways to Fire Up Your Creativity," *Working Woman* (July 1989), p. 94.
[18]Edward Glassman, "Creative Problem Solving," *Supervisory Management* (January 1989), pp. 21–22.

EXHIBIT 12-6

Individual Creativity Traits
Source: Adapted from
*Leadership: Researching
Findings, Practice, and Skills*
(Boston: Houghton Mifflin,
1995), p. 253.

Creativity

Here is a series of sixteen dots. Your task is to connect all sixteen dots using only six lines. You must draw these lines continuously, meaning that you cannot lift your pen once you've begun. You may cross a line, but you cannot retrace a line that exists.

Special Challenge

If you succeeded in connecting all sixteen dots, here's another challenge for you. Using one continuous line, circle each dot only once. That is, when you are finished, there will be only one dot in each circle. Again, you can cross lines, but you cannot retrace one.

Inspiration in the creative process is similar. **Inspiration** is the process of prior efforts successfully coming together suddenly and the answer becoming clear. Had President Kennedy been alive on that night in July 1969, his inspiration would have been realized as astronaut Neil Armstrong took his "one small step for man, one giant leap for mankind."

Although inspiration leads to euphoria, the creative work is not complete. It requires an innovative effort. **Innovation** is the process of taking creative ideas and turning them into a useful product, service, or way of doing things. Thomas Edison is often credited with saying, "Genius is one percent inspiration and ninety-nine percent perspiration." That ninety-nine percent, or the innovation, involves testing, evaluating, and retesting what has been found. It is usually at innovation stage that you become more involved with others in what you had been working on. Accordingly, your human relations skills will be critical for implementing the new idea. Even the greatest invention may be delayed or lost if you cannot effectively deal with others in what the creative idea is supposed to do.

➤ **Inspiration**
the process of prior efforts successfully coming together suddenly and the answer becoming clear

➤ **Innovation**
the process of taking creative ideas and turning them into a useful product, service, or way of doing things

*S*o how did you do? Were you able to achieve your goal in relatively little time? For most of us, solving this puzzle takes as long as thirty minutes. Let's look at one possible solution. The arrows indicate line direction.

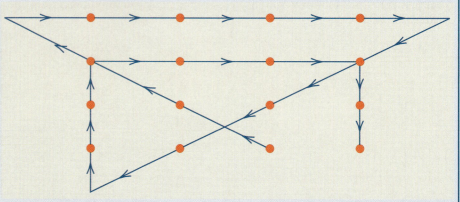

The Cultural Component

Most people have difficulty with this problem because they try to solve it without going beyond the dots. We impose constraints on our thinking and creativity— barriers that really don't exist. As a result, we lose out on reaching a greater potential.

We must therefore open our minds and look for solutions that go beyond our self-imposed boundaries. We must seek creative solutions when things appear impossible. Those who do will have a better time adapting and adjusting to the changing environment we face each day of our lives.

Solution to the Special Challenge

For those of you who accepted the special challenge, here's a solution for you to consider. Again, arrows indicate the direction of the line.

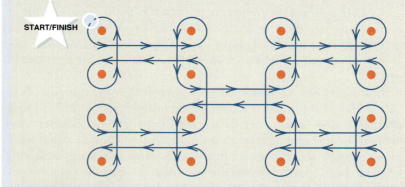

START/FINISH

Extra Effort

What does this exercise tell you about how you approach problems? How do you see creativity helping you in your college courses? In reaching your career goals? Although creativity can stretch our minds further than they've been stretched before, are there times when creativity should not be used? Describe one situation and how creativity may have blocked your success.

Becoming More Creative

1. **Think of yourself as creative.** Although this is a simple suggestion, research shows that if we think that we can't be creative, we won't be. Just as the little engine in the children's fable says, "I think I can," if we believe in ourselves, we can become more creative.

2. **Pay attention to your intuition.** Every one of us has a subconscious mind that works well. Sometimes answers come to us when we least expect them. For example, when we are about to go to sleep, our relaxed mind sometimes helps us come up with solutions to problems we face. We need to listen to this premonition. In fact, creative people often keep a notepad near the bed and write down those great ideas when they occur. That way, they are not forgotten.

3. **Move away from your comfort zone.** Every individual has a comfort zone in which certainty exists. But creativity and the known often don't mix. To be creative, we need to move away from the status quo and focus ourselves and our mind on something new.

4. **Engage in activities that put you outside your comfort zone.** Not only must we think differently, we need to do things differently. By encouraging in activities that are different to us, we challenge ourselves. Learning to play a musical instrument or learning a foreign language, for example, opens the mind and allows it to be challenged.

5. **Seek a change of scenery.** As humans, we are creatures of habit. Creative people force themselves out of their habits by changing their scenery. That may mean going into a quiet and serene area where we can be alone with our thoughts.

6. **Find several right answers.** Just as we see in bounded rationality, we seek solutions that are good enough. Being creative means continuing to look for other solutions even when we think we've solved the problem. We may just find a better, more creative solution.

7. **Play your own devil's advocate.** Challenging yourself to defend your solutions helps you develop confidence in your creative efforts. Second-guessing may also help you find more correct answers.

8. **Believe in finding a workable solution.** Along with believing in yourself, you also need to believe in your ideas. If you don't think you can find a solution, one won't be found. Having a positive mental attitude, however, may become a self-fulfilling prophecy.

9. **Brainstorm with others.** Creativity is not always an isolated activity. When we bounce ideas off others, a synergistic effect occurs.

(Continued)

SUMMARY

This summary corresponds to the learning outcomes found on page 278.

1. Both external and internal forces can foster change. External forces for change include the marketplace, government regulations, technology, and economic changes. Internal forces of change include long-range planning, new equipment, the workforce, compensation and benefits, and employee attitudes. The calm waters metaphor views change as something that occurs in a relatively stable and predictable organization that is disturbed by an occasional crisis. Under these circumstances, change involves a three-step process: unfreezing, changing, and refreezing. The whitewater rapids metaphor views change as continual, unpredictable, and caused by a dynamic environment.

2. You may resist change because of the uncertainty it creates, your concern for personal loss, or a belief that it might not be in your organization's best interest.

3. Organization development is an activity designed to facilitate long-term organization-wide changes. Its focus is to constructively change the attitudes and values of organizational members so that they can more readily adapt to and be more effective in achieving the new directions of the organization.

4. Conflict is the perceived differences between individuals that result in some form of interference or opposition. The three views of conflict are the traditional view, which holds that all conflict should be avoided; the human relations view, which holds that conflict is natural and inevitable in any organization; and the stimulating view, which holds that some conflict is necessary for an organization to perform effectively. Conflict can be positive when it supports the goals of the organization and its members.

5. The five popular conflict-handling techniques are avoiding, accommodating, forcing, compromising, and collaborating. Avoiding involves withdrawing from or suppressing the conflict and is useful when emotions are running high or when more assertive action may create a bigger problem. Accommodating attempts to maintain harmonious relationships by placing another's needs and concerns above your own and is useful when the dispute isn't that important to you. Forcing involves satisfying your needs at the expense of the other party and works well when a quick resolution on important issues is needed. Compromising requires you and the other individual to give up something of value and is appropriate when the two of you are about equal in power. Finally, collaborating involves satisfying the collective interests of those in the dispute and is best used when your time pressures are minimal and when all involved seriously want a win-win solution.

6. Conflict can be stimulated by advocating that conflict is natural, through the use of ambiguous messages or by playing the role of a devil's advocate.

7. Creativity is the ability to combine ideas in a unique way or to make unusual associations between them. Creativity is a function of four processes: the per-

ception stage, the incubation stage, the inspiration stage, and the innovation stage.

8. Inspiration is the process of prior efforts successfully coming together suddenly and the answer becoming clear. Innovation is the process of taking creative ideas and turning them into a useful product, service, or way of doing things.

REVIEWING YOUR UNDERSTANDING

1. What internal and external forces create the need for change?

2. Describe two views of change. Which of the two most directly affects you? Explain.

3. List three reasons you may resist change. Give an example of each.

4. Describe three popular organization development techniques.

5. What is conflict? Contrast the traditional, human relations, and stimulating views of conflict.

6. What skills are necessary to properly handle conflict?

7. What are five primary conflict-handling techniques?

8. Why would you ever want to stimulate conflict?

9. What characteristics do creative individuals possess?

10. Identify and explain four steps involved in the creative process.

ANSWERS TO CHECKING YOUR UNDERSTANDING

1. b **2.** d **3.** a **4.** b **5.** d **6.** c **7.** d **8.** b

LEARNING TOGETHER

A. It has been said, "For change to take place, you must first go outside your comfort zone." Do you agree or disagree with this statement? Why or why not? Identify at least ten things or instances that support or do not support this statement. Debate the issues with classmates.

B. Form a group of four to six people. Come up with a skit that illustrates a conflict. Act out the scenario involving the conflict for the rest of the class, without identifying the conflict. Then, role-play a resolution to the conflict using one of the five ways of handling conflict.

C. Form a group of no more than three people. One person should serve as the recorder for the group; the other two will be talkers. In five minutes, brainstorm as many uses for a rubber band as you can. No suggestion is to be rejected, no matter what it is. After five minutes, go over the list and talk about it relative to the text's discussion on creativity and innovation. How many of the group's ideas could become innovations?

D. Brainstorm as many ideas you can possibly think of for using a six-inch piece of string and a two-inch cube of clay. Be creative. In class, share your list and vote on the ten most creative things to do with the string and piece of clay. Discuss why most creative people spend some time daydreaming.

E. Debate the statement, "Creativity is 1 percent inspiration and 99 percent perspiration." Describe why, then, "creativity is only as good as the ability to put it into practice or take action."

Troutwein Manufacturing

When Pauline, Bill, Wesley, Adria, and Janet heard their company was restructuring, they panicked. Each of the employees had invested about twelve years working for Troutwein Manufacturing, Inc.—these five employees represented more than sixty years of service to the firm. Wesley, being the positive person he always was, suggested to the rest of his fellow workers that they knew a lot more than some of the newer workers. Their team probably would be called on to assist in the restructuring effort. Anyway, he was going to volunteer to get involved.

Over the next few weeks, Pauline became very skeptical of nearly everything and everyone. She wondered why the company was restructuring, now that the company had just landed a large contract for steel pipe casings that would keep everyone extremely busy for at least seven months. In fact, it was the biggest contract the company had negotiated in the last three years. Pauline thought it was strange, too, that their team supervisor, Ida Patchett, was having more team meetings with them. Pauline felt on edge most of the time and actually was starting to pick "little fights" with her co-workers. Ida had several discussions with Pauline and other workers about the conflicts that kept springing up. After sending a second reprimand memo to Pauline, Ida decided she would have to employ other techniques to handle the conflicts that were getting more and more frequent.

Rumor had it that the Madison plant where Ida's team worked would be shut down completely. Bill and Pauline immediately set out on a campaign to find out when. Adria, on the other hand, decided to identify ways she could deal with whatever the outcome would be. She talked about how it might be fun to move to Toledo to work in Troutwein's steel beam factory. She envisioned that another environment might be good for all of them, to get them out of their rut and become more creative as they had been in their early years.

Although Janet and Ida had become extremely good friends, they seemed to be spending less and less time together lately. Pauline speculated that Ida was going to be retained by the company and didn't want to continue fostering a friendship with Janet, who would be terminated.

When the day came for the restructuring plan to be announced, none of the team was ready for what they heard. All of them would continue working together, but the company was taking a big step in expanding its business into the international market and would actually be hiring more employees. A company survey would soon be distributed to employees to identify ways to incorporate the change. What a surprise to all of them! Pauline was still skeptical because she was sure this was just a way to keep the employees busy while the executives of the company were deciding which jobs to cut and which employees to fire.

Questions

1. What were the factors that contributed to Troutwein employees understanding change?

2. Describe how each of the employees at Troutwein viewed change.

3. What organization development efforts on the part of the company were being planned to facilitate the change? What other efforts would have been helpful to employees in understanding the changes that were going to take place?

4. Discuss the views of conflict that were (or could have been) present in this case. What conflict-handling techniques might Ida be considering to address her team's problems?

5. How could the team have benefited from viewing the situation as a creative challenge?

part five

MAKING THE CONNECTIONS

For several chapters, you have had the opportunity to explore a variety of topics related to human relations. You should have a better understanding of who you are, what has shaped your personality, how you interact with others, and potential problems you may face—both personally and at work. We also introduced topics related to organizational behavior, focusing on organizational structures and communications, and various issues that an organization might face. Finally, we looked at how individuals behave within an organization.

We have looked at you as a person and a worker; we have explored the components of an organization; we have explored the realities of the world of work. It's now time to pull all these pieces together. A common thread in many of these previous discussions was an element that affects your career and your life. This part, then, looks at the topic of matching organization to person, employer to employee. Most important, we emphasize your maintaining a happy and healthy work and personal life. Part five contains two chapters:

chapter **13**

EMPLOYMENT PRACTICES: GETTING AND KEEPING EMPLOYEES

chapter **14**

CAREER SUCCESS: GETTING AND KEEPING JOBS

chapter

13

EMPLOYMENT PRACTICES: GETTING AND KEEPING EMPLOYEES

*L*earning Objectives

After reading this chapter, you will be able to:

1. Describe the employment process and discuss the influence laws have on employment decisions.

2. Explain the difference between job descriptions and job specifications.

3. Identify and describe four recruiting options used in the employment process.

4. Describe why employee selection is like a hurdle race.

5. Discuss the importance of reliability and validity in employee selection.

6. Explain the importance of orientation for new employees.

7. Identify the purposes of performance evaluations and describe how employee performance is appraised.

8. Explain the discipline process.

9. Describe what a union is; explain the employment-at-will implications in an organization.

Several months before Jamie Wells was to graduate from college, she began her efforts to find a job. But not knowing what to expect and having little idea of how organizations make decisions about whom to hire, Jamie began contacting companies asking about employment opportunities for someone who was getting a degree in mass communications. Many people explained to her that they were not hiring now, but maybe in the near future, and if she'd like, she could send them some information about herself for their files. But one organization was different. A company representative asked Jamie to come to his office sometime in the next two weeks, and he'd be able to immediately tell her whether she had a job. Something appeared unusual to Jamie, but she was adventuresome. In fact, the intrigue of the unknown was somewhat exciting to her. So, Jamie scheduled an appointment with the company representative for the following Tuesday, and she spent the next few days preparing for the event.

Dressed exquisitely in her dark blue Alberta Ferretti pinstripe suit and carrying her new hand-sewn Tumi black leather attaché case, Jamie entered the company's employment office Tuesday morning at precisely nine-thirty A.M. But instead of being greeted by a receptionist, she encountered two doors.[1] On door one was a sign, "Those who have gone to college," and on door two was a sign "Those who have not attended college." Being in her last semester at school, Jamie entered door one. Immediately, she encountered two additional doors. On door one was "3.55 or better grade point average," and on door two was "all other GPAs." Having a 3.78 grade point average, Jamie opened and walked through the first door. Once again, she found herself facing two more doors. On door one was "Majored in radio and television," and on door two was "All other majors." Being a mass communications major with a focus on print advertising and newspaper journalism, Jamie opened door two. There she found a pamphlet thanking her for her interest in the organization and a hallway that led her out of the building.

What Jamie experienced is clearly absurd. But it does point to one important element. Every organization hires, trains, and evaluates employees differently. Although the employment processes of organizations do have some unique differences, many elements are consistent in most organizations. That's the focus of this chapter—giving you some idea of what you need to know about the employment process and how it affects you.

An Overview of the Employment Process

*E*xhibit 13-1 introduces the key components an organization takes an individual through during the employment process. It represents nine activities or steps (the yellow-shaded boxes) that an organization attempts to follow. This is done to find and hire competent, long-term, high-performing employees.

The first three steps represent getting the right kinds of employees in terms of the skills, knowledge, and abilities they possess. This advance planning results in deciding how many employees to hire, where to recruit them, and how to select the best candidates who fit the organization's needs. Together, the focus of these three steps is identifying and selecting competent employees. Once an organization has hired its employees, it begins the process of adapting them to the organization and ensuring that their job skills and knowledge are kept current so as to prepare them for tomorrow's jobs. This is done through orientation and training and development efforts. The last

---

[1]This story was directly influenced by an example in Arthur Sloan, *Personnel: Managing Human Resources* (Upper Saddle River, N.J.: Prentice-Hall, 1983), p. 127.

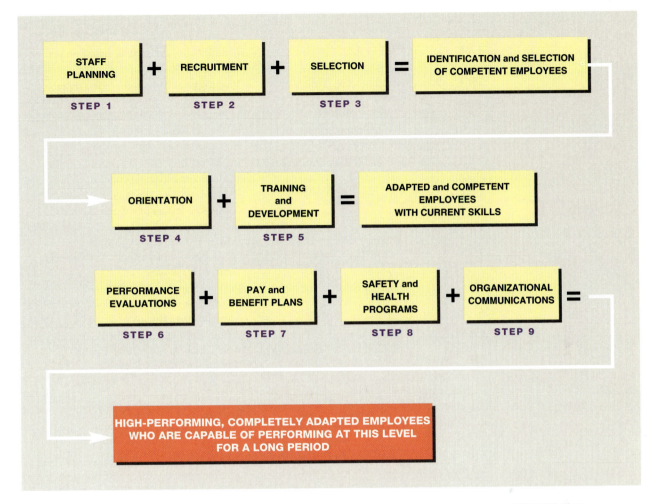

EXHIBIT 13-1

The Employment Process

steps in the employment process help supervisors identify performance problems and correct them, and help employees sustain a high level of achievement during their association with the organization. This is accomplished through effective performance evaluation systems, pay and benefit plans, safety and health programs, and organizational communications to keep employees aware of what is going on.

Notice in Exhibit 13-1 that the external environment influences the entire employment process. Although many of the factors introduced in Chapter 2 directly affect our employment (globalization, downsizing, diversity, and so on), the greatest influence comes from a number of laws that mandate that employers treat all their employees fairly. Let's look at the protection employees are provided.

Laws Promoting Equal Opportunity for All

Since the mid-1960s, the federal government has greatly expanded its influence over employment decisions by enacting several laws and regulations. (See Exhibit 13-2.) As a result of this legislation, your employer must ensure that equal employment opportunities exist. This means that decisions regarding whether you will be hired, fired or promoted must be made without regard to race, sex, religion, age, color, national origin,

Year	Law or Regulation	Description
1963	Equal Pay Act	Prohibits pay differences based on sex for equal work
1964	Civil Rights Act, Title VII (amended in 1972)	Prohibits discrimination based on race, color, religion, national origin, or sex
1967	Age Discrimination in Employment Act (amended in 1978)	Prohibits age discrimination against employees between ages 40 and 65
1973	Vocational Rehabilitation Act	Prohibits discrimination on the basis of mental or physical disabilities
1974	Privacy Act	Gives employees the legal right to examine letters of reference concerning them
1978	Pregnancy Discrimination Act, Title VII	Prohibits dismissal because of pregnancy alone and protects job security during maternity leaves
1978	Mandatory Retirement Act	Prohibits the forced retirement of most employees before age 70; later amended to eliminate the upper limit
1986	Immigration Reform and Control Act	Prohibits unlawful employment of aliens and unfair immigration-related employment practices
1988	Polygraph Protection Act	Limits an employer's ability to use lie detectors
1988	Worker Adjustment and Retraining Notification Act	Requires employers to provide 60 days' notice before a facility closing or mass layoff
1990	Americans with Disabilities Act	Prohibits employers from discriminating against, and requires reasonable accommodation of, essentially qualified individuals with physical or mental disabilities or the chronically ill
1991	Civil Rights Act	Reaffirms and tightens prohibition of discrimination; permits individuals to sue for punitive damages in cases of intentional discrimination
1993	Family and Medical Leave Act	Permits employees in organizations with 50 or more workers to take up to 12 weeks of unpaid leave each year for family or medical reasons

EXHIBIT 13-2

Significant Employment Legislation

or any disability. Decisions affecting your job that can be proved to have been made solely based on such criteria are generally regarded as illegal.[2]

The key word here, however, is *proved*. Proving that something inappropriate was used in an employment decision about you is difficult at best. And even if it can be shown, an organization may have the limited right to make such a decision. In such a

---

[2]We need to understand that although federal laws are most dominant in protecting our employment rights, state and local laws, too, give additional rights. For example, at the federal level, marital status or sexual orientation is not covered. However, Maryland does cover marital status, and California covers sexual orientation. Accordingly, employees should explore the employment rights of the state in which they reside.

UNLOCKING YOUR POTENTIAL *13-1*

Equal Opportunity Employment

Almost every organization knows that its hiring practices must meet the requirements of employment laws. As a result, rarely today will you find an organization that blatantly excludes certain groups of people. But this is not the only way discrimination can occur. Employment practices that appear harmless may, in fact, keep certain people from having an equal chance. For example, listed below are several situations that you may see in the employment process. After reading each one, check whether you feel it is a safe or a risky practice for an organization to be using. Notice, too, that we are not saying *legal* or *illegal*. That's up to a court to determine. We want to know only if it is okay to do, or if it could create problems for the organization.

	Safe	Risky
1. "Wanted: Recent college graduate to teach first grade in the local public school."	☐	☐
2. A waiter in an exclusive restaurant was fired when his supervisor found out he had tested positive for HIV.	☐	☐
3. You want to take twelve weeks off without pay to care for your new child during the busiest part of your work year, and your supervisor denies the request.	☐	☐
4. A Broadway theater hires a woman for the job of washroom attendant and assigns her to the men's washroom.	☐	☐
5. An applicant who uses a wheelchair is denied a job as a computer programmer. This seventy-five-person company states that the job is on the third floor and that there are no elevators. Furthermore, door openings to offices are not wide enough for a wheelchair to pass safely, thus creating a safety hazard for the individual.	☐	☐
6. The company policy states: "Applicants applying for jobs in the organization must have, at a minimum, a high school diploma."	☐	☐
7. A pilot for Continental Airlines celebrates his sixtieth birthday. The following day, he is no longer permitted by his supervisor to fly commercial flights as he has been doing for the past twenty-three years.	☐	☐
8. "Wanted: Sales rep to sell medical supplies to regional hospitals. The successful applicant must have five years of sales experience."	☐	☐

case, an exception is made. Exceptions, however, can occur only for job requirements that are referred to as *bona fide* occupational qualifications. For instance, age is a determining factor for pilots. For reasons associated with passenger safety, commercial pilots must be removed from the first seat in the cockpit on celebrating their sixtieth birthday. Regardless of the skills, dexterity, or experience sixty-year-old pilots may have, they're not permitted to fly a commercial airplane. Accordingly, removing them from their jobs at age sixty—though it may appear discriminatory—is legal.

As we saw in Chapter 2, our world of work is rapidly changing. With that change has come an influx of people from all parts of the globe seeking jobs in the United States. In order for all of us (regardless of race, religion, gender, or nationality) to get along and work well together, we must develop and practice sensitivity toward one another. But many U.S. organizations that seem to embrace this idea may simply be paying lip service to the issue. For example, can they truly be sensitive to individuals from different cultures when they require all their employees to speak only English at the work site? First of all, is that legal? Generally, yes. At least that's what the Supreme Court has indicated.

Employers have identified the need to have a common language spoken at the work site. They claim it's needed so that they can communicate effectively with all employees—especially when safety matters are at stake. It's also a way for them to know if their employees are making fun of the organization or harassing other workers.

Nonetheless, workers in today's organizations speak many different languages. It's estimated that about thirty-two million U.S. employees speak a language other than English. What about their need to speak their language, to communicate effectively with their peers, and to maintain their cultural heritage? To them, being required to speak only English is discriminatory.

Should employers be permitted to require their employees to speak only English in the workplace? Should employees be forbidden to speak their language even if it has nothing to do with their work or does not create a safety hazard? Or do you believe in the adage, "When in Rome, do as the Romans do"? What's your view on this hotly debated issue?

But criteria such as age cannot be used in other situations. For example, airlines today have flight attendants of both sexes and of varying ages. In the early 1960s, airlines hired almost exclusively flight attendants who were young, attractive females. But age, beauty, and gender are not bona fide qualifications for this job, and therefore these criteria had to be dropped. The key for the organization, then, is that whatever it uses to distinguish between those whom they feel can or cannot do the job must be based on job-related factors.

> **affirmative action programs**
> programs that ensure that an organization's decisions and practices enhance the employment, upgrading, and retention of members from protected groups, such as minorities and women

Many organizations have **affirmative action programs** to ensure that their decisions and practices enhance the employment, upgrading, and retention of members from protected groups, such as minorities and women. These organizations not only intend to refrain from overt discrimination, but also actively seek to hire and promote members from protected groups.

Starting the Hiring Process

Employers recognize that they cannot do everything themselves. Many times the business grows to the point where help is needed. But hiring help is not an aimless activity. Instead, supervisors recognize that certain tasks need to be accomplished, and performing these tasks properly requires certain types of people. Accordingly, employers are interested in finding employees who are capable of completing those tasks

KEYS TO UNLOCKING YOUR POTENTIAL *13-1*

*T*hings aren't always as they appear. Laws may guard against a particular practice. But those same laws may also give your employer a freedom to act. Let's review each employment situation introduced in Unlocking Your Potential 13-1 and explain why it's either safe or risky.

1. *"Wanted: Recent college graduate to teach first grade in the local public school."* This ad is risky. Although it is not stated, a recent college graduate is typically younger than forty. Thus, this could violate the Age Discrimination in Employment Act.

2. *A waiter in an exclusive restaurant was fired when his supervisor found out he had tested positive for HIV.* This practice is risky. Under the 1991 Americans with Disabilities Act, an employer cannot make an employment decision about you based on a physical or medical disability. And HIV-positive status, as well as AIDS, is protected under this act.

3. *You want to take twelve weeks off without pay to care for your new child during the busiest part of your work year, and your supervisor denies the request.* As this statement is presented, it is risky. Under the Family and Medical Leave Act of 1993, organizations employing fifty or more individuals must grant time off without pay (up to twelve weeks each year, taken at once or in phases) for family matters (such as giving birth to or adopting a child) or for medical reasons. But the employer is required to give only up to twelve weeks each year (taken at once or in phases). So denying a request for fourteen weeks off is proper.

4. *A Broadway theater hires a woman for the job of washroom attendant and assigns her to the men's washroom.* This action is safe. In fact, denying this woman the job could potentially be seen as sex discrimination under the Civil Rights Act of 1964.

5. *An applicant who uses a wheelchair is denied a job as a computer programmer. This seventy-five-person company states that the job is on the third floor and that there are no elevators. Furthermore, door openings to offices are not wide enough for a wheelchair to pass safely, thus creating a safety hazard for the individual.* This company action is risky. Under the Americans with Disabilities Act, a company must make every reasonable effort to accommodate disabled individuals. Sufficiently wide doorways, curb cutouts, elevators, and the like must be provided.

6. *The company policy states: "Applicants applying for jobs in the organization must have, at a minimum, a high school diploma."* This practice, though seemingly harmless, is risky under the Civil Rights Act of 1964. Even though everyone is being held to the same requirement, there may be jobs where the high school diploma has no direct relationship to performing the job. Thus it could exclude certain people.

7. *A pilot for Continental Airlines celebrates his sixtieth birthday. The following day, he is no longer permitted by his supervisor to fly commercial flights as he has been doing for the past twenty-three years.* As you may have seen in the text, this is a safe practice. It's mandated by the Federal Aviation Administration (FAA). Even though the Age Discrimination in Employment Act is designed to prevent us from treating people who are over age thirty-nine differently,

(Continued)

some exceptions do apply. Forcing a pilot to retire from the captain's seat on his or her sixtieth birthday is one of those.

8. *"Wanted: Sales rep to sell medical supplies to regional hospitals. The successful applicant must have five years of sales experience."* As written, this ad could be risky; when a number such as *five years* is stated, the organization may have to prove that it's a bona fide qualification. For example, is one year of experience repeated five times better than four years of progressive experience? Or should a person who has four years and ten months of experience be excluded? That's why you'll more likely find employment ad statements concerning experience to be vague.

Extra Effort

Given the many laws that are designed to protect you in the employment process, it's important for you to understand what protection you may have. Remember, too, that we've been addressing federal laws. Each state has the right to add to these laws and make the guidelines more demanding.

Contact several employers in your area to find out what employment laws affect them the most. Ask them how they've adjusted their practices to meet the laws. Because the Americans with Disabilities Act and the Family and Medical Leave Act of 1993 are relatively new laws, you may want to find out what effect either of these has had on them. Your college, too, may be able to provide some information about how it is changing its practices to comply with these more recent laws.

that will help achieve the organization's overall objectives. They begin this process by gaining an understanding of what is involved in each job. This is done through what we call a job analysis.

A **job analysis** defines the jobs that exist within the organization and the employee behaviors that are necessary to successfully perform those jobs. For instance, what does an international photographer who works for *National Geographic* magazine do? What minimal knowledge, skills, and abilities are necessary for adequate performance of the photographer's job? How do the job requirements for an international photographer compare with those for a domestic photographer or for the photo librarian? Job analysis can answer these questions. It seeks to determine the kind of person needed to fill each job and concludes with job descriptions and job specifications.

A **job description** is a written statement of what employees do, how they do it, and why it is done. It typically states the job content, to whom the employee reports, and the conditions of employment. A **job specification,** on the other hand, states the minimum acceptable qualifications that an employee must possess to perform a given job successfully. It identifies the knowledge, skills, and abilities needed to do the job effectively.

Job descriptions and specifications are important documents when an organization begins to recruit and select employees. For example, the job description can be used to describe the job to you—especially in advertising the opening. The job specification keeps the attention of those who hire you on the list of qualifications necessary for you to perform the job. Properly using these two documents helps the organization hire the best employee while making the employment process fair for all job candidates.

> ▶ **job analysis**
> a process that defines the jobs that exist within the organization and the employee behaviors that are necessary to successfully perform those jobs

> ▶ **job description**
> a written statement of what employees do, how they do it, and why it is done

> ▶ **job specification**
> a written statement of the minimum acceptable qualifications that an employee must possess to perform a given job successfully

1. Which one of the following statements best reflects what is meant by an organization being an affirmative action employer?
   a. The organization agrees to abide by employment laws.
   b. The organization actively seeks to hire women and minorities.
   c. The organization hires women and minorities but not white males.
   d. The organization hires women and minorities into the lowest level of the organization.

2. Which one of the following statements is false?
   a. Job analysis is the process of determining what each job entails.
   b. What employees do and how they are to do it are provided in a job description.
   c. Job outcomes, reporting relationships, and working conditions are all part of the job specification.
   d. Job specifications state the minimal qualifications needed to be successful in a job.

Recruiting and Selecting Employees

*O*nce supervisors decide they need to hire individuals who possess certain skills, they can begin to do something about it. Using the information gathered through job analysis to guide them, recruitment begins. **Recruitment** is the process of locating, identifying, and attracting capable applicants. Given the local labor market, the type or level of the position being sought, and the size of the organization, you should expect the organization to use a variety of ways to recruit. But keep in mind that what supervisors do in the recruiting process is designed to favor them. They generally want many individuals to apply so that they have more choices in selecting the person they think will be most successful on the job.

➤ **recruitment**
the process of locating, identifying, and attracting capable job applicants

The Recruitment Process

Although employers use many ways of recruiting, the four that will more than likely affect you are newspaper advertisements, employee referrals, school placements, and the Internet. Let's look at each of these.

Newspaper Advertisements. The most popular way organizations let us know about job openings is through newspaper advertisements. Given the wide distribution of newspapers, the organization can reach many individuals at once. In turn, many interested applicants will send in résumés, hoping that they will be one of the few to be advanced to the next stage of the hiring process. A problem you might encounter with advertisements, however, is that you may miss job opportunities. Companies tend to advertise in local papers. So, for example, if you live in Richmond, Virginia, and a job that is perfect for you is on the West Coast and advertised in the *San Diego Union-Tribune*, you may never know about the opportunity. Accordingly, you may need to look at job advertisements in such national newspapers as *The Wall Street Journal*, the *New York Times*, the *Los Angeles Times*, or the *Chicago Tribune*.

If you've not paid much attention to the employment section of your local newspaper (especially the Sunday edition), you might find it worth your while to check it out. An example of an organization's advertisement for its positions is provided in Exhibit 13-3. Notice how the organization gives information about the position and what is needed to qualify for the job. Also look at what is being requested. When the ad asks for a résumé and salary requirement, give them that information. Failure to respond

EXHIBIT 13-3
A Sample Advertisement

properly indicates that you cannot follow directions. After all, you'll have to follow directions on the job, so it gives the employer a job-related reason not to consider you for the position. Because this is one of the tricks used in the hiring process, knowing how to respond is critical for your job search success.

Employee Referrals.   In some companies, employers may ask employees if they know someone who could handle the job that is being filled. In such instances, the organization often values input from trusted employees who know the organization well and who know the kinds of skills and abilities that are needed. Besides, they know employees wouldn't recommend a person for the job who couldn't handle it. That's because an employee's reputation in the organization is at stake with a referral. Employers know that referring someone happens primarily when the employee is reasonably confident that the referral won't make him or her look bad. You've heard it before: Sometimes it's not what you know but who you know that is important. In the hiring process, this is referred to as networking. Talking to people you know—family, friends, professors, and others—about job openings they are familiar with is an excellent way of finding employment opportunities.

But realize that simply knowing someone today may not be enough. Companies are sensitive to such issues as nepotism (hiring someone related to an employee), a need for new blood in the organization, and diversity. Depending on the organization's culture, employers may pay less attention to these referrals. A male employee, for example, is more likely to recommend a male friend for a job. That won't help much if the organization is interested in increasing its female workforce. Nevertheless, employee referrals can open doors for you, and you should explore this opportunity whenever possible.

School Placements.   Educational institutions at all levels offer opportunities for you to find job openings. Most schools, colleges, and universities operate placement services where potential employers can review your credentials and interview you. Whether the educational level required for the job involves a high school diploma, specific vocational training, or a college background, school placements serve as a golden opportunity for you in finding entry-level positions in an organization.[3] Recognize also that though finding job openings in school placements is usually viewed as a means for inexperienced students to locate a job, this may not be the case. Those of you with considerable work experience who have returned to school to upgrade your skills or who are interested in pursuing other career opportunities will also find this to be a good source for identifying job openings.

Moreover, staff in school placement centers can also serve you well. Staff in these centers are generally available to help you put your résumé together, to prepare you for the interview, and to offer several other tips. You should visit your college's placement center well in advance of searching for a job. It will be time well spent.

The Internet. Newspaper advertisements and employment agencies may be on their way to extinction as primary sources for identifying job candidates. The reason: Internet recruiting.[4]

Nearly four out of five companies currently use the Internet to recruit new employees—increasingly by adding a recruitment section to their Web site. As almost every organization—small as well as large—creates its own Web site, these sites become natural extensions for finding new employees. Organizations planning to do a lot of Internet recruiting often develop dedicated sites specifically designed for recruitment. The sites contain the typical information you might find in an employment advertisement; qualifications sought, experience desired, benefits provided. But the organization is also able to showcase its products, services, corporate philosophy, and mission statement. Making this information available helps the organization improve the quality of applicants, because those whose values don't mesh with the organization's tend to self-select themselves out. The best designed Web sites include an online response form so applicants don't need to send a separate résumé by mail, e-mail, or fax. Applicants need only fill in a résumé page and hit the Submit button.

Aggressive job candidates are also using the Internet. They set up their own Web pages to sell their job candidacy. When they learn of a possible job opening, they encourage potential employers to "check me out at my Web site." There, applicants have standard résumé information, supporting documentation, and sometimes a video in which they introduce themselves to potential employers. Finally, Internet recruiting isn't the choice of only those looking to fill high-tech jobs. As computer prices fall, access costs to the Internet decrease, and the majority of working people become comfortable using the Internet, online recruiting will be used for all kinds of nontechnical jobs—from those paying thousands of dollars a week to those paying $7 an hour.

The Selection Process

No matter how successful you may have been in finding job openings, the fact remains that no one ever gets a job without first experiencing the selection process. The **selection process** is a prediction exercise; that is, it is a method designed to predict which individuals will be successful if hired. *Successful* in this case means performing well

> **selection process**
> a method designed to predict which individuals will be successful if hired

---

[3]Christopher Caggiano, "Beyond Campus Recruiting," *Inc.* (April 1998), p. 115.

[4]This section based on information from Michelle Neely Martinez, "Get Job Seekers to Come to You," *HR Magazine* (August 2000), pp. 42–52; R. Maynard, "Casting the Net for Job Seekers," *Nation's Business* (March 1997), pp. 28–29; V. Pospisil, "Recruitment Added to Web Sites," *Industry Week* (April 21, 1997), p. 12; E. I. Schwartz, "A New Reality," *Business Week* (February 9, 1998), p. ENT 7; and J. Martin, "Changing Jobs? Try the Net," *Fortune* (March 2, 1998), pp. 205–208.

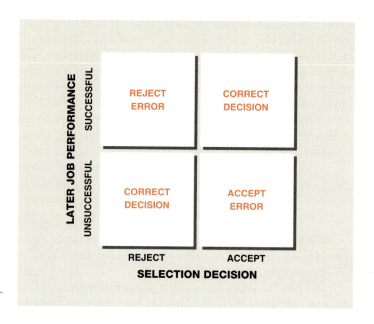

EXHIBIT 13-4
Selection Outcomes

on the criteria the organization uses to evaluate employees. In filling a sales position, for example, the selection process should be able to predict which individuals would generate a high volume of sales; for a position as a high school teacher, it should predict who would be an effective educator. Consider, however, that any selection decision about you can result in four possible outcomes. As shown in Exhibit 13-4, two of these outcomes would indicate correct decisions, but two would indicate errors.

A decision to hire someone is correct when the applicant was predicted to be successful and later was productive on the job. Likewise, rejecting an applicant is a correct decision if the employer predicted that the person would be unsuccessful on the job. In the former case, the applicant was successfully accepted; in the latter, properly rejected. Problems occur when employers make errors by rejecting applicants who would later have performed successfully on the job (reject errors) or hiring those who subsequently perform poorly (accept errors). These problems are, unfortunately, far from insignificant for the employer. A generation ago, reject errors meant only that the costs of selection would be increased because the organization would have to fill the jobs again. Today, however, selection techniques that result in reject errors may indicate that an organization's hiring process is not fair for everyone. What applicants need is the assurance that the organization's hiring actions are both reliable and valid. Let's briefly look at these two important selection terms.

> **reliability**
a criterion that addresses whether a selection device used in making a decision about an individual measures the same thing consistently

Reliability and Validity.   **Reliability** is a criterion that addresses whether a selection device used in making a decision about an individual measures the same thing consistently. For example, if a test is reliable, your score should remain fairly stable over time, assuming that the characteristics it is measuring are also stable. No selection device you encounter can be effective if it is low in reliability. That is equivalent to weighing yourself every day on an erratic scale. If the scale is unreliable—randomly fluctuating, say, ten to fifteen pounds every time you step on it—the results will not mean much. For an organization to make a correct decision about your employment prospects, its selection devices must possess an acceptable level of consistency.

> **validity**
a proven relationship between a selection device and some relevant criterion

Any selection device that an organization uses—such as application forms, tests, interviews, or physical examinations—must also demonstrate **validity**. That is, there

EXHIBIT 13-5

The Selection Hurdles

must be a proven relationship between the selection device and some relevant criterion. For example, the law prohibits the organization from using a test score as a selection device unless there is clear evidence that, once on the job, those with high scores on this test outperform those with low test scores. The burden is on the organization, especially if challenged, to show that any selection device used is related to job performance.

Selection Hurdles. Whenever you look for a job, you can expect to be put through several activities all designed to help the organization make the correct employment decision. The most common of these are completion of an application form, written and performance-simulation tests, interviews, and a background investigation. In some special cases, you may even have to pass a medical examination. Let's briefly review each of these devices and why they are used. (See Exhibit 13-5.)

Almost all organizations require you to fill out an application form. It may be a form on which you give only your name, address, and telephone number. At the other extreme, it might be a comprehensive personal history profile, detailing your activities, skills, and accomplishments. Applications are used primarily to create an equal playing field for all job candidates. It is often said that the closest we come to perfection is when we put our résumé together. We tend to put things on a résumé that may be important to us, but not to the organization. Besides, every résumé is different. An application form puts all information into a consistent format for the reviewers and gives the organization an opportunity to get just the information it needs to make a correct decision.

Typical written tests you may encounter include tests of intelligence, aptitude, ability, and interest. Using tests that relate directly to the job allows the organization to make a quick decision about one's job candidacy. For example, if you are applying for a job as a word processor, but can't type eighty words per minute with fewer than two mistakes, you won't be able to handle the job. This test quickly separates successful and unsuccessful candidates. More and more organizations are expanding testing of job candidates to include assessing just how well they'd do on the actual job. Think about that for a moment. What better way to find out whether an applicant for a technical writing position at Microsoft can write technical manuals than by having him or her do it in a simulated work environment? Such tests give applicants the opportunity to show what they really can do. That's about as job related as a test can be.

The interview, along with the application form, is an almost universal selection device. Not many job seekers have ever obtained a job without one or more interviews. In fact, getting a job at Disney involves being interviewed by about forty individuals.[5] The irony of this process is that the value of the interview in determining whether you will be successful on the job has been the subject of considerable debate.[6]

Job interviews can be useful in making a decision about you, but too often they're not. In a typical interview, you are asked a set of essentially random questions in an informal setting. Although you may be unaware of what has happened, the result is that this disorganized interview usually provides little valuable information. However, when interviews are structured and well-organized, and when all job seekers interviewed answer common questions, interviews can be effective predictors.[7] That's what organizations have been trying to teach their interviewers. And though progress is being made, it is not uniformly practiced. Unfortunately, all kinds of potential biases creep into interviews. The most notable of these are identified in Exhibit 13-6.

If you've been successful getting through the interviews, before you are hired, an organization will typically conduct a background investigation on you. Background investigations are intended to verify the information you gave on your application form. Why must they do this? Sadly, organizations report that almost one-third of all applicants exaggerate their backgrounds or experiences—misrepresenting dates of employment, job titles, past salaries, or reasons for leaving the job—when completing their applications.[8] In other words, some people lie.

Finally, depending on the job you've applied for, you may be required to pass a medical examination. That's because for the few jobs with certain physical requirements, the medical examination is directly related to success on the job.

---

[5]Ronald Henkoff, "Finding, Training, and Keeping the Best Service Workers," *Fortune* (October 3, 1994), p. 118.
[6]Michael M. Harris, "Reconsidering the Employment Interview: A Review of Recent Literature and Suggestions for the Future," *Personnel Psychology* (Winter 1989), pp. 691–726.
[7]Robert L. Dipboye, *Selection Interviews: Process Perspectives* (Cincinnati, Ohio: South-Western, 1992), p. 6.
[8]Commerce Clearing House, *Human Resources Management: Ideas and Trends* (May 17, 1992), p. 85.

Bias may influence your interview if your interviewer:
- Uses prior knowledge about you in his or her evaluation
- Has a stereotype of what a good applicant is
- Favors applicants who share his or her own attitudes
- Puts too much emphasis on negative information
- Makes a decision about you in the first five minutes of the interview
- Forgets what you said in the interview minutes after your interview ends

EXHIBIT 13-6
Potential Problems with Your Interview

Companies, however, have to be very careful when using the medical examination as a hurdle in the selection process. That's because even if you have a disability, that still may not be enough to disqualify you from the job. If it does, the company's action may be a violation of employment laws. In the majority of cases, organizations use the medical examination for insurance purposes, but only after you've been hired. Depending on their health insurance coverage, some companies won't provide health benefits for a pre-existing condition. For example, if you hurt your back on a previous job—and that employer was liable for the injury—any future expense for medical care of your injured back won't be paid by your current employer's health insurer.

Congratulations, You Made It.   If you've cleared all the hurdles, congratulations! The job is yours. But now what? Obviously, you show up for work. Yet it's much more than that. When starting a new job—especially in a new organization—you need to get acquainted with your new surroundings. You'll also have to learn specifically how your new organization wants the job performed. Very shortly after beginning work, then, you'll be exposed to orientation and training.

Orientation and Training

*W*hen an organization has performed its recruiting and selecting activities, it should have hired competent individuals who can perform successfully. But successful performance on the job requires more than an individual possessing certain skills. For instance, before you can be productive, you must adapt to the organization's culture and be trained to do the job in a manner consistent with the organization's objectives.

Orientation to the Organization

Once you have been offered the job—and accept it—you need to be introduced to the job and organization. This introduction is called orientation. **Orientation** is an organizational procedure that introduces new employees to an organization's objectives, history, philosophy, procedures, and rules. Orientation also gives relevant employment policies and benefits such as work hours, pay procedures, overtime requirements, and benefits. During your orientation period, you'll also probably be given a tour of the organization's physical facilities so that you'll know your way around. The major objectives of orientation are to reduce the anxiety you'll feel as you begin a new job and to familiarize you with the organization, the job, and the people with whom you'll work.

➤ **orientation**
an organizational procedure that introduces new employees to an organization's objectives, history, philosophy, procedures, and rules

✓ Checking Your Understanding *13-2*

3. What is the difference between reliability and validity in the employment process?
   a. Reliability means consistency. Validity means job-relatedness.
   b. Validity refers to making correct employment decisions. Reliability refers to an employee's continuous successful performance.
   c. Reliability means job relatedness. Validity means consistency.
   d. Validity and reliability refer to the same thing in the employment process.

4. Which one of the following would you typically not be exposed to in an organization's orientation program?
   a. an introduction to the organization's culture
   b. an explanation of the goals of your work unit
   c. an extensive review of your work experience
   d. an overview of employment policies

Job orientation expands on the information you received while being recruited. You should be informed about the goals of your work unit and be told how your job contributes to the unit's goals. This understanding will be important; it will lead to establishing your specific duties and responsibilities, which tells you a lot about how your performance is to be evaluated. Finally, orientation includes an introduction to your co-workers, who may help make your adjustment into the work unit as smooth and anxiety-free as possible. This is an important time for you, as well as for your employer. After all, considerable money has been spent getting you to this point. The last thing an employer wants to see is a surprise resignation only a week or two into your job.

Training and Development: For Today and Tomorrow

Every organization needs to have well-trained and experienced employees who successfully perform the jobs that need to be done. This is more true today than at any time in U.S. history. Given the changing world of work—especially the technological advancements—you must continuously learn. Not surprisingly, to assist you in this investment, organizations often provide opportunities to improve your skills. They do this by offering training.

Training is a learning experience that focuses on improving an employee's ability to perform his or her job. Training concentrates on enhancing your skills and abilities so that you can be more productive in your present job. Reality tells us that no matter how educated you are, you need to learn the organization's way. You need to understand how to apply what you bring to the job in a manner that is consistent with the organization's policies and practices. For example, selling for Frito-Lay may appear no different than selling for Utz. In both cases, you're selling snack foods. But you need to learn a new territory for your new job at Frito-Lay. Furthermore, Frito computerizes its selling process, and orders are processed directly into your hand-held computer.[9] Then at the end of the day, you send your data to the company, which routes it to the shipping department for delivery scheduling. Understanding the ins and outs of this process requires training.

Many different types of training methods are available. For the most part, however, they can be classified in two ways: on-the-job and off-the-job training methods. The more popular of these are summarized in Exhibit 13-7.

Organizations also have a vested interest in preparing you for tomorrow's jobs. As your job and career progress, new skills and abilities will be required of you. To be ready to accept greater challenge requires further development. For example, if you become the sales supervisor in your territory, the skills needed will be different from those you currently possess in your sales job. You'll be required to supervise several sales representatives and demonstrate a number of supervisory skills and competencies. Therefore, to groom you for this position of greater responsibility—requiring more advanced skills, knowledge and abilities—an organization may invest in your future by providing employee development opportunities.

How Will Your Performance Be Evaluated?

*M*ention the term *performance evaluations*, and almost immediately there's a nervous reaction. Why? Most of us don't like to be judged, and that's what performance evaluations do. You know how you've been working, the effort and the hours you've

> **training**
> a learning experience focusing on improving an employee's ability to perform his or her job

---

[9]Jeffrey Rothfeder and Jim Bartimo, "How Software Is Making Food Sales a Piece of Cake," *Business Week* (July 2, 1990), p. 54.

Sample On-the-Job Training Methods

Job rotation	Lateral transfers allowing employees to work at different jobs. Provides good exposure to a variety of tasks.
Understudy assignment	Working with a seasoned veteran, coach, or mentor. Provides support and encouragement from an experienced worker. In the trades industry, this may also be an apprenticeship.

Sample Off-the-Job Training Methods

Classroom lectures	Lectures designed to convey specific technical, interpersonal, or problem-solving skills.
Films and videos	Using the media to explicitly demonstrate technical skills that are not easily presented by other training methods.
Simulation exercises	Learning a job by actually performing the work (or a simulation). May include case analyses, experiential exercises, role-playing and group interaction.
Vestibule training	Learning tasks on the same equipment that one actually will use on the job, but in a simulated work environment.

EXHIBIT 13-7
Training Methods

put into a project. Then to have someone, such as your supervisor or a professor, analyze your work and say it didn't measure up or that it was just satisfactory, is frustrating. These things, though, don't have to happen if organizations have in place effective performance appraisal processes.

Performance appraisal is a process organizations use to make objective decisions about individuals as employees. These decisions include such things as determining pay increases and training needs. Keep in mind, however, that performance appraisals also provide the necessary documentation to support a decision to terminate someone. A properly operating performance appraisal process includes three elements. First, you need to know how you've been performing over a period of time. This item is what most associate with performance evaluations. It's feedback given by someone, such as your supervisor, about the work you did. Second, the evaluation should identify areas where you may be weak or where you need some improvement. Only by identifying your weaknesses can you begin to overcome them. Like the term paper that you get back with only a grade of C on it, little helpful information is given. But if the reason for the grade is identified—such as using dated sources or poorly written paragraphs—you can focus on what needs correcting. (Before any of this can occur, there's a prerequisite: setting performance goals, which is discussed next.) Finally, your evaluation has to be used as documentation. Although the documentation may serve the organization's purposes more, it can help you, too. For example, suppose your work has been satisfactory over the past several years, and you have appraisals to prove it. Being fired today for performance reasons isn't consistent with your past evaluations. Maybe something else has happened—perhaps you caught your supervisor doing something unethical, and now he or she wants to get rid of you. Copies of your documentation can help support your cause that the firing is unjust.

> **performance appraisal**
> a process organizations use to make objective decisions about individuals as employees

Setting Performance Goals

In the first step in the goal-setting process, the organization establishes performance standards for each job. (See Exhibit 13-8.) In the second step, employees and their supervisors establish work goals jointly for their particular jobs. What is ultimately

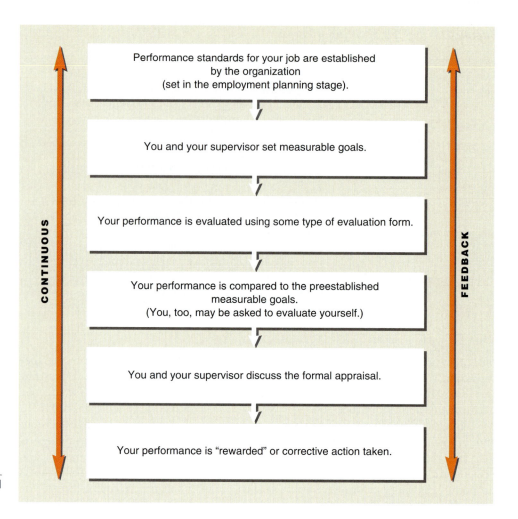

EXHIBIT 13-8

The Performance Appraisal Process

agreed upon should be guided by information that top management has set for the organization as a whole. Organizational goals and duties as specified in job descriptions, then, lead to establishing precise work activities for employees. Performance goals should be clear and objective. If they aren't, employees will have difficulty understanding them. More important, they won't know on what behaviors and standards they are being evaluated.

Generally, with established individual performance goals, you'll know what specific contributions you're making toward your unit's goals. For this to occur, however, four elements generally must exist: specific goals, participation, specified time periods, and feedback.

The specific goals you'll be held accountable to should be concise statements of expected accomplishments. It's not adequate, for example, merely to be required to cut costs, improve service, or increase quality. You can't easily measure these goals. Instead, statements such as cutting costs by 6 percent, improving service by processing all credit card applications within seventy-two hours of their receipt, or increasing quality by keeping returns to less than 1 percent of sales are examples of specific objectives. When these are present, you know precisely what you need to be doing.

Employees at Datametrics set some challenging goals, for it is through their efforts that the Woodland Hill, California, company can be successful. And its president, Sid Wing, knows precisely that. Sure, good performance is rewarded with pay increases. But Wing prefers to go one step beyond. Outstanding employee performance results in public recognition of the individual's achievement—something Datametric's employees value!

Having these expectations given to you doesn't work well either. They should not be unilaterally set by your supervisor. Instead, you should have an active role in determining what will be accomplished. In that case, you'll both jointly choose the goals and agree on how they will be achieved. Each of these goals will also have a concise period in which it is to be completed. Typically, the period is three months, six months, or a year.

Finally, for all this to work, there must be feedback on your performance. An effective evaluation process provides you with continuous feedback on how well you're progressing toward your goals. Ideally, this is accomplished by meeting periodically with your supervisor. What you have been doing is monitored. Any deviations that arise are corrected. Remember, your supervisor has something at stake here, too. His or her success is contingent on you—and everyone else in your work unit—meeting performance goals. So your supervisor should do whatever he or she can to help you succeed. There will still be the official performance appraisal meeting, but that should be just a formality. If you've set your goals properly, if you know what is expected of you, if you and your supervisor talk about your goals frequently, and if you get help in your weak areas, there should be no surprises in the end. In such a case, the evaluation process can be a positive experience.

Having Your Performance Appraised

When a supervisor evaluates you, he or she can use one or more of several methods. The organization usually will have a performance evaluation procedure that supervisors are expected to follow. Generally speaking, however, that procedure will fall into one of three categories: comparing you to preset standards, comparing you to other employees, or comparing you to established objectives. We explain the various types next and summarize them in Exhibit 13-9.

Preparing for the Performance Evaluation

1. **Focus on what is expected of you.** When an employer pays you to work, they expect, if not demand, that you reach a certain level of performance. Whether or not you have the benefit of having mutually set goals with our supervisor, you have clues about what you are supposed to be doing. Your job description or your supervisor's direction can provide this. Yet, remember, everything about your job cannot be identified. You will be expected to do the extra things needed to help your organization reach its goals.

2. **Recognize the importance of the appraisal process.** Performance appraisals are emotional, time-consuming events. If they didn't have to be done, they probably wouldn't be done. Performance appraisals are designed to do three things: give you feedback on how well you've performed in the past, identify areas where you need some development, and provide the legal documentation the organization requires for your files.

3. **Keep a record of your accomplishments.** Supervisors cannot be with employees every minute of the workday, nor would you, as an employee, want them to be. So supervisors may miss or lack information about something you've done. Each employee has a responsibility to keep that information on himself or herself. Set up a file and simply drop notes into it throughout the year about the exceptional things you've accomplished. Provide dates, times, and something about the accomplishment.

4. **Prepare for the formal appraisal by evaluating yourself.** A number of organizations today require their employees to evaluate themselves as part of the appraisal process. If it's not a requirement, ask your supervisor if you can do a self-evaluation as part of the process. This can serve a useful purpose. In your self-evaluation, be honest with yourself. Don't exaggerate your accomplishments—but don't short-change yourself either on what you've done. If you've kept good records in step 3, you'll have documentation to help you in this evaluation. Use this data to rate your performance. Further, as part of the evaluation, identify your strengths and the areas where you need more development. When finished, give your supervisor a copy of your evaluation. You're now ready for the formal meeting.

5. **Listen to your supervisor's appraisal of your performance.** Having to sit silently and listen to another person tell you about the good and bad things you've done at work is difficult. However, you must force yourself to actively listen. You're going to hear both positive and negative things. That's all part of this process. Your supervisor often sees things about your work that you don't. Your self-evaluation may prepare you for this—especially if you've focused on both your strengths

and weaknesses. Nonetheless, you're bound to be nervous, but so, too, may be your supervisor. Remember, even if the information is negative, you're not being attacked personally. It's your performance, not you, that's at issue.

6. **Address your concerns.** The heart of the evaluation is to have a frank discussion about your performance. After you listen to your supervisor, there may be some information that you need to share with your supervisor. You're not trying to make excuses; that would be a mistake. But maybe you need to clarify some things or correct a misunderstanding. Remember, your feedback skills will help you convey this information.

7. **Set a plan of action.** If there are no concerns about your work, congratulations. You're doing a splendid job. But even here, you can't sit back on your past successes. You must begin planning with your supervisor what work activities you'll do next and what you can do to continue to grow in your career. If you need improvement in some areas, don't take it as an insult. Although it is hard to hear, your supervisor may, in fact, be doing you a favor. Work with your supervisor on how you can correct this weakness, what steps you will take, when you will do it, and what help your supervisor will give. In either case, follow your plan.

8. **Summarize what has happened.** Before your evaluation is over, summarize what took place in the meeting. Let your supervisor know that you understood what was discussed. Thank your supervisor and begin implementing your action plan.

Category	Advantage	Disadvantage
Compared to preset standards		
• Written essay	Simple to use	Evaluation of writer's ability vs. actual performance
• Critical incident	Rich, behaviorally based examples	Time-consuming; lacks quantification
• Graphic rating scales	Provide quantitative data; less time-consuming	Do not provide depth of job behavior assessed
Compared to other employees	Compares employees to one another	Unwieldy with large number of employees
Compared to established objectives	Focuses on end goals; results-oriented	Time-consuming

EXHIBIT 13-9
Performance Appraisal Methods

Preset Standards.   The most widely used evaluation systems compare you to preset standards. What you do on the job is independent of what everyone else does. For example, tests in college often use a preset standard. Your grade on an exam is usually based on some standard (often 100 percent). A score of 95 is excellent, but a grade of 55 isn't.

Although the grade is important to you, how it was determined should carry much weight, too. At work, under preset standards, you'll more than likely be evaluated through written essays, critical incidents, or graphic rating scale instruments. Realize that the instruments used are not perfect. Each comes with its pluses and minuses.

The written essay requires no complex forms or extensive training to complete. However, your appraisal, good or bad, may be determined as much by your supervisor's writing skill as by your actual level of performance. The use of critical incidents focuses a supervisor's attention on your critical or key job behaviors that separate effective from ineffective job performance. He or she writes down little anecdotes describing what you did that was especially effective or ineffective. The key here is that only your specific behaviors are cited, not vaguely defined statements sometimes attributed to your personality traits. One of the oldest and most popular appraisal methods is the graphic rating scale. This method lists a set of performance factors such as quantity and quality of work, job knowledge, cooperation, loyalty, attendance, honesty, and initiative. Your supervisor goes down the list of factors and rates you (usually on a scale of 1 to 5) on how he or she feels you've met each requirement. After all factors are evaluated, an overall composite score is calculated. That is, on a scale of 1 to 5, with 5 being the highest, you might be evaluated at 3.7. What the 3.7 means is usually up to the organization; for instance, everyone between 3.55 and 4.05 might get a 3 percent raise.

Compared to Other Employees. These methods have one thing in common. You were evaluated based on how well your performance matched some preestablished or absolute criteria. Multiperson comparisons, on the other hand, compare your performance to those of one or more other employees. Thus, this method is a relative, not an absolute, measuring device. The three most popular uses of this method are group order ranking, individual ranking, and paired comparisons.

The group order ranking requires a supervisor to place you into a particular classification, such as "top fifth" or "second fifth." When this method is used to appraise, all employees in the unit are evaluated as a whole. If, for example, there are twenty employees in the department, only four can be in the top fifth. Of course, four must be relegated to the bottom fifth. The individual ranking approach requires a supervisor merely to list employees in order from highest to lowest. Only one individual can be best. However, in a department of 20, the difference between the first and second employees is assumed to be the same as that between the fourteenth and fifteenth employees. That's not always correct. Furthermore, even though some employees may be closely grouped, there can be no ties. Everyone must have a different ranking. In the paired-comparison approach, you are compared to every other employee in the unit and rated as either the more productive or the less productive employee of the pair. After all paired comparisons are made, you are assigned a summary ranking based on the number of "more productive" scores you received. Since this approach ensures that you are compared to every other employee, the entire process becomes unmanageable when large numbers of employees are being assessed.

Compared to Established Objectives. Just a few pages ago we introduced a preferred appraisal that involves both you and your supervisor. But the methods of evaluation discussed here don't reflect that process. Unfortunately, in a number of organizations, supervisors and employees don't meet to set mutual goals.

Where they do, the appraisal process is very straightforward. You are evaluated on how well you accomplished the mutually established set of objectives that were determined to be critical to the successful completion of your job. Those objectives were concrete, verifiable, and measurable. Such a process focuses on end goals. It allows you the opportunity to achieve your objectives without having to be constrained by certain barriers. That is, it focuses on the ends rather than the means. Assuming, of course, that your work effort is both legal and ethical, this appraisal process gives you the discretion to choose the best path for achieving your goals.

When Performance Falls Short

So far this discussion has focused on the performance appraisal process. Though it is designed to help you be productive and achieve work-related goals, we need to answer some important questions: What if you are not performing in a satisfactory manner? What can you expect the organization to do? The answers to these questions lie in two activities: employee counseling and discipline.

Employee Counseling.   If, for some reason, you are not working up to par, your organization needs to find out why. If it's because you are mismatched for the job (a hiring error) or because you don't have adequate training, something relatively simple can be done; you can be put into a job that better matches your skills or be trained in how to do the job more effectively. But what if the problem is not associated with your abilities, but your desire to do the job? When that happens, it becomes a discipline problem. Although there are often formal discipline procedures in an organization, a more progressive organization may be inclined to counsel you. **Employee counseling** is a process designed to help employees overcome performance-related problems. Rather than viewing the performance problem from a punitive point of view (discipline), employee counseling attempts to uncover why you've lost the desire to work productively and to find ways to correct the situation. In many cases, you don't go from being a productive employee to a poor one overnight. Rather, it happens gradually and may be a function of something that is occurring in your personal life.

> **employee counseling**
> a process designed to help employees overcome performance-related problems

Remember the discussion of stress and the reasons employers have employee assistance programs? Employee counseling is consistent with that philosophy. Just as it's costly to have employees quit shortly after they've been hired, it's also costly to fire someone. The time spent recruiting, selecting, orienting, training, and developing an employee translates into money. If an organization can use various efforts and interventions to help you overcome personal problems—and get you back on the job quickly—it just might be more beneficial for them. That's the intent of employee counseling. But make no mistake about it, employee counseling is not meant to lessen the effect of your poor performance, nor to reduce your responsibility to change work behavior. It's designed to help you. If you won't or can't accept that help, then more punitive actions will take place—the disciplinary process.

Disciplinary Procedures.   What specifically do we mean when we use the term *discipline* in the workplace? **Discipline** refers to actions taken by a supervisor to enforce the organization's standards and regulations. It generally follows a typical sequence of four steps: verbal warning, written warning, suspension, and dismissal. (See Exhibit 13-10.)

> **discipline**
> actions taken by a supervisor to enforce the organization's standards and regulations

The mildest form of discipline is the **verbal warning.** A verbal warning is a temporary record of a reprimand, which is then placed in a supervisor's file. This verbal warning typically states the purpose, date, and outcome of the feedback session with you. If the verbal warning is effective, no further disciplinary action is needed. However, if you fail to improve, you'll encounter more severe action: the written warning. The **written warning** is a written record of a reprimand, which becomes part of an official personnel file and the first formal stage of the disciplinary procedure. In all other ways, however, the written warning is similar to the verbal warning. That is, you are advised in private of the violation, its effects, and potential consequences of future

> **verbal warning**
> a temporary record of a reprimand, which is then placed in a supervisor's file

> **written warning**
> a written record of a reprimand, which becomes part of an official personnel file and the first formal stage of the disciplinary procedure

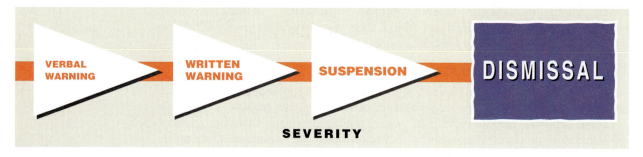

VERBAL WARNING → WRITTEN WARNING → SUSPENSION → DISMISSAL

SEVERITY

EXHIBIT 13-10
The Discipline Process

> **suspension**
> time off without pay as a disciplinary action

> **dismissal**
> removal from one's job

violations. Further, after a period, if no further disciplinary problems arise, the written warning is removed from your file.

A **suspension,** time off without pay, may be the next disciplinary step. It is usually taken only if the prior two steps have not achieved the desired results—although exceptions do exist where suspension may be given without any prior verbal or written warning if the infraction is serious. Why would your supervisor suspend you? One reason is that a short layoff, without pay, is potentially a rude awakening. It may convince you that your supervisor is serious and help you fully understand and accept responsibility for following the organization's rules.

Your supervisor's ultimate disciplinary punishment is **dismissal,** removal from one's job. Although dismissal is often used for the most serious offenses, it may be the only feasible alternative for your supervisor if your behavior seriously interferes with the organization's operation.

Many organizations may follow the process described here, but recognize that it may be bypassed if your behavior is extremely severe. For example, stealing or attacking another employee with intent to inflict serious harm may result in immediate suspension or dismissal. Regardless of any action taken, however, discipline should be fair and consistent. That is, the punishment you receive should be appropriate for what you did, and others doing the same thing should be disciplined in a like manner.

Belonging to a Union

Most of the activities that occur in the hiring, training, and appraising processes in an organization are conducted between the employer and the employee. In fact, most organizations prefer it that way—dealing with you one-on-one. For example, if you need skills training, they can set up a program for you to attend. If you have a complaint, your supervisor gets involved first. But this two-way street is not always the case. Under certain circumstances, you may be represented by a third party. That third party is, of course, a labor union.

What Is a Labor Union?

> **union**
> a group of workers, acting together, seeking to promote and protect their mutual interests through collective bargaining

A **union** is a group of workers, acting together, seeking to promote and protect their mutual interests through collective bargaining. Although it is true that only about 13 percent of the private sector workforce is unionized,[10] the successes and failures of unions affect all segments of the workforce in two important ways. First, since major industries in the United States—such as automobile, steel, and electrical manufactur-

---

[10]U.S. Department of Labor, *Statistical Abstracts of the United States,* 1999 (Washington, D.C., GPO, 1999), p. 452.

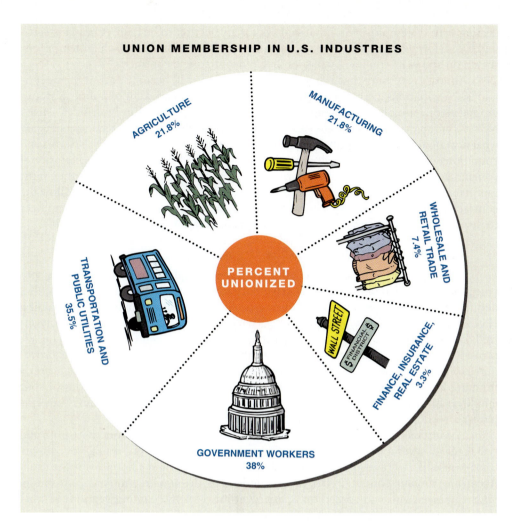

UNION MEMBERSHIP IN U.S. INDUSTRIES

AGRICULTURE
21.8%

MANUFACTURING
21.8%

WHOLESALE AND RETAIL TRADE
7.4%

PERCENT UNIONIZED

FINANCE, INSURANCE, REAL ESTATE
3.3%

TRANSPORTATION AND PUBLIC UTILITIES
35.5%

GOVERNMENT WORKERS
38%

EXHIBIT 13-11
Union Membership in U.S. Industries

ers, as well as all branches of transportation—are unionized, unions play a major role in some of the important sectors of the economy. (See Exhibit 13-11.) Second, any gains achieved by unions often spill over into other nonunionized sectors of the economy. So, the wages, hours, and working conditions of nonunion employees at a Toledo, Ohio, grocery store may be affected by an agreement reached between the United Auto Workers and the Chrysler Corporation at the latter's Toledo Jeep facility.

How Do You Become a Union Member?

You cannot awake one morning and decide that you want a union to deal with your employer for you. Even if you're upset at your employer, or if the organization has done something you believe to be terrible treatment of its employees, unions can't help you overnight. They simply cannot enter the picture that quickly. Instead, before a union can represent you, it must launch, and win, a **certification election,** in which a union must win a majority of eligible voting workers before it can be certified.

Nothing official happens until at least 30 percent of your co-workers who could be represented by the union sign authorization cards. The authorization card, however, doesn't force the employer to recognize the union as your representative. Instead, it indicates only that you wish this particular union to be considered your representative in

> **certification election**
an election in which a union must win a majority of eligible voting workers before it can be certified

dealing with the employer and that you ask for an election to be held. A union is certi-fied if a majority of eligible voting workers vote for the union. If and when that occurs, the union and your employer will soon begin negotiating a contract.

Almost everything that affects your employment will become part of the negoti-ations. Negotiations are often give-and-take events. There are a lot of political, strate-gic games that are played during negotiations. That's expected. But both sides usually have a common goal: to reach the best agreement possible. Yet neither side gets exactly what it wanted. Instead, the final outcome of negotiations is a compromise—terms and conditions of employment with which both parties can live. As long as a majority of you and your co-workers vote to approve this agreement, it will explicitly guide most aspects of your job for the next few years. Your employer will be required to follow the contract exactly as it's written. There will be little or no opportunity for your employer to deviate from the contract language, which is something that few employers like.

Does Your Union Constrain the Organization?

> **collective bargaining agreement**
an agreement that defines such things as wages, work hours, criteria for promotions and layoffs, training eligibility, and disciplinary practices

When a union represents you, your employer is required to implement very spe-cific practices spelled out in the **collective bargaining agreement,** an agreement that defines such things as wages, work hours, criteria for promotions and layoffs, training eligibility, and disciplinary practices. That's what you really asked for when you union-ized (common practices fair to all workers), and what you reinforced when you ap-proved the contract. For instance, your compensation, what benefits you get, proce-dures to follow for determining who works overtime, how you are disciplined, criteria for attending training programs, and the like are no longer unilateral options of your employer. Instead, such decisions have already been reached in negotiations. Your em-ployer's freedom to act on employee issues, therefore, is constrained.

For instance, suppose you have had an excellent year. Your productivity is up and you received several letters of commendation from customers. As a result, your super-visor would like to reward you, with say, a 10 percent raise and a bonus. But she can't. According to your contract, your raise is defined in the agreement. And your union, your employer, and you agreed on a 2 percent raise for the coming year. Now don't misinterpret what this example is saying. Sure, when a situation that would benefit you can't occur, you may think the union has hurt you. But situations like that may be rare. Even so, for the union to be successful, it must treat everyone alike. Otherwise, the purpose of the union is diminished. Yet employers may cite an event like the one in the example during organizing drives to show their employees why unionizing may not be in their best interest. Remember, this can be a brutal game.

> **management rights**
an employer's right to run his or her business as effectively and efficiently as possible

As always, there are two sides to this story. Clearly, unions prevent employers from making unilateral decisions when it comes to dealing with employees. But it stops there. Not everything that happens in the organization is subject to negotiation. Your employer still has the opportunity to run the business as efficiently as possible. Those things that don't directly affect your employment, then, are outside the scope of nego-tiations. These are called **management rights,** an employer's right to run his or her business as effectively and efficiently as possible. For example, your employer is not re-sponsible for negotiating over such items as products to produce, their selling prices, the size of the workforce, or the location of operations. Needless to say, your employer wants to have as many issues as possible labeled management rights, and reserves the right to make decisions about those issues without having to consult or negotiate with your union. Obviously, your union would prefer having more of these items subject to negotiations.

Are unions constraining or helpful? That's a big question. Its answer, however, lies in how the union and the employer get along. If they despise each other, and little trust between them exists, serious problems are going to arise. Yet if they view each other as important components in doing what's right for employees and for the business, their relationship can be a positive one.

Building Cooperative Labor-Management Relations

The history of work relationships in the United States is filled with instances where unions and management fought each other tremendously. Not only were these confrontations verbal, but at times they erupted into violent acts where people were seriously injured or killed. Unfortunately, events such as these just made matters worse—pitting one side against the other. But it doesn't have to be that way.

Even though company officials may view a union's presence as constraining them, unions can be beneficial for the employer. In fact, under the best of circumstances, unions can actually be helpful to the organization in achieving its goals. It all depends on the relationship between the two groups. For example, both the organization and the union have to make some decisions about how they'll work with, or against, the other side. If it's the latter, that relationship is often characterized as confrontational.

In the **confrontational relationship,** a relationship between company officials and the union that is represented by the "we-they" syndrome, both company officials and the union oppose each other. That means, any gains "we" make (whichever side is the *we*) come at the expense of "them." It's a win-lose situation, and victory carries with it an emotional cost. In many cases, this confrontational relationship leads to lengthy standoffs. When that occurs, rather than lose, one or both sides stop making the effort to reach an agreement. The baseball strike of 1994, the dispute between Caterpillar and the United Auto Workers, and the dispute between USAir and its pilot's union all attest to this trend in labor-management relationships. Sadly, when these work stoppages occur, productivity is lost, relationships between the parties sour, and years of momentum are halted. And yet, although these events often make headline news, fortunately they are not happening everywhere. Instead, many unions and company officials have recognized that they need each other. In the labor-management arena, this is called a cooperative relationship.

A **cooperative relationship** is one in which company officials actively seek input from union members about a variety of issues at work. These issues may focus on determining ways of increasing productivity, enhancing quality, or finding ways of improving efficiency. In other words, the relationship reflects a "we-we" syndrome—achieving gains for everyone. That means that both labor and management begin to think as one.[11]

Undoubtedly, many individuals see cooperation being inconsistent with an environment that is built on taking sides. Fostering that perception, however, may serve few long-term purposes. It may condemn us to reliving the past. Instead, we need to look at instances where cooperation flourishes and see the benefits that it can generate. For instance, the agreement between General Motors and the UAW at its Saturn plant in Spring Hill, Tennessee, is one example of how progress can be made in the spirit of cooperation.[12] Workers at the Saturn plant are paid a salary, just like professional-level employees in the organization. Moreover, union members sit on various organizational decision-making committees, giving them input into many of the things that affect them at work. And to foster an environment of teamwork, significant effort is made to

> **confrontational relationship**
> a relationship between company officials and the union that is represented by the "we-they" syndrome

> **cooperative relationship**
> a relationship in which company officials actively seek input from union members about a variety of issues at work

---

[11]See, for example, Peter Nulty, "Look What the Unions Want Now," *Fortune* (February 8, 1993), pp. 128–135.

[12]See, for example, Ross Laver, "Joining Hands," *MacLeans* (April 15, 1991), p. 46.

EXHIBIT 13-12

An Example of an Employee Handbook Disclaimer

This handbook is not a contract of employment. Employment in the organization is at will, and either you or the organization may end employment without cause or without having to use an established procedure.

enhance quality and productivity.[13] Successful efforts at Saturn, as well as in organizations in other major industries, reveal that confrontation needn't be the standard means of interaction between these two groups.[14]

Employment at Will

Before we leave the discussion of employment practices, there is one other important aspect to consider: Your employee handbook is of little use if you don't read it. Although the organization may go to great lengths to make sure the handbook gives pertinent information and is written in a way that is understandable, no organization can make you read it. In fact, although most prefer that you do read the handbook, most will simply have you sign a sheet of paper acknowledging that you've received your copy. This is done for legal reasons to protect the organization—especially if the organization reserves the right to fire you at any time, for any reason. In business, this is called **employment at will,** an organizational policy under which an employee can be fired for a good reason, a bad reason, or no reason at all. It's likened to the fact that you can quit at any time you want. Therefore, why shouldn't an organization have the same right in deciding who works for it?

Although employment at will raises an ethical issue, U.S. common law generally permits such policies. Therefore, one of the first things you'll probably see in your handbook is a disclaimer that looks something like that in Exhibit 13-12. But don't let employment at will scare you. Organizations use it primarily as legal protection in the event that they must fire someone who is not doing his or her job. Even though many individuals work at the will of the employer, terminating productive employees is not logical.

> ➤ **employment-at-will**
> an organizational policy under which an employee can be fired for a good reason, a bad reason, or no reason at all

---

[13]David Woodruff, "At Saturn, What Workers Want Is . . . Fewer Defects," *Business Week* (December 2, 1991), p. 117.

[14]Keith L. Alexander, "USAir's Flight Plan Leaves Little Room to Maneuver," *Business Week* (October 17, 1994), p. 48; and Keith L. Alexander & Stephen Baker, "If You Can't Beat 'Em, Buy 'Em," *Business Week* (October 24, 1994), pp. 78–81.

SUMMARY

This summary corresponds to the Learning Outcome, on page 301.

1. The employment process seeks to staff the organization and sustain high employee performance through employment planning, recruitment, selection, orientation, training and development, and performance appraisals.

2. Since the mid-1960s, the U.S. government has greatly expanded its influence over employment decisions by enacting new laws and regulations.

Because of the government's effort to provide equal employment opportunities, all employment decisions must be made without regard to race, sex, religion, age, color, or national origin. Extensive financial penalties can be imposed on organizations that fail to follow these laws and regulations.

3. A job description is a written statement of what you do on a job, how you do it, and why it's done. A job specification states the minimum acceptable qualifications that you must possess to perform your given job successfully.

4. Organizations can use several methods for recruiting employees. The more popular include newspaper advertisements, employee referrals, school placements, and the Internet.

5. Employee selection is likened to a hurdle race because you are faced with several events that you must pass. Failure to pass any one event, like failing to clear a hurdle, eliminates you from the employment race.

6. The quality of any selection device is decided by its validity and reliability. If a selection device isn't reliable, then it cannot be assumed to be a consistent measure. If a device is not valid, then no proven relationship exists between it and relevant job criteria.

7. Every new employee experiences anxiety when starting a new job. Orientation attempts to reduce this anxiety by familiarizing you with the organization, your job, and people with whom you'll be working.

8. Performance evaluations are used to make objective decisions about your work as employees. They should provide you feedback on your past performance, identify areas where you may need improvement, and serve as documentation for your employer. Your performance can be appraised by having it compared to some preset standards, by comparing you to other employees, or by comparing your performance to established objectives.

9. The discipline process consists of a verbal warning, a written warning, a suspension, and finally dismissal. This process is usually progressive, but steps may be skipped depending on the severity of one's behavior.

10. A union is a group of workers, acting together, seeking to promote and protect their mutual interests through collective bargaining. Some organizations believe that a collective bargaining agreement (which covers such things as wages, hours, and working conditions) constrains them, because these areas are spelled out in the contract stating how management must act. Their freedom to act unilaterally on employee issues is, therefore, not permitted.

11. Employment at will refers to a situation in organizations where an employee can be fired for a good reason, a bad reason, or no reason at all. Similar to employees having the right to quit whenever they want, employment at will gives employers the right to terminate employees whenever they want.

REVIEWING YOUR UNDERSTANDING

1. Do you feel that the government should be able to influence the employment process of organizations through legislation and regulations? Support your view.

2. What is a bona fide occupational qualification and how can it be used?

3. Identify some possible sources for finding new employees. Which source do you believe will best reach you? Why?

4. How do job descriptions differ from job specifications?

5. What's the difference between an accept error and a reject error? Explain how one error can be more likely to violate employment laws.

6. Identify the potential problems we may face with employment interviews. How can organizations ensure that problems are reduced?

7. How are orientation, training, and employee development similar? Different?

8. Explain the different performance appraisal methods using preset standards.

9. "When we are having a performance problem, being counseled corrects the problem faster and better than if we are disciplined." Do you agree or disagree with this statement? Discuss.

10. Assuming that an organization treats its employees well, do you think that joining a union would benefit employees? Explain your position.

11. "Employment at will is a 'downer.' For employees to be effective, they can't work under the constant threat of job loss. As such, organizations need to freely give up their right to employment at will and create a more positive work environment." Do you agree or disagree with this statement? Explain your position.

ANSWERS TO CHECKING YOUR UNDERSTANDING

1. b **2.** c **3.** a **4.** c

LEARNING TOGETHER

A. In groups of two or three, develop a question-naire to identify what companies should look for in hiring, training, and appraising employees. Then contact a public relations firm, employ-ment agency, or local business's personnel rela-tions office to get your questions answered. Compare your results with those of other groups. Draw some conclusions about this exercise.

B. Invite a union and a nonunion affirmative action officer from two businesses to come and speak to your class. As a class, or in groups of six to eight, prepare a list of concerns or issues you want the affirmative action officers to address. After the presentations, have a class debate about what you learned and identify the business where you might prefer to work. Discuss why you may be interested in one business over the other and why more than just union or nonunion issues may be influencing your decision.

C. In your community, where are the best places or what are the best sources to look for a job? What role, if any, should networking play in your job search? What cultural diversity elements, if any, influence your choices? Once you have collected information on these and related questions, share your findings with a classmate. Together, formu-late a game plan for a good job search. Outline your game plan, identifying all the elements you think would help you and others in a job search. Make an attractive, eye-catching bulletin board for your classroom that depicts your findings.

Maldonado Book Binders

Jackson Frieberg works for Maldonado Book Binders, a family-owned printing and bookbinding firm. Maldonado, in its forty-eighth year of operation, has earned an excellent reputation in serving the needs of a Midwestern community of 300,000 people. Jackson has been with the firm for nine years and was promoted to the director of quality control two years ago. He is the only non–family member on the managerial team. Rita Maldonado, a granddaughter of the firm's founder, took over his job of customer service manager when he was promoted. She has hired two customer service clerks who work directly with customers.

Over the nine years Jackson has been with the company, he has worked in several areas of the company's operations. He has a keen knowledge of the services the company delivers and has an exceptional ability to estimate the cost and time needed for the customized jobs that represent over 90 percent of the firm's business. For example, take the customer who wanted fifty junior-sized notebooks with a leather covering and gold embossing. Jackson was able to help the customer identify a more reasonable way to do the job, since the customer did not have a realistic view of what the project would cost. He presented samples to the customer, outlined the project specifications, and delivered the notebooks two days before the estimated delivery date. The result was a very satisfied customer. Jackson feels strongly that if he can satisfy customers and still help make the business profitable, he has fulfilled his job.

In recent months, business volume has slowed even though the profits appear to be fairly stable. The atmosphere in the company is a little more tense and there seem to be more customer complaints. Jackson feels the basic problem is Rita; it appears she is encouraging her employees to tell the customer almost anything to get business. In addition, he has found that the majority of estimates given to customers are billed out at 10–20 percent higher than the estimates. Jackson recalls vividly that the skills Rita brought to the job were nowhere in alignment with the job specifications.

Jackson is in an awkward position. He needs to share his concerns with management, yet Rita is part of the management. He recalls how Rita was hired—near the end of the position search. She was not in the applicant pool. When the customer service managerial job became open two years ago, Maldonado advertised for applicants to fill the position. In the job ad, the company specified qualifications of the job. Jackson interviewed all candidates and ranked the top three. He suggested that management provide orientation and a period of training that Jackson volunteered to conduct. He even outlined a plan for appraising performance once the person was hired.

Questions

1. Identify the problems with the hiring, development, and appraisal processes associated with Rita's hiring at Maldonado Book Binders. Categorize the problems under three or four general headings and, in groups, identify good practices associated with each.

2. What influences were present in hiring Rita? What laws were broken? Why or why not?

3. Discuss the pros and cons of training for Rita.

4. If Jackson is correct in his assessment, what disciplinary action should be taken in this case? What role should Jackson play in this assessment and how could this affect him?

5. What advice could you offer to improve the overall hiring practices at Maldonado?

CAREER SUCCESS: GETTING AND KEEPING JOBS

*L*earning Outcomes

After reading this chapter, you will be able to:

1. Define *career*.

2. Identify the purpose of career planning.

3. Describe the five stages of careers.

4. Explain how a résumé is a sales tool.

5. List six conclusions research has shown about interviews in organizations.

6. Define *impression management*.

7. Identify eight tips for excelling in an interview.

8. Explain what can be done to assist in surviving the first few months on the job.

9. List three useful methods for making career success a reality.

10. Describe how spirituality can play a role in organizational life.

Three generations ago, getting a job was much different than today. As major industrial players in world economics, U.S. companies grew larger and more powerful. As they did, so, too, did jobs for hundreds of thousands of people. After significantly completing their education, many of these individuals landed jobs that promised many of them some level of security. Doing good work was often rewarded with pay increases and, at times, promotion up the proverbial organizational ladder. Then, after some forty years of giving to the organization, these seasoned workers retired with a pension that should have made their remaining years financially secure.

Sadly, this picture doesn't exist to the extent it did fifty years ago. The work world has changed. Job security for even the most secure jobs has dwindled. For example, some 40,000 AT&T workers, many of whom had ten to thirty years with the company, have seen their jobs eliminated.[1] Some were lucky enough to find something else to do in the company—but that was rare. Even government jobs—once thought of as jobs for life—have become less secure; federal, state, and local governments have had to resort to permanent layoffs. For workers today, this means that reaching personal work goals will become more challenging.

Undoubtedly, your personal and work-related goals are important to you. Although they may not always go as well as planned or even as well as you would hope, you still must pay close attention to them. The unexpected complexities and difficulties in achieving these objectives will require a more concerted effort on your part—and a better understanding of what you want.

Careers

*T*he term **career** has a number of meanings. In popular usage, it can mean advancement ("He's moving up in his career"), a profession ("She has chosen a career in medicine") or stability over time ("He's a career military person").[2] For our purposes, we will define *career* as "the pattern of work-related experiences that span the course of a person's life."[3] By this definition, it is apparent that we all have or will have careers. The concept is as relevant to transient, unskilled laborers as it is to engineers and physicians. Any work, paid or unpaid, pursued over an extended period can constitute a career. In addition to formal job work, careers may include schoolwork, homemaking, or volunteer work.

> ▶ **career**
> pattern of work-related experiences that span the course of a person's life

The Value of Developing Your Career

Because careers have different meanings to different people, and what is considered a successful career has changed, the value of developing your career has expanded. Success is no longer a function of your income level, the size of your office, or how high a position you achieved in the organization. It may now include how well you have reached your potential, how prepared you are for the challenges you'll face tomorrow, or having greater responsibilities and increased autonomy in the work you do.

As you think about developing your career, one helpful aspect to consider is career planning. **Career planning** is a process involving the identification of major work-related and personal goals that one wants to achieve. In this analysis, you'll need to come

> ▶ **career planning**
> a process involving the identification of major work-related and personal goals that one wants to achieve

---

[1]George J. Church, "Disconnected," *Time* (January 15, 1996), pp. 44–45.
[2]Douglas T. Hall, *Careers in Organizations* (Santa Monica, Calif.: Goodyear, 1976); and J. Van Maanen & E. H. Schein, "Career Development," in J. R. Hackman & J. L. Suttle, eds., *Improving Life at Work: Behavioral Sciences Approaches to Organizational Change* (Santa Monica, Calif.: Goodyear, 1977), pp. 341–355.
[3]Jeffrey H. Greenhaus, *Career Management* (New York: Dryden Press, 1987), p. 6.

UNLOCKING YOUR POTENTIAL *14-1*

Are You Prepared to Work in the 21st Century?

*P*reparing yourself for the future of work is a continuous process. For each of the following twenty items, circle the appropriate response, based on a 5-point scale regarding how well the statement reflects your thinking, where 5 is most like you, and 1 is least like you.

	Most Like Me				Least Like Me
1. I don't let personal matters affect me while I'm at work.	5	4	3	2	1
2. I believe in my abilities to do an excellent job.	5	4	3	2	1
3. I am open to constructive suggestions that can help me become a better performer.	5	4	3	2	1
4. I have a positive attitude.	5	4	3	2	1
5. I like to know why things are done as opposed to what effects they have.	5	4	3	2	1
6. I like to find out why things happen.	5	4	3	2	1
7. I try to learn something new every day.	5	4	3	2	1
8. I believe the status quo must constantly be reviewed to validate its existence.	5	4	3	2	1
9. I share my work-related problems with others in the organization.	5	4	3	2	1
10. I plan to continue my education after graduating from college.	5	4	3	2	1
11. I know that my job adds value to my organization.	5	4	3	2	1
12. I anticipate what skills and competencies may be needed in the future to be a successful worker.	5	4	3	2	1
13. I practice my current skills frequently to keep them current.	5	4	3	2	1
14. I try to learn new skills by watching others work.	5	4	3	2	1
15. I know what skills I need to develop and how I will develop them.	5	4	3	2	1
16. My peers view me as a competent co-worker.	5	4	3	2	1
17. I think there are better ways of doing most things.	5	4	3	2	1
18. I am a risk taker.	5	4	3	2	1
19. I do what I can to maintain my health.	5	4	3	2	1
20. I know what I need to do to improve my performance.	5	4	3	2	1

Source: Adapted from W. Richard Plunkett, *Supervision: Diversity and Teams in the Workplace* (Upper Saddle River, N.J.: Prentice- Hall, 1996), p. 40, Exhibit 2-2.

to grips with what investment you're willing to make for your career.[4] For instance, making a decision about your major in college is one of the first steps you'll need to consider. If you plan to become an attorney, you'll need to begin taking courses—such as political science, logic, and debating—that will prepare you for law school and ultimately your career. Careers in law, as well as many other areas, also require an investment in obtaining advanced degrees. The cost of the education, as well as the time involved, must be factored into your analysis. In other words, are you willing to spend the next ten years of your life adequately preparing for your chosen profession?

Career planning also involves thinking about your future in terms of what you want to achieve. If your goal is to run your own company or achieve a high-level, decision-making position in an organization, you need to identify what or who will help you reach that goal. You must also think about what you may have to give up. For example, if your desire is to run a successful small business, you may be looking at working six to seven days a week, putting in upwards of eighty hours a week. If that's what it will take, then you must be prepared to make such a commitment. But remember, this commitment may result in less time to pursue other interests you have.

Finally, you need to think about your personal life. What goals have you set for yourself? Are they compatible with your work-related goals? Would, say, the eighty hours over six days a week interfere with your personal life? Probably, but there's no reason a happy medium cannot be found. You must make that choice. Some career activities may not be conducive to family life. The long hours involved in running your own business, traveling constantly on your job, or being on call twenty-four hours a day, for example, may create conflict between what you want and what you can do. For instance, if having and raising a family is most important to you, then you need to look for a career that will meet your requirements. Working at home, part-time work, or other work alternatives may better serve your needs.

Remember, however, that like the world around you, your career choice and life goals may change. What you decide today may have to be altered in five years to reflect new goals you've set or as a result of change thrust on you. Most of us, research tells us, will have twelve or more jobs in our lifetime in as many as four distinct careers. Irrespective of where they are, they seem to follow a particular pattern. These patterns are called career stages.

Career Stages

One of the most popular ways of analyzing and discussing careers is to view them as a series of stages.[5] Progression from the beginning of a career to its end is a natural occurrence that happens to everyone. In this section, we'll look at a five-stage model that applies to most people during their adult years regardless of the type of job they do.

Most individuals begin to form ideas about their careers during their elementary and secondary school years. Their careers begin to wind down as they reach retirement age. The stages that most individuals will go through during these years are

---

[4]See, for instance, E. P. Cook, "1991 Annual Review: Practice and Research in Career Counseling and Development, 1990," *Career Development Quarterly* (February 1991), pp. 99–131.

[5]See, for example, Donald E. Super, *The Psychology of Careers* (New York: Harper & Row, 1957); Edgar Schein, *Career Dynamics: Matching Individual and Organizational Needs* (Reading, Mass.: Addison-Wesley, 1978); and Daniel J. Levinson, C. N. Darrow, E. B. Klein, M. H. Levinson, & B. McKee, *A Man's Life* (New York: Knopf, 1978).

Planning for Your Career

Career planning is designed to assist you in becoming more knowledgeable of your needs, values, and personal goals. This can be achieved through a three-step self-assessment process.*

1. **Identify and organize your skills, interests, work-related needs, and values.** The best place to begin is by drawing up a profile of your educational record. List each school you attended from high school on. What courses do you remember liking most and least? In what courses did you score highest and lowest? In what extracurricular activities did you participate? Did you acquire any specific skills? Have you gained proficiency in other skills?

   Next, begin to assess your occupational experience. List each job you have held, the organization you worked for, your overall level of satisfaction, what you liked most and least about the job, and why you left. It's important to be honest in covering each of these points.

2. **Convert this information into general career fields and specific job goals.** After completing step 1, you should have some insight into your interests and abilities. Now you need to look at how these can be converted into the kind of organizational setting or field of endeavor with which you will be a good match. Then you can become specific and identify distinct job goals.

   What fields are available? In business? In government? In nonprofit organizations? Your answer can be broken down further into areas such as education, finances, social services, or health services. Identifying areas of interest is usually far easier than pinpointing specific occupations. When you have identified a limited set of occupations that interest you, you can start to align these with your abilities and skills. Will certain jobs require you to move? If so, would this be compatible with your geographic preferences? Do you have the educational requirements necessary for the job? If not, what additional schooling will be needed? Does the job offer the status and earning potential that you aspire to? What is the long-term outlook for jobs in this area? Does the career suffer from cyclical employment? Since no job is without its drawbacks, have you seriously considered all the negative aspects? When you have fully answered questions such as these, you should have a relatively short list of special job goals.

3. **Test your career possibilities against the realities of the organization or the job market.** The final step in this self-assessment process is testing your selection against the realities of the marketplace. You can do this by talking with knowledgeable people in the fields, organizations, or jobs you desire. These informational interviews should provide reliable feedback on the accuracy of your self-assessment and the opportunities in the fields and jobs that interest you.

*Irving R. Schwartz, "Self-Assessment and Career Planning: Matching Individuals and Organizational Goals," *Personnel* (January–February 1979), p. 48.

KEYS TO UNLOCKING YOUR POTENTIAL *14-1*

The purpose of Unlocking Your Potential 14-1 was to draw your attention to four critical areas for career success: your attitudes toward work, your knowledge, your skills, and your abilities.

For each group of questions, place your circled response on the line next to each statement. That is, if you circled a 5 for statement 1, place a 5 on the line next to number 1 here. When you have completed transferring your circled numbers for each statement, total each column and place that total in the box at the end of each column.

Attitude Readiness

1. _____
2. _____
3. _____
4. _____
5. _____
   ☐
   Total
   AR

Knowledge Awareness

6. _____
7. _____
8. _____
9. _____
10. _____
    ☐
    Total
    KA

Skill Assessment

11. _____
12. _____
13. _____
14. _____
15. _____
    ☐
    Total
    SA

Ability Focus

16. _____
17. _____
18. _____
19. _____
20. _____
    ☐
    Total
    AF

Each of the four areas has a maximum of 25 total points. Your scores should be viewed separately. That is, you'll have a composite score for each of the four areas. Scores of 16 to 25 indicate that you are properly preparing yourself in this area. That means that you recognize the need to keep making appropriate changes where necessary. Scores between 10 and 16 indicate that you are making progress on this criterion, but there are areas where improvement is needed. Scores below 10 indicate that you may be creating a situation where you will not be properly prepared for the world of work in the twenty-first century. You will need to look at the types of questions asked in the respective column, and determine what you may be able to do to correct this potential deficiency.

Extra Effort

For any of the criteria where your scores fall below 16, develop a plan of action regarding what you may be able to do to correct this. Consider this activity part of a proper career-planning process.

Carole Wright thought she had her career well laid out. She was going to be an accountant and rise up the corporate ladder just like her two older brothers. A University of Florida graduate, she quickly began to fulfill her plan. After passing the CPA exam, she landed a good job with one of the big accounting firms. From there, career progressions were going as planned. But then something happened. The promotions stopped having the excitement associated with them. Accounting work lost its luster. So at age forty, she quit and started a construction company. Today, three years and nine custom homes later, she's working as hard as ever, but enjoying life more than at any time before. Carole Wright has cemented a new foundation for her career and built a thriving business on top of it!

exploration, establishment, midcareer, late career, and decline. These stages and the challenges most will face are shown in Exhibit 14-1.

The age ranges for each of the five stages in Exhibit 14-1 are provided as general guidelines. They should not be interpreted as the ages when events must occur. As such, someone who makes a career change to another line of work at age forty-seven will have many of the same establishment-stage concerns as someone starting at age twenty-one.

Exploration. Individuals often make decisions about their careers prior to entering the workforce on a paid basis. Information from relatives, teachers, friends, and the media helps them narrow career choice alternatives and leads them in a certain direction.

During the exploration stage, individuals will be looking at potential careers to see what they like or don't like. They form attitudes and prepare themselves for work. The exploration period ends for most individuals when they make the transition from school to work.

Establishment. The establishment stage begins with the search for work and includes getting that first job, being accepted by peers, learning the job, and gaining the first tangible evidence of success or failure in the real world. During the establishment stage, performance improves; mistakes are made, yet learned from; and responsibilities increase. However, individuals in this stage have yet to reach their peak productivity and rarely are they given work assignments that carry great power or high status. During this stage, one can anticipate expending a lot of time and energy on his or her career goals.

Midcareer. Many people do not face their first severe career dilemma until they reach the midcareer stage.[6] This stage represents a period when performance may

---

[6] Jaclyn Fierman, "Beating the MidLife Career Crisis," *Fortune* (September 6, 1993), p. 51.

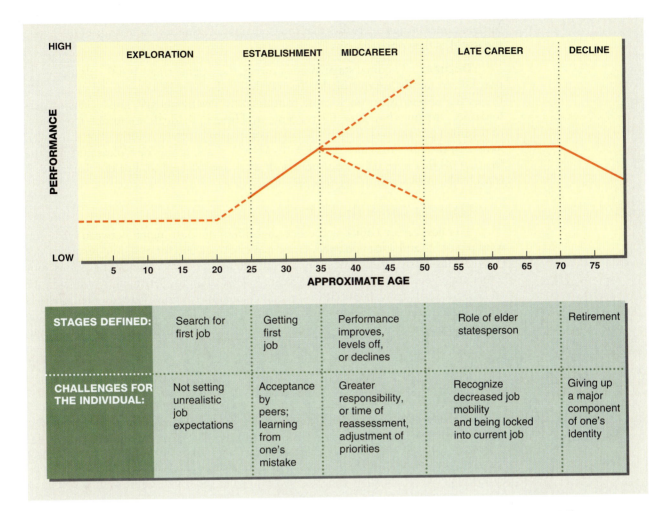

	EXPLORATION	ESTABLISHMENT	MIDCAREER	LATE CAREER	DECLINE
STAGES DEFINED:	Search for first job	Getting first job	Performance improves, levels off, or declines	Role of elder statesperson	Retirement
CHALLENGES FOR THE INDIVIDUAL:	Not setting unrealistic job expectations	Acceptance by peers; learning from one's mistake	Greater responsibility, or time of reassessment, adjustment of priorities	Recognize decreased job mobility and being locked into current job	Giving up a major component of one's identity

EXHIBIT 14-1

Career Stages
Source: D. T. Hall, *Careers in Organizations* (Glenview, Ill.: Scott Foresman and Company, 1976), p. 57. Reprinted with permission of the author.

improve (continuing to advance), decline (loss of interest), or level off (plateauing). Those who continue to advance get more responsibility and greater rewards. Others may have to reassess what they want out of a career and possibly make some changes— either in career choice or personal goals.

In the past fifteen years, one career issue receiving a lot of attention has been those individuals who have plateaued. Restructuring organizations, downsizing, and reengineering have reduced upward mobility chances for many employees. As a result, many career plans have been halted, which has led to anxiety and frustration for some.[7]

Late Career. For those who continue to grow through the midcareer stage, the late career is usually a pleasant time when one is allowed the luxury to relax a bit and enjoy playing the part of the elder statesperson. During the late career, individuals are no longer expected to outdo their levels of performance from previous years. Their value to the organization lies heavily in their judgment, built up over many years and through varied experiences, and sharing with and teaching others based on the knowledge they have gained. For those who have stagnated or deteriorated during the midcareer stage,

---

[7]Frederic M. Hudson, "When Careers Turn Stale," *Next* (Lakewood, Calif.: American Association of Retired Persons, 1994), p. 3.

the late career brings the reality that they will not have an everlasting impact or change the world as they once thought.

Decline. The final stage in one's career, the decline stage, is difficult for everyone, but, ironically, is probably hardest on those who have had continued successes in the earlier stages. After decades of continued achievements and high levels of performance, the time has come for retirement. These individuals are forced to step out of the limelight and to relinquish a major component of their identity. For those who have seen their performance deteriorate over the years, it may be a pleasant time; the frustrations that have been associated with work are left behind. For the plateaued, it is probably an easy transition to other life activities.

Making a Career Decision

The best career choice is the one that offers the best match between what you want out of life and what you need. Good career choice outcomes should result in a series of positions that give you an opportunity to be a good performer, make you want to maintain your commitment to your career, lead to highly satisfying work, and give you the proper balance between work and personal life. A good career match, then, is one in which you can develop a positive self-concept, do work that you think is important, and lead the kind of life you desire.[8] Before any of these can happen, though, you need to get into an organization. In the next section, we look at how that can be accomplished.

Getting into the Organization

*A*ssuming, of course, that you have planned in some capacity for the type of career you are interested in, it's now time to begin to make those career goals a reality. When someone in the organization decides to hire employees, information is often sent out announcing the job. If you see that announcement and feel that there's a potential match between what you can offer and what the organization wants, you need to throw your hat into the "hiring ring."[9]

One of the more stressful situations you will face happens when you apply for a job. This occurs because generally there are no specific guidelines to follow to guarantee you success. However, several tips may increase your chances of finding employment. Even though getting a job interview should be one of your major goals in the hiring process (another is actually being offered the job), being offered an interview requires hard work. Therefore, you need to view getting a job as your job at the moment.

Competition for most jobs today is fierce. Thus, you cannot wait until the last minute to enter the job market. Your job hunt must start well in advance of when you plan to start work. You should consider about seven to nine months as the normal lead time for getting a job. That's particularly true if you hope to land a position in May after graduating. In that case, your job search should begin sometime around September of your senior year. Although you may not need the entire time, starting in March may be too late.

---

[8] D. E. Super, "A Life-Span Life Space Approach to Career Development," *Journal of Vocational Behavior*, vol. 16 (Spring 1980), pp. 282–298. See also Cook, *1991 Annual Review*, pp. 99–131; M. Arthur, *Career Theory Handbook* (Upper Saddle River, N.J.: Prentice-Hall, 1991); and Louis S. Richman, "The New Worker Elite," *Fortune* (August 22, 1994), pp. 56–66.

[9] Material for this section is adapted from David A. De Cenzo and Stephen P. Robbins, *Human Resource Management*, 5th ed. (New York: Wiley, 1996), appendixes A and B.

How is starting in the fall helpful? There are two advantages. First, it shows that you are taking an interest in your career and that you are planning. You are not waiting until the last minute to begin, and this reflects favorably on you. Second, starting in the fall coincides with many companies' recruiting cycles. If you wait until March to begin the process, some job openings may have already been filled. For specific information regarding the company recruiting cycles in your area, visit your career development center, which should be able to give you helpful information.

Given that you will be getting a head start on the hiring process, the next step is to prepare a résumé.

Preparing Your Résumé

Every job applicant needs to circulate information that reflects positively on his or her strengths. That information needs to be sent to prospective employers in a format that is understandable and consistent with the organization's hiring practices. In most instances, this is done through the résumé.

No matter who you are or where you are in your career, you need a current résumé. Your résumé is typically the only information source that a recruiter will use in determining whether to grant you an interview. Therefore, it must be a sales tool; it must give accurate information that supports your candidacy, highlights your strengths, and differentiates you from other job applicants. Identifying these strengths can take a long time, but you must give them much thought and express them in ways that speak well of you. The information in the résumé must also be listed in a way that is easy to read. An example of the type of information that should be included is shown in Exhibit 14-2.

It is important to pinpoint a few key themes regarding résumés that may seem like common sense, but are seldom followed. First of all, your résumé must be printed on a quality printer—or at the very least, professionally typed. The style of font should be easy to read (for example, Courier). Avoid any style that may be hard on the eyes, such as a script or italics. Look at the résumé in Exhibit 14-3. It contains exactly the same information as shown in Exhibit 14-2, but what a difference. A recruiter who must review two hundred résumés a day is not going to slow down and strain to read the script type; valuable information may not come across. So, use an easy-to-read font and make the recruiter's job easier.

Note also that some companies today are using computer scanners to make the first pass through résumés. In a matter of moments, computers can be programmed to scan each résumé for specific information such as key job elements, experience, work history, education, or technical expertise.[10] The use of scanners, then, has created two important criteria for résumé writing.[11] The computer matches key words in a job description. Thus, in creating a résumé, you should use typical job description phraseology. Additionally (and this goes back to the issue of font type), you should use a font that is easily read by the scanner; if it isn't, your résumé may be put in the rejection file.

Your résumé should be copied on good-quality paper (no off-the-wall colors). Sure, there are certain types of jobs—such as a creative artist position—where this suggestion may be inappropriate. For the rest, however, use a standard white or cream-colored paper. There are many definitions of good-quality paper, but you can't go wrong with a 20-bond-weight paper that has some cotton content (about 20 percent).

---

[10]See, for example, Julia Lawlor, "Scanning Résumés: The Impersonal Touch," *USA Today* (October 7, 1991), p. 7B.

[11]Terry Mullins, "How to Land a Job," *Psychology Today* (September–October 1994), pp. 12–13.

RESUME OF:	**LESLIE SMITH** **1430 West Avenue** **Center City, OK 41111**
CAREER OBJECTIVE:	A multitalented individual seeking employment in a progressive, print media organization that provides a challenging opportunity to combine exceptional writing and computer skills.
EDUCATION:	STATE COMMUNITY COLLEGE A.A., DESIGN AND PUBLICATION (MAY 1998) STATE UNIVERSITY B.S., MASS COMMUNICATIONS AND PUBLIC RELATIONS (MAY 2000)
EXPERIENCE: 12/98 to present	STATE UNIVERSITY CAMPUS NEWSPAPER, EDITOR *Primary Duties:* Responsible for the design, editing, and publishing of a weekly college student newspaper. Supervised eight student staff writers and two photographers. Served as a newspaper liaison to faculty and staff committees. Managed annual budget of $150,000.
9/96 to 9/98	STATE COMMUNITY COLLEGE OFFICE OF STUDENT RELATIONS, STAFF ASSISTANT *Primary Duties:* Responsible for preparing timely draft copies of public relations material used in college catalogs and recruiting brochures. Coordinated final printing with external vendors.
12/93 to 6/94	STATE HIGH SCHOOL YEARBOOK STAFF *Primary Duties:* Responsible for coordinating photo sessions and layout design. Involved in fund raising through contacts with community organizations.
SPECIAL SKILLS:	Experienced in desktop publishing and in application software. Fluent in speaking and writing Spanish. Certified in CPR.
SERVICE ACTIVITIES:	Vice president, Student Government Association Volunteer, Meals-On-Wheels Volunteer, United Way
REFERENCES:	Available on request.

EXHIBIT 14-2
A Sample Résumé

By all means, don't send standard duplicating paper—it may look as if you are mass-mailing résumés. Even though you probably *are* mass-mailing résumés, don't make it so obvious. The cost might seem an expense you would rather not incur, but remember that your competition may be doing it—and if you have to spend a few dollars to make a few copies, consider it a wise investment.

The last point on résumés, one that shouldn't have to be mentioned, concerns proofreading. Because the résumé is the only representation of you the recruiter has, a sloppy résumé can be deadly. If it contains misspelled words or is grammatically incorrect, your chances for an interview will be significantly reduced. Proofread your résumé, and if possible, let others proofread it too.

RÉSUMÉ OF: LESLIE SMITH
              1430 West Avenue
              Center City, OK 41111

CAREER   A multitalented individual seeking employment in a progressive,
OBJECTIVE: print media organization that provides a challenging opportunity to
              combine exceptional writing and computer skills.

EDUCATION: STATE COMMUNITY COLLEGE
              A.A., DESIGN AND PUBLICATION (MAY 1998)
              STATE UNIVERSITY
              B.S., MASS COMMUNICATIONS AND PUBLIC
              RELATIONS
              (MAY 2000)

EXPERIENCE: STATE UNIVERSITY
12/98 to present   CAMPUS NEWSPAPER, EDITOR
              Primary Duties: Responsible for the design, editing, and
              publishing of a weekly college student newspaper. Supervised eight
              student staff writers and two photographers. Served as a
              newspaper liaison to faculty and staff committees. Managed annual
              budget of $150,000.

9/96 to 9/98   STATE COMMUNITY COLLEGE
              OFFICE OF STUDENT RELATIONS, STAFF
              ASSISTANT
              Primary Duties: Responsible for preparing timely draft copies of
              public relations material used in college catalogs and recruiting
              brochures. Coordinated final printing with external vendors.

12/93 to 6/94   STATE HIGH SCHOOL
              YEARBOOK STAFF
              Primary Duties: Responsible for coordinating photo sessions
              and layout design. Involved in fund raising through contacts with
              community organizations.

SPECIAL SKILLS: Experienced in desktop publishing and in application software.
              Fluent in speaking and writing Spanish. Certified in CPR.

SERVICE   Vice president, Student Government Association
ACTIVITIES: Volunteer, Meals-On-Wheels
              Volunteer, United Way

REFERENCES: Available on request.

EXHIBIT 14-3
A Sample Résumé (with font change)

In addition to your résumé, you need a cover letter. Your cover letter should contain information that tells the recruiter why you should be considered for the job. The cover letter should not be an oversell letter, but one that highlights your greatest strengths and indicates how these strengths can be useful to the company. Cover letters should also be tailored to the organization. Your cover letter should contain some information citing why the organization getting your résumé is of interest to you. That shows you've taken some time and given some thought to the job you're applying for.

One of the biggest turnoffs a recruiter may experience in reviewing résumés is the "To Whom It May Concern" letter. This tells the recruiter that you are on a fishing expedition and are sending out hundreds of résumés in hopes of generating some

1. Which one of the following is not associated with the meaning of the term *career?*
   a. advancement
   b. educational major
   c. stability over time
   d. a profession

2. The _____ stage of careers involves searching for work and getting that first job.
   a. late career
   b. exploration
   c. establishment
   d. midcareer

3. Which one of the following statements is most accurate with respect to résumés?
   a. Having an updated résumé is not as critical when you have been on the job more than three years.
   b. Printing a résumé on bright colored paper—like hot pink or sunshine yellow—helps make the résumé stand out and thus increases the likelihood that the reviewer will read it.
   c. Résumés today are more likely to be initially read by a computer scanner. Therefore, key words that describe the job should be included in the résumé.
   d. The content of the résumé is more critical than its appearance. Accordingly, how it relates to one's potential for successful performance on the job creates the biggest impact for someone reviewing it.

positive response. This technique seldom helps your job hunting. Writing to a specific person has a much greater effect. You may not always have the recruiter's name and title, but with some work, you can get it. Use whatever resources you can. Telephone the company in question and ask for it; most receptionists will give out the recruiter's name and title. If you just can't get a name, go to the Internet (you may also find this information in the reference section of a library) and locate publications such as Standard and Poor's *Register of Corporations* or Moody's *Industrial Manual.* These publications usually list the names and titles of officers in the organization. If everything else fails, send your résumé to one of the officers—preferably the officer in charge of employment or administration—or even to the president of the organization. This is much better than a "To Whom It May Concern" salutation on a cover letter.

Like the résumé, the cover letter should be flawless. Proofread this as carefully as you do the résumé. Finally, sign each cover letter individually. A real signature has a much better effect than a duplicate.

Excelling at the Interview

If you have made it through the initial screening process, chances are good that you may be called in for an interview. Although you may be excited, some caution is in order. Remember that interviews play a critical role in determining whether you will get the job. Up to now, all the recruiter has seen is your well-polished cover letter and résumé. Therefore, prepare for one of the more stressful face-to-face encounters you'll ever have in achieving your career goals: the interview.

The reason interviews are so popular is that they help the recruiter determine whether you are a good fit for the organization in terms of your level of motivation and interpersonal skills.[12] Popularity aside, however, how interviews are conducted can be

---

[12]For a discussion on this and its appropriateness to the interviewing process, see "The Right Fit," *Small Business Reports* (April 1993), p. 28.

UNLOCKING YOUR POTENTIAL *14-2*

Potential Interview Problems

Listed here are several behavioral items that may take place in an interview. Place a check in the appropriate column, depending on whether you believe the behavior will positively or negatively influence the interviewer's evaluation.

	Positive Influence	Negative Influence
1. Dressing appropriately	☐	☐
2. Being assertive	☐	☐
3. Expressing information clearly	☐	☐
4. Showing interest and enthusiasm	☐	☐
5. Having a career plan	☐	☐
6. Having confidence and poise	☐	☐
7. Emphasizing money	☐	☐
8. Being willing to start at the bottom	☐	☐
9. Rationalizing mistakes made	☐	☐
10. Being courteous	☐	☐
11. Demonstrating maturity	☐	☐
12. Citing instances of problems with previous employers	☐	☐
13. Being interested in the company and the job	☐	☐
14. Making good eye contact	☐	☐
15. Being able to laugh at self	☐	☐
16. Arriving exactly at interview time	☐	☐
17. Raising questions about the organization and the job	☐	☐
18. Showing appreciation by sending a thank-you card to the interviewer	☐	☐

Source: Adapted from Victor R. Lindquist, *The Northwestern Lindquist-Endicott Report 1989* (Evanston, Ill.: Northwestern University, 1988).

problematic. Exhibit 14-4 presents a summary of the research that has been conducted on interviews.

Although items such as those listed in Exhibit 14-4 shouldn't be part of your interview, it's important for you to understand that they may exist. Why is this knowledge important? If you know how the interviewer may react in the hiring process, it can help you avoid making a costly mistake. Additionally, many of the biases that may exist in the interview may be overcome through a technique called impression management. **Impression management** refers to an attempt to project an image that will result in achieving a favorable outcome.[13] For example, if you can say or do something

> ➤ **impression management**
> an attempt to project an image that will result in achieving a favorable outcome

---

[13]For a more detailed discussion of impression management, see Amy L. Kristof & Cynthia Kay Stevens, "Applicant Impression Management Tactics: Effects on Interviewer Evaluations and Interview Outcomes," in Dorothy P. Moore, ed., *Academy of Management Best Papers Proceedings*, August 14–17, 1994, pp. 127–131.

EXHIBIT 14-4

Conclusions about Interviews

- Interviewers hold a stereotype of what represents a good applicant.
- Interviewers tend to favor applicants who share their attitude.
- The order in which applicants are interviewed influences an evaluation.
- Negative information is given unduly high weight.
- Decisions about the candidate are made in the first four or five minutes of the interview.
- Interviewers tend to forget much of the interview's content within minutes of its conclusion.

that is viewed favorably by the interviewer, then you may create a more favorable impression of yourself. Take a situation where you find out in the early moments of the interview that your interviewer values workers who are well-rounded—meaning they are capable of balancing work and personal responsibilities. Making statements of being an individual who likes to work hard but also one who reserves time to spend with family and friends may result in your creating a positive impression. You need to understand, too, that interviewers generally have short and inaccurate memories.[14] Research has shown that most remember only about half of what you say. Although taking notes can help them remember more, what they remember most will be the impressions you make—both favorable and unfavorable.[15] Given this background information on interviews and interviewers, what can you do to increase your chances of excelling in the interview?

First of all, do some homework. If you haven't already done so in your search of to whom to send résumés, go to the Internet and get as much information as possible on the organization. Don't fall into the trap that one applicant did when interviewing for a job at IBM: He didn't even know what IBM stood for. Gather as much data as possible so that you sound as though you know a bit about the company. This will be time well spent since it creates a perception of you as an individual who takes charge. Many interviewers may look at you favorably (impression management) if you have read about a recent company venture in such publications as *Business Week*, *Fortune*, or *The Wall Street Journal*. In fact, the job you are interviewing for may be directly related to that venture. So be sure to go to the interview prepared.

The night before the interview, get a good night's rest. Eat a good breakfast to build your energy level, since the day's events will be grueling. As you prepare for the interview, keep in mind that your appearance is going to be the first impression you make. Dress appropriately. Even though appearance generally is not supposed to enter into the hiring decision, it does make an impression about you. In fact, one study suggests that 80 percent of the interviewer's perception of you in the interview comes from his or her initial perception of you, based primarily on your appearance and body language.[16] Therefore, dress appropriately and be meticulous in your attire.

---

[14]Reported in Robert E. Carlson, Paul W. Thayer, Eugene C. Mayfield, & Donald A. Peterson, "Improvements in the Selection Interview," *Personnel Journal* (April 1971), p. 272.

[15]Robert L. Dipboye, *Selection Interviews: Process Perspectives* (Cincinnati, Ohio: South-Western, 1992), p. 201.

[16]Kirsten Schabacker, "Tips on Making a Great First Impression," *Working Woman* (February 1992), p. 55.

Make a point of arriving early—about thirty minutes ahead of your scheduled interview. It is better for you to wait than to have to contend with something unexpected, such as a traffic jam that could make you late. Arriving early also gives you an opportunity to survey the office environment and possibly gather some clues about the organization. For instance, if the atmosphere is friendly and cheerful, this may indicate that the organization puts considerable emphasis on employee satisfaction. Again, use any hint you can pick up to increase your chances of making a favorable impression.

As you meet the recruiter, give him or her a firm handshake. Make good eye contact and maintain it throughout the interview. Remember, your body language may be giving away secrets about you that you don't want an interviewer to pick up. Sit erect and maintain good posture. At this point, you are probably as nervous as you have ever been. Though this is natural, try your best to relax. Recruiters know you'll be anxious, and a good one will try to put you at ease. Being prepared for an interview can also help build your confidence and reduce nervousness. You can start building that confidence by reviewing the questions most frequently asked by interviewers, shown in Exhibit 14-5. More important, however, since you may be asked these questions, you should begin to develop responses to them. But let's add a word of caution here. The best advice is to be yourself. Don't go into an interview with a prepared text and recite it from memory. Have an idea of what you would like to say, but don't rely on verbatim responses. They will only frustrate you if you forget them and may ultimately make you look foolish.

You should also try to go through several practice interviews if possible. Universities often have career days on campus, when recruiters from companies are on site to interview students. Take advantage of them. Even if the job does not fit what you want, the process will at least help you become more skilled at dealing with interviews. You can also practice with family, friends, career counselors, student groups to which you belong, or your faculty advisor.

There's another issue that you should consider with respect to interviewing. You must be prepared to deal with the stress, or pressure, interview, as well as interviews in which potentially discriminatory questions are asked.[17] The point of these tactics is to "see how you react when you're pressured and to test your professionalism and confidence."[18] These questions may appear rude or even demeaning. But remember, they are designed to rattle you. If you lose control, chances of a job offer are slim.

When the interview ends, thank the interviewer for his or her time and for giving you this opportunity to talk about your qualifications. But don't think that selling yourself has stopped there. As soon as you get home, type a thank-you letter and send it to the recruiter. You'd be amazed at how many people fail to do this. This little act of courtesy has an impact, so use it to your advantage. Then sit back and wait to see what happens.

When the Good News Arrives

Depending on the hiring process an organization uses, at some point (usually after several interviews), a job offer is made. Assuming that you have been successful

---

[17]See Jundra Woo, "Job Interviews Pose Risk to Employers," *The Wall Street Journal* (March 11, 1992), p. B1; and Joann Keyton & Jeffrey K. Springston, "What Did You Ask Me?" *National Business Employment Weekly* (Spring 1991), p. 32.
[18]Stephen M. Pollan & Mark Levine, "How to Ace a Tough Interview," *Working Woman* (July 1994), p. 49.

1. What goals have you set for yourself? How are you planning to achieve them?
2. Who or what has had the greatest influence on the development of your career interests?
3. What factors did you consider in choosing your major?
4. Why are you interested in our organization?
5. Tell me about yourself.
6. What two or three things are most important to you in a position?
7. What kind of work do you want to do?
8. Tell me about a project you initiated.
9. What are your expectations of your future employment?
10. What is your GPA? How do you feel about it? Does it reflect your ability?
11. How do you solve conflicts?
12. Tell me about how you perceive your strengths. Your weaknesses. How do you evaluate yourself?
13. What work experience has been the most valuable to you and why?
14. What was the most useful criticism you ever received and from whom was it?
15. Give an example of a problem you have solved and the process you used.
16. Describe the project or situation that best demonstrated your analytical skills.
17. What has been your greatest challenge?
18. Describe a situation involving conflict with another individual and how you dealt with it.
19. What were the biggest problems you have encountered in college? How have you handled them? What did you learn from them?
20. What are your team-player qualities? Give examples.
21. Describe your leadership style.
22. What interests or concerns you about the position or the company?
23. In a particular leadership role you had, what was the greatest challenge?
24. What idea have you developed and implemented that was particularly creative or innovative?
25. What characteristics do you think are important for this position?
26. How have your educational and work experiences prepared you for this position?
27. Take me through a project where you demonstrated skills.
28. How do you think you have changed personally since you started college?
29. Tell me about a team project of which you are particularly proud and your contribution to it.
30. How do you motivate people?
31. Why did you choose the extracurricular activities you did? What did you gain? What did you contribute?
32. What types of situations put you under pressure, and how do you deal with the pressure?
33. Tell me about a difficult decision you have made.
34. Give an example of a situation in which you failed, and how you handled it.
35. Tell me about a situation when you had to persuade another person to your point of view.
36. What frustrates you the most?
37. Knowing what you know now about your college experience, would you make the same decisions?
38. What can you contribute to this company?

EXHIBIT 14-5

Fifty Frequently Asked Interview Questions

39. How would you react to having your credibility questioned?

40. What characteristics are most important to a good manager?

41. What challenges do you seek in a position?

42. Are you willing to relocate or travel as part of your career?

43. What two or three accomplishments have given you the most satisfaction?

44. Describe a leadership role of yours, and tell why you committed your time to it.

45. How are you conducting your job search, and how will you make your decision?

46. What is the most important lesson you have learned in or out of school?

47. Describe a situation where you had to work with someone who was difficult. How was the person difficult, and how did you handle it?

48. We are looking at a lot of great candidates; why are you the best person for this position?

49. How would your friends describe you? Your professors?

50. What else should I know about you?

Source: Victor R. Lindquist, *The Northwestern Lindquist-Endicott Report 1989* (Evanston, Ill.: Northwestern University, 1988), p. 15.

EXHIBIT 14-5
Fifty Frequently Asked Interview Questions

in your efforts at landing the job, it's now time to go to work. Although there's a natural excitement associated with starting a job, you should be aware of some aspects of those first few months. In this section, we'll look at some suggestions about how to survive in the organization and ways that you can continue to make inroads in achieving your goals.

Adjusting to the Job

Shortly after you've been hired, many organizations will work hard at helping you adjust to your new surroundings. You will likely be put through some sort of orientation program as the organization begins its socialization process. This process will include representatives from the administration, the employment department, and your work unit who attempt to make you feel welcome and help you understand what is expected on the job. Their actions notwithstanding, one aspect remains important. It will be up to you to demonstrate certain behaviors in an effort to survive the new job. Let's look, then, at some ways that can help you make a smooth transition from outsider to effective employee.[19]

Surviving the First Few Months. No one can precisely predict what you will need to do your first few months after joining an organization. What may work or what is acceptable in one organization may be totally irrelevant in another. That's because too many unique factors may exist that will require you to behave in a particular way. Even so, the following suggestions appear to be universally useful in creating a positive image of you. (See Exhibit 14-6.)

Learn everything you can about the organization. During orientation, you'll be given an overview of the critical aspects of the organization. Recognize that these are just the highlights. There's much more to learn about the organization. Read any material you

---

[19]For a good review and self-directed approach to surviving your first month on the job, see Elwood N. Chapman, *Your First Thirty Days: Building a Professional Image in a New Job* (Menlo Park, Calif.: Crisp, 1990).

KEYS TO UNLOCKING YOUR POTENTIAL *14-2*

*M*any factors can lead to creating a favorable impression of you in an interview; likewise, several can lead to an unfavorable impression. Even though favorable versus unfavorable is in the eye of the evaluator, many interviewers agree on some general interpretations. Let's see how they would rate the items presented in Unlocking Your Potential 14-2.

	Positive Influence	Negative Influence
1. Dressing appropriately	☑	☐
2. Being assertive	☑	☐
3. Expressing information clearly	☑	☐
4. Showing interest and enthusiasm	☑	☐
5. Having a career plan	☑	☐
6. Having confidence and poise	☑	☐
7. Emphasizing money	☐	☑
8. Being willing to start at the bottom	☑	☐
9. Rationalizing mistakes made	☐	☑
10. Being courteous	☑	☐
11. Demonstrating maturity	☑	☐
12. Citing instances of problems with previous employers	☐	☑
13. Being interested in the company and the job	☑	☐
14. Making good eye contact	☑	☐
15. Being able to laugh at self	☑	☐
16. Arriving exactly at interview time	☐	☑
17. Raising questions about the organization and the job	☑	☐
18. Showing appreciation by sending a thank-you card to the interviewer	☑	☐

Extra Effort

Undoubtedly, many of the items that reflect a positive influence may appear to be common sense. For the most part, that is correct. Yet you need to remember that though they may be positive, if you fail to do them properly, each of them can become a negative influence. For example, whereas good eye contact has a positive influence, a lack of good eye contact may have the opposite effect. Let's look at those statements that have a negative influence.

Statement 7 may have a negative influence if you overemphasize what the job pays and the benefits it provides. Clearly, this is important information to you, but there's a time and place to discuss it. If you appear to be interested only in the money, an interviewer is going to view this negatively.

Statement 9 may create a negative influence in that it may appear you are blaming others for a problem you yourself may have. If it appears you are making excuses to cover yourself, this can lead to an unfavorable impression. Interviewers like to see that you are realistic and that you understand your strengths and weaknesses.

Statement 12 may be viewed less than favorably because it may indicate you are hard to please or get along with. It's pretty much understood that you probably won't be leaving an employer whom you felt was the greatest employer on earth. By badmouthing a previous employer, you are indicating that you didn't learn anything from the experience or, worse yet, that you may not be a loyal employee. Remember, one day you'll probably be leaving this organization, too. Do you think they want to hire someone who they know may speak ill of them in the future?

Finally, statement 16 is unfavorable because it may indicate you did not plan well enough. Although you just barely made it, had you experienced a minor delay for some reason, you might have been late.

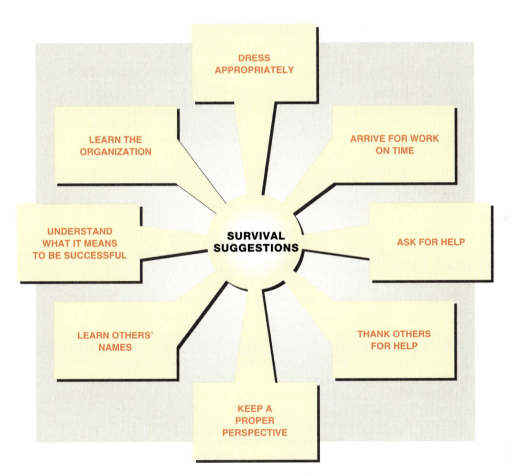

EXHIBIT 14-6
Survival Tips

can—such as the employee handbook, company newsletter, or departmental reports—that explains where the organization is heading, what it does, and why it is doing so. Talk to as many people as you can to get a better appreciation for what they do and how it fits in with the organization goals. Be open to and observant about what you are being told. Remember, you are getting another person's perception of activities and events. Although these perceptions may be accurate, don't make sweeping generalizations about what is being said. Even in an orientation overview, some individuals may allow politics or their own dissatisfaction to taint the picture they are describing. Your role is to listen attentively to what is being said, but do not put yourself in a position where you have to choose sides. The people you contact should be not only from your department, but from various other parts of the organization. You may find that in some organizations, these meetings are formally arranged as part of your orientation. In others, you may have to make these contacts yourself at times that won't interfere with your regularly scheduled work.

Arrive for work on time. The first couple of months of work in a new job set the stage for how you are going to be perceived by organizational members. One of the first things you'll be letting others know about you is whether you are dependable and punctual. This means showing up every day you are expected to be there and arriving for work on time. You shouldn't be asking for time off during these initial weeks. In fact, in many organizations, you are not eligible for paid vacation until you've been on the job for some time—perhaps six months. If your organization grants you personal leave days immediately after starting work, save these for use later on. As with vacation time, you may also have to wait to be eligible for sick leave. If you truly do get sick in the first six months, a personal leave day can be used for the time off. However, the idea here is to be present on the job.

Dress appropriately. More than likely, you came to the interview well-dressed. That's a tip that everyone usually follows. But what happens when you actually start the job? It depends. You should dress in a manner that is consistent with what others in your department wear. If your job is in an office, then proper attire may include dressier clothing. The issue here is not to go overboard in your attire or accessorizing so that you dramatically stand out. Rather, it is to be properly dressed according to organizational and departmental norms. Irrespective of what the dress code may be, one element must be evident: your hygiene. You should come to work clean and groomed. That means such things as bathing regularly and wearing clean clothes.

Know what it takes to be successful. As part of your new job, performance expectations should be set. Doing good work and making progress in your job are important. But it's also important to understand what else may be expected of an employee. Find out what the successful people have done. Likewise, attempt to understand what factors are attributed to those who have been less than successful. Model the behaviors of the successful people and make every effort to avoid the behaviors associated with those who have failed.

Learn the names of organizational members. Whether or not you meet with people in a formal orientation, one aspect that can leave a positive impression with others is to learn their names. Knowing others by name indicates a level of respect for them and shows that you've taken the time and made the effort to familiarize yourself with other organizational members.

Ask for help when you need it. You'll be learning a lot during the first few months on the job. That's normal. You'll have to become accustomed to new techniques and skills and many other facets of organizational life. You are expected at some point to master these, but you may not have to do that alone. When you need help, ask for it. As a new employee, you have a golden opportunity to ask almost any question and to get a response as well as some assistance. Don't view asking for help or saying you don't know something as a sign of weakness in the first few months on the job. In fact, if you didn't ask for some help, you could be viewed as a know-it-all. And that's not a perception you'd like to leave with others.

Remember to say "Thank you." When you do get help, in whatever capacity it is, don't forget one important aspect of human relations. Say "Thank you," and let those helping you know how much you appreciate what they are doing for you. Sometimes in the hustle and bustle of organizational life one may forget this act of kindness. Make saying "Thank you" a part of your everyday vocabulary.

Keep things in perspective. There's a holistic aspect of work that is sometimes overlooked. No matter what happens, life should go on. You need to develop a sense of humor and laugh about certain things—even yourself. While taking your work seriously, don't forget that you're dealing with others. Sometimes feelings and emotions must be taken into account. New employees, too, are often so gung-ho for a time that their co-workers do things to bring them into organizational reality. More than one rookie has had a practical joke played on him or her. For instance, you might come to your office and find that all of your furniture has been removed, or your pen tops have all been glued shut. Expect something to happen. But try not to overreact. Although it may be embarrassing to be the brunt of a good-natured practical joke, it's often done when your co-workers feel comfortable with you. It may also be the last test you'll encounter. In fact, the practical joke becomes a rite of passage.

When the Boss Is Demanding.   Not everyone has the pleasure of working for someone who is concerned enough about his or her employees to make the work environment warm and friendly. Although the trend in organizations is to develop supervisors who are more coaches and facilitators as opposed to taskmasters, demanding supervisors still exist. In fact, even someone who is a coach can be demanding. But the job must be done.

No matter how your supervisor interacts with you, you need to keep several things in mind. Your work needs to be done on time, and it must be quality work. Anything short of that target may temporarily derail your career track. Just because a supervisor appears to be professionally interested in you—and makes every effort to create a positive work environment—does not mean that work is less important. When push comes to shove, if your supervisor doesn't reach his or her goals (which is a function of what you and your co-workers accomplish), his or her tenure as a supervisor may be short-lived. Your good work, then, makes the supervisor look good.

Another item of importance is recognizing that you may work at some point in your career for a supervisor you don't respect. Whatever the reasons for the personality conflict, you cannot let it get the best of you. Granted, it's not an enjoyable time for you—and probably not for your supervisor, either. But locking heads or badmouthing your supervisor may be the wrong thing to do. More than likely, you'd lose.[20] That's because your supervisor plays a major role regarding whether you stay employed. Therefore, you must accept what you've been dealt for the time being and continue to perform well on the jobs you've been assigned. Smile, be courteous, and do your job. Remember, you're not trying to make a new friend. You're just trying to get your work done. In fact, keeping a cool head under the circumstances and performing well may end up being your ticket out of the situation—even with the recommendation of that demanding supervisor.

Preparing for the Future

Doing a good job and interacting well with others are vital components for promoting your career growth. But at some point, you'll need to expand your current

---

[20]See Mary Ann Emely, "Is It Ever OK To Go over My Boss's Head?" *Executive Female* (May–June 1995), pp. 64–65.

horizons in an effort to move closer to achieving your career goals. An important factor in reaching your goals is the realization that you, and you alone, are responsible for making it happen.[21] No matter what anyone tells you, organizations today cannot guarantee career success. In fact, as you read various parts of this text, you should recognize that an organization's commitment to its employees is short-term. Few, if any, jobs offer the security they did two decades ago. Accordingly, you must accept full responsibility for advancing your career. Although an organization may assist you in a number of ways—such as providing career counseling or skills training—*your* planning and effort may make career success a reality. Several suggestions can help you in this endeavor: accepting challenging jobs, continuing your education, and changing jobs when necessary.

Accepting Challenging Jobs.   When it comes to your career, taking the path of least resistance is probably ineffective. When your job becomes easy or routine, you stop growing personally and professionally. The goal is not to have one year of experience, over and over again. To help reduce this effect, you should continuously look for and accept challenging opportunities. When you face something new, you're taking some risk. But with that risk comes some payoff. Research has shown that those who take on challenging jobs often are usually more successful in their careers.[22]

A new challenge broadens your work horizons. It gives you new experiences and provides exposure to new and unique organizational activities. Each of these, plus the positive image you create for yourself in willingly accepting the challenges, makes you a more valuable employee.

Continuing Your Education.   When students graduate from college, there's a sense of accomplishment. A goal was set, and it was achieved. But graduating from college doesn't mark the end of your education. Rather, as strange as it may seem, it really signifies the beginning.

In a changing world, skill requirements and required competencies continuously change. To reach your career goals, you will need to continuously keep yourself up to date. This means continuing your education by working toward advanced degrees, attending training seminars to learn new skills, or retooling by starting your education over again in another field. In whatever form it takes, one statement can safely be made: Your education never stops. Therefore, never stop learning.

Changing Jobs When Necessary.   In addition to continuing your education and training to keep up to date and learn new skills, you should recognize that changing jobs periodically can help you foster a successful career.[23] The important element in a job change is that it offers you an expanded range of experiences and new challenges. Changes that you make may include accepting a promotion that gives you

---

[21]Hal Lancaster, "Managing Your Career: You, and Only You, Must Stay in Charge of Your Employability," *The Wall Street Journal* (November 15, 1994), p. B-1; and "Do It Yourself: Even Employers That Provide Career Help Urge Self-Reliance," *The Wall Street Journal* (March 3, 1992), p. A-1.

[22]A. Cohen, "Career Stage as a Moderator of the Relationship Between Organizational Commitment and Its Outcomes: A Meta Analysis," *Journal of Vocational Psychology* (March 1991), pp. 253–268; see also T. W. Lee, S. J. Ashford, J. P. Walsh, & R. T. Mowday, "Commitment Propensity, Organizational Commitment and Voluntary Turnover: A Longitudinal Study of Organizational Entry Processes," *Journal of Management* (January 1991), pp. 15–32.

[23]H. G. Kaufman, *Obsolescence and Professional Career Development* (New York: AMACOM, 1974); J. R. DeLuca, "Strategic Career Management in Non-Growing Volatile Business Environments," *Human Resource Planning* (January 1988), pp. 49–61; B. Nussbaum, "A Career Survival Kit," *Business Week* (October 7, 1991), pp. 98–104; and A. Gates, "Career Management: Hell No! I Won't Plateau," *Working Woman* (October 1990), pp. 100–105.

greater responsibility. It may involve making a lateral move that entails similar responsibility but new experiences. You might also find that in order to move your career forward, you may even have to take a step backward in a job you hold. These actions may happen in your current organization or in another one.

If you have planned your career and update that plan whenever necessary, you may find that the quickest path to achievement may not be a straight line. You may have to move around frequently—both in jobs and in areas in where you live—to put yourself in a better position to attain your career goal.

Maintaining a Healthy Work and Personal Life

*A*n old adage states that "all work and no play" makes for a dull individual. Although your professional development depends greatly on how well you excel in the organization, any discussion of a career needs to be tempered with some of the realities of life.

Work Hard, Play Hard

Undoubtedly, to achieve your career goal, you are going to work diligently. You'll plan accordingly, expend a lot of effort through the years, and, someday, possibly be in a position to say you've made it. But that single focus on making it can create problems for you; carrying something to an extreme may lead to a weakness. Hard work is no exception.

This is not to imply that you can sit back and wait for something to be given to you. That strategy won't work. It happens now and then, but it's not how the vast majority of us reach our goals. You cannot disregard that there's more to life than hard work. When you are working, you work as diligently as you can—and that may be for hours and days on end. But you've also got to give something back to yourself—a time to revitalize yourself. You need to make time for the relaxing part of life—whatever that may be for you. Get a hobby, play a sport, spend time with your family, join a health spa, volunteer in the community, and so on. You need to play and have some excitement in your life, too. In fact, finding the time to play may also help keep you well-rounded, enable you to make contacts and friendships outside work, and keep your level of stress down.

Keeping Life Properly Focused

When describing the American culture, researchers have noted that the American people are one of the most materialistic groups in the world. Many Americans often desire bigger, more extravagant things. They try to surround themselves with luxury and all the amenities that make life easier. To afford such a lifestyle, however, requires substantial cash and credit. Accordingly, these individuals may view a career somewhat differently. Instead of viewing their careers in terms of what they really would like to do, they see them in terms of the amount of income those jobs can produce. As a result, some work at jobs they absolutely loathe just to have a particular income level. That's not how things are supposed to be.

Life can offer you much more. It's there for your taking. Don't misinterpret what is being said. There's nothing wrong with working hard and making it. As long as you do so in a proper and ethical way, it's something of which you can be proud. But you need to recognize, too, that material possessions aren't the end-all in life. There's a humanity and **spirituality** (things coming from your heart) that also needs to be present. Your spiritual life can bring you a level of fulfillment that no material possession will ever be able to match.

> ➤ **spirituality**
> things coming from one's heart

Whenever most individuals hear the word *spirituality*, they naturally associate it with religion. Although spirituality is an important component of most religions, it's not a formalized religion that is the concern here. Rather, by spirituality, we are referring to **empathy** toward others. Empathy is caring and compassionate concerns you have for others. Spirituality reflects the quiet time you spend in deep thought focusing on your inner self. It means doing things that benefit other people—people to whom you may have no connection whatsoever. Spirituality means helping those in need, not only by giving money but also by freely donating your time and energy. It's getting involved in your community—giving something back to a world that has been good to you. Spirituality also means acting in an ethical manner—doing the right thing—even when there's pressure to do otherwise. That may involve not taking advantage of someone else's misfortune or standing up for someone who has been wronged—especially when it's not popular to take that stand. It's finding ways of easing an individual's pain and letting him or her know you are available to help. Spirituality also focuses on family and personal life values and keeping them in proper perspective to work. Spirituality is a way of life—that inner sanctum of respecting yourself and your fellow human beings.

Choosing the Healthy Life

A healthy life does for the body what training and education do for the mind and spirituality for the soul. Much has been reported over the years about the American

**VALUE JUDGMENT:
Will Only the Strong Survive?**

In the animal kingdom, there's a saying that only the strong survive. In the wild, the animal that is the quickest or the strongest has the advantage at being toward the top of the food chain. Being more powerful or the swiftest, then, is handsomely rewarded. But what about humans? Is survival in our world based on being the strongest?

Many cases can be built to support this premise. Military strength has been shown to help a nation defend itself or avert invasions by an opposing country. Professional sports, as well as the entertainment industry, reinforce that being very competitive has its advantages. Those who want it more, that have the desire to climb to the top, frequently succeed. And this success is often achieved at the expense of someone else's mistakes. For instance, take a football running back who fumbles deep in his own end of the field. As a result of his misfortune, the opponent has now received great field position. This is not a result of the players' great ability to move the ball down field. Rather, it's because they capitalized on an opponent's mistake.

Obviously, in professional sports, or even military matters, there's a good reason behind this behavior. It's how the game is played. But does that imply that in organizations where there is competition for positions of responsibility or for generating a good bottom line that one has to be overly competitive? Can organizational members achieve more as a coordinated group of individuals, as opposed to every person being out for himself or herself? Will those who genuinely help others succeed be overrun by others who take advantage of their kindness? Does acting in an ethical and compassionate manner have a place in organizations today? Or is such behavior present primarily when everything else is in place—such as the bottom line being met? What's your opinion on the applicability of compassion in organizations today?

4. Which one of the following would be the most valid reason for arriving approximately thirty minutes early for an interview?

    a. It reveals your respect for the interviewer's time and would make you available if the interviewer wants to start the interview earlier than scheduled.

    b. It provides an opportunity for you to practice prepared responses to frequently asked interview questions with actual organizational members.

    c. It reveals that you have good time management skills and prepare for the unexpected.

    d. It gives you the opportunity to observe the atmosphere of the organization.

5. Which one of the following was not identified as a suggestion for surviving the first few months on a new job?

    a. accepting challenging assignments

    b. learning everything you can about the organization

    c. dressing appropriately

    d. saying "Thank you" to those who help you

6. Which one of the following would best reflect the existence of spirituality in your career?

    a. doing things that not only benefit you, but that also benefit someone else

    b. acting ethically in your professional and personal life

    c. attending religious services regularly

    d. all of the above

---

population getting flabbier and experiencing more diet-related medical problems—such as high blood pressure, heart disease, diabetes, and arthritis.[24] As a result, the Departments of Agriculture and Health and Human Services have for the first time strongly advocated an exercise regime, in addition to proper nutrition, in their *Dietary Guidelines for Americans.*[25] What does that mean for you? The latest recommendations on nutrition are that you need to eat a variety of foods that are low in fat and high in grains. (See Exhibit 14-7.) Furthermore, fatty foods (such as most fast foods) should be eaten in moderation, with no more than 30 percent of your daily total caloric intake coming from fat. Instead of ingesting high levels of fat, you should be eating more fruits, vegetables, and grain products. But even then, the rule of thumb is still eating them in moderate amounts.

One of the problems with diets that you may encounter in your busy schedule is having the time to eat properly. Because you may constantly be on the go, eating foods that are more convenient to prepare or dining out could become the norm. Unfortunately, when you do, you often eat foods that are not the most nutritious for you. Rather, they are often the ones that contain the most fat. That's not to say that it's impossible to eat nutritious fast foods. It simply means that it takes a concerted effort to focus primarily on foods that are better and healthier for you.

In addition to a proper diet, you need to exercise. A regular exercise program has been shown to help you maintain a proper weight, while preventing many of the medical problems being overweight may cause. That's because exercise burns the extra calories you have stored in your body and helps turn flab into muscle mass. Exercise has also been shown to reduce cholesterol levels in your blood—the bad cholesterol that leads to heart disease. So how frequently and for how long do you need to exercise? Answers

---

[24]See, for example, Michele Meyer, "The Smart Diet," *Working Woman* (June 1995), pp. 59–62; and David Stipp, "New Weapons in the War on Fat," *Fortune* (December 11, 1995), pp. 164–174.

[25]Colleen Peirre, "New Dietary Guidelines Add Exercise," *The Baltimore Sun* (January 23, 1996), p. 5E.

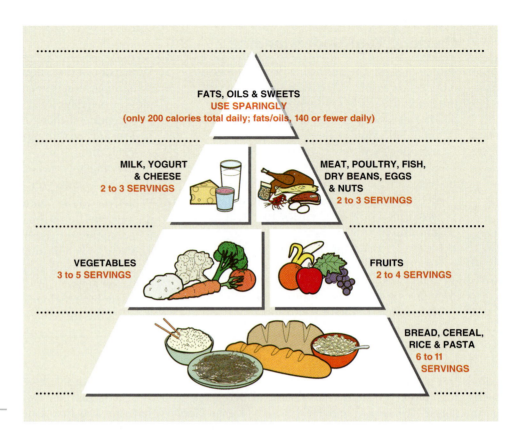

EXHIBIT 14-7
Nutrition Guidelines

to those questions have evolved through the years. Many have subscribed to the suggestion that you need at least twenty minutes of aerobic exercise (increasing your heart rate) three times a week. Guidelines offered early in 1996 suggest that more is needed. That is, you should make an effort to spend at least thirty minutes a day in some form of moderate exercise. (See Exhibit 14-8.)

Like diet, exercise is another element that impinges on your time. Whether you can exercise three days a week or dedicate yourself to a seven-day exercise regime may not be the issue; what is, however, is that you are getting some sort of exercise. Sitting behind a desk and moving only your pencil isn't enough. Midlife spread is something that nature nastily does to all of us. Proper exercise and diet, however, can slow down the aging process. So eat well and get some exercise. You'll feel better about yourself. You'll also probably feel better about those around you.

Realize Life Is Not a Fair Game

Why do some people always appear to have good luck? Why does it appear that everything they do is successful? Why are they always at the right place at the right time?

Life is not always fair. Some people are dealt a hand that makes you wonder how such things can happen. An infant can be born with a serious birth defect or stricken with an incurable form of cancer. An athletic actor can sustain a terrible neck injury that leaves him paralyzed from the neck down. A nine-year-old girl can be swept off the street while riding a bike, only to be found days later—the victim of an horrendous crime. Employees are laid off after years of productive service to an organization with little or no hope of ever reviving their careers. And this list can go on.

EXHIBIT 14-8

Moderate Exercise Possibilities (30-Minute Workouts)

Undoubtedly, being laid off is no comparison to the loss of life or a serious medical condition. You must realize, however, that there are no guarantees in life—either your personal or professional one. Although many of you may attain great things, others may never reach their career goals, or sadly, may have to deal with one of life's more challenging events. No one knows whom, where, or when these things may strike. Therefore, you cannot adequately prepare for an unexpected event. What you can do, however, is accept that these events do occur.[26] If you ever do experience misfortune in your life, you will have to deal with it. Ironically, there may be some truth to the saying that you are only given what you can endure. You'll need to draw on all of your strength and skills—human relations included—to help you make the best of any ordeal. Some sadness or depression is normal. But when that depression starts getting the best of you—to the point where you start thinking about injuring yourself—you need help. Remember, you don't have to deal with whatever is bothering you by yourself. Others care for you and are available to assist you however they can. Don't ever forget that family, friends, or your spirituality may provide that calming shoulder to lean on.

---

[26]For an interesting discussion of career setbacks, see Patricia Sellers, "So You Fail. Now Bounce Back," *Fortune* (May 1, 1995), pp. 48–66.

Some Concluding Remarks

*C*ongratulations. You have successfully finished this book. We hope you have found it useful in providing information and a foundation for building an understanding about your personal and professional life. You've been exposed to a lot of things. Recognize that each of these takes time for you to fully understand and for you to master. But treat these lessons as you would any worthwhile learning effort. That means you get out of it what you put in. In the years ahead, you'll be interacting with many people from all walks of life. Your success will depend, in part, on the extent of your human relations skills. Build on what you've learned. Practice enhancing your human relations skills whenever possible. But most important, remember some of the key aspects we've discussed. Be positive and create a positive image for others to see. Deal with others ethically and be sincere in what you do. Give them the respect and dignity they deserve. Dedicate yourself to working hard, but also find the time to relax. And realize that no matter how far you go in life, the greatest success you may ever achieve is having an inner peace, shared with family and friends—people you love and who love you.

Good luck and may all of your human interactions be positive.

SUMMARY

This summary corresponds to the Learning Outcomes found on page 332.

1. A career is the pattern of work-related experiences individuals have over the course of their lifetime. It includes formal job work, schoolwork, homemaking, and volunteer work.

2. Career planning is a process involving the identification of major work-related and personal goals one wants to achieve.

3. The five stages of careers include exploration, establishment, midcareer, late career, and decline. During the exploration stage, individuals make decisions about potential careers, examining what they like or don't like. In the establishment stage, individuals begin the search for work, including getting that first job. The midcareer stage involves continuous improvement in performance, leveling off in performance, or the beginning of a decline in performance. The late career is a period in which individuals are no longer expected to outdo levels of performance from previous years; however, they are expected to share their knowledge with less experienced employees. The final career stage, decline, marks a time for retirement.

4. A résumé is considered a sales tool in that it is usually the only piece of information a potential employer has about a candidate. The résumé should provide accurate information that supports an individual's employment candidacy, highlighting strengths that the individual would bring to the job.

5. Six conclusions regarding interviews are as follows: Interviewers hold a stereotype of what represents a good applicant; interviewers tend to favor applicants who share their attitude; the order in which applicants are interviewed influences an evaluation; negative information is given unduly high weight; decisions about the candidate are made in the first four or five minutes of the interview; and interviewers tend to forget much of the interview's content within minutes of its conclusion.

6. Impression management refers to projecting an image that will result in achieving a favorable outcome. Impression management, then, involves doing those things that will favorably impress an evaluator.

7. Suggestions for excelling in an interview include the following: Gather as much information as possible about the organization; get a good night's rest before the interview; eat a good breakfast to give you energy for the interview day; dress appropriately for the interview; arrive for the interview about thirty minutes ahead of schedule; greet the interviewer with a firm handshake; prepare responses for the most frequently asked interview questions; and thank the interviewer for his or her time.

8. Suggestions for helping a new employee survive the first few months on the job include learning everything about the organization you can, arriving for work on time, dressing appropriately for work, understanding what it means to be successful, learning the names of organizational members, asking for help when it is needed, thanking others for their help, and keeping work-related activities in proper perspective.

9. Three useful methods for making career success a reality are accepting challenging jobs (to broaden your work experiences), continuing your education (keeping up to date with skill and technology changes), and changing jobs when necessary (providing an expanded range of experiences and new challenges).

10. Spirituality can play a role in organizational life by focusing on caring and compassion for other people and doing things in an unselfish manner. This may involve good interactions with others, giving back to the community in which you work, and acting ethically.

REVIEWING YOUR UNDERSTANDING

1. What is meant by the term *career?*

2. Describe what you can do to help in your career planning.

3. "Career stages and a person's age evolve together." Do you agree or disagree? Explain.

4. Explain why having an effective résumé is critical for gaining entry into an organization.

5. What are the major problems associated with interviews? What can you do to overcome these potential obstacles?

6. "Doing something that one would normally not do to create a favorable impression in an interview is acting unethically." Do you agree or disagree with this statement? Discuss.

7. What recommendations would you make to a colleague who has asked you how best to succeed in an interview?

8. Explain what you can do to help make your career goals a reality.

9. "Being spiritual and being effective in business today are incompatible. Surviving in a dog-eat-dog world requires one to be ruthless and to capitalize on the misfortunes of others." Do you agree or disagree with this statement? Explain your position.

10. How are proper diet and physical fitness related to career success?

ANSWERS TO CHECKING YOUR UNDERSTANDING

1. b   2. c   3. c   4. d   5. a   6. b

LEARNING TOGETHER

1. Invite a guest speaker from the state employment office, your campus placement office, or a professional job service to visit your class. The day before the speaker comes to class, have your fellow students compile a list of questions to ask the speaker based on your reading of this chapter.

2. In groups of three, role-play an interview. The third member of the team should be the evaluator, taking notes of "dos and don'ts" that could help all of you improve the interviewing process. After doing two or three role plays, ask another teacher or administrator in your school (or a businessperson) to conduct mock interviews in your class. Discuss the "do's and don'ts" of the role plays that were conducted. Are you ready for an interview? If not, do more role-playing.

Career Issues and You

Several of your friends have decided that it is necessary to spend some time planning their careers if they are going to be successful. They spend time thinking about and discussing their futures and what goals they think they would like to pursue. They do a lot of research on several careers, but still are having difficulty deciding on the direction they should take to have a successful career.

Then one of your friends suggests that the self-assessment in your *Human Relations: Personal and Professional Development* book would be a good place to start. Together you decide to discuss the dimensions of life success: achievement of status and wealth, contribution to society, good family relationships, personal fulfillment, and security. Once you score your assessment, you find the assessment to be quite revealing. You can hardly wait to see how your friends scored.

When your friends come together again to discuss the assessment each had done, you find that you are able to expand your knowledge and understanding of the six dimensions. You suggest continuing your discussions beginning with a focus on the career stages of exploration, establishment, midcareer, late career, and decline. Several others agree, and off you go to do some research.

The discussions of career stages lead to discussions on how to make a career decision, how to get your foot in the door of a potential employer, preparing a résumé and developing a portfolio of your work, writing cover letters, and practicing interviewing techniques. You and your friends feel you are now well-prepared for a good job search. Off each of you goes to find a job.

You are pleased to report to your friends that you have just been hired. You and your friends are excited about your job, but you are a bit apprehensive about your new job even though you have been preparing for this for a very long time. Your friends suggest that you continue meeting to discuss their job searches and to help in adjusting to work. You are finding this support mechanism very helpful in surviving the first few months of your job. You also have a lot of things you can pass on to others about job survival—arriving on time for work, learning about the organization, dressing appropriately, understanding how to be successful, learning others' names, keeping a proper perspective, and asking and thanking others for help. You have arrived!

Questions

1. Have you really arrived? What will you do if you have co-workers with whom it is impossible to work? What will you do if your boss is demanding? What will you do if the work environment is boring and you don't feel challenged?

2. Identify some of the things you can do to prepare for the future.

3. In groups of three or four, discuss some of the ways you can maintain a healthy work and personal life.

4. What will you do if you get laid off? Discuss some contingency plans that would be good to have in case the job doesn't work out.

5. Make a plan of how you intend to reach your career goals. When should you start to implement your plan?

GLOSSARY

Accommodating (conflict handling technique) An attempt to maintain harmonious relationships by putting another's needs and concerns above one's own.

Active listening Having empathy with the sender—that is, placing oneself in the sender's position while reserving judgment on the message's content and carefully listening to what is being said.

Adhocracy An organizational structure that is characterized as low in complexity, low in formalization, and decentralized.

Affiliation A connection with an organization.

Affirmative action programs Programs that ensure that an organization's decisions and practices enhance the employment, upgrading, and retention of members from protected groups, such as minorities and females.

Alcoholic An individual for whom alcohol has become a crutch, and for whom overindulgence reduces that person's ability to function effectively.

Apathy A condition that exists when a person has little or no drive, or simply doesn't care.

Application form A form that puts all job application information into a consistent format for reviewers, and gives the organization an opportunity to obtain only the information they need to make a correct decision.

Assumed similarity The "like me" effect; a perception of others influenced more by an individual's own characteristics than by those of the person observed.

Attitudes Statements that reflect values—either favorable or unfavorable—concerning objects, people, or events.

Authoritarianism A belief that there should be differences in status among people in organizations.

Authority The rights inherent in a job to give orders and expect the orders to be obeyed.

Authorization cards Cards signed by employees indicating that they wish a particular union to be considered as their representative in dealing with the employer, and that they prefer that an election be held.

Autocratic leader Someone who can best be described as a taskmaster. This individual leaves no doubt as to who is in charge and who has the authority and the power in the group. He or she makes all decisions affecting the group and tells others what to do.

Autonomy The freedom and independence an individual has in scheduling work and in determining procedures to be used in carrying it out.

Avoiding (conflict handling technique) Withdrawing from or suppressing a conflict.

Baby boomers (born between 1946 and 1964) This group is the largest in the workforce. They are regarded as career climbers—at the right place at the right time. Mature workers view them as unrealistic and workaholics.

Baby busters (born 1965 and after) Workers who are viewed as being less committed, less rule bound, selfish, unwilling to play by the rules, and more involved in their own gratification. They are also seen as having an intolerance of baby-boomers and their attitudes. *See also* Baby boomers.

Background investigations Verification of applicant background and experience—such as dates of employment, job titles, past salaries, or reasons for leaving the job.

Behavioral stress Symptoms of this type of stress include decreased productivity, increased absenteeism and turnover, and increased smoking and alcohol consumption.

Blind spots Things others know about an individual but that the individual does not know about him- or herself.

Body language Gestures, facial configurations, and other movements of the body.

Bona fide occupational qualification (BFOQ) A job qualification accepted by law that may appear to be discriminatory.

Brainstorming A technique for overcoming conformity pressures that may keep a group from developing creative alternatives.

Bulletin board Centrally located boards that contain postings on job openings, upcoming company-sponsored events, new policies, and so on.

Bureaucracy An organizational structure that breaks down jobs into simple, routine, and well-defined tasks.

Burnout Chronic emotional distress.

Calm waters A metaphor illustrated by Kurt Lewin's three-step description of the change process. According to Lewin, successful change requires unfreezing a current activity, changing to something new, and refreezing the new change to make it permanent.

Career The patterns of work-related experiences that span the course of a person's life. Any work, paid or unpaid, pursued over an extended period of time.

Career planning A process involving the identification of major work-related and personal goals that one hopes to achieve.

Centralization Concentration of power or authority in a central organization or unit.

Certification election A process in which a union must win a majority of eligible voting workers who vote for the union before it can be certified.

Change To alter; transform; convert.

Change agents People who act as catalysts and assume the responsibility for influencing the change process.

Channel A medium through which a message travels.

Character How one defines oneself and the way one shows this to others through his or her behavior.

Charisma Magnetism to an individual that inspires followers to reach goals that are perceived as difficult or unpopular.

Charismatic leaders Individuals with compelling vision or a sense of purpose; those with an ability to communicate that vision in clear terms that their followers can easily and readily understand; a demonstrated consistency and focus in the pursuit of that vision; and an understanding of their own strengths.

Code of ethics A formal document that states an organization's primary values and the ethical rules it expects employees to follow.

Coercive power Power based on the use of fear.

Collaboration All parties in conflict seek to satisfy their collective interests. This is the ultimate win–win situation.

Collective bargaining agreement An agreement that defines such things as wages, work hours, criteria for promotions and layoffs, training eligibility, and disciplinary practices.

Collectivism A social framework in which individuals expect others in groups of which they are a part to look after them and protect them when they are in trouble.

Common knowledge Information that is known by both parties in two-way communication.

Communication The transference and understanding of meaning.

Communication differences Disagreements arising from semantic difficulties, misunderstandings, or noise in the communication channels.

Communication process Stages of communication that include the sender, the message, encoding, the channel, decoding, the receiver, and feedback.

Company-wide meetings Meetings at which all organizational members get the same information at the same time.

Complexity The number of differences that exist in an organization.

Compromise A situation in which two or more individuals give up something of value in order to achieve a common goal or to arrive at a decision.

Conceptual skills The mental ability to coordinate a variety of interests and activities. The ability to think in the abstract, analyze information, and make connections between data.

Conflict The perceived incompatible differences that result in some form of interference or opposition.

Conformity pressures Pressures felt by individuals who have a desire to be accepted by a group to which they belong or wish to join.

Confrontational relationship Actions of company officials and the union represented by the "we-they" syndrome that often leads to lengthy stand-offs.

Consensus building An attempt to develop a solution that is acceptable to most members of a group.

Consultative participative leadership A leadership role in which the leader uses the input of followers as an information-seeking exercise.

Contingent workforce Individuals who "sell" their services to an organization, including those who are hired for short periods of time to perform specific tasks which often require special job skills, and who are employed when an organization is experiencing significant deviations in its workflow. When the special needs are fulfilled, these workers are let go. They often do not receive the employee benefits that are provided to core workers.

Cooperative relationship   A relationship in which company officials actively seek input from union members about a variety of issues at work.

Cooperativeness   The degree to which one attempts to ease conflict by satisfying the other person's concerns.

Core employees   Workers who hold full-time jobs in organizations and provide some essential job tasks that require commitment and permanence in the organization. These individuals receive all benefits that are given to full-time employees.

Creativity   The ability to combine ideas in a unique way to make unusual associations between them.

Critical incidents   A performance appraisal method that focuses a supervisor's attention on critical or key job behaviors that separate effective from ineffective job performance.

Cultural environment   A country's legal, political, economic, and cultural systems.

Cultural shock   A sensation of confusion and frustration that occurs when we are first exposed to a different culture.

Decline stage   A stage in which retirement-age individuals are forced to step out of the limelight and to relinquish a major component of their identity to allow the next generation of workers to take over power and control of an organization.

Decoding   Translation of the sender's message.

Democratic participative leadership   A participative leader may allow followers to have a say in what is decided.

Devil's advocate   A person who purposely presents arguments that run counter to those proposed by other individuals in a group. This is the role of the critic, even to the point of arguing against positions with which one may actually agree.

Discipline   Actions taken by a supervisor to enforce the organization's standards and regulations.

Dismissal   Removal from one's job; firing.

Downsizing   Reshaping or restructuring of an organization by reducing the number of workers employed. Primary goals of downsizing include greater efficiency and reduced costs.

Downward communications   Any information delivered by any means to an individual from anyone who has a higher position in the organization.

Dress codes   Norms developed to dictate the kind of clothing that should be worn to work.

Drive   The desire to exert a high level of effort given to a task.

Driving force   A method that can be used by a supervisor to direct an employee's behavior away from some current activity.

Dysfunctional tension   Tension that creates a sense of hopelessness due to repeated failure to fulfill a need.

Effort   A measure of the intensity with which one approaches a task; outward behavior designed to achieve a personal goal.

Electronic media   Any technological means of enhancing communications.

Electronic meeting   A blend of the nominal group technique with computer technology, this technique allows for the networking of up to 50 people per session, in which issues are presented and group members are required to type their responses on computer screens.

Emotion barrier   The interpretation of a message in various ways depending on the emotional state of the receiver.

Empathy   Caring and compassionate concern for others.

Employee Assistance Programs (EAPs)   Programs designed to help employees overcome their personal problems and to return them to the job as soon as possible.

Employee counseling   A process designed to help employees overcome performance-related problems.

Employee development   A process designed to help employees grow in skills and knowledge about their job and the jobs of others in their unit and organization.

Employee handbook   A tool that serves both employees and employers, providing important information regarding what the company is about, its history, and employee benefits.

Employee referral   A recommendation by an employee of someone who can handle a job that is currently open.

Employment at will   An organizational policy under which an employee can be fired for a good reason, a bad reason, or no reason at all.

Encoding Conversion of a message into symbolic form.

Establishment A period that begins with the search for work and includes getting one's first job, being accepted by peers, learning the job, and gaining the first tangible evidence of success or failure in the real world.

Esteem needs Internal esteem needs include self-respect, autonomy, and achievement; external esteem include status, recognition, and attention.

Ethics The rules or principles that define right and wrong conduct.

Ethnocentric view A view that the values, morals, customs, and laws of one's culture are better than those of any other culture.

Expectancy theory A belief that an individual will act in the way his or her supervisor wants if that person believes he or she will be rewarded.

Expert power Power based on an individual's expertise, special skill, or knowledge.

Exploration An individual's search for information from others about his or her career prior to entering the workforce on a paid basis.

Extinction Elimination of a behavior due to withheld negative or positive reinforcement.

Fact Anything that is actual or true.

Feedback Information given back to you; the response received by asking the receiver to restate a message in his or her own words. Direct and clear information about one's performance.

Filtering The deliberate manipulation of information to make it appear more favorable to the receiver.

Flextime A system whereby one agrees to work or is required to work a specific number of hours per week but is free to vary the hours of work, often within certain limits.

Forcing (conflict handling technique) An attempt to satisfy one's own needs at the expense of another party.

Formal groups Groups assigned by supervisors in which specific tasks must be accomplished.

Formalization The rules, regulations, and policies that exist to guide behavior.

Fox An analytical person who studies everything and values logic, process, and truth.

Free-rein leader Someone who gives followers total autonomy to make the decisions that will affect them. After establishing overall objectives and general guidelines, followers are free to establish their own plans for achieving their goals.

Friendship group A group formed on the basis of something that each individual member has in common.

Function group A group formed through the formal authority relationships that exist in an organization.

Functional tension "Hype" that gives us the energy to perform. For example, getting "pumped up" by stepping long and hard—even pulling an "all nighter."

Gantt chart A bar chart used by managers as a scheduling device for planning and controlling work. It shows the relationship between work planned and completed on one axis and time elapsed on the other.

Global village A view that the world and organizations in it are no longer constrained by national borders and that, to be effective in business, people must adapt to cultures, systems, and techniques that are different from their own.

Grapevine An unofficial, unauthorized, and unsupported way that communications take place in an organization. Also referred to as "the rumor mill," the grapevine frequently represents a fast and sometimes accurate source of information.

Graphic rating scale A set of performance factors such as quantity and quality of work, job knowledge, cooperation, loyalty, attendance, honesty, and initiative.

Grievance procedure An internal dispute procedure spelled out in a labor contract.

Group Two or more who come together to achieve certain objectives.

Group cohesiveness The degree to which group members are attracted to one another and share group goals.

Group order ranking A performance appraisal classification system in which all employees in a unit are evaluated as a whole. Supervisors must rank employees in order from highest to lowest.

Groupthink A tendency to withhold unpopular views in order to give the appearance of agreement to those in charge.

Halo effect A general impression about an individual based on a single characteristic such as intelligence, sociability, or appearance.

Hawthorne Studies Studies that attempted to examine the effect of work factors such as lighting and ventilation levels, individual pay plans versus group wage plans, and length of workday and workweek.

Hidden potential Anything an individual may be capable of accomplishing but hasn't yet become aware of.

Hierarchy of needs A hierarchy that consists of five independent needs, including physiological needs, safety needs, social needs, esteem needs, and self-actualization needs. In this theory of motivation, each lower level need must be substantially satisfied before one moves up to the next need.

Horizontal structures An employee grouping with a flat structure in which work is performed in teams that represent employees from across the organization or who possess a variety of skills.

Hostile environment An environment in which the unwelcome actions of another create an abusive work setting for an individual. (*See also* Sexual harassment.)

Human relations The study of the interactions between people.

Human relations movement A twentieth-century organizational movement characterized by the belief that satisfied workers will be productive workers.

Human relations skills The ability to work with, understand, and motivate others.

Human relations view of conflict A view that conflict is a natural and inevitable outcome in any organization. Accordingly, conflict need not be harmful but, rather, has the potential to be a positive force in contributing to an organization's performance.

Hygiene factors Factors that create job dissatisfaction.

Impression management An attempt to project an image that will result in achieving a favorable outcome.

Incubation A waiting period for the "hatching" of an idea; during this time one collects massive data that is stored, retrieved, studied, reshaped, and finally molded into something new.

Individual ranking A ranking method that requires a supervisor to list employees in order from highest to lowest.

Individualism A social framework in which individuals look after their own interests and those of their immediate family.

Industrial Revolution An eighteenth-century period that saw the advent of machine power, mass production, and expansion of the railroads. Workers became "cogs" in the wheels of production and faced difficult work conditions.

Inference A conclusion drawn without fact, but based on probabilities.

Informal groups Groups formed to fulfill a need for individuals to be social.

Innovation The process of turning a creative idea into a useful product, service, or way of doing things.

Inspiration The moment when all prior efforts successfully come together suddenly, like a flash of light, and the answer suddenly becomes clear.

Interest group Individuals who band together to promote their own interests.

Intergroup development An attempt to achieve the same results among different work groups by changing attitudes, stereotypes, and perceptions that a group may have for another group. In doing so, better coordination among groups can be achieved.

Internal dispute (complaint) procedure A way for employees to question actions that have occurred in the organization, and to seek the organization's assistance in correcting the problem.

Interpersonal communications Interaction that exists between two or more people in which the parties are treated as individuals rather than objects.

Interpersonal style The way in which an individual interacts with and communicates with others.

Interview A face-to-face meeting for the evaluation or questioning of a job applicant.

Job analysis A method that defines the jobs that exist within the organization and the employee behaviors necessary to perform those jobs successfully.

Job characteristics model A model represented by five core characteristics or dimensions including skill variety, task identity, task significance, autonomy, and feedback.

Job description A written statement of what employees do, how they do it, and why they do it.

Job enrichment The assumption of some of the tasks typically performed by a supervisor.

Job rotation Rotation of individuals to different jobs. Job rotation allows employees to diversify their activities and offsets the occurrence of boredom.

Job specification A written statement of the minimum acceptable qualifications that an employee must possess to perform a given job successfully.

Johari Window A model designed to explain communications relationships and interactions with others. It is based on the premise that when two individuals interact, certain factors must be taken into account.

Karoshi Sudden heart attacks caused by overwork.

Language barrier The interpretation of words and the language used according to different meanings given to them by different people. Receivers use their definition of the words communicated.

Late career A time when one is allowed the luxury to relax and enjoy playing the part of the elder statesperson. Individuals in late career are no longer expected to outdo their levels of performance from previous years. Their value to the organization lies heavily in their judgment and experiences, and in the ability to share with and teach others based on the knowledge they have gained.

Lateral communications Communications among peers.

Leadership The ability to influence others to act in a particular way. A leader inspires followers to accept challenges and achieve goals that may be viewed as difficult.

Leadership traits Qualities such as intelligence, charm, decisiveness, enthusiasm, strength, bravery, integrity, and self-confidence that separate leaders from nonleaders.

Learning The process of bringing about relatively permanent change through experiences.

Legitimate power Power that is based on an individual's position in an organization—a formal title.

Line authority Authority that entitles a supervisor to direct an individual's work.

Lions Individuals who like to control things.

Locus of control The location or center of control or authority.

Loyalty norms Standards for demonstrating loyalty toward one's organization or supervisors.

Machiavellianism A characteristic named after Niccolo Machiavelli, who taught how to gain control and manipulate others. An individual high in Machiavellianism is practical, maintains emotional distance from others, and believes that ends can justify means. The view "If it works, use it" is consistent with those who have high Mach.

Management rights An employer's opportunity and right to run his or her business as effectively and efficiently as possible.

Matrix structure An organizational structure that groups employees by the jobs they do and by the products they produce.

Mature workers Workers born shortly after the Great Depression, who are considered security oriented and who are viewed as having a committed work ethic.

Medical examination Examination by a doctor that one must pass before being hired.

Mentor Typically a more experienced and more senior member of the organization who acts as an individual's support system within the organization.

Message A physical product conveyed by a sender, who encodes and passes the message by means of a channel. A message can take the form of speech, writing, gestures, facial expressions, and so on.

Midcareer A period when performance may improve, decline, or level off. Those who continue to advance get more responsibility and greater rewards. Others may reassess what they want out of a career, and possibly make some changes, in either career choice or personal goals.

Morale A measure of how happy an individual is with the way things are going on the job.

Motivation One's willingness to exert effort to achieve organizational goals that also lead to satisfying individual needs. Three main components of motivation are effort, organizational goals, and needs. A motivated person exerts a greater effort to perform a task than someone who is not motivated.

Motivation-hygiene theory A belief that one's attitude toward work can determine one's success or failure.

Motivators Factors that increase job satisfaction.

Multinational corporations (MNCs) Corporations that maintain significant operations in two or more countries simultaneously, but are based in one home country.

Multiperson comparisons Comparison of an individual's behavior to the behaviors of one or more others.

Myers-Briggs Type Indicator (MBTI) A method of identifying personalities that uses four dimensions of personality to identify 16 different personality types.

Need for achievement The drive to excel, to succeed in relation to a set of standards, to strive to succeed.

Need for affiliation (nAff) The desire for friendly and close interpersonal relationships.

Need for power (nPow) The need to make others behave in a way that they would not have behaved otherwise.

Negative reinforcements Unpleasant responses to an individual's actions or behaviors that discourage repetition of such behaviors.

Networking skills Skills that provide one with the ability to socialize and interact with outsiders—those not associated with one's unit.

Newsletter A method of providing employees with information about organizational activities and anything else of interest.

Noise Disturbances that interfere with the transmission of a message.

Nominal group A technique that restricts discussion among group members, who are required to operate independently.

Nonverbal communication Communication that is neither spoken nor written; the body language or intonation that sends the receiver a message. If verbal and nonverbal cues are not aligned, communication may be distorted.

Norms Acceptable standards that are shared by a group's members.

Open door policy A policy of trust and respect for all organization members, in which one is permitted to participate in discussions regarding work activities and can talk with his or her supervisor about anything when he or she is available.

Operant conditioning Learning as a behavioral change that is brought about by a function of its consequences.

Organization A planned grouping of people to accomplish a specific purpose or goal.

Organization design Implementation of various degrees of complexity, formalization, and centralization to form an organization's structure.

Organization development (OD) An organizational activity designed to facilitate long-term organizational-wide changes.

Organization structure An organization's framework.

Organizational behavior (OB) A field of study concerned specifically with the actions of people at work.

Organizational chart A chart that shows reporting structure, communication flows, and who's in charge.

Organizational communications Programs designed to keep one current regarding what is happening in an organization, as well as ensuring that one is knowledgeable of the applicable policies and procedures.

Organizational culture The values, symbols, rituals, myths, and work practices that are shared by organizational members.

Organizational socialization A process offered by many organizations to help individuals adapt to its values.

Organizational structure An organization's framework.

Organizational surveys Surveys that present a set of statements or questions written to solicit specific information about an individual's job, coworkers, supervisor, and so on.

Orientation An organizational procedure that introduces new employees to an organization's objectives, history, philosophy, procedures, and rules.

Paired comparison Each employee is compared to every other employee in the unit and is rated as either the more productive or less productive employee of the pair.

Pareto's Law of Optimality A law that states that in most things an individual does, 20 percent of the items account for 80 percent of the results.

Parochialism A situation in which individuals see things through their own eyes and from their own perspective.

Participative leadership style A leadership style in which input from followers is actively sought for many of the activities in the organization.

People skills Skills that help to coach, facilitate, and support others.

People-centered leader Someone who emphasizes interpersonal relations with those they lead. This leader takes a personal interest in the needs of his or her followers and interactions are characterized as trusting, friendly, and supportive.

Perception A process by which an individual organizes and interprets sensory impressions to give meaning to his or her environment.

Performance appraisal A process organizations use to make objective decisions about individuals as employees.

Personality traits The combination of various psychological traits used to classify a person. Terms used to describe people in terms of personality traits include quiet, passive, loud, aggressive, ambitious, extroverted, introverted, loyal, tense, sociable, and so on.

Physical fitness A regular exercise program.

Physiological needs Food, drink, shelter, sexual satisfaction, and other bodily requirements.

Physiological symptoms of stress Symptoms of stress that relate to internal medical changes, including increased heart and breathing rates, higher blood pressure, headaches, backaches, and stomachaches. At the extreme, they can lead to heart attacks and strokes.

Politics Attempts to influence the advantages and disadvantages of a situation.

Positive attitude A frame of mind that reflects seeing good in oneself, in others, and in what one does.

Positive reinforcements Positive reactions/responses to our actions.

Power The ability to influence others to do the things one would like to have them do.

Power distance The acceptance by society of the fact that power in institutions and organizations is distributed unequally.

Prestige The distinguished grading, position, or ranking of a group; the stature derived from belonging to a particular group.

Principles of management Fundamental or universal truths of management.

Procrastination Putting off for tomorrow things that should be done today.

Psychological symptoms of stress Symptoms include tension, anxiety, irritability, boredom, and procrastination. When these symptoms are present, we begin to lose interest in things around us and begin to feel overwhelmed.

Punishment Penalty for specific undesirable behaviors.

Pygmalion effect An effect that reflects the opinions and expectations of others toward an individual. Sooner or later one's behavior adjusts to their perceptions.

Quality of work life (QWL) The degree to which workers are motivated, supported, and encouraged by their work environment.

Quid pro quo Getting something for giving something.

Readiness (of followers) How able and willing a follower is to complete a task.

Recruitment The process of locating, identifying, and attracting capable job applicants.

Reengineering Evaluation and alteration of most of the work done in an organization. Reengineering efforts lead to improvements in production quality, speed, and customer service.

Referent power Power based on possessing personality traits that others respect.

Referents Those people or things to which we compare ourselves.

Reliability A way of addressing whether a selection device used in making a decision about us measures the same characteristic consistently.

Responsibility An obligation to do what is expected of us.

Restraining forces A method used by a supervisor to reduce things that hinder your movement from current activity.

Reward power Power based on the ability to distribute anything that others value.

Risk propensity The degree to which an individual is willing to take chances.

Role A set of expected behaviors attributed to someone who occupies a given position in society.

Role ambiguity A situation in which an individual is unclear about what is expected.

Role conflict A conflict between work and family responsibilities.

Role overload A situation that exists when one has more work than time in which to complete it.

Safety needs Need for security and protection from physical and emotional harm.

Saint Bernards People who truly value pleasing others.

School placements Opportunities offered by educational institutions to find job openings, especially entry-level positions, in an organization.

Scientific management A set of principles designed to make employees more productive while providing greater profits for the organization that could be shared with employees.

Secrets Privately held information.

Selection process A method designed to predict which individuals will be successful if hired.

Selective perception Interpretation of objects and events based on personal interests, background, experience, and attitudes.

Self-actualization needs Need for growth, for achieving one's potential, and for self-fulfillment; the drive to become what one is capable of becoming.

Self-disclosure Sharing information about oneself.

Self-esteem The degree to which you like or dislike yourself; feelings of self-worth.

Self-serving bias A person's tendency to take credit for their successes while putting blame for their failures on others.

Sexual harassment Any unwanted activity of a sexual nature that affects an individual.

Shared values Organizational cultures that govern how its members should behave.

Simple structure An organizational grouping that appears to have almost no structure—one that is low in complexity, has little formalization, and has its authority centralized in a single person.

Situational leadership A leadership style that adjusts to the maturity level of the follower for a given set of tasks. Given a follower's ability and willingness to do a specific job, a situational leader will use one of four leadership styles: telling, selling, participating, or delegating.

Skill variety The variety of tasks that lets one use different skills and talents.

Social learning theory A view of learning as an ongoing interaction between an individual and his or her environment.

Social loafing A tendency for individual group members to slack off when a group as a whole is held responsible for completing a task.

Social needs Need for affection, belongingness, acceptance, and friendship.

Social obligation The foundation of a business's social involvement.

Social responsibility An obligation, beyond that required by law and economics, for a firm to pursue long-term goals that are for society's good.

Social responsiveness A moral standard to do those things that make society better and not to do those that could make it worse.

Social-learning theory The view of learning as an ongoing interaction between an individual and his or her environment.

Span of control Range of control or authority.

Spirituality Feelings and beliefs coming from one's heart. A spiritual life can bring one a level of fulfillment that material possessions will never be able to match.

Staff authority Positions created to support, assist, advise, and generally reduce informational burdens of supervisors.

Standardized jobs Jobs that are broken down into a number of steps, each step of which is completed by a separate individual.

Status A social rank or the importance one has in a group.

Status symbols Items that clearly demonstrate one's status in an organization.

Stereotyping Judging someone on the basis of one's perception of the group to which he or she belongs.

Stimulating view of conflict A view that encourages conflict on the grounds that peaceful, harmonious organizations become rigid and stagnant. When that happens, organizational members fail to recognize the need for change.

Stress An individual's feeling when faced with opportunities, constraints, or demands that are perceived to be both uncertain and important.

Stressors Personal and organization factors that cause stress.

Substance abusers Individuals who partake of illegal substances.

Suggestion program A program designed to allow employees the opportunity to tell organization members what they are doing inefficiently, and what they should do to make the organization better.

Survey feedback Efforts designed to assess attitudes about changes encountered and to identify perceptions of the change taking place.

Suspension Time off without pay.

Task group A collection of people brought together to accomplish a specific task.

Task identity The ability to complete the whole job or an identifiable piece of work.

Taskmaster Someone who uses power, politics, and status to keep employees down. Working under such an individual can affect our attitudes and behaviors toward supervisors and organizations.

Task significance The effect a job has on the lives or work of other people.

Task-centered leadership behaviors Behaviors that focus on the technical or task aspects of a job.

Task-oriented leader An individual who has a strong tendency to emphasize the technical or task aspects of the job. This individual's major goal is to ensure that employees know precisely what is expected of them and to provide any guidance necessary for goals to be met.

Teambuilding An activity that helps a group set goals, develop positive interpersonal relationships, and clarify the role and responsibilities of each team member. Its primary focus is to increase group trust and openness toward one another.

Technical skills Tools, procedures, and techniques that are unique to a specialized situation.

Theory X A negative view of the nature of human beings.

Theory Y A positive view of the nature of human beings.

Therbligs A classification scheme that labels seventeen basic hand motions, thus allowing a precise way of analyzing the exact elements of any worker's hand movements.

Three-needs theory A theory that three major personality characteristics motivate one at work: need for achievement (nAch), need for power (nPow), and need for affiliation (nAff).

Time management A tool used to help schedule both one's personal and professional life.

Total quality management (TQM) A quality revolution inspired by a small group of quality experts taking place in both business and the public sector. It is a philosophy of management that is driven by customer needs and expectations.

Traditional view of conflict A view that all conflict is bad and has a negative effect on organizations and their members. In this view, conflict is seen as destructive.

Training A learning experience focusing on improving an employee's ability to perform his or her job.

Transactional leaders Leaders who motivate their followers in the direction of established goals by clarifying role and task requirements.

Transformational leaders Leaders who pay attention to the concerns and developmental needs of individual followers; they change followers' awareness of issues by helping those followers look at old problems in new ways.

Transnational corporations (TNCs) Corporations that do not seek to repeat domestic successes by managing foreign operations from home. Decision making in such organizations takes place at the local level, and individuals in the host countries, called *nationals*, run operations in each country. Products and marketing strategies are uniquely tailored to each country's culture.

Type A personality An individual who is time driven, aggressive, and competitive, with a strong desire for achievement. *See also* TYPE B PERSONALITY.

Type B personality An individual who is relaxed and easygoing, even tempered, flexible, and friendly. This type is less time conscious, accepts change easily, and isn't as likely to experience the anxiety-related ailments that affect its Type A counterparts. *See also* TYPE A PERSONALITY.

Uncertainty avoidance A social framework characterized by an increased level of anxiety and uncertainty.

Union A group of workers acting together, seeking to promote and protect their mutual interests through collective bargaining.

Unity of command Clear lines of authority defining who is in charge and who answers to whom.

Upward communications Any information delivered by any means to an individual from anyone in a lower position in the organization.

Validity A proven relationship between a selection device and some relevant criterion.

Value system Beliefs formed over time by taking in and processing thousands of pieces of information from varied sources.

Values Strongly held beliefs that guide an individual's behavior.

Verbal intonation   The emphasis given to words or phrases.

Verbal warning   A temporary record of a reprimand that is then placed in a supervisor's file.

Vocational preferences   Occupational interests based on personality and the proper matching of individuals to jobs and resulting productivity.

Weakness   A strength carried to extreme—something one does too much of or acts out inappropriately.

Wellness programs   Organizationally sponsored events designed to keep employees healthy and to prevent problems from developing. Programs include smoking cessation, weight control, blood pressure control, stress management, and physical fitness.

White water rapid   A concept of change that takes into consideration that an individual's surroundings are both uncertain and dynamic.

Workforce diversity   Differences that diverse groups bring to the workplace, such as gender, nationality, age, and race.

Work teams   Formal groups composed of individuals responsible for the attainment of a goal.

Written essay   A performance appraisal method that often relies as much on a supervisor's writing skill as on an employee's actual performance.

Written tests   Tests that measure intelligence, aptitude, ability, and interests.

Written warning   The first formal stage of the disciplinary procedure, the written warning becomes part of an employee's personnel file.

Index

PHOTO CREDITS

Chapter 1 p. 10, Gary Moss Photography
Chapter 2 p. 27, Dan Bryant Photographs
Chapter 3 p. 53, Erica Freudenstein/
Corbis/SABA Press Photos, Inc.
Chapter 4 p. 82, David Butow/Corbis/
SABA Press Photos, Inc.
Chapter 5 p. 102, Peter Cade/Stone
Chapter 6 p. 139, Tomas Sodergren
Chapter 7 p. 168, Norma Jean Gargasz
Photography

Chapter 8 p. 199, Ferguson and Katzman
Photography, Inc.
Chapter 9 p. 221, Robbie McClaran
Chapter 10 p. 230, Gary Laufman Photography
Chapter 11 p. 265, Terry Parke Photography
Chapter 12 p. 290, Tony Savino/JB Pictures Ltd./The
Image Works
Chapter 13 p. 319, Amy Cantrell Photography
Chapter 14 p. 338, Bryan Whitney Photography